"If the virtual corporation becomes our new business model, then the managers who survive will need all the virtual experts they can find. And this book is the place to start."

Jeffrey Tarter
Editor and Publisher, *Soft•letter*

"The power of this book is in how well it presents the logic behind the software tools it so ably describes. Readers are given hands-on guidance on the use of a wide variety of software programs that have emerged in recent years to enhance managerial decision-making. More importantly, they get practical insights into when and why a particular program should be used and how the results should be interpreted. As PC-based management tools grow in power and number, guides such as *The Digital MBA* will become increasingly important additions to the executive's bookshelf."

Jay Paap, Ph.D.,
Partner, Data and Strategies Group

"*The Digital MBA* can improve your management batting average. Seasoned executives or business beginners will benefit from strategic planning software programs that show how to make more good decisions and fewer bad ones—more hits and fewer embarrassing whiffs. *The Digital MBA* combines smart coaching with risk-free practice—a learning opportunity for both novices and old pros."

Robert M. Randall, Managing Editor, *Planning Review*
Co-editor of *The Portable MBA in Strategy* (New York: Wiley, 1994)

"Most people have not anticipated how quickly software will support the complex analytical work and day-to-day management processes described and demonstrated in *The Digital MBA*. Exploring these **first-of their kind** software products will stimulate thinking and generate interesting discussions about the nature of our work and who can perform it."

Gloria Gery, Performance Support Consultant
Author of *Electronic Performance Support Systems* (Tolland, MA: Gery Associates, 1991)

"As a teacher of entrepreneurship and marketing courses related to high technology, we encourage use of the latest software tools to boost managerial productivity and effectiveness. This book serves a critical need in our classroom as well providing a method for continual learning by our graduates."

Professor Tom Byers
Haas School of Business, UC Berkeley
School of Engineering, Stanford University

"I wish they had state of the art tools and educational resources like *The Digital MBA* and its companion CD during my MBA education. Even years after my graduation I find it to be an invaluable resource. This book and the CompuServe GO MBAWARE forum should be found in every managers tool box."

Joel Diamond, Online Director, WUGNET, CompuServe
MBA 1983, Temple University

"People often ask me, 'How can computers help executives think?' The concept of expert systems (or MBA-ware) is a key component to my answer. Executives and others know surprisingly little about commercial expert systems, and they could benefit tremendously from learning about their effectiveness."

Mary E. Boone, author of *Leadership and the Computer* (Rocklin, CA: Prima, 1993)

What They're Saying About MBA-ware...

"MBA-ware brings you the latest knowledge and techniques for managing organizations in both the public and private sectors."

> Professor Michael R. Reich, Harvard University
> Creator of *Political Mapping: Computers-Assisted Political Analysis*

"MBA-ware has revolutionized productivity, similar to the evolution of the personal computer."

> Jeanne Butler
> Director, Transport Technologies Contracting

"'It's been shown in many fields that self-study with computers is a faster way to apprehend content' than reading books, says John Sviokla, an assistant professor at Harvard Business School."

> William M. Bulkeley, "With New Planning Software, Entrepreneurs Act Like M.B.A.'s," *Wall Street Journal*, June 2, 1992

"..Imagine a mix of project management programs, rules-based expert systems, and forecasting software, and you start to get an idea of what MBA-ware is all about."

> Don Willmott, "Wharton in a Box," *PC Magazine*, November 9, 1993

"Rather than simply providing facts, figures, and a format to make work easier, MBA-ware actually analyzes data you supply and advises you on a course of action. Applications so far include planning and tracking complex projects, devising negotiation strategies, and automating management chores, such as writing personnel policies and job descriptions—tasks most managers would gladly surrender to a silicon chip."

> Nancy K. Austin, "MBA-In-A-Box," *Working Woman*, November, 1993

"The first generation of personal computer software was clerical...The next generation of PC software was designed to inform or entertain us...Now a new category is emerging that blends the other two. It does clerical work, but it knows more than a mere spreadsheet or word processor program. Call it, if you will, middle-manager software...Let's be realistic. Computer programs aren't going to replace the critical element of judgment in business management. But their creators may find new ways to speed up bureaucratic chores and perhaps even to inspire the bureaucrats to higher achievements."

> Richard A. Shaffer, "Can a PC Make You a Sharper Manager?" *Forbes*, February 30, 1995

"Built around knowledge bases covering marketing, finance, negotiating, forecasting, and planning, MBA-ware is said to be ideal for executives involved in downsizing, because often fewer staff members means broader responsibilities; the software can help managers undertake tasks they haven't been trained to perform. MBA-ware is characterized by its ability to analyze and advise, not just manipulate data."

> Tom Farre, Editor-in-Chief, "Goodbye Expert Systems, Hello MBA-ware," *Reseller Management*, October, 1993

"Expert system programs are used by many companies in many different ways. In general, they are programs that tap the collective wisdom of human experts who are interviewed on how they might respond to any given circumstance. Their responses are codified and entered into a knowledge base that can be used by a computer."

> Peter Lewis, "For Face-to-Face Talks, Ask Your Machine First," in "The Executive Computer," *New York Times*, July 21, 1991

The *Digital* MBA

Edited by Daniel Burnstein

Osborne **McGraw-Hill**

Berkeley New York St. Louis San Francisco
Auckland Bogotá Hamburg London Madrid
Mexico City Milan Montreal New Delhi Panama City
Paris São Paulo Singapore Sydney Tokyo Toronto

Osborne **McGraw-Hill**
2600 Tenth Street
Berkeley, California 94710
U.S.A.

For information on translations or book distributors outside the U.S.A., or to arrange bulk purchase discounts for sales promotions, premiums, or fundraisers, please contact Osborne **McGraw-Hill** at the above address.

The Digital MBA

1234567890 DOC 998765

ISBN 0-07-882099-5

Publisher	**Proofreader**
Lawrence Levitsky	Stefany Otis
Co-editor	**Indexer**
Michael R. Shirer	Sami Menefee
Acquisitions Editor	**Computer Designer**
Scott Rogers	Peter F. Hancik
Project Editor	**Illustrator**
Nancy McLaughlin	Marla Shelasky
Developmental Editor	**Series Design**
Scott Spanbauer	Jani Beckwith
Copy Editor	**Quality Control Specialist**
Kathryn Hashimoto	Joe Scuderi

Cover Design
Ted Mader Associates

About the Author...

Daniel Burnstein, Esq., is the president and founder
of The Management Software Association and
is a consultant for the American Management
Association. He developed multimedia software
for Harvard Law School for five years and is
currently a member of the Massachusetts Honor
Roll of Innovation and Discovery.

Contents

PART I
Managing People and Projects

PART II
Strategic and Financial Planning

PART III
Business Process Modeling

Foreword

by Nancy K. Austin
Austin Associates, Inc.

Why spend two years and $25,000 chasing an MBA at Wharton when your desktop computer can give you the same expertise with a single keystroke? No, that's not a trick question. It's the downright irresistible challenge posed by the savvy contributors in this intelligent, first-of-its-kind book. You are about to dip your toes into—courtesy of this field guide—a wide-open terrain known as decision-support software. Call it MBA-ware for short.

This book arrives at a topsy-turvified time for managers. As any business school student can tell you, the practice of management simply isn't what it used to be. The pace of commerce is in hyperdrive. New developments in any kind of business—from telecommunication to financial services to basic manufacturing—seem to hit at least twice a day. No doubt about it, since I completed my own MBA program (UCLA, class of '77, practically in the dark ages), the whole marketplace has been a perfect pandemonium. Slow and steady management skill may have won yesterday's race, but it's surely the quickest route to disaster now (in this new world, you'd better be quick or you'll be dead).

No wonder a fleet-footed vanguard is taking over from the old guard. Owing to cutthroat competition, the emergence of a highly skilled and educated work force and portable, powerful, time-saving technology, managers everywhere are rethinking the tried-and-not-so-true tenets they grew up with. If the *New York Times Magazine* is right in declaring that "Microsoft's only factory asset is the human imagination," then practically everything we've been taught about the job of management should be turned on its head. Imagination, something managers were once paid to drive out of the corporation, is now our most urgent requirement. It took, for example, real imagination (not to mention technical know-how) to dream up a smart toothbrush, whose row of blue bristles fade halfway to white when it's time to replace it. And since the service and smarts embedded in such "mundane" products will just keep growing, only those who are quick on their feet and who have a genuine passion to learn, all the time, will be able to keep up. Forget about competing on the cost of labor with low-wage countries. All we have to leverage these days is our know-how. Period.

Might as well face it: Ye Olde Management Models don't work so well anymore. Here comes a new, smartened-up kind of organization, one that grants each inhabitant real elbowroom, one that is fast and flexible and alert, where the only true asset is the human mind. So long, muscle-bound chains of command! Take a hike, warring business functions. Hello self-managed teams, open books, and unfettered information flow! Welcome to what writer Bruce Tucker called "the new economy—that unplanned, unlooked for, but suddenly-upon-us world in which information technology levels the competitive playing field, innovation counts for more than experience, speed beats size, brains beat big money, and product life cycles grow as short as the life of a hit record." Only more so.

Today's work force has to run very lean and very mean to rack up dramatic performance improvements where they count the most—in quality, service, innovation, and speed. It's the only way to produce genuine value for the customer, and whoever gets there first wins. But since every industry is moving at a head-spinning pace, the time needed to acquire and polish important new skills is hard to come by. Frontliners need to know their way around budget and P and Ls, managers need to brush up on managing performance expectations without crowding their teams, and everybody wants to know how to make better decisions. Classroom training can help plug gaps, of course, but prolonged absences from the daily grind aren't usually practical (somebody has to pick up the slack). And then there are the inevitable questions about whether classroom training sticks anyway (the jury is still out).

Knowledge is unconquerably the prime source for added value in your company. So the question becomes: how do we continuously create, use, and leverage the knowledge that resides in our own firm? Suppose we figured out how to learn more readily and to make better use of it. Perhaps the learning could be self-paced, unassisted, and delivered just in time anyplace, anytime. Suppose the learner could be directed through the steps involved in, say, setting up crystal-clear performance expectations and helping a team work through a complex project. And suppose the student could tap into the collected wisdom of the best experts in a given field—how to create workable written policies, maybe, or how to negotiate that next big contract with a notoriously difficult supplier. Now, that would be something.

The book you are holding *is* that something. It's about software, yes, but that's only part of the story. It's really about the care and feeding of know-how and putting it to productive use. Even if you're a novice manager, you can easily and quickly use the interactive electronic tools you find here to solve problems and manage complex projects, and that's just for starters. You can beef up your negotiation skills, make sure your company's health and safety conditions are all they should be, hone your leadership ability, create a new product plan and introduction, and prepare a comprehensive business forecast (without first submitting to remedial instruction in statistical analysis). Think of it as an MBA-in-a-box—and more.

To put it another way, this wild new economy of ours is located in the human mind; it's what you know (and refreshing and expanding it) that counts. In *The Twilight of Sovereignty: How the Information Revolution Is Transforming Our World* (New York: Scribners, 1992), former Citicorp chair Walter B. Wriston observes that "intellectual capital will go where it is wanted, and it will stay where it is well treated. It cannot be driven; it can only be attracted." You know: Feed your head. And you have found the perfect place to start.

Preface

"Armed with Business Insight, a new expert system for strategic analysis, we analyzed the Applications Business Systems division of IBM (AS400), a multibillion-dollar unit. After collecting our answers to questions on a wide variety of topics—including organizational factors, human resources, product benefits, packaging, market definition, sales processes, and financing—the software was able to synthesize an accurate and coherent strategic plan. Based on our experience with other strategic planning tools, we believe that Business Insight is breaking new ground in a wide-open market. One question we skeptically asked ourselves when we began this exercise was, Will this software really give us any insights we hadn't thought of?' The answer is, surprisingly, it did...it also provided new insights in the areas of competitive rivalry, upside potential for earnings, and advertising."

Mark McNeilly and Steve Gessner, market analysis and strategy advisors, Systems Strategy department, IBM, *Planning Review,* March/April, 1993

It used to be that employees at billion-dollar business organizations had regular access to specialized expertise not generally available to smaller firms. However, with the recent wave of management layoffs, this is not always the case. To meet the need at both large and small firms for on-demand consulting, some 100 software companies, largely unknown to each other and the computer press, have started a quiet revolution in business software. These software publishers have created smart business applications that embed information and also serve as performance support tools. Most of these software programs combine the functions of a tool and a just-in-time learning environment to help users perform sophisticated tasks, on-site, with the mind of a manager.

In 1983, three small software companies began to ship some of the earliest MBA-ware programs. These visionary companies were: ExpertChoice, with content by Tom Saaty and others in Pittsburgh, PA; Ronstadt's Financials, by Lord Publishing, now in Dana Pointe, CA, devised by Bob Ronstadt, then of Babson College; and Experience In Software in Berkeley, CA, inspired by pioneer negotiation expert, Gerard I. Nierenberg, Esq. Each of these pioneering companies is busy and growing twelve years later. The persistence of these electronic performance-support companies is not a small feat given the turbulent software industry. Other products followed.

Business Insight, a program that helps the user develop business strategies was created by the former Operations Manager and Manager of Strategic Planning at Intel's Systems Division. This program builds on their years of successful experience and the research of more than 30 marketing experts, including Michael Porter, Philip Kotler, and others.

More recently, another MBA-ware company has appeared with a market-positioning product. Enterprise Support Systems of Norcross, GA was started by an author, with six book titles and a busy consulting practice, who decided to put his expertise into software. Instead of being a client—paying $50,000 for a week of consulting and viewing software results—a company can now purchase the Product Planning Advisor for one-fiftiethth of the week's consulting cost and answer the positioning questions themselves. Use of the software at Rolls Royce Industrial Power Group resulted in a return to profitability.

Peter Lewis of the *New York Times* Spots a Trend

In 1990, Peter Lewis reviewed an employee review program, Performance Mentor, from a company of the same name in Palo Alto, CA. This review had a wonderfully

"Use of the Product Planning Advisor resulted, in part, in a turnaround from substantial losses to profitability. Carpenter noted that the process of using this tool provided a variety of benefits to Rolls Royce: (1) managers of every product/service line must consistently address the same questions, particularly questions related to market and technology issues—this consistency makes plans much easier to communicate, and plans can be integrated; (2) using this software has increased his staff's business skills; and (3) an immediate payoff of better plans faster."

W. J. Carpenter, *Business Process Re-Engineering: Promoting Cross-Functional Ownership of Processes,* Newcastle, England: Rolls Royce Industrial Power Group, 1993

provocative headline, "I'm Sorry; My Machine Doesn't Like Your Work," and in it Lewis wrote:

> Managers at most companies are required to give performance evaluations to their workers on a regular basis, usually at least once a year. While some executives say they enjoy the opportunity to provide thoughtful, constructive feedback that will help the worker meet clearly defined performance objectives, others—the majority, perhaps—would rather go to the dentist.

Lewis later reviewed a negotiation support system that I created, Negotiator Pro. It was a relatively unknown program until the headline in the Sunday *New York Times* business section appeared on July 21, 1991: "Before Going Face to Face Consult Your Machine." In the review, Lewis wrote:

> Most business deals require some type of negotiation, whether it is to forge a labor contract or figure out how to get people to work together effectively. Few executives, however, have formal training in negotiation skills. So when the negotiations are hardball, some companies are turning to software. Negotiator Pro...is based on the premise that negotiation is more of a skill that can be learned than an art, and that a computer, which is inherently devoid of any personality, can help an executive plan an effective negotiation with other humans by examining their personality types.

After getting over the shock of having my software plucked from the shadows of obscurity by the *New York Times,* I was struck by an unstated connection between what these software programs were doing, beyond expert systems. Being new to the field, I assumed there were only a few categories of software: spreadsheets, databases, word processors, utilities, and "other." I realized that there was an emerging new category of software for assisting business users. Typically, the software embedded business knowledge and married content with a practical tool. While none of the programs pretended to be magic bullets—they asked up front for intelligent input from the user—they shared a number of key characteristics: they all embedded knowledge, they did not talk down to the user, and, best of all from management's point of view, they did not take the user away from his or her desk.

To test out these observations, I contacted William Bulkeley of the *Wall Street Journal.* "There is a new category of software," I claimed. He was appropriately skeptical, but after investigating the story, he wrote an article in June, 1992 entitled "With New Planning Software, Entrepreneurs Act Like MBAs." In this article, he described the software as *MBA-ware.* I was gratified to see that a respected business and technology-oriented journalist was receptive to what we were trying to communicate.

Shortly after the article appeared, the presidents of several of these companies began to talk, and even though some of us were competitors, we decided to band together to educate computer users, pundits, and the sales channels. By June, 1993, we hired an executive director and started throwing pebbles against the windows of the gatekeepers of the computer and business world as The Management Software Association.

Early discussions with Norman Wu of Avantos Performance Systems, Inc., Michael Troy of KnowledgePoint, Gary Deines of Inform, Rebecca Lord Ronstadt of Lord Publishing, and others centered on articulating our mission. We realized that our software programs shared the following characteristics:

> ➤ Used the power of the computer to assist the business user

> ➤ Were not books on a disk

> ➤ Had a modest expert system, hypertext, algorithms (formulas), or all three

> ➤ Provided day-to-day and solution-oriented assistance

> ➤ Were knowledge-driven without being academic

Our shorthand description of MBA-ware evolved to "Software that embeds management expertise via an expert system, algorithms, hypertext, or all three." MBA-ware has proved to be the right label to distinguish these content-oriented applications from other already recognized "management" applications, such as spreadsheets, financial planners, and project management programs.

What Is the Market for Such Products?

Angelo Pabon, Vice President of operations at Blue Shield in San Juan, Puerto Rico, was told one morning that he was going to have a meeting with the president regarding the status of a project that he had put on the back burner due to more pressing priorities. He walked into the meeting at 10:00 A.M. to find that his presentation was the most complete of those discussed. Pabon also used business software to plan a new strategic computer system for Blue Shield and for various civil defense projects for his National Guard command.

As Jon Zilbur, Editor in Chief of *PC Computing Magazine,* put it recently, "The people interested in MBA-ware have job descriptions that say nothing about computers, but who rely heavily on computers to do their jobs." In the U.S., there are approximately 12 million managers, about three million government managers, three million in upper-level sales, and two million professionals of the legal and financial stripe. What percentage of this potential market are looking for answers supplied by MBA-ware? In 1983, the percentage was quite low, but it has grown steadily. After all, when the first companies started up, the typical $5,000 business computer was a DOS machine with 128K and no hard disk! Executives, who previously prided themselves on not typing, now fight to get the first hot laptops and accounts on the Internet. More significantly, MIS personnel have to provide remote access to company data for VPs, or else they fear for their jobs.

How Is MBA-ware Used?

There is a general perception that men do not like to ask for directions, but here is one who does ask for help. Perhaps one of the best things about being president of the TMSA trade association is that I get to try all of the programs described in this book. My measuring stick has been to ask "What does this product do for my daily operations?" In this section, I will briefly highlight the benefits my company has experienced from the software in this book, interspersed with comments from other users.

I operate a small software company that employs three people full-time and four others part-time. Like most other small business owners, I find myself running full tilt—a copywriter one minute, software content provider the next, then application designer, strategic planner, then using the next minute to catch my breath and meet with technical staff.

"As the Finance Director of a $200 million food processing company, I rely on SmartForecasts to forcast the sales of hundreds of our key product items every month. Its built-in expert system has more than tripled our productivity. In only a few minutes, SmartForecasts produces highly accurate forecasts which drive our overall business planning process."

Robert Denny, Director of Finance, Pierre Frozen Foods (a subsidiary of Hudson Foods)

To keep track of the many projects at my company and in my volunteer work outside the company, I regularly use two programs from Experience In Software: Project KickStart and The Idea Generator Plus. I use these programs to help me quickly expand project ideas into coherent projects with goals, deadlines, and task assignments. Often, I need that list of steps and issues to keep me going in the right direction on a project.

Given my "sort of vague" leadership style, I decided to develop individual mission statements and goals for everyone in the company. This seemed like a good idea since we are engaged in a variety of tasks, and sometimes it is hard to see the forest for the trees. To do this, I used ManagePro from Avantos Performance Systems, Inc. of Emeryville, CA. Once we set up our mission statements, goals, and deliverables, we decided we were much better off singing from the same score.

The vice president of manufacturing for Polk Audio, Craig Georgi, has to supervise everyone from materials managers to quality assurance and production hourly workers. He uses ManagePro to track, organize, and analyze how well he and his team are doing. "It's easy to sit down and praise somebody, but it doesn't always work out that way," Georgi says. "People have weaknesses as well as strengths, and your job as manager is to make certain that people understand both areas. While ManagePro can't save you from the less pleasant aspects of the job, it does help you organize your thoughts and gives you empirical data upon which to make a balanced judgment. And if you present that data to the people involved, they often come to the same conclusions that you do."

At Computerland, a $32 million retailer and service provider, every product on the shelf is used in-house before it is put on the shelf. Debra Gibb is Computerland's Vice President of Technology. Gibb has made Review Writer an integral part of her own performance reviews. "It helps us to state clearly the rules by which we govern our business and evaluate employees. While each department is different the package helps assure that the criteria for evaluation is consistent and fair throughout the company."

Recently I had to prepare a performance review document for Kim, our marketing person. Although I knew Kim was consistently performing beyond the call of duty, I had trouble remembering what she had done over the previous six months. All I could remember was the past ten days. I tried out several employee review products, including Review Writer by Avantos Performance Systems, Inc. and PerformanceNow! by KnowledgePoint. A particularly attractive feature of Review Writer is the feature that allows the user to review the employee's mission statements and objectives that have been created in ManagePro. This helped remind me of Kim's initiative in a highly successful sales campaign several months ago. Review Writer was also recently put through the paces at Computerland of Southern California.

One of my greatest weaknesses has been in keeping track of the financial status of my company. I first used Ronstadt's Financials, and more recently, Destiny Business Information & Planning System from The Planet Corporation of Worcester, Massachusetts. Both of these programs provided professional-looking financials and, more importantly, a sense of the financial underpinnings of the company on a month-to-month basis. Destiny has a feature to quickly show my return on investment (ROI) and other ratios.

"As the VP of the Environmental Controls and Service Division in a company with 22 employees, I use Destiny for budgeting—to set up my operating expenses for our accountant. I am not trained in accounting. Before Destiny I used a spreadsheet, but I find Destiny is a lot easier because a lot of forms are already in there. It takes me 25 percent less time now to do my reports, and this year when I gave my reports to the controller, he said there was a better breakout of numbers and generally more information than last year. Since I was able to break out the costs with more detail, I only had to present two revisions, where previously I generally had to do four revisions."

Ed Hashey, Vice President, Environmental Controls and Service Division, Thermos Engineering, Worcester, MA

As my company has continued to grow, I have been faced with a number of critical decisions where I didn't always know where I was headed. A good example was a recent offer from Softkey, a larger software publisher, to develop a consumer product to help people buy and sell their homes. The difficult issue was whether my company should develop and publish the software as an affiliated label or let the larger publisher put it under its brand. DPL, a tool for decision analysis from Applied Decision Analysis, Inc. in Menlo Park, CA, helped analyze this opportunity in graphical ways.

DPL is specifically designed to address the options and the issues of uncertainty involved in decision-making. It has a unique combination of decision tree and influence diagrams. DPL worked with one large company to help them decide whether or not to expand its manufacturing plant. The decision was risky. The company decided that once all of its critical uncertainties were identified it could refine the initial estimates to capture additional knowledge about the variables. They wanted a chart could be built showing for price: its low, baseline, and high levels with estimates of uncertainty attached. Then a decision tree was built in the software. The expanded tree was viewed as a graph. Then users created a risk profile as an alternative way to view the tree information. DPL plotted the distribution of profits. During the course of the analysis, key uncertainties were identified and decision options were invented.

Another important task for us has been to try to understand all of the different processes found within my firm, Negotiator Pro Company. Even though we are a small company, efficiency is just as important to us as it is to the larger corporations. The fact of the matter is, we need to get the most from the few employees we have. A new generation of software helped us use computers to model our business processes and to reengineer our order-taking process. In this category of business software, Imagine That, Inc. of San Jose, CA, publishes their Extend package.

A major communications company used Extend shortly after it had gone through deregulation—it wanted to restructure its operations. There were numerous redundancies and multiple competing legacy systems. Each organizational unit provided a team of employees who were experts in their processes. The employees identified alternative processes, and these were modeled using Extend. Some ideas that looked good in concept were rejected after being modeled, taking into account such factors as training, staffing, cost, cycle time, etc. This was an iterative effort: alternatives were modeled, data was analyzed, new questions were raised, and the design was modified several times.

Another tool for modeling we used in my company was ithink, from High Performance Systems, Inc. in Hanover, NH. ithink is a tool that is used in industry and academia to simplify the modeling process. ithink helped convince my company to outsource the fulfillment process because it had identified the efficiencies of scale that the move would accomplish.

Fireman's Fund Insurance Company decided to build an ithink model of their $800 million-dollar reinsurance business in the summer of 1994. Dominic Bosque, Director of Business Reengineering for Fireman's, found that by using ithink software, the company could identify some $8 million dollars in immediate savings and potential long-term savings of $20 million dollars—without needing any investment in new hardware or software.

Once the reengineering process was done, I completed my revised business plan and entered some preliminary sales figures into a spreadsheet in order to make sales projections. Using two statistical forecasting products, SmartForecasts and Forecast Pro, the future sales predictions were not very encouraging. They reinforced the product marketing advice I had gotten from Business Insight. I realized I needed to change my product development direction, and I develop a series of "specific solutions" rather than generic tools. I called Softkey the next day, and a deal was struck a few days later. Statistical forecasting applications have a wide range of uses.

"I have been using Forecast Pro and its predecessor since 1987. From exponential smoothing models to Box-Jenkins and dynamic regression, the features of Forecast Pro have quadrupled the productivity of my analysis. The user-friendly interface dramatically reduces the model development and forecasting cycle. I also use Forecast Pro to develop time-dependent risk model specifications."

Sam O. Sugiyama, President, Economic & Engineering Consultants

There are a number of other MBA-ware tools for forecasting sales, financials, and other events. Some decision makers are using the Monte Carlo engine found in @RISK, from Palisade Corporation in Newfield, NY and Crystal Ball, from Decisioneering in Denver, CO. I personally found Monte Carlo simulation to be a very useful tool to use in analyzing risks associated with our new product launches.

"@RISK is used by a major foreign bank in New York City to build analytical models to support new product development. It used the program to evaluate potential new products and to forecast returns over a five-year period. While many of the costs were straight-line items, some of the projected income streams involved a lot of variability and a substantial use of @RISK. This was particularly true in the case of hybrids, where there were multiple income sources for a variety of transactions."

Craig Jennings, CompuTrainers Corporation, New York, NY

Future Developments in MBA-ware

During its first two years of existence, The Management Software Association has succeeded in getting its message about MBA-ware out to publications ranging from *Fortune* to *Working Woman*. It has presented its companies to the major software trade association, The Software Publishers Association, as well as journalists and resellers. Recently, TMSA has made arrangements to distribute information on the Internet and CompuServe.

In my personal opinion, the future of MBA-ware will likely see a merging of MBA-ware with decision-support engines to assess business information and business uncertainty, anticipate human behavior in negotiations, and help with other challenges. At the same time, traditional business tools, such as spreadsheets and project management software, will move toward the MBA-ware model and incorporate expert systems and online multimedia tutoring.

Eventually, all business software will have sophisticated data visualization capabilities to let the user visually "walk around" data sets and find new relationship patterns. There will be embedded software "agents" to locate relevant data and expertise on our own local area networks, as well as on the Internet.

Additionally, the future "manager's workstation" will have voice recognition. The manager will start his or her day by saying, "I have to do a report for the board on next year's sales forecasts, and I am worried they will not go along with my proposed reorganization or my increased budget." The computer will respond, "Do you want to finish your sales forecasts or work on the business reorganization diagram you left off yesterday at 5:49 P.M.? You might want to use the negotiation preparation planning software to get your arguments organized for the board; last time, you found that a useful exercise. And speaking of exercise, perhaps you should take a run instead of going to lunch today."

As the MBA-ware companies evolve, their products will become intelligent tutoring systems that build an image of the user so that the software will operate in an intuitive fashion. Software will increasingly be measured by its invisibility. Users of a successful MBA-ware program will be impressed by their (own) ideas, and the software that helped will be something in the background.

I hope you will enjoy the short essays on MBA-related skills in each of the chapters of this book. You are encouraged to *play* with all the applications on the accompanying CD-ROM and to test their ability to help with *your* management problems.

For an ongoing dialog, I encourage you to contact me through the GO MBAWARE Forum on CompuServe.

Acknowledgments

The bulk of the credit and thanks for this book goes to the wonderful co-authors who took time from their busy schedules to write the book. Each of them is eminently qualified to write at length about his or her particular topic; most have extensive formal training in their area of expertise, and all have considerable real-world management experience, from inside major corporations to positions as consultants to their own software companies. As the book evolved, it demanded considerably more time and effort on their part than was originally envisioned. However, our faith in their knowledge and abilities was confirmed as each new demand was met in full.

This book could not have come about without the talented editorial assistance—not to mention unflagging energy and good humor—of my co-editor, Michael Shirer. Mike, currently a graduate student, is executive director of The Management Software Association. In addition to contributing his wordsmithing ability, Mike always asked the right "why" questions. Mike's wife, Karen, and his colleagues at MIT deserve a hearty thanks for forgiving his absence from their activities as a result of this project.

The overall structure for the book, which became a melding of a computer book and a business book, came largely from inspired thinking on the part of

Larry Levitsky, Jeff Pepper, and Scott Rogers at Osborne McGraw-Hill. Scott Spanbauer made significant improvements in the content of the chapters with his commonsense brand of editing. Editorial Assistant Kelly Vogel, Project Editor Nancy McLaughlin, and Copy Editor Kathryn Hashimoto devoted many hours of attention both to the little details and to the big picture. Our able agent, Bill Gladstone, helped with negotiations and assured us that books of merit are interactive affairs that only take final shape as they move towards completion.

Lastly, I would like to dedicate this book to my wife, and friend, Jacquelyn Borck and my children, Adam, Julia, and Michael, without whose love and support I never would have completed this project. Their love shone through the dark days and regularly brought sunshine into my heart.

Introduction

This book offers the manager and business owner—who is busy struggling to meet deadlines and profit projections—a quick primer on both business tasks and a new category of business software that assists managers with sophisticated management tasks. These tasks are the ones that cause us to rub our foreheads several times each week.

The goals of the book are (1) to inform the reader about substantive business management topics, (2) to illustrate how new information technologies can help managers do their job better, and (3) to provide a look at some working models of the software.

This is not a complete reference work on any particular topic, nor is it meant to replace a seminar on these subjects. However, the reader should get a good briefing on a wide range of business skills, ranging from communicating with your staff to redesigning your business processes. And readers can play with the full-working evaluation versions of the software contained on the inside back cover.

Who Should Read This Book?

This book is for managers, executives, and business owners at *all* levels who recognize the need for assistance with the tasks involved in running a business. For small business owners—who simultaneously face the challenges of forecasting inventory and sales, performing market analysis, managing employees, and reaching agreements with vendors—there just isn't enough time in the day to become a specialist in all business functions. For managers in larger corporations, where layoffs may have occurred, the in-house specialist may no longer be available.

For both large and small businesses, there is an emerging category of "smart" software that assists with complex management tasks and guides users through the process. With varying sophistication, most of these programs explain the basic business issues involved and provide a tool to undertake a number of sophisticated business functions. The book and its programs are also useful for human resource development (HRD) courses and for graduate and undergraduate business courses.

As this book has taken shape, it has become clear that it could not be all things for all people. It is definitely *not* the book for those who love to spend time doing the following:

> ➤ Configuring spreadsheets with hundreds of macros to create complex plans

> ➤ Attending advanced seminars on human resources, business processes, statistics, and systems analysis

> ➤ Reading marketing journals written by business school professors for other professors

> ➤ Adding in special utilities to automate project management software to track staff

> ➤ Reading and rereading textbooks on statistics and market analysis

> ➤ Using Fortran to build Monte Carlo simulations and other statistical tools

This book will be useful for businesspeople at all levels of management who want to do the hard tasks better. The book is also for MIS and human resource directors who need to be up-to-date on useful business-oriented applications. After reading the book and looking at the software, the reader should have a fuller grasp of the MBA-ware concept and understand the software and what it does as well as its limitations. The future of this software category will also be discussed.

How the Book Is Structured

The book is divided into four sections, with advice and software to help overcome the challenges that arise in the following categories:

> ➤ Part 1: Managing People and Projects

> ➤ Part 2: Strategic and Financial Planning

> ➤ Part 3: Business Process Modeling

> ➤ Part 4: Sales and Financial Forecasting

Part 1, "Managing People and Projects," addresses some of the tasks most commonly faced by those vested with management authority. In addition to project creation (brainstorming), planning, and execution, the chapters in this section discuss employee performance reviews, tracking and analyzing accidents and near-accidents in the workplace, and negotiation. Part 2, "Strategic and Financial Planning," covers the how-to's of creating an integrated business plan and strategy, from an accounting *and* a marketing perspective. Part 3, "Business Process Modeling," introduces the latest methods and tools for modeling and analyzing the processes and decisions that shape a business. Part 4, "Sales and Financial Forecasting," covers risk analysis and statistical forecasting, two important topics that are often neglected because of their quantitative nature.

Each chapter follows roughly the same format. The first section of each chapter offers a primer on the substance of managing people and projects, business planning, decision analysis and process modeling, and risk analysis and sales forecasting. The second part of each chapter briefly gives a sense of why that particular business challenge is difficult and what substantive methods are used to approach that challenge without a computer. For readers who want to learn more about these ideas and methods, we have included a set of references for additional reading in Appendix A. The balance of each chapter is devoted to an overview of a particular MBA-ware application, its design and features, and a walk-through of the software as applied to a sample problem.

Each of the programs discussed in depth can be found on the CD-ROM included with this book. These are full-working evaluation copies for you to test-drive using the easy-to-follow instructions in the chapter tutorials. The programs are limited in that they cannot save or print. However, these are not slide-show demos. Most contain data or models unavailable outside this book.

Instructions for viewing the evaluation programs can be found on the very last page of the book. There you will also find instructions on how to unlock the full-featured versions of six programs encrypted on the CD by the disc's producer, CD-Direct. These full versions can be utilized immediately; simply call CD-Direct to make payment arrangements. Within minutes, users can be gaining the full benefit of the programs, with all the manuals following shortly in the mail.

At the back of this book are four pages of offers by the publishers of these programs, with special discounts on the price of their software for readers who take a slower route and order directly from the publishers.

PART 1

Managing People and Projects

CHAPTER 1

Software Tools for Managing People and Goals

by W. Norman Wu, President & CEO
Avantos Performance Systems, Inc.

Imagine a business environment in which change is slow and managers have plenty of highly experienced and motivated employees ready to attack any market opportunity or competitive challenge. It seems easy to succeed. Employees know what they need to do, and have plenty of time to do it. As a result, managers can be somewhat "sloppy" in the way they manage. They don't have to clearly communicate or agree on objectives up front. The experienced employees just "know" what's expected of them and do it. And if there *is* some misunderstanding, there's plenty of time for a midcourse correction. Oh, if business were only so easy!

Now imagine a business environment in which change is rapid, managers are presented with new market opportunities or competitive challenges almost every day, and they have lots of inexperienced or unmotivated employees who are stretched thin. *Welcome to the real world!* Communication is all important. The manager must assume a role like the conductor of a well-timed orchestra. Not only does he or she make sure that there is a clear understanding of where the group is headed and how each individual contributes to the overall success of the team, but the manager also monitors progress, gives people feedback and coaching to help them hit their goals and improve their skills, and rewards and recognizes their achievements so that they'll try harder to meet their responsibilities.

This chapter will describe the challenges that managers face in today's rapidly changing business environment, traditional (noncomputer-based) approaches to meeting these challenges, early computer-based attempts to assist in these areas, and the emergence of second-generation software tools for effective people and goal management. It concludes with descriptions and tours of how ManagePro®, an integrated performance management tool, and Avantos Review Writer™, a performance review writing tool, can help managers meet their goals and manage their people more successfully.

The Changing Business Management Environment

Managers have never faced such a demanding business environment as they do today. Short product life cycles, changing customer needs, and intense, often global, competition means that decisions must be made faster. Companies are downsizing and organizational structures are flattening. Fewer layers of management mean each individual has more responsibility. For those who manage projects, it means responsibility for meeting more goals and objectives. For those who manage people, it also means accountability for more individuals. Gone are the days when managers had four to seven people reporting directly to them. Today, ten or fifteen "direct reports" is not uncommon.

More than ever, today's managers are being held accountable to produce results. But as the business environment has grown more complex, and managers' responsibilities ever greater, those results have become harder to achieve. How have managers tried to cope in this new era of rising expectations and expanding responsibilities? By churning through a steady progression of management fads such as Total Quality Management, Continuous Improvement, Self-Directed Work Teams, Empowerment, and Business Process Reengineering. The list goes on and on.

While these New Age management concepts offer hope and salvation for the overstressed manager, they often end in frustration. It's not that these concepts are inherently bad. They are just very difficult to implement. And more often than not,

they are simply band-aids for ineffective underlying management processes—basic
management practices that are effective in theory, but difficult to put into practice.

Management Skills: The Growing Challenge

Are today's managers equipped to handle the burdens wrought by the increasing
complexity of their jobs? Not fully. A study commissioned by Avantos indicates
that 75 percent of managers in midsize companies (100 to 2,000 employees) think
effective people management is critical to success. And while most managers think
they possess above-average people management skills, 85 percent recognize that
there is room for improvement.

More dramatically, *Inc.* magazine found that two-thirds of the 500 CEOs
surveyed in 1991 blame declining U.S. competitiveness on mediocre management.
The same survey found that managing people is second only to cash flow as CEOs'
major management concern.

A May, 1992 *Inc.* magazine poll revealed that 54 percent of managers spend
most of their time managing people (see Figure 1-1). The same poll indicated that

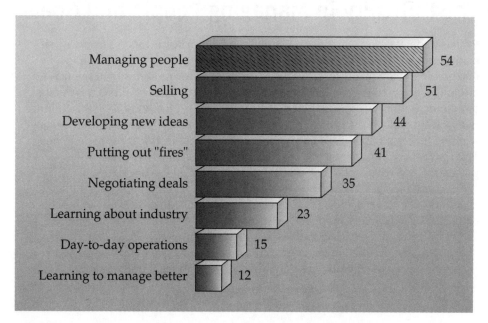

FIGURE 1-1.   *How managers spend their time (multiple responses account for
total percentages exceeding 100). (Source:* Inc. Magazine, May, 1992)

31 percent of owners/founders, 38 percent of CEOs, and 44 percent of top managers feel they "don't know enough to run the company effectively."

Sixty percent of the managers surveyed who reported feeling in control of their responsibilities spend 60 percent of their time managing people, versus the 47 percent spent by low-confidence managers. A similar survey by *Inc.* listed "managing people" as the third most popular answer out of eight key issues that managers said they most need to know more about. According to this survey, 35 percent of managers said they needed to know more about managing people.

In the face of these rising challenges, corporate America is investing heavily in management training. For companies that can provide it (typically, larger companies with over 1,000 employees), management training is a good start. Still, there remains a significant gap between *learning* management concepts and *applying* the processes to actual day-to-day work. It is not unusual for a manager to return from such training with the best of intentions, only to fall immediately back into familiar, ineffective patterns. In the best of circumstances, a manager will work diligently to apply one or two newly learned concepts at a time.

The Difficulty in Managing People and Goals

Why is it that these management processes, which make as much sense for the manager as for the conductor of the well-timed orchestra, are so difficult to implement in the real business world? It's because they require structure and discipline. Many managers learn these management processes in business school or training seminars sponsored by their companies. Yet the half-life of this training is invariably short—the training just doesn't stick. Managers come back from training and find a dozen phone calls to return and lots of people asking for their advice. They have the will but not the way to put these management processes into practice. The course materials end up gathering dust on the bookshelf.

Because of today's hectic business environment, it is more important than ever for managers to delegate authority and communicate effectively with their employees. And as the American work force grows more diverse with varied sets of skills, experience, capabilities, needs, and values, managers face more challenges than ever before in terms of creating, delegating and tracking goals, communicating expectations, ensuring predictable and consistent performance, and managing professional growth.

Creating and Communicating Clear Business Goals

Managing a successful business or department involves a hierarchy of goals. These are the key business goals that must be achieved for you and your business team to succeed. These goals may be high-level corporate goals, such as:

> ➢ Double sales in three years

> ➢ Increase operating profit to 18 percent

> ➢ Achieve recognition as the worldwide leader in toy robot

Or they may focus on a particular department or activity:

> ➢ Reduce employee turnover by 25 percent

> ➢ Achieve 99 percent customer service satisfaction

> ➢ Develop the industry's fastest widget

Whatever the appropriate level, these are your business' *primary* goals—the goals that you and your team are being held accountable for. Goals are usually the product of some form of analysis—industry analysis, market analysis, or analysis of the competition. For a more detailed discussion of how industry structure analysis is done and how it can be used to generate primary goals, see Chapter 5, "Industry Structure Analysis and Strategic Business Planning."

Primary goals are often supported by a number of supporting goals or subgoals. If your primary goal is to achieve 99 percent customer satisfaction, several subgoals might be necessary to accomplish it. For example,

> ➢ Implement Total Quality Management program

> ➢ Liberalize return policies

> ➢ Computerize customer service department

Once the primary goals and the appropriate subgoals have been identified, these goals need to be agreed to by the members of your team. An up-front agreement on goals is especially important to delegating tasks and empowering people effectively—what needs to be done, who's going to do what, when each part needs to be done, and what specific level of results are acceptable. Having a clear set of goals and subgoals that everyone recognizes makes it easier to monitor progress and facilitates the performance review process, a subject that will be discussed later in this chapter. From a team member's perspective, the process looks like Figure 1-2.

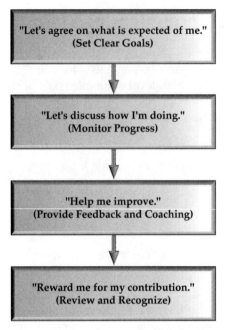

FIGURE 1-2. *The performance management process*

Traditional Ways of Managing People and Goals

Having gone through management training, many managers try (with varying degrees of success) to develop a system to help them put the newly learned concepts into practice. William Benson and Edward Kappus, two well-known management development consultants, suggest a number of ways to set goals, monitor progress, provide feedback and coaching, and give performance reviews and rewards in *Managing People: Your Competitive Edge in the 90's.*

Setting Goals

Ambiguity about goals is the single most critical barrier to employees' achievement, productivity, and work happiness. It causes as much as a 20-50 percent deviation in the way people spend their time, and thus deeply affects productivity. And the better your people are, the more assumptions they will make if they don't have clear goals.

For these reasons setting goals is the right way to begin managing your people. You and your direct reports can develop carefully thought-out and SMART goals. A set of goals is SMART if the goals are:

➤ **Specific** Be as clear and precise as necessary to avoid misinterpretation or multiple interpretations.

➤ **Measurable** Quantify whatever you can and qualify more subjective expectations by stating what the outcome will be if the goal is achieved.

➤ **Achievable** Both you and your direct report should be able to say "we can do it."

➤ **Related** Ensure that your goals are related to the business plan, your expectations, and your direct report's growth.

➤ **Time-bound** Set specific dates for both intermediate and end results. The more complex, difficult, important or long-running the goal is, the more checkpoints you will want for interim adjustment and coaching.

Some examples of SMART goals:

➤ Stabilize market share and sales volumes in two key markets by October 1, achieving a 60 percent or higher market share in Colorado for Brand C and a +25 percent sales volume in Illinois for Brand D.

➤ Reduce voluntary attrition in the manufacturing area for full-time, salaried workers from 18 percent to 9 percent annualized rate by November 1.

➤ Manage a 23-hour customer service turnaround time from problem reporting to problem diagnosis and customer feedback, with 19 of 20 customers satisfied/very satisfied with the service, as measured by next year's customer opinion survey.

Monitoring Progress

After you and your direct reports have set clear goals and they have begun work, you must monitor their progress. But how closely should you be involved? As managers, one of our people management challenges is finding the right balance between being an "ever-present" manager and a "never-present" manager. The balance you choose defines the balance of empowerment and intervention required to manage each employee and goal.

Empowerment is another word for delegation. Empowerment defines how much responsibility and authority you've given to your direct reports. Intervention is the amount of involvement your staff members require from you in order to complete their tasks. If an employee has demonstrated a willingness and ability to do the task, then "empower high and intervene low"; if not, then "empower low and intervene high."

There are four management responsibilities in monitoring any direct report's progress:

1. Keep yourself informed of direct report progress. Progress meetings are one of the most important ways for you to stay informed.

2. Keep your staff informed. Providing all appropriate information to direct reports is part of your job. Ask yourself frequently "If I were the employee, what information would I like to have to do this task?"

3. Keep your staff equipped for the tasks they must perform. Make sure that at least the minimum resources are available, that backup support is accessible when needed, and that peers who need to help one another do not have conflicting objectives.

4. Keep your direct reports on the right track. Sometimes corrective action is important to keeping on track. If the problem needing corrective action is inadequate performance, then feedback and coaching are in order.

Providing Feedback and Coaching

In the everyday world of work, most of us often reach stress points trying to accomplish all that is expected in a limited time. Often, we find the need to abbreviate, postpone or even eliminate activity that does not show up on our bottom line. Placing feedback and coaching activity into this "abbreviate or postpone" category is a mistake, even though many times one may not see the direct linkage to the bottom line. One executive put it succinctly: "In most companies, nothing is more important or less immediate than providing feedback and coaching to direct reports."

Most people get very apprehensive when they don't know how their boss views their performance, and this often affects their bottom-line results. Some performance expectations, even some jobs, have very visible measures of success, such as sales quotas or assembly line output, or finished pages per day, but these measures are not substitutes for knowing what the boss thinks.

In addition, most direct reports will have at least one goal that is more subjectively measured. These goals require special attention. But whether or not progress is easily measured by employees, the need to hear it from a manager is still imperative. There is too much at stake to allow staff members to make assumptions about the boss's perspectives. Feedback should be explicit and it should be provided on a regular basis.

Coaching is the other side of feedback. A coaching relationship between any manager and direct report requires trust, which you can earn by following these guidelines:

> Coach for the employee, not yourself. Your direct reports must sense that you really care and believe they lack something that is needed.

> Ensure your staff that you are able and willing to help in an ongoing way.

> Learn coaching skills and practice using them.

> ➤ Make sure that SMART performance expectations are in place and communicated before starting any coaching activity.

> ➤ Be open, honest, and nonthreatening in communicating both good and bad news.

Reviewing and Recognizing

Professionally written performance appraisals are one of the most important and fundamental documents that a manager creates. An effective review can serve as an excellent reward for an employee's contribution. If employees know that their appraisals are directly driven by their contributions, then they will try harder to meet agreed-upon goals and objectives.

In addition to formal performance reviews, other forms of recognition include increased responsibilities, promotions, merit increases, bonuses, stock option grants, public thank-you's, personal letters of thanks or commendation, plaques, certificates, and such psychological recognition as asking employees for their input or letting them make important presentations.

The Difficulty in Writing and Giving Effective Performance Reviews

Beyond the difficulty of handling the day-to-day tasks of keeping the goals and projects of several different people under control while coaching and developing these people effectively, lies another tactical but very important managerial task: the performance review. Many problems and pitfalls (from incomplete documentation to fear of legal repercussions) face managers as they sit down to write appraisals.

The Chinese philosopher Tsin Yu once remarked that the Imperial Rater seldom evaluates men on their merits, but often on the Rater's own personal biases. Today, some 17,000 years later, too many organizations still have Imperial Raters of their own—managers who put too little thought and effort into evaluating the people they supervise. This problem is especially evidenced by the all-important written appraisal, which is often based on imperfect memory rather than careful record-keeping, and on criteria that changes direction in the proverbial breeze.

Managers know that a professionally written review is valuable to the company and the employee, and can prevent subsequent complications to their relationship. But the pain of actually producing the document often leads to procrastination and a rushed job. The result is inconsistent at best and unfair—or even illegal—at worst.

A performance review may seem like a private transaction between manager and employee. In most cases, the document is filed away and never read again. But for the past 30 years, society has sought ways of ensuring that an employee's livelihood is protected against the capricious whim of a careless or even vengeful manager and is instead based on clear objectives and careful record-keeping. The written appraisal stands alone as the record of how an organization views an employee. As such, it is one of the most important and fundamental documents a manager creates.

Formal performance appraisals in the United States date back to the early 1900s in government and military jobs. In these sectors, the tradition of promotions based on merit required an objective measurement of performance and hence the written evaluation was created. This tradition moved to the industrial workplace after World War I and into the general work environment after World War II. But while most large organizations were conducting appraisals by the early 1950s, the programs were based on rough measures of performance; grades were issued for such traits as "initiative" or "motivation."

The turning point in appraisal writing came in the mid-1960s when federal guidelines demanded a more objective and systematic means of evaluating employees—one that could, if necessary, be defended. These federal mandates have gone a long way toward making the appraisal process more fair, but in doing so, they have put more pressure on managers to produce a truly professional document.

Most of the guidelines have come from the Equal Employment Opportunity Commission (EEOC). The rules are straightforward. They stipulate that:

➤ Employees not be discriminated against because of race, color, sex, age, creed, or national origin

➤ Employees performing similar jobs must be paid equally

➤ People with handicaps have equal opportunity

In 1978, the EEOC further stipulated that the appraisal accurately reflect job-related performance, that is, it must be based on *facts*, not impressions.

Common Problems with Written Appraisals

The most common pitfall associated with written appraisals is a lack of employee performance records. Too often in writing an evaluation, managers try to reconstruct an entire year's performance without any documentation. But records, not mere observations, play a big role in producing a professional-quality appraisal. All good managers informally take note of performance factors (such as communication, analytical abilities, or leadership skills) during the course of a year. Few of them take the time to establish a record-keeping system in which the information can be deposited for quick and easy retrieval.

Vague Evaluation Criteria

A second major pitfall in writing evaluations is in not establishing strong performance criteria and therefore not directly addressing the issues related to performance. During any review process, it is imperative that managers not only keep in mind an employee's job description but explicitly state the major goals for the review period.

Managers should also keep in mind that performance objectives must be specific. Goals should be expressed in clearly worded and measurable terms. Not every goal can be quantified, of course, but the opportunity to do so should not be overlooked. By defining the measurement basis up front, managers can better address the issues that count.

The Lack of Weighted Grades

A third area where written appraisals can go off track is the failure to rank the relative importance of an employee's various goals and objectives. Obviously, all of the things an employee is asked to do are not of equal importance. Is punctuality as important as teamwork? Is analytical problem solving as important as maintaining key relationships? When "grading" an employee's performance, managers need to consider the nature of their position on the business team, which aspects of the position are critical to achieving the team's primary goals, and then evaluate their overall performance, giving the most weight to position-critical tasks.

It is important to remember that each position on the team requires a different set of skills, and therefore involves a different set of weights. Punctuality is clearly more important for any part of your team that deals with the public (marketing and sales) than for personnel who work most effectively on their own schedule (programmers or R&D staff). A similar comparison can be made for "people skills" versus analytical skills. The point is that each position deserves to be evaluated on the basis of the appropriate criteria.

Unfortunately, on most preprinted corporate evaluation forms, managers have no opportunity to rank those categories that are most important to the position. Instead of being able to assign relative weights to various performance factors, the forms may simply ask the manager to rate the employee's performance as satisfactory/unsatisfactory, or to use some other scale that ignores the importance of that factor to the employee's position. As a result, managers are forced to use the same, equally weighted criteria to rate every position.

Poorly Written Evaluations

A manager is not expected to be an attorney, of course, and in most cases good common sense will go a long way. But written evaluations should be free of inflammatory and problematic language, as well as overly subjective or unsubstantiated impressions. For this reason, an evaluation should be edited as much for misleading statements as for good spelling.

One other factor contributing to a poorly written evaluation is worth noting: writer's block. Good writing is difficult, and the fear of a blank screen or paper form is well-founded. But waiting until the last minute to write an evaluation does justice to neither you nor the employee. Writing under pressure can lead to inaccuracies, omissions, and poor phrasing that reflects poorly on both parties. Maintaining an ongoing record of your direct reports' performance contributes to a clearly written report by spreading the process out over the entire review period, allowing you to choose your words carefully.

Traditional Software Approaches

Along with word processors, PC-based spreadsheets and databases represent the major horizontal applications designed to increase productivity across all business categories. However, these applications are, in effect, generic application "shells" or "frameworks" that must be structured and designed around a specific objective. Right out of the box, spreadsheet and database applications do nothing to help a manager meet his or her primary goals or manage people. And most business managers lack the time or technical skill to customize software to meet their needs.

Some managers have tried more specific project-management software, such as Microsoft Project or Symantec's Time Line, to manage their goals and people. While these programs have some useful tools, such as outliners that break high-level goals and projects into subgoals, tasks, and Gantt charts, the underlying philosophy is oriented toward resource allocation. The belief is that to successfully meet these goals, one simply allocates man-hours (or woman-hours) and costs effectively. Thus, 10 percent of Jack is assigned to this task and 20 percent of Sally to another task. There is no recognition that Jack and Sally are individual people with different skills, experiences, and behaviors and are not machines, nor that success is more driven by the effectiveness with which one delegates and how one coaches and rewards their performance.

Thus, the main focus in project management software is on finding critical paths and leveling resources. If one is building an aircraft engine, where hundreds or even thousands of tasks have to be completed to stay on schedule and the resources allocated to those tasks are more or less equal, then project management software is appropriate. However, most managers have to allocate a mixture of human and material resources. Lacking the means to distinguish between the resources being allocated, traditional project management software may not offer the most appropriate resource allocation method for every manager.

Managers have also tried to use personal information managers (PIMs) such as NetManage's ECCO or Lotus Organizer. These tools are focused on providing a convenient place to organize and store information. One can certainly store notes about people's goals and performance on a PIM. But because PIMs are designed to be generic depositories of information, there is little support for structured and disciplined management processes. One still needs to proactively apply effective delegation, tracking, coaching, and recognition skills.

A variety of specialized "expert systems" are available to help managers in their jobs. These tend to be black-box, rule-based products that offer advice based on user answers to a structured set of questions. Acumen and Praxis software, both from Acumen International of San Rafael, California, offer guidance reports improving one's interpersonal managerial effectiveness. DISC software from Carlson Learning analyzes your behavioral style and offers suggestions for improvement.

Second-Generation Software to Manage People and Goals

Unfortunately, traditional software approaches fall short of meeting the goal and people management needs of most business managers. Today's managers need turnkey solutions that integrate databases with expert advice and planning tools to provide real-time facilitation for effective management processes. They require a *complete* solution, including tools that provide the structured processes and management discipline critical to success.

A number of second-generation software tools that address various aspects of people management have recently emerged. These include Avantos Performance Systems' ManagePro software for real-time support of people and goal management processes and three software-based performance appraisal tools: Avantos' Review Writer, KnowledgePoint's PerformanceNow!, and Austin-Hayne's Employee Appraiser.

The rest of this chapter provides an overview of Avantos' ManagePro and Review Writer, followed by guided tours of the working models found on the CD-ROM included with this book. These working models are full-featured versions of the two applications. However, you will not be able to print, export, or cut and copy your data from either product.

ManagePro Features and Design Goals

ManagePro is an integrated software tool to support goal and people management. It provides a variety of planning tools, a networked database, and onscreen management advice to help users plan and track the business goals of individuals and groups.

ManagePro provides the following features:

➤ The **Goal Planner** helps you articulate business objectives, define supporting goals, and delegate them to subordinates and teams.

➤ **Structured forms** guide you step by step as you input information.

➤ A **performance database** helps you track progress versus goals.

➤ The **Goal Status Board** helps you focus your time and energy on those group goals requiring your intervention.

➤ The **People Status Board** graphically provides a way to monitor progress on goals.

➤ **Online reference material**, **tutorials**, and **expert advice** reinforce effective management techniques and help you to diagnose and deal with tricky performance issues.

➤ The **Assistant** collects information for review from each of ManagePro's three areas of focus: goals, people, and actions.

➤ The **To Do List**, **Action List**, **Goal Timeline**, and **Calendar** are tools that help you track information on your projects and people.

➤ **Multiuser** and **cross-platform features** support collaborative efforts in work groups even if the group uses different kinds of computers on a network.

➤ **Data exchange** (Windows DDE), **document attachment**, and **E-mail** features link ManagePro to other applications and let you send messages based on ManagePro data.

Review Writer Features and Design Goals

Avantos Review Writer was designed to help managers write more timely and more thorough performance reviews and to help them avoid costly wrongful-termination lawsuits. The product guides the user through the process of creating effective performance appraisals that are based on predefined goals set by the manager and employee, and that state specific criteria to be fulfilled during the year, resulting in clear expectations and fewer surprises for the employee at the time of the review.

Review Writer offers the following features:

➤ The **Performance Log** lets managers keep an ongoing list of comments regarding each employee throughout the entire review period and allows managers to import key performance data from ManagePro.

➤ **QuickBuild Mode** leads managers step-by-step through the process of writing the entire review.

➤ **Predefined templates** are available for general job types, including managers, team members, sales/service people, and clerical workers.

- ➤ Layouts can be **configured** to match a company's existing appraisal form in terms of content.

- ➤ The **Performance Factor Rater** accesses a library of over 14,000 paragraphs of sample text linked to over 70 performance factors, behaviors, and skills.

- ➤ The **Goal Rater** facilitates evaluation of results versus specific predefined goals and objectives.

- ➤ An **onscreen advisor** is based on the work of Dr. William Swan, an authority on performance review writing and author of *How To Do a Superior Performance Appraisal.*

- ➤ Goal and/or performance factor **weighting** allows the software to calculate an overall weighted average rating for the performance review.

- ➤ **Legal Check**™, a language-checking facility designed by employment law firm Orrick, Herrington & Sutcliffe, monitors the wording of the review for inappropriate, discriminatory, or overly vague words.

Now that you have read about the features and goals of ManagePro and Review Writer, you are probably wondering what they look like onscreen. The following tutorials take you through a self-guided tour of ManagePro and a more detailed walk-through of Review Writer. However, before the tutorials can be started, you need to download the two products from the CD-ROM included with this book, following the instructions found inside the back cover.

The ManagePro Guided Tour

ManagePro offers several tutorials for users with varying needs and abilities. First-time users should select the "Guided Tour (Basic) with Sample Database" in order to learn about all of ManagePro's features and how to use them. The Basic Guided Tour is an interactive tutorial that will take you about 30 minutes. After the Basic Guided Tour has been completed, users can then select either "Creating Your First Database," which walks the user through a database creation tutorial, or "Guided Tour Accessing a Manager's Database," which demonstrates some additional features of ManagePro, including a limited access feature for managers who choose to give their employees access to selected parts of their database. However, to get the most from either tutorial, the Basic Guided Tour should be completed first. The following procedure can help you get started.

To start ManagePro for Windows after downloading the program from the CD-ROM:

1. Open the Program Manager group that contains the ManagePro icon ( ).

2. Double-click the icon.
   To begin the Guided Tour:

3. Select Tutorial from the Help menu.

4. Select the "Guided Tour (Basic) with Sample Database" option from the Choose a Tutorial window and click Begin. ManagePro displays the table of contents for the Guided Tour (Basic) with Sample Database:

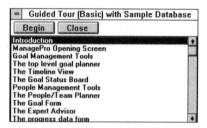

The table of contents for every tutorial works the same way. Simply select a topic that interests you. To get the Guided Tour underway:

5. Click the Begin button to start the Guided Tour at the Introduction (the default topic). Alternatively, you can double-click on any topic in the Guided Tour's table of contents to jump directly to that topic.

After ManagePro has started, the Tutorial window appears at the bottom of the workspace (see Figure 1-3).

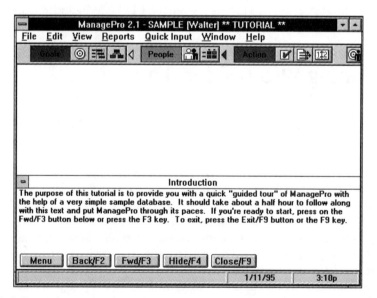

FIGURE 1-3. *The Tutorial window provides instructions for using ManagePro*

The Tutorial window offers instructions and explanations about running the tutorial and familiarizing yourself with the program. The buttons that appear across the bottom of the Tutorial window are listed here:

BUTTON	FUNCTION
Menu	Click this button to return to the Guided Tour table of contents.
Back/F2	Click this button or press F2 to move back one tutorial screen.
Fwd/F3	Click this button or press F3 to move forward one tutorial screen.
Hide/F4	Click this button or press F4 to toggle between hiding the Tutorial window (so you can see the full screen) and showing it again.
Close/F9	Click this button or press F9 to exit the tutorial and return to the ManagePro window.

Now that you've familiarized yourself with the Tutorial window, you are ready to read the tutorial instructions and to start the tutorial itself.

1. Click the Fwd/F3 button (or press F3) and read the Running the Tutorial instructions.

2. Click the Fwd/F3 button (or press F3) again when you're ready to move ahead, and the Tutorial window displays the next topic.
   Follow the instructions in each topic. We won't repeat these instructions here. As you choose commands from menus, open windows, and so on, you are already using ManagePro.

3. When you have finished the Guided Tour, click the Close/F9 button (or press F9).

Walk-Through of Avantos Review Writer

After downloading Review Writer from the CD-ROM, you can start the application from Windows by following these steps.

1. Open the Program Manager group that contains the Review Writer icon (Review Writer).

2. Double-click the icon.

The first time you start Review Writer, it displays a special Welcome message and requests one-time information about yourself and your preferences for writing reviews in the Set Options For Review Writer dialog box. In addition to asking your name and position, Review Writer asks you to choose an optional password, to select a "voice" for your report (2nd or 3rd person) and a rating scale (four or five point Expectation, Performance, or Numeric scales are available).

NOTE
After you set these options, Review Writer thereafter skips the Welcome message and Set Options For Review Writer dialog box when you start the application. If you select Cancel instead of setting these options, the application gives you another opportunity to do so the next time you start Review Writer.

Deciding How to Use Review Writer

After you have completed the Set Options dialog box, and each subsequent time you start Review Writer, the Review Writer main window (Figure 1-4) becomes the first screen you see. The main window lets you decide how to use Review Writer by asking you to click one of the three buttons shown. These three buttons allow you to do the following:

➤ **QuickBuild Mode** takes you step by step through the process of writing a review from start to finish with the help of Review Writer. For more

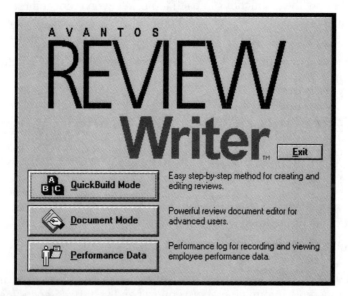

FIGURE 1-4. *The Review Writer main window*

information about how to use QuickBuild Mode, see the "Creating a Review in QuickBuild Mode" section next.

➢ **Document Mode** goes to the Review Writer Document window where all of its tools and commands are at your fingertips. Select this mode if you prefer writing the review yourself, asking Review Writer for help when you need it.

➢ **Performance Data** opens the Add/Edit/View Performance Data dialog box, where you can enter performance data for selected employees. Entering the data regularly can help you write an accurate performance review by reminding you of an employee's progress throughout the year.

Creating a Review in QuickBuild Mode

The first time you use Review Writer, you should use the QuickBuild mode to begin creating a performance review. QuickBuild mode guides you through the process step by step. Perform each of the following sets of sequential steps in order. You can take a break any time and return to the process later by opening the review and continuing where you left off.

Step 1: Create or Open a Review

The first step in writing a review is creating a new review. Once you have created a review, you can stop any time and open it later to resume your work.

1.1 Click the QuickBuild Mode button in the Review Writer main window. The QuickBuild main window will appear (Figure 1-5).

At the left of the window, the seven steps of building a review fall into three major groups:

➢ **Set Up Review Form** Create or open a review and define the form and content of your review.

➢ **Write Review** Rate success in meeting goals, rate performance categories, and write the review summary.

➢ **Scan and Print Review** After viewing or editing the entire document, use AdvisorScan to check quality (completeness and originality), spelling, and legal language issues (potentially inappropriate or sensitive words or phrases). In a full version of Review Writer, AdvisorScan would also allow you to print or export your review. However, the print and export options have been disabled in the demonstration version you will be viewing.

As you can see in Figure 1-5, the first step, "Create or Open a Review," is the only step that initially appears as a button. After you complete the first step, the second step becomes a button that you can click. Once you complete the second step, all the remaining steps change from icons with descriptive text to active buttons, as they are enabled. This means you can work on the third through seventh steps in any order you like. Again, all seven steps must be completed before the review is finished.

1.2 At the top left of the QuickBuild main window, click the Create Or Open A Review button. The Create/ Open Review dialog box appears:

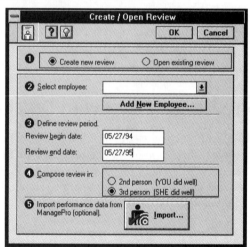

This box lets you create a new employee review or open an existing one. The Create New Review button at the left side of Section 1 is initially selected, which means that Sections 2 through 5 contain options for creating a new review. Note

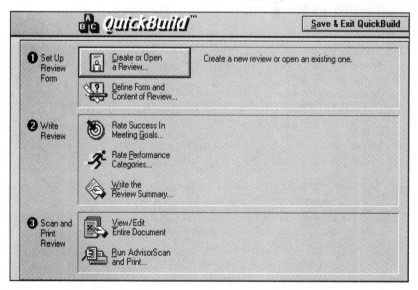

FIGURE 1-5. *The QuickBuild main window*

that the default review period covers the year ending with today's date. This period can be modified by entering new dates. Section 4 also enables you to change the default "voice" (2nd or 3rd person) that you selected when you started the application for the first time. If you click the Open Existing Review button in Section 1, the options in the panel change to those of an existing review. Once you have completed the QuickBuild tutorial, you can use this button to review your work.

1.3 Click the Add New Employee button below the Select Employee drop-down list box. The Add/Edit Employee dialog box appears:

In this box you can enter information about the person. You must enter the first name, last name, and gender. In addition, you can enter a job title, job description, employee number, level, and familiar name; this information is optional.

TIP
Be sure to specify a familiar name, if any, and the employee's gender. Review Writer uses these when providing suggested text. You can also enter a formal name in the Familiar Name text box if you want Review Writer to call a person by their formal name, such as Ms. Underhill.

1.4 Enter the appropriate information for the employee and click OK.
Review Writer redisplays the Create/Open Review dialog box, inserting the name of the employee in the Select Employee box. You can accept the default settings for the Review Begin Date, Review End Date, and Compose Review In boxes, or you can change the settings if you prefer. The Review End Date is used to uniquely identify this review from any other you might create for an employee. If you try to create multiple reviews and use the same Review End Date for more than one of them, Review Writer lets you know you are trying to create a duplicate review. To create a distinct second review for the employee, simply choose a different Review End Date. You can also import performance data for the person from your ManagePro database by clicking the Import button.

1.5 When you're satisfied with the information entered in the Create/Open Review dialog box, click OK.

Review Writer returns to the QuickBuild main window, changing its title to show the name of the employee, followed by the review end date. It also adds a check mark inside the first button. You have now completed Step 1 (Create or Open a Review) with the help of QuickBuild.

Step 2: Define Form and Content of Review

The second step in creating a review in QuickBuild mode is defining its form and content.

2.1 Click the Define Form And Content Of Review button in the QuickBuild main window. Review Writer displays the Define Form And Content Of Review dialog box (Figure 1-6).

On the left side of this dialog box, you can click a card's numbered tab to bring that card to the front and set its options. Changes made on the cards affect the Review Contents section on the right side of the dialog box.

As part of completing a review, you must set the options that become available after clicking each of the first three cards: Select Template, Define Goals, and Select Categories. The last card, Optional Steps, lets you move sections to and from

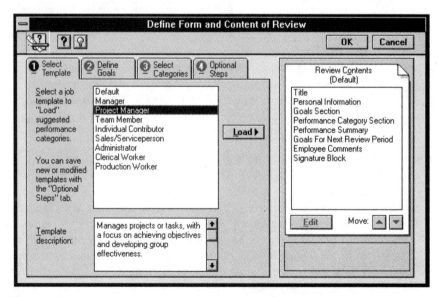

FIGURE 1-6. *The Define Form And Content Of Review dialog box with the Select Template card at the front*

the review contents, specify weighting, and save a template. Each of the cards and the options they offer are described in the following sections.

Select Template   In the Select Template card, you can select an existing template to use for the review. A template can define any combination of the following items: performance categories, goals, and weighting. Review Writer provides predefined templates designed for different job types. Brief descriptions of the positions that correspond with these templates can be found at the bottom-left of the Select Template card. If you have already set other options, such as goals or performance categories for the review form, Review Writer tells you that if you select a template now, any previous selections you have made will be lost.

2.2 To select a template, highlight the most appropriate template from the list and click the Load button. Note that the review contents on the right of the dialog box change to reflect the general requirements of the position you are reviewing.

2.3 When you have selected your template, click the tab on the Define Goals card.

Define Goals   In the Define Goals card, you define the major goals for the last review period. In the full version of Review Writer, you also have the option of importing these goals from your ManagePro database.

2.4 Define goals for the review according to the following instructions:

➤ To add a goal to the Review Contents section, enter the information in the Goal Title, Description, Due Date, and Measurement Basis text boxes and click the Add button.

➤ To delete a goal from the Review Contents section, select it in the Review Contents and click the Delete button.

➤ To edit a goal in the Review Contents section, select it in the Review Contents and click the Edit button. Review Writer moves the information about the goal to the Define Goals card so that you can make changes.

➤ To move a goal or other item in the Review Contents section from one position to another, select the goal and click the Move up or down buttons.

2.5 When you have finished defining the goals, click the tab on the Select Categories card.

Select Categories   In the Select Categories card you can move performance categories that you want to include from the list of available performance categories into the Review Contents section. You can also move categories out of the Review Contents section and create new categories of your own.

2.6 Select categories for the review according to the following instructions:

➤ To move a performance category into the Review Contents section, select it in the list at the left and click the Move button that points toward the Review Contents section at the right.

➤ To move a performance category out of the Review Contents section, select it in the Review Contents section and click the Move button that points toward the list of available categories at the left.

➤ To create a new performance category, click the Add New Category button. Review Writer displays the Add/Edit Performance Category dialog box. Enter a name and description for the new category, then click OK. Review Writer automatically adds your new performance category to the list of those available.

➤ To edit a performance category in Review Contents section, select it and click the Edit button. Review Writer displays the Add/Edit Performance Category dialog box with information for the selected performance category in the text boxes. Make changes and click OK to save the new information.

➤ To move a performance category or other item from one position to another in the Review Contents section, select it and click the Move up or down button.

2.7 When you have finished selecting the categories, click the tab on the Optional Steps card.

Optional Steps   In the Optional Steps card, you can select sections and move them to or from the Review Contents section, click the Set Weightings For Review button to set the relative weight of goals and performance categories, or click the Save Form For Later Use button to save your current settings as a reusable template that you can use for other reviews. Sections of this card can be moved or edited.

2.8 To adjust the weightings for the review, follow these steps:

a. Click the Set Weightings For Review button. Review Writer displays the Set Weightings For Review dialog box, shown here:

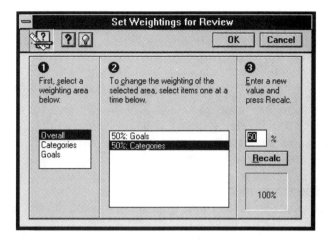

b. Select a category from the list in Section 1: Overall, Categories, or Goals.

c. Select an item from the list in Section 2.

d. Enter a new percentage in Section 3 and click the Recalc button. Review Writer equally adjusts the weight percentages of the other items in the category to total 100 percent.

e. Repeat for all the items and categories in your template.

f. Click OK when you have finished them all. This returns you to the Define Form and Content Of Review dialog box.

2.9 To save the form settings as a template, follow these steps:

a. Click the Save Form For Later Use button. The Save Form As Template dialog box appears:

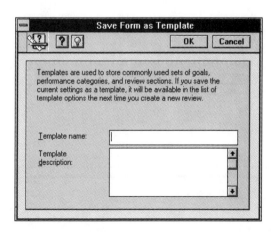

b. Enter a template name and description. Then click OK. Review Writer automatically saves the review contents and form settings.

2.10 After you finish working with the Define Form And Content Of Review dialog box and its cards, click OK This takes you to the Review Writer Document window where you can examine your review form or edit it.

2.11 When you finish defining the form and content of the review, click Continue. Review Writer returns to the QuickBuild main window and adds a check mark if you have completed Step 2. Steps 3 through 7 in the window are now active buttons. You are now ready to begin Step 3.

Step 3: Rate Success in Meeting Goals

The third step in creating a review with QuickBuild is rating the employee's success in meeting his or her goals.

3.1 Click the Rate Success In Meeting Goals button in the QuickBuild main window. Review Writer displays the Goal Rater dialog box (Figure 1-7).

NOTE
To select the Related Performance Data card or the All Performance Data card, click the card's tab. Use the up and down scroll boxes to move through the text.

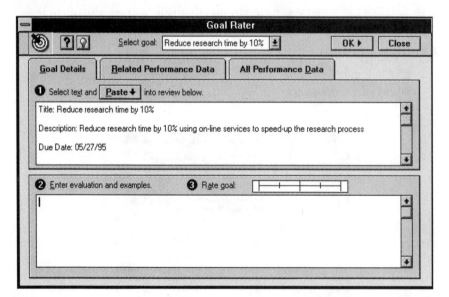

FIGURE 1-7. *The Goal Rater dialog box*

3.2 Start with the first goal that appears in the Select Goal drop-down list box. To select any text you want to include in the rating, click the Paste button to move it into the Review Text area.

3.3 To select a goal rating, point at the Rate Goal scale and click the mouse button when you see the appropriate rating.

As you move the pointer above the scale, Review Writer displays the rating value that will be applied to the current goal if you click at that point. When you click the mouse, Review Writer places a check mark in the Rate Goal scale according to the rating you've selected.

3.4 Edit your evaluation message in the Enter/Edit Evaluation And Examples text box.

3.5 Click OK when you finish evaluating the current goal. Review Writer automatically displays the next goal or you may choose a different goal to evaluate from the Select Goal drop-down list box. Review Writer returns to the QuickBuild main window if you have finished evaluating goals.

3.6 Click Close when you finish evaluating goals.

Review Writer displays the QuickBuild main window, and adds a check mark inside the third button if you've completed Step 3.

Step 4: Rate Performance Categories

The fourth step in creating a review with QuickBuild is rating the employee's performance categories levels.

4.1 Click the Rate Performance Categories button in the QuickBuild main window. Review Writer displays the Performance Category Rater dialog box (Figure 1-8).

4.2 Start with the first performance category in the Select Category drop-down list box or choose a different performance category from the Select Category drop-down list box if you prefer. The performance categories you see in the drop-down list box are the ones you added to the Review Contents section.

NOTE
To view the Related Performance Data card or the All Performance Data card, click the card's tab. Use the scroll bar to move up and down in the text.

4.3 Select a performance factor from the Select Factor drop-down list. Review Writer changes the three Rate Statements to apply to the performance

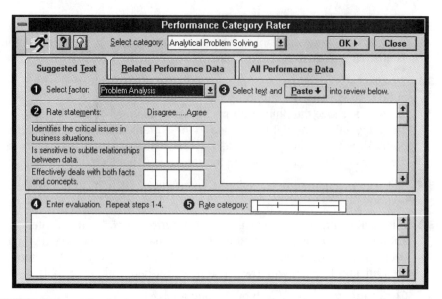

FIGURE 1-8. *The Performance Category Rater dialog box*

factor you select. Note that Review Writer only allows you to set an overall rating for those performance categories you create in Step 2.

4.4 Click the check box that indicates your level of agreement or disagreement with each of the three statements.

As you move the pointer above a check box, Review Writer displays the value that will be selected if you click that check box. Your options, from left to right, are Strongly Disagree, Disagree, Neutral, Agree, and Strongly Agree. The combination of responses you give determines the suggested text that Review Writer provides for a particular performance factor.

After you have selected your level of agreement with all the statements, Review Writer displays the suggested text in Section 3 on the right side of the dialog box. The text is already selected.

4.5 Click Paste to add the text to the Enter/Edit Evaluation and Examples text box.

If you prefer, you can select only portions of the suggested text that you want to paste into the evaluation. You can also edit the suggested text using basic Windows text editing techniques. If you are unfamiliar with how to edit text, see your Microsoft Windows user's guide for more information.

Once the evaluation text has been edited and entered, the importance of the category to overall performance needs to be rated.

4.6 Select a category rating by pointing at the Rate Category scale and clicking when you see the appropriate rating.

As you move the pointer over the scale, Review Writer displays the rating value that will be applied to the current category if you click at that point. The default rating values are Unsatisfactory, Meets Minimum, Meets, Exceeds, and Far Exceeds.

NOTE
You can change the rating values by selecting a different rating scale. To do this, choose the Options command from the Tools menu, select Preferred Rating Scale, and choose a different rating scale from the drop-down list. Review Writer also lets you create your own custom rating scales.

4.7 Click OK to accept your entries and begin rating the next performance category.

4.8 Repeat these steps for all of your chosen categories.

When you've finished the last performance category, Review Writer redisplays the QuickBuild main window, and adds a check mark inside the fourth button if you've completed Step 4.

Step 5: Write the Review Summary
The fifth step in creating a review with QuickBuild is writing the review summary.

5.1 Click the Write The Review Summary button in the QuickBuild main window. Review Writer displays the Write Summary Sections dialog box with the All Ratings card at the front (Figure 1-9).

NOTE
To view the All Ratings and Text card or the All Performance Data card, click the card's tab.

5.2 Choose a summary section from the Select Section drop-down list box.

5.3 Select the text in the scrolling text box (Section 1) and click Paste to add that text to the Enter Overall Summary Message text box. If you are working on the performance summary, be sure to select an overall performance rating.

5.4 Point at the Rate Performance scale and click when you see the rating value you want. As you move the pointer, Review Writer displays the rating value that will be selected if you click at that point. The default choices are Unsatisfactory, Meets Minimum, Meets, Exceeds, and Far Exceeds.

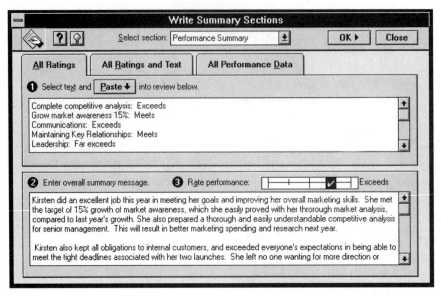

FIGURE 1-9. *The Write Summary Sections dialog box with the All Ratings card at the front*

NOTE
You can change the rating values by selecting a different preferred rating scale. To do this, choose the Options command from the Tools menu, select Preferred Rating Scale, and choose a different preferred rating scale from the drop-down list box.

5.5 Edit the overall summary message in the text box if necessary.

5.6 Click OK to continue with the next summary section.
   If this is the last section, Review Writer redisplays the QuickBuild main window, and adds a check mark inside the fifth button if you've completed Step 5.

Step 6: View/Edit Entire Document
The sixth step in creating a review with QuickBuild is viewing and editing the entire document.

6.1 Click the View/Edit Entire Document button in the QuickBuild main window. Review Writer displays the Review Writer document window (Figure 1-10) with the complete text for the review.

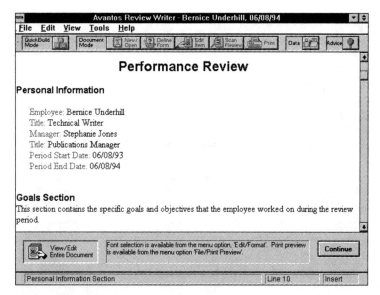

FIGURE 1-10. *The Review Writer document window*

In this window, each goal and performance category is weighted and briefly described, followed by the employee's evaluation text. Light gray text is used to identify information that cannot be edited. At the bottom of the window, a message bar appears, letting you know that you can view or edit the review text or click Continue to go back to the QuickBuild window when you are ready.

6.2 Click Continue when you finish viewing or editing the review document. Review Writer returns to the QuickBuild main window and adds a check mark inside the sixth button if you've completed Step 6.

Step 7: Run AdvisorScan and Print

The final step in creating a review with QuickBuild is running AdvisorScan. With the fully enabled version of Review Writer, you would also be able to print the review or export it to its own file as part of this step.

7.1 Click the Run Advisorscan And Print button in the QuickBuild main window. Review Writer displays the Advisorscan And Print dialog box (Figure 1-11).

AdvisorScan can check your review text for quality (completeness and originality), spelling, and inappropriate language, as described in the following sections.

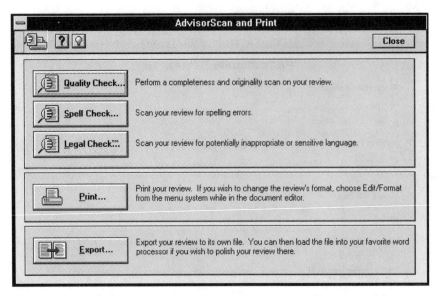

FIGURE 1-11.   *The Advisorscan And Print dialog box*

Quality Check   To perform a quality check of your completed review, click the Quality Check button. Review Writer displays the Quality Check dialog box (Figure 1-12). Examine AdvisorScan's evaluation of originality and completeness. When you are finished reviewing AdvisorScan's evaluation, click OK to return to the AdvisorScan dialog box. If the review needs to be revised, changes can be made by clicking the View/Edit Entire Document button in the QuickBuild main window, which places you in the Review Writer Document window (Step 6 earlier).

Spell Check   To perform a spell check on your review, click the Spell Check button in the AdvisorScan and Print dialog box. If AdvisorScan finds no unrecognized words, it displays the "Spelling Check Complete" message. Click OK to return to the Advisorscan And Print dialog box. If AdvisorScan finds a word that is not in the dictionary, it displays a dialog box, as shown here, across the bottom of the Document window.

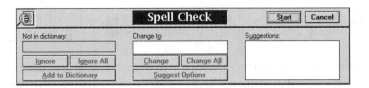

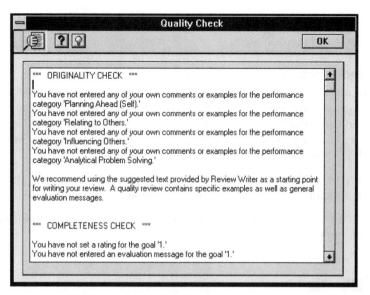

FIGURE 1-12.   *The Quality Check dialog box*

The spell check function works much like the ones found in most popular word processing applications. The dialog box shows the unrecognized word, offers suggestions if any are available in the dictionary, and lets you select one of the suggested words, ignore the word the speller doesn't recognize, add a correctly spelled new word to the Review Writer dictionary, or type your own replacement.

After you respond to the last unrecognized word, Review Writer displays a message that tells you the spelling check is complete. Click OK. This returns you to the AdvisorScan And Print dialog box.

Legal Check   To perform a language check, click the Legal Check button in the AdvisorScan and Print dialog box. If AdvisorScan discovers any words or phrases that are potentially inappropriate or sensitive, it displays the Document window with a Legal Check dialog box, as shown here, across the bottom of the window.

You can substitute replacement words or phrases in the Document window to resolve these legal language issues.

Printing and Exporting The Advisorscan And Print dialog box also includes the appropriate buttons for printing your performance reports and/or exporting these reports to another file. Like the other Review Writer features, printing and exporting are completed through a straightforward set of dialog boxes. However, these features have been disabled in the demonstration version of Review Writer found on the CD-ROM.

7.2 To run Quality Check, Spell Check, or Legal Language Check, simply click the appropriate button in the AdvisorScan and Print dialog box.

7.3 When you are finished, click the Close button to return to the QuickBuild main window.

Conclusion

Today's business environment is increasingly complex and competitive. Companies are constantly growing and changing. Competitive pressure means decisions must be made faster. As a result, existing management processes and systems are being stretched to the limit. Small businesses with meager support staffs have become the norm; large companies are flattening and downsizing. Individual managers everywhere face a growing scope of responsibility, with accountability for more goals and people than ever before. Consequently, it is more important now than ever for managers to delegate authority and to communicate effectively with their employees.

Although this problem can be addressed through additional management training, a significant gap remains between *learning* management concepts and *applying* the processes to actual day-to-day work. These trends are driving the need for a new generation of productivity tools that help managers learn and apply proven management processes: tools that harness the power of the personal computer to help businesspeople manage their top priorities—business goals and people.

This new breed of software already exists: MBA-ware. These programs integrate key software components—graphical user interfaces (GUIs) to reduce the learning curve, application-specific databases to store critical management information, various planning and productivity tools with which to view and manipulate that data, and knowledge bases and expert systems to reinforce training—to deliver a highly focused, easy-to-use support tool designed to meet the most pressing needs of today's business manager. You have just read about two of these programs: ManagePro and Review Writer from Avantos Performance Systems. In the chapters that follow, you will learn more about 12 other MBA-ware applications.

CHAPTER 2

Managing Occupational
Illness and Injury Costs

by Bryan Pfaffenberger,
University of Virginia, and
Harry Smith, Safety Software

At the dawn of the industrial age, little thought was given to worker safety. This inattention had fatal results. For instance, 525 work-related deaths occurred in 1906 in one county alone (Allegheny, Pennsylvania). Over the subsequent four years, approximately three-quarters of the work force in this county missed work due to work-related injuries and accidents. Conditions such as these led to a public outcry for industrial regulation, an outcry met in the U.S. with industrial safety and workers' compensation laws at the state level. Varying from state to state, these laws shared the philosophy that workplace-related injuries and illnesses should be compensated for by the employer, even if the malady is not attributable to the employer's negligence. Subsequently, the federal Occupational Safety and Health Act of 1970 (OSHA) mandated federal regulation of workplace health and safety conditions.

Keeping records related to occupational illnesses and injuries is both a good idea and it is required by law. More than one million firms are required to keep records using the federally mandated Form 200 (Log and Summary of Occupational Injuries and Illnesses). Although Form 200 is not submitted to OSHA at present, the agency recently announced plans for periodic submissions of the document by firms to the agency. In the meantime, OSHA levies stiff penalties on firms that fail to comply with OSHA's record keeping mandate. According to one industry observer, OSHA finds record keeping violations easy to punish because the investigation requires relatively modest expenditures. In the two decades following OSHA's creation, record keeping violations were the most cited violation, resulting in fines of at least $1,000 *per error*. In other words, if OSHA determines that six cases should have been recorded, the fine is $6,000. If OSHA further determines that the error was serious and willful, the fine is multiplied by a factor of seven. The largest record-keeping fines, in such multisite industries as meat packing and automobile manufacturing, have exceeded $1 million.

A business may respond to regulation in two ways: negatively, by seeing it as a burden, or positively, by seeing it as an opportunity. As this chapter explains, risk control management can be transformed from mere recordkeeping into a significant opportunity for cost reduction, and it can become an integral part of total quality management (TQM). And as every businessperson knows, reducing costs translates into increased profits. This chapter explores methods to facilitate cost reduction through risk control management, surveys the role of computer applications in risk control management, and introduces the OSHALOG.200 Series™, a database with an expert decision-tree module.

Risk Control Management: Improve Profits and Be Ethical

Risk control is not only humane and ethical, it is also in management's best interest, since unsafe practices are often time-consuming and costly. From 1926 to 1976, safety contests, safety regulations, and other proactive safety-management programs led to a remarkable 75 percent decline in the frequency and severity of disabling work-related injuries. However, reductions in work-related injuries and illnesses have not occurred fast enough to offset the almost unbelievable growth in costs related to occupational safety.

A 1993 study disclosed that even as workplaces were getting safer, costs for workers' compensation claims were rising dramatically. In 1991, 10.9 out of every 100 employees made workers' compensation claims, a figure that dropped to 10.1 out of each 100 employees in 1993. But employers' costs per claim jumped 35 percent in the same period. To many industries, the costs of providing occupational safety seem completely out of control:

> ➤ In 1991 alone, workers' compensation costs consumed $62 billion, up 300 percent from just ten years earlier. Costs at one company, Olsten Corp., a Pennsylvania janitorial services company, reached $10.3 million annually.

> ➤ From 1991 to 1992, seven out of nine manufacturing industries experienced increases of more than 15 percent in workers' compensation costs. In some industries, the increases threatened the firms' very existence: transportation equipment manufacturers, for example, reported a 138 percent increase.

According to a 1994 survey in *Risk Management*, the leading safety management journal, the cost of uncontrolled risk rose 10 percent in just one year (1993) for U.S.-based organizations. During the same year, workers' compensation costs rose 7 percent, while the cost of liability risk financing rose a whopping 18 percent.

The reasons for spiraling costs are many: the rise of state workers' compensation programs, the growing burden of paperwork, the awarding of spectacular damages by juries angered by employer negligence, and the concomitant explosion of insurance rates for workers' compensation coverage. Workers' compensation costs have become sufficiently worrisome that more than one-third of U.S. firms make siting decisions based principally on state-to-state variations in workers' compensation laws.

In short, an injury prevented is money saved. For every workplace injury or illness that is prevented by loss control management, the savings go beyond medical bills, legal bills, and increased insurance rates. These savings include additional funds that would otherwise have been spent on investigation time, recruitment, retraining, building and tool damage, production delays and interruptions, missed shipments, and paperwork—expenses that can total as much as 50 times the cost of the medical bills and compensation costs alone. Firms committed to reducing costs quickly discover that reducing work-related injuries and illnesses is one of the quickest routes to significant savings—and higher profits.

TQM, ISO 9000, SPC

The current interest in total quality management (TQM), ISO 9000 (a quality standard), and SPC (statistical process control) all relate to the same goal as safety record keeping—tracking business processes to improve the bottom line. Safety is one of the key processes that make up your business. The measurement of safety losses is as integral to a business' operating costs as measuring losses from theft, defects, and mean time between failures. Safety issues, like quality issues, require a commitment from management to integrate the process into ongoing operations. Safety, like quality, simply doesn't work if it is only done on Friday afternoons.

Measurement: The Key to Loss Control Management

An effective loss-control management program begins with a positive and proactive program that makes workplace safety a top management priority. Such a program minimally includes worker indoctrination, rules and practices, standardized job procedures, hazard correction, skills training, protective equipment, and group meetings. But even the best program cannot prevent loss-producing incidents. In even the most safety-conscious firms, unforeseen circumstances may produce what appear to be totally unpredictable accidents, resulting in property damage, injury, and even loss of life.

In the aftermath of such an incident, everyone involved is keenly aware of the meanings implied by the word "accident"—an unpredictable, unpatterned, inexplicable incident that conforms to no known pattern. For loss-control management, these connotations are unfortunate: they mislead. Loss-producing incidents typically stem from patterns that can be observed and quantified. Accidents are caused by dangerous habits, unsafe conditions, inadequate procedures, improper attitudes, deficient skills, inattentive operation, and lack of training. Underlying these causes are the behavioral patterns of employees at all levels. For instance, a study of 1,000 fatal accidents in the U.K. disclosed that 60 percent of the accidents could be attributed to such behavioral factors as poor supervision, inadequate training, or the adoption of unsafe work systems.

The central question in loss-control management is whether such patterns can be detected before they result in loss-producing incidents. And the answer, unequivocally, lies in detailed recordkeeping and the analysis of these records. Analysis can reveal patterns that would otherwise not have been obvious, even to a trained observer. In Figure 2-1, for example, it is immediately obvious that the bulk of injuries have been inflicted on workers' backs, followed by fingers and eyes. This information, which was taken from an actual study of injuries incurred at a manufacturing firm, suggests that injury-related costs can be reduced immediately by focusing on the causes of these particular injuries.

The Importance of Smart Recordkeeping

One example should suffice to demonstrate the importance of smart recordkeeping as well as the massive cost savings that can result from the measurement and analysis of safety-related incidents. Rosendin Electric Company instituted a measurement program in the early 1990s, which sought to record every work-related safety incident, regardless of whether it produced actual losses. A subsequent analysis disclosed a fact that no one had previously realized, namely, that more than half of the firm's injury-related losses involved back and eye injuries. After pinpointing the problem areas, managers revised safety regulations and acquired additional safety equipment. The results? Between October, 1992 and October, 1993, the frequency of workers' compensation claims declined by more than one-third, and the severity of these claims declined by 10 percent. The firm estimates that these claim reductions alone saved over $350,000. In some states, OSHA utilizes state workers' compensation records to target firms for potential record-keeping violations, and if discrepancies are found, fines are sure to follow.

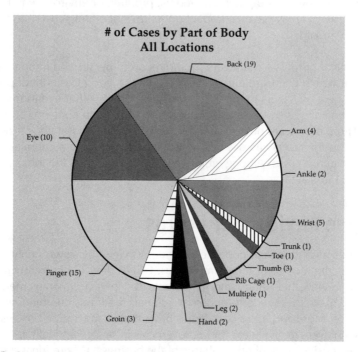

FIGURE 2-1.   *Injuries by body part*

OSHA Regulations and the Issue of Recordability

OSHA has published complex regulations that determine whether or not an event is recordable. Many of the reasons underlying OSHA's definitions relate to the fact that these records must be standardized to comply with the data for the U.S. Department of Labor's Bureau of Labor Statistics annual surveys. Hence the "OSHA perspective and definition" of an event often differs from what most businesspeople may use for their own purposes.

With respect to the recording of occupation-related injuries and illnesses, a decision must be made each time a malady is recorded—namely, whether it is *recordable* or *nonrecordable* according to OSHA guidelines:

> **Recordable Events** OSHA requires that management record these injuries and illnesses. All these events must appear on Form 200 (Log and Summary of Occupational Injuries and Illnesses).

> **Nonrecordable Events** These are events for which OSHA does not require record-keeping—"near-misses" or "accidents" without injuries, damage, or loss to property, equipment, materials, product, or environment. However, these events may have an impact on a firm's operating costs and long-term safety record.

For analytical purposes, managers *should* record illnesses and injuries other than those for which OSHA requires recordkeeping. A good loss control program should encourage managers to record near-misses, or any other events that could conceivably be connected to occupational safety and health concerns and liabilities. These events are not required by Form 200 and do not appear on the form. However, managers can use this information to get a more complete picture of the injuries and illnesses among employees, both on and off the job, as well as other potential loss areas.

Employee Review of Records

It is considered a good idea to permit employees to view their own safety records, without seeing the records of other employees. OSHA does not currently require employees to review their injury and illness entries. However, management's willingness to make these records accessible signals the firm's commitment to a safe workplace. More and more companies have started suggestion box systems that solicit employees to give ideas for improvements in safety, production, marketing, sales, product design, and all other phases of the business. Where ideas have a dramatic impact on the bottom line, the employees often receive recognition and sometimes earn cash bonuses.

Traditionally, union locals, shop stewards, and business agents have offered formal and informal advice for business process improvement. While still an area of controversy, the new worker-management circles, quality circles, and self-directed teams have also been active in the safety area. The controversy has arisen over the applicability or nonapplicability of the labor management statutes. Nonetheless, where a cooperative management style can harness the creative insights of those on the front lines of a business, the benefits are quickly apparent.

Approaches to Loss-Control Management

Keeping records of occupation-related injuries and illnesses provides the key to significant cost reduction. With paper-and-pencil methods, however, this opportunity is rarely exploited to the fullest. The advent of inexpensive but powerful personal computers, coupled with high-quality database management software, provides precisely the solution needed by managers who wish to track injury and illness data but would not otherwise have the time.

Paper-Based Records vs. Computer Database Systems

To make a long story short, old-style paper-based file records are simply inadequate compared to a computer database management program. Such programs enable the user to design a custom data entry form, the first step in record-keeping. These forms resemble a card in a library card catalog with distinct areas (called *fields*) for each type of information that is recorded. Unlike a library card catalog, however, a database program provides powerful, computerized tools for sorting and organizing this information. By means of a *query language*, a programming language in which the user can ask questions of the database, it is also possible to analyze the data. Examples of the kinds of queries one could ask of an injury- and illness-related database for a firm include

> ➤ Which department is experiencing the most frequent injuries?

> ➤ What part of the body is most frequently injured by our employees?

> ➤ Which job categories generate the fewest injuries?

The answer to these queries could then be produced as either a report (a tabular printout) or as a graph.

Database software provides the tools managers need to keep the necessary records, query the recorded data, and generate informative reports and graphs. However, general database programs such as dBASE and Paradox come with their own liability, namely, the difficulty of customizing the program so that it records the needed data, enables useful queries, and produces the right reports and graphs. Users can spend hundreds of hours learning how to program these applications and many more hours actually creating a customized database application that proves useful for risk reduction. In addition, any person attempting to design such a system would need training and background in risk control management concepts and terminology to design an effective application. For these reasons, managers are turning to a new generation of smart database applications created specifically for use in loss control management rather than creating their own.

Software for Safety Management

The advent of powerful relational database systems has enabled software developers to create powerful knowledge-based applications that bring the tools of the safety professional to managers whose expertise lies in other areas. The integration of quality systems and safety management has resulted in the creation of valuable software tools for the forward-looking organization.

Several software applications have been developed for safety management, including WARE from Systems Software Group, Ann Arbor, Michigan, and Industrial Health 2000 from Software 2000, Inc. of Hyannis Port, Massachusetts. Each of these programs aid managers in keeping the necessary records required to print an OSHA-approved version of Form 200, along with the necessary customization tasks—creating the data form, programming the queries, and generating the reports. More specifically, with these applications, managers can perform the following tasks:

> ➤ Enter all the necessary information about every illness and injury required by OSHA Form 200.

> ➤ Enter information about other illnesses, injuries, near-misses, or accident/loss causing events, even if OSHA does not require you to do so. You can use this information to help you understand the broader patterns of illnesses and injuries in your organization.

> ➤ Edit the information to make sure that it is accurate and complete.

> ➤ Print all the events on which OSHA requires information on an OSHA-approved facsimile of Form 200.

Enhanced versions of these applications provide additional data collection options, reporting for one or multiple locations, and advanced graphing choices.

MBA-ware for Loss-Control Management

Today's best MBA-ware software embeds task-specific knowledge and experience that guides managers toward optimal decisions. The same is true of the OSHALOG.200 Series, an MBA-ware application developed specifically for loss-control management.

As outlined earlier, managers can enter the details of all employee injuries and illnesses, whether or not the incidents are recordable according to OSHA regulations. In OSHALOG software, if the user is not sure whether an event is recordable, the program can test for its recordability by guiding the user through a series of structured questions and answers using an embedded decision tree. OSHALOG's decision tree filters the incident information, using OSHA's criteria and definitions, to assist in determining which incidents are OSHA-recordable. Employees can also view their OSHA-recordable records, if they wish, without viewing their supervisor's comments. To keep records up-to-date, the user can edit the data that has been entered. Managers have the option of creating custom reports, which produce printouts of the recorded data sorted by severity, department and supervisor, job title, employee last name, part of body affected, injury classification, and illness classification.

Even though OSHA does not require firms to keep records of nonrecordable injuries and illnesses, it is good policy to record them. With OSHALOG, data pertaining to nonrecordable injuries and illnesses is taken into account in producing analyses, such as accident factor analyses. This data can help a manager form a more complete picture of the patterns of injuries and illnesses in the workplace.

Creating Custom Reports

The initial motivation for using an advanced loss control management application such as OSHALOG, WARE, or Industrial Health 2000 is the legal requirement to maintain the records needed to produce an accurate Form 200. All the programs permit managers to keep records of nonrecordable as well as recordable incidents, and within this information can be found important clues to injury and illness patterns in the workplace. Some useful criteria for building custom reports and looking at the data include the following:

➤ **All Cases** All the events for the specified time period in case number order.

➤ **Severity of Event** All the events for the specified time period, sorted in decreasing order by the amount of lost or restricted time. For each case, you see the department name, supervisor's name, employee's name, the date of the record, the illness or injury description, the part of the body affected, and the affected side.

➤ **Department/Supervisor** All the cases for the specified time period, orted by department. Within a department, cases are sorted by supervisor. For each supervisor, you see a list of all the cases alphabetized by the employee's last name. Each case lists the amount of lost or restricted time, and you also see summaries for lost or restricted time by supervisor and by department.

➤ **Job Title** All the cases for the specified time period, sorted by job title. Within a job title, cases are alphabetized by employee last name. For each case, you see the amount of lost or restricted time. For each job title, you see totals for the amount of lost or restricted time.

➤ **Employee Last Name** All the cases for the specified time period, sorted by employee last name. For each case, you see the amount of lost and restricted time. For each employee, you see totals for the amount of lost and restricted time. Repeaters are grouped together.

➤ **Part of Body** All the cases for the specified time period, sorted by the part of body affected. Within a body part category, cases are sorted by department. Within a department, cases are alphabetized by employee last name. For each case, you see the amount of lost or restricted time. You also see summaries of lost or restricted time for each body part.

➤ **Injury** All the cases for the specified time period, sorted by the injury description. For each injury description, cases are sorted by department. You see a summary of the lost or restricted time for each department, and you also see totals of lost or restricted time for each injury.

➤ **Illness** All the cases for the specified time period, sorted by the illness description. For each illness description, cases are sorted by department. You see a summary of the lost or restricted time for each department, and you also see totals of lost or restricted time for each illness.

➤ **Employee Verification** The employees who have verified their records with an employee review option.

Performing Queries to Analyze Data

Once a customized report has been created, managers should analyze the data by performing queries. A *query* is a question that is asked of the data, such as "How many injuries have there been for each body part?" The result of a query is a new table, organized in a way that helps you to understand the data. Many queries are more easily analyzed in a graph format, which permits the manager to detect patterns in the data that are highlighted by visual cues.

Unlike generic database programs, which require users to learn complex procedures or even programming skills to frame effective queries, the new generation of loss control management software offers the user the simplicity of choosing complex but ready-made queries from a menu that embeds the insights of an experienced safety expert. The following queries are typical of those available:

> ➤ **Body Part Reports** A graphical display or printed tabular report of the total number of cases by part of the body that was affected, limited by the time frame you specify.

> ➤ **Job Title** A table of injuries organized by job title, department, and injury description.

> ➤ **Department by Supervisor** A table of all injuries and illnesses for the specific time frame, sorted by department and supervisor. This report differs from the Department/Supervisor report discussed in the previous section in the following way: the display of data can be limited by the legal status, location, or other classification.

> ➤ **Lost Time Injury by Supervisor** A table or graph of the injuries that resulted in lost time, sorted by supervisor.

> ➤ **Events by Lost or Restricted Time** A table (grouped by department) of the number of events as well as the number of days away and restricted days.

Analyzing Accident Patterns

Advanced loss control management software can enhance a manager's ability to understand the patterns of accidents in an organization by enabling him or her to query the software for *accident factors,* such as the reason for the accident, the location of the accident, the type of corrective action undertaken, the hazardous material involved, and more. Users can create and use custom data fields to track information unique to their organization or analytical needs. These features are critical for management, safety personnel, and others who wish to adopt a proactive program to identify and correct the underlying causes of workplace accidents. With this capacity, managers can create analytical categories that can be used to code incidents with customized information, including the following cuts of the data:

➤ **Equipment/Machinery/Tools** These are the implements that your employees use every day, such as strapping machines, grinders, drills, or nonhazardous materials.

➤ **Hazardous Materials** These are the hazardous chemicals, substances, or materials that your employees work with, such as benzene, toluene, or insulation.

➤ **Location of Accident** These are specific locations within your organization where accidents have occurred or are likely to occur, such as the metal fabrication shop, the aisle next to the assembly line, or the stockroom.

➤ **Operation Being Performed** These are the specific tasks that your employees perform, such as wrapping, grinding, stacking, or honing.

➤ **Operation Frequency** These are codes for identifying how often the operation is performed (such as hourly, daily, weekly, or monthly).

In addition to the above customizable entry fields, loss control management software typically offers untitled fields that can be used for any purpose. Managers can use these fields to track special costs, such as related vehicle, liability, property, equipment, or environmental costs. Having this data is useful for providing corporate managers with the data necessary for improving business processes.

Predictions from Data

Once the user has entered incidents into a safety management software program, it is possible to ask more probing queries of the data. By using these queries, a manager can gain greater insight into where incidents are more likely to occur. The following reports can quickly pinpoint problem areas:

➤ **Job Title** Displays a table of injuries organized by job title, with department and injury description.

➢ **Department by Supervisor** Displays a table of injuries and illnesses for the specific time frame, by department and supervisor, restricted to workers' compensation cases, if desired.

➢ **Lost Time Injury by Supervisor** Displays a table of the injuries that resulted in lost time, sorted by supervisor.

➢ **Total Loss by Supervisor** Displays the total estimated losses for each event, by supervisor.

➢ **Events/Lost Time/Restricted Time by Department** Displays a table, grouped by department, of the number of events as well as the number of lost or restricted days.

Body-part analyses are particularly useful to reveal the existence of problem areas that might have otherwise gone unnoticed. In these analyses, these programs can produce tables and graphs that summarize data regarding the affected portion of the body, such as the back or the eyes, grouped by department, job title, equipment used, operation performed, and more. The following reports are useful for those seeking to reduce occupational risk: all events by body part or disease, body part or disease by department, body part or disease by job title, body part or disease by cost, body part or disease by accident type, body part or disease by equipment, body part or disease by hazardous material, body part or disease by accident location, body part or disease by operation performed. Most of the advanced loss control management applications can generate these reports without any difficulty.

In summary, firms everywhere are faced with rapidly escalating workers' compensation costs. By identifying those areas where costs are accelerating most rapidly and dealing with the accident case factors proactively, a safety manager can significantly reduce these avoidable costs, thereby improving the firm's bottom line.

A Walk-Through of the OSHALOG Demo

The preceding sections have introduced you to the OSHA requirements for complete and accurate accident and injury records and the role of advanced loss control management software in tracking and analyzing these records. The remainder of this chapter will walk you through a demonstration version of the OSHALOG.200 Plus software on the CD-ROM included with this book. This is a fully functioning version of OSHALOG.200 Plus with two exceptions: the demo will not print reports nor will it run on a network. Also included with the demo is sample data from a small widget manufacturer for the year 1994. You can enter as many additional cases as you wish, and you can run queries (reports) on the demonstration data or on any data you may have entered. There are also two *full* versions of OSHALOG.200 available on the CD-ROM (OSHALOG.200 Plus and OSHALOG.200 Manager Plus) that can be downloaded and enabled after contacting CD-Direct according to the instructions at the end of this book.

Getting Started with OSHALOG

The following instructions for loading and operating OSHALOG.200 Plus are written with the computer novice in mind.

Loading Instructions: DOS

To install your OSHALOG demo application, place the CD-ROM in your drive. Type the CD-ROM drive letter (typically D or E) followed by a colon, for example, **D:**.

1. Press ENTER to change the active drive.

2. At the CD-ROM drive prompt, type **CD\OSHALOG** and press ENTER.

3. Now type **DEMO** and press ENTER.

4. Follow the instructions on the screen. Be patient—a large file is being loaded.

Loading Instructions: Windows

1. Open File Manager and click on the CD-ROM drive icon.

2. Click on the OSHALOG subdirectory.

3. Double-click on the file DEMO.EXE.

4. Follow the directions on the screen and be patient—a large file is being loaded.

Starting OSHALOG from DOS

1. Type **CD\OSHALOG** and press ENTER. If you just loaded OSHALOG from DOS, you will already be at the OSHALOG prompt.

2. Type **OSHALOG** and press ENTER.

Starting OSHALOG from Windows

1. Open File Manager and click on the OSHALOG subdirectory of your hard drive.

2. Double-click on the file OSHALOG.BAT.

If you want to set up OSHALOG as a program item, it has its own icon file called OSHALOG.ICO, which is located in the same subdirectory. To load the OSHALOG icon:

1. Open the program group into which you wish to place the OSHALOG icon by double-clicking on the group icon in the Program Manager.

2. Open the File menu and select New.

3. Click on Program Item, then click on OK.

4. Type **OSHALOG** in the Description box.

5. Click in the Command Line box and type **OSHALOG**.

6. Click in the Working Directory box and type the directory path (e.g., **C:\OSHALOG**).

7. Click on Change Icon.

8. Click on Browse.

9. Select the drive OSHALOG is installed on.

10. Double-click on the drive letter in the Directories box.

11. Scroll the directories and double-click on OSHALOG.

12. Click in the List Files Of Type box and select icons {*.ico}.

13. Double-click on OSHALOG.ICO.

14. Click on OK in the next three dialog boxes.

15. Double-click on the OSHALOG icon to start OSHALOG.

Running OSHALOG

When you see the program screen, you will be prompted for a password.

1. Type **DEMO** in capital letters. (You will not see the password DEMO as you type it. OSHALOG has password protection to keep confidential information secure.)

2. Press ENTER.

You are now ready to begin your OSHALOG session. The next section provides an overview of OSHALOG commands.

How to Use OSHALOG's Features

The OSHALOG.200 software incorporates a number of features that make it a powerful loss control management tool. The importance of these features was discussed earlier in the chapter. What follows is a brief description of these features and instructions on how they should be used.

The main menu is the point of entry for all actions in OSHALOG. Use your LEFT-ARROW or RIGHT-ARROW key to move from one menu choice to the next. Pressing ENTER selects that menu choice. You can also select a menu item by pressing the first letter of the menu item (e.g., F for Fast Entry or T for Test Recordability).

Fast Entry

The Fast Entry command enables you to enter all your new incidents, accidents, and first-aid cases, both recordable and nonrecordable. When the Input screen opens, be sure to note that some of the fields contain an asterisk (*). These fields are linked to OSHALOG's Lookup tables. To enter data into these fields, you will need to press F1. To see how Fast Entry works, enter a recordable accident for yourself:

1. Highlight Fast Entry, if necessary, and press ENTER.

2. The next screen asks if this is a recordable or nonrecordable event. Press R or highlight Recordable and press ENTER.

OSHALOG allows you to change the recordable or nonrecordable status of an event at a later time through the editing functions (see the "Edit Tables" section later in this chapter).

3. The next choice is whether this is an injury or an illness. Select Injury and press ENTER. This will bring up the Recordable INJURY Input screen (Figure 2-2).

4. The system will then ask you to enter the number of cases that you plan to record. Type **1** and press ENTER.

5. Enter your Social Security number. Notice as you type the numbers, the dashes are automatically entered for you. Press either TAB, ENTER, or the RIGHT-ARROW key to move to the Employee ID #. If you do not use ID numbers, just press ENTER.

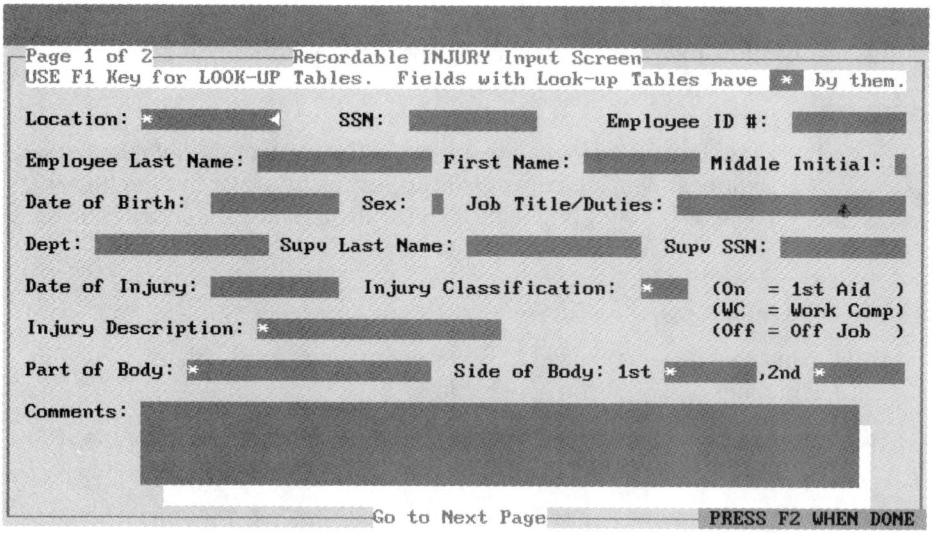

```
┌─Page 1 of 2──────────Recordable INJURY Input Screen──────
│ USE F1 Key for LOOK-UP Tables.  Fields with Look-up Tables have [*] by them.
│
│ Location: [*          ◄]    SSN: [          ]      Employee ID #: [          ]
│
│ Employee Last Name: [          ]     First Name: [        ]  Middle Initial: [ ]
│
│ Date of Birth: [        ]    Sex: [ ]  Job Title/Duties: [          ↲]
│
│ Dept: [          ]    Supv Last Name: [          ]    Supv SSN: [        ]
│
│ Date of Injury: [        ]    Injury Classification: [*    ]  (On  = 1st Aid  )
│                                                               (WC  = Work Comp)
│ Injury Description: [*                   ]                    (Off = Off Job  )
│
│ Part of Body: [*             ]      Side of Body: 1st [*    ] ,2nd [*    ]
│
│ Comments: [                                             ]
│           [                                             ]
│
│ ──────────────────Go to Next Page──────────── PRESS F2 WHEN DONE
```

FIGURE 2-2.   *The Recordable INJURY Input screen*

6. Type your last name and press ENTER. Note that the program is case-sensitive, so be sure to type in any information accurately.

7. Continue filling out the form until you reach Date Of Birth.

8. Type in the number of your birth month, then press the SPACEBAR. Note that the slash is put in for you. Enter the number for the day you were born, press the SPACEBAR, and then enter the year you were born.

9. Continue filling in the form until you reach Date Of Injury. Let's say the injury happened today. Pressing the SPACEBAR three times will put in today's date.

10. Note that the Injury Classification field has an asterisk in it. To open the related Lookup table, press F1. Highlight the item describing the injury classification you need using the down arrow and then press F2 to select it. Notice that you can select among first-aid cases, workers' compensation cases, and even those that occurred off the job (the latter costs you money too, one way or another—lost productivity, employee benefits, decreased efficiency of those who are at work, etc.). Use On for first-aid cases, WC for workers' compensation cases, or Off for off-the-job cases (i.e., at home).

11. Move on to Injury Description. Press F1 for the lookup table.

12. Use the arrow keys to move to the item you want and press F2 to select.

13. Repeat the process for Part Of Body and Side Of Body.

NOTE
These lookup tables can be modified if your needs require more or additional detail. (See the "Edit Tables" section later in this chapter.) You also have a Comments field for any additional information you'd like to add for this case.

14. Press PAGE DOWN.

15. On the next page, you need only answer the questions with an **X**, or with the number of days when applicable.

16. Press F2. Then enter the last two digits of the year of the accident (i.e., **95**). The year value must be between 86 and 99.

17. Press ENTER. You have just simply and quickly entered your first recordable case in OSHALOG.

The procedure for entering the information about an illness is basically the same as that for entering information about an injury. The Recordable ILLNESS Input screen is shown in Figure 2-3.

```
┌Page 1 of 2────────────Recordable ILLNESS Input Screen──────────────────┐
│USE F1 Key for LOOK-UP Tables.  Fields with Look-up Tables have ▓ by them.│
│                                                                          │
│ Location: ▓          ◄   SSN: ▓              Employee ID #: ▓            │
│                                                                          │
│ Employee Last Name: ▓            First Name: ▓        Middle Initial: ▓  │
│                                                                          │
│ Date of Birth: ▓         Sex: ▓   Job Title/Duties: ▓                    │
│                                                                          │
│ Dept: ▓            Supv Last Name: ▓            Supv SSN: ▓              │
│                                                                          │
│ Date of Illness: ▓       Illness Classification: ▓   (On  = 1st Aid  )   │
│                                                      (WC  = Work Comp)    │
│ Illness Description: ▓                               (Off = Off Job  )   │
│                                                                          │
│ Part of Body: ▓             Side of Body: 1st ▓     ,2nd ▓               │
│                                                                          │
│ Comments: ▓                                                              │
│           ▓                                                              │
│           ▓                                                              │
│                                                                          │
│                ─────Go to Next Page─────       PRESS F2 WHEN DONE        │
└──────────────────────────────────────────────────────────────────────────┘
```

FIGURE 2-3. *The Recordable ILLNESS Input Screen*

Test Recordability: Built-in Expert Decision Tree

OSHALOG has a built-in decision tree to help you determine if an incident is indeed recordable. This is very helpful if someone other than the human resources manager, safety manager, or occupational health nurse is entering the information. Through a series of questions, OSHALOG's knowledge-based decision tree filter determines whether an incident may be recordable. If it is, OSHALOG will take you directly to the Fast Entry screen. To enter the event, follow the instructions outlined above. If OSHALOG determines that the incident is *not* recordable, you will be advised to enter it as nonrecordable. Should that occur, you can override the recommendation and make it recordable anyway. While Test Recordability is usually correct, it is the employer's (your) decision to make that final choice.

Case Review

This feature allows employees to review their OSHA recorded cases (without your comments being viewed) and documents their name, Social Security number, and the date of review. A custom report, Employee Review, can be printed showing who has reviewed their cases and when. It's a good tool to improve communications with your employees and to demonstrate and communicate management's concern about accident prevention, while helping to improve those intangible areas of employee morale and attitude that affect productivity and costs.

1. Select Case Review from the main menu by using your LEFT-ARROW or RIGHT-ARROW key to highlight it, then pressing ENTER, or by pressing C.

2. Now you can review "your OSHA recordable cases" just as an employee would. Use your Social Security number and review the case you just entered, by following the instructions on the screen.

Edit Tables

To review, update, or change cases already entered, or to modify the Part of Body, Injury or Illness Description lookup table, choose Edit Tables.

1. From the main menu, press E, or highlight Edit Tables and press ENTER. The menu choices at the top of the screen will change.

   We will add "Near-Miss" to the Injury Description lookup table. Since near-misses usually result in exposure to a potential injury or illness, you can classify and document your near-misses as nonrecordable events and thus be able to analyze them. Remember, a near-miss tells you something is wrong. OSHALOG is designed to capture and analyze ALL events. By documenting and analyzing near-misses, you can head off losses and injury situations before they occur.

2. Using your RIGHT-ARROW key, highlight Injury Description and press ENTER.

3. Using your DOWN-ARROW key, go to item 16, and press INSERT. You have now made a "space" alphabetically.

4. Press ENTER and type in **Near-Miss**.

5. Press F2 to save.

This is how easy it is to customize the lookup tables for your business. You can do the same for Illness Description and Part Of Body. The OSHALOG.200 Manager Plus program has additional lookup tables for accident factors, including equipment, machinery, tools, hazardous materials, location of event, operation performed, and operation frequency.

Main Data Table   Now, let's edit the Main Data table. The Edit Tables feature offers a powerful search capability.

1. From the main menu, press E for Edit Tables. The Main Data table will already be highlighted.

2. Press ENTER.
   You are now on the first page of the first case of your documented events or cases. You will note that these tables look much like the Input screen except for the dialog at the bottom of the screen. Be sure to read this information before you proceed.

NOTE
The search feature is case- and context-sensitive unless wild cards are used (see the next section). If you are searching for a last name and it was originally entered in capital letters, you will need to use all caps for the search value.

As an example, let's look for case number 11. All you need to do is place your cursor in the field you wish to search.

3. Put your cursor in the Case # field. Press CTRL-Z.

4. You will see a flashing cursor in the upper-left corner of the screen asking for a Value. Type in the value **11**.

5. Press ENTER. The system will search and bring up case number 11.

6. You can also search all of the other fields. Place the cursor in the Last Name field. Press CTRL-Z.

7. Type in your last name. (Be sure to type it in exactly as you did earlier in the walk-through.)

8. Press ENTER.

NOTE
When editing the Main Data table, use the BACKSPACE key to erase the information in a given field. If the DELETE key is used, the entire record will be deleted. To restore a deleted record, press CTRL-U.

You now see the case as it was entered. As the status of events change, you can change any of the information you originally entered and add any additional comments you may need. To make changes in the details of a case, simply place the cursor in the field where the changes need to be made and edit the existing information or add new data as needed. To change the status of an event from recordable to nonrecordable, or vice versa, all you need to do is add or erase the last two digits of the year in which the event occurred. This information is entered in the green dialog box for the first field at the bottom of the Edit OSHALOG Main Data Table window. Adding the year makes the event recordable. Erasing the year makes it a nonrecordable event.

Wild Cards   A wild card can also be used in your search value. The wild card is two periods (..), which can be placed at the front, middle, or end of the search value. An example would be

1. Press CTRL-Z. Type **JO..** and press ENTER. You will first see an event for JONES.

2. Press ALT-Z. You will now see an event for JOHNSON.

3. Pressing ALT-Z again will continue to search the field for that value.
   If you were looking for employees whose first names ended in Y, you would use ..Y as the value. When you use the wild card, the search is *not* case-sensitive. Wild cards can be helpful when searching for specific entries or types of entries. You will be able to locate any entry quickly and easily.

4. Press F2 to leave Edit Tables and return to the main menu.

Reports
The Reports section of OSHALOG is where you see the real benefits of computerizing your safety records.

➤ From the main menu, press R for Reports, or highlight Reports and press ENTER.

The Log And Summary Reports option prints the Form 200 Log and Summary by selected year, and can be used at any time. When the February deadline for posting your Form 200 comes around, you can simply print it and post it.

Custom Reports   Under Custom Reports, you can generate a number of additional reports at the push of a button, including: All Cases in case number order; Severity of Event, which shows cases by the amount of lost or restricted time; Department by Supervisor; and Job Title, which classifies the cases by job title, employee last name, part of body, injury description, illness description, and employee review.

Queries And Analysis   With Queries And Analysis, OSHALOG really goes to work for you. Not only do you get tabular reports such as Body Part Report by Department or Job Title, Reports of Injuries or Illnesses by Job Title, Lost Time Injuries by Supervisor, and Events Lost Time/Restricted Time by Department, but you can also generate report graphs. These reports are first shown to you on the screen, and then you are offered the option of printing the results. This is useful when you need a quick answer to your question, but not a printed report, or you need to change or adjust the parameters of your query.

NOTE
Because these complex queries are done "on the fly" in memory (RAM), when a report sequence is begun, it must run through the complete sequence.

First, let's look at a table for the Total Number of Events by Body Part.

1. Press Q for Queries And Analysis.

2. Press B for Body Part.

3. Press T for Total Number of Events.

Next, you will need to give a date range for the events you would like to graph.

1. Enter the beginning date by typing **1** and pressing the SPACEBAR.Then type **1** again and press the SPACEBAR. Type **94** and press ENTER for the beginning date (the date should read 1/1/94).

2. To enter the ending date, type **12** and press the SPACEBAR. Then type **31** and press the SPACEBAR. Type **94** for the ending date and press ENTER.

3. Press ENTER again to see the Answer table of Total Number of Events by Body Part.

Now let's look at the pie graph report for the Total Number of Events by Body Part.

1. Press F2 to leave the table.

2. Press N and then ENTER when asked if you would like to print the table.

REMEMBER
This is a demo version of OSHALOG, which will not print.

3. Press ENTER to see the graph.
   You will see a graph titled "Answer." The table and graph are given this label because they are the program's answer to the user's query. This is how your graph will look when you print it. If you wish to edit the graph in any way, such as rearrange the pie shapes, you can do so by rearranging their order in the Answer table. The procedure is similar to the one described earlier for editing tables.

4. Press ENTER and change the order of the Table for Body Parts.

5. To change the order of the Table, first create a space in the list by using the DOWN-ARROW key to move the cursor to the point where you want to insert a particular body part, then press INSERT. Type in the name of the body part and the number of events associated with that body part. Then, delete the body part from its previous point in the list by highlighting it and pressing DELETE.

6. Press F2 for your report.

7. Press ENTER, then press N and ENTER again when asked if you wish to print.

Additional Features of the OSHALOG.200 Series

In addition to OSHALOG.200 Plus, the OSHALOG.200 series offers the Manager Plus module, which provides additional user-defined lookup tables for equipment, machinery, tools, hazardous materials, location, operation performed, and operation frequency. These tables allow you to zero in on problem areas with querying and reporting capabilities, including bar graphs and pie charts. The secondary descriptors, ranging from hand tools and specific hazardous materials to vehicles and any kind of equipment or job being performed, allow you to precisely describe your operations and any accident factors.

There are also predefined lookup tables for basic or primary accident type, cause, and corrective action. You can capture workers' compensation cost factors and associate these with the various accident factors, so management will know where they are losing dollars and what the basic causes are so that appropriate corrective action can be undertaken.

OSHALOG.200 Manager Plus claims-tracking and proactive claims-management capabilities enable you to better manage your workers' compensation cases and control your overall workers' compensation costs and premiums. With the unlimited narrative capability and additional user-defined alphanumeric and financial fields of Manager Plus, other event information and cost factors can be documented as well, from medical histories and follow-up treatment, repair costs, or pollution cleanup costs to whatever information you need to capture and document related to each event.

Under Reports, the Manager Plus Queries and Analysis section has three subsections. The Body Part Reports section lets you associate any part of the body with other accident factors. The Queries section, which is similar to Queries in the 200 Plus, offers additional report formats. The Summaries section gives you financial information for upper-level management, including the bottom-line-oriented Executive Summary with both actual and indirect costs for the various accident factors and by department.

Manager Plus accepts data for multiple locations, and it can import data from OSHALOG.200 Plus. You don't even need a wide area network (WAN). That means you can have a standardized data collection system that can export data to a central (corporate) database while providing a useful tool for local management. This sort of versatility is becoming increasingly important for organizations with multiple locations, each of which will be required to submit their Form 200 logs *directly* to OSHA in Washington, D.C.

Conclusion

Risk control and safety management share the same foundation as total quality management. Safety management concepts and practices, like those of TQM, must be an *integral* part of an organization's culture and day-to-day operations to be effective. Near-misses resulting in no injuries, or "accidents" without injuries, damage, or loss to property, equipment, materials, product, or environment are red flags, but only *if* someone is watching and recording these warning signs.

The outcome of accidents that do result in injuries and material losses are significant—repair, cleanup, replacement, rework, losses in productivity etc. Direct workers' compensation costs to employers today are only the tip of the proverbial iceberg. Indirect expenses, such as those just mentioned, usually range from 10 to 30 times greater than actual "claim" expenses.

All job-related accidents and incidents are "errors." If errors are not documented, measured and analyzed, they cannot effectively be controlled or eliminated. This is the rationale underlying statistical process control procedures.

As more of the world moves to ISO 9000 standards, automated systems to document, analyze, and control errors, accidents, and incidents will be utilized.

Safety management must become part of ongoing day-to-day operations and processes to be both effective and *cost-justified*. Weekly, monthly, or quarterly safety functions to meet even minimal OSHA or insurance requirements are a waste of both time and money if there is no commitment to improve processes. Processes for improvement must become an everyday integrated process.

OSHA requires more than one million firms to keep records of occupation-related injuries and illnesses, and it levies stiff fines if these records are not kept. But this recordkeeping requirement should be viewed as an opportunity rather than a burden. By recording all data concerning workplace injuries and illnesses, a manager can create a database that exposes any underlying patterns. OSHALOG.200 Series applications can help transform an onerous recordkeeping requirement into an opportunity for creating a safer and more humane work environment—and significantly reducing costs.

CHAPTER 3

Negotiation and Computers

by Daniel Burnstein, Esq.
Negotiator Pro Company

How do you negotiate a budget with your controller? A legal dispute with a former partner? Hammer out a merger? Convince a skeptical loan committee that a new venture is worthwhile? Negotiations have always been a challenge. Preparation by itself cannot replace the intuitive sense that an agreement is possible or the look in someone's eye that reveals a problem, but a prepared mind can better plot a course and take advantage of subtle clues. This chapter will outline the modern method for negotiation preparation and discuss interest-based bargaining that helps illuminate the underlying needs of all the parties. The chapter ends with a walk-through of Negotiator Pro software.

Negotiation in Everyday Life

Whether at work or at home, everyone negotiates every day. We all negotiate budgets, work tasks, evaluations, purchases, sales contracts, office space, car and home purchases, time for dinner, who does the chores, and what movie or TV program to watch. While we cannot avoid negotiations, we can improve our influence quotient (IQ).

In spite of the fact that almost everyone negotiates every day, and many negotiate as a significant part of their workday, there is surprisingly little recognition of negotiation as a specialization other than amongst contract compliance departments, labor-management negotiators, intellectual property lawyers, licensing departments, and professional mediators. There are only a few small national organizations of negotiators. Otherwise, there is no professional organization dedicated generally to the promotion of negotiation. Since Adam and Eve negotiated over the apple, there has almost never been a job titled "negotiator." It is almost as if we tend to hide the fact that a negotiation is going on from others—and ourselves. Perhaps this is why negotiation has been generally neglected as an area for study and improvement. Historically, the great negotiators kept their insights to themselves and the rest of us bumbled along without a system to prepare, improve, or measure the real effectiveness of our negotiations.

Negotiation Since Machiavelli

The literature on negotiation has evolved from a smattering of books by early pioneering thinkers of diplomacy and court intrigue. The first "modern" manual of realpolitik was *The Prince* by Machiavelli. Published in 1513, *The Prince* advised rulers to divorce negotiation from religion and ethics. Two hundred years later, a somewhat more honorable tome, *On the Manner of Negotiation with Princes*, was written by deCallieres as a study of the practical side of international diplomacy. Thereafter, the literature of negotiation remained remarkably sparse until the 1940s, when a resurgence of interest began. Since then, our understanding of negotiation has been advanced through the work of experts in economics and game theory, labor, psychology, law, and intercultural business negotiation.

Just as mediation and alternative dispute resolution (ADR) have started to receive greater attention in law and business education, more and more state and federal courts have begun to offer dispute resolution programs as alternatives to trials. The concept of a "multidoor courthouse," where there are a range of alternatives to litigation, was pioneered by Professor Frank Sander of Harvard Law School. The growing acceptance around the country of this concept suggests that people are seeing the court as a center for dispute resolution, whether through litigation, mediation, arbitration, or negotiation. A parallel private movement is growing to replace litigation with arbitration and mediation, often using retired judges and law professors. Most of these dispute resolution professionals are using an interest-based negotiation approach, as described in the sections that follow.

Elsewhere, public attention has been drawn to dramatic negotiation successes in the Middle East, Northern Ireland, and Haiti, as well as to the negotiation failures in the former Yugoslavia. When negotiations fail, as with the 1980 flight controllers' strike, the 1994 baseball negotiations, and the partisan disputes over a universal health plan, the consequences of *not* reaching an agreement are noticeable. Herb Cohen, a pioneer in negotiation training and author of *You Can Negotiate Anything*, recalls: "When I was on the radio in the early days, people would call up and say why do you have this bum on the air—all he does is manipulate people. They thought dealmaking was inherently unethical." Now, negotiation is gaining recognition as a valuable *skill worthy of study and improvement.*

There has also been a revolution in the way business and law schools teach negotiation. Prior to 1980, very few graduate or professional schools offered formal training in negotiation. Now almost every graduate program has begun to teach the concepts behind negotiation—usually interest-based bargaining—in courses on negotiation, ADR, mediation, labor law, human relations, and business management.

Strategies of Negotiation

A fundamental challenge for every negotiator is to form and act on a strategic plan for a particular negotiation. There are only three strategic approaches used for negotiating: cooperative, competitive, and principled. It is possible to be effective or ineffective at each of these strategies. In the opinion of the author and many other negotiation experts, the most powerful strategy to follow is that of the effective principled negotiator.

The *cooperative negotiator*, as described by Gerald Williams (a leading negotiation researcher, attorney, and professor at Brigham Young University) generally shares interests (underlying needs), background information, and exhibits mutual concern for all parties. The effective cooperative negotiator is consistently honest and straightforward without being reckless. When they negotiate, effective cooperatives assume good faith and focus a lot of their energy on building the relationship. However, the ineffective cooperative often carries this interest in the other party too far. Ineffective cooperatives will trade away some of their interests to establish a better relationship with the other side. Ineffective cooperatives also tend to ask for exactly what they want and fail to leave themselves bargaining room.

In contrast, the *competitive negotiator* assumes that you are out to get him or her. The ineffective competitive negotiator stands out as extremely indirect and hard-nosed. He or she will denigrate your proposals, withhold information about interests (needs), refuse to share important data or indicate true settlement ranges, and use force to get his or her way. Ineffective competitives are often so paranoid about revealing their true needs that their negotiations sometimes break off in failure, when the other side would have been willing to accommodate their needs if only those needs had been disclosed and explained. Effective competitives succeed in negotiations because they are able to steamroll their opposition without forcing them to walk away. However, many people do walk away from discussions with competitive negotiators—and as a result, lose out on deals that would have been to their benefit.

The *principled negotiator*, as described by Roger Fisher and William Ury in their best-selling negotiation book *Getting to Yes: Negotiating Agreement Without Giving In*, focuses on the reasons for a negotiation to succeed instead of trying to be nice or tough. The effective principled negotiator will try to establish a good working relationship in order to more efficiently explore the other side's interests. The ineffective principled negotiator will reveal his or her vulnerabilities before a relationship has been built and will ignore the subtle, nonverbal dynamics of the negotiation.

What is the best approach to influencing others in the less-structured playing field of modern corporations? The *principled* negotiator seeks out the interests of all the parties. This has been called the "win-win" or "Getting to Yes" approach (after the best-selling book by Fisher and Ury). It combines a number of aspects that go beyond what is thought of as a cooperative or competitive strategy. A principled negotiator uses principles or reasons to come up with a fair resolution that has the goal of satisfying his or her side well and the other side at least acceptably. This approach does not require that either side be "nice." It is a powerful and useful way of being more effective and more efficient. A principled negotiator should

- ➢ Bargain over interests, not positions. Ask a million questions to find out what motivates the other side; don't assume you know what they want or why.

- ➢ Separate the people from the problem.

- ➢ Focus on interests, not positions. Don't be fooled by demands—look under the demands for interests and concerns.

- ➢ Invent options for joint gains.

> ➤ Require objective criteria and the use of principles (reasons) for positions.

If the other side doesn't play along, the principled negotiator should

> ➤ Develop alternatives.

> ➤ Use negotiation jujitsu. Welcome the thrusts of the other side, explore their complaints, and ask them what would result if you were to adopt their proposal.

> ➤ Tame the hard bargainer who uses dirty tricks by recognizing the tactic, raising it explicitly, and questioning the tactic's legitimacy and desirability.

> ➤ Prepare "yesable" propositions, backed by reasons or principles, containing action items that can be responded to with a yes or no.

The *principled* approach to negotiation has been criticized for appearing to suggest that negotiators have to be "nice" to each other or that one has to blindly trust the other negotiator. This is not true. The principled approach does not suggest that one simply reveal all of one's vital interests (needs) up front. In *Getting to Yes*, Fisher and Ury note that "good faith negotiation does not require total disclosure." A number of other criticisms have been leveled at the approach. Critics argue that both sides must agree in advance to use principled negotiation and therefore the approach is inherently unrealistic in a world of competitive bargainers. These criticisms are answered in a subsequent book by William Ury, *Getting Past No: Negotiating Your Way from Confrontation to Cooperation*. This book presents a plan for dealing with difficult people using the interest-based bargaining model described next.

Why Use Interest-Based Bargaining?

Without time to reflect, you must act solely according to your immediate impulses: fight or flight. Will the other side give me what I want? Which side has the power to get their way? A better way of handling negotiation is emerging, however. In the past two decades, interest-based bargaining has moved into the mainstream of commercial and diplomatic negotiations in such diverse venues as the United Nations, The Asian Development Bank, The New England Bank, Motorola, the Naval War College, and the Federal Board of Mediation and Conciliation.

Interest-based bargaining has been widely embraced by thousands of governmental agencies and private corporations because it is more efficient in terms of the time and resources needed to reach agreement: less is left on the table; more is achieved in each trip, letter, and call; there are better long-term relations;

parties are less defensive and there is less stress; fewer deals crumble needlessly; overhead costs go down; and there is less disruptive behavior.

So how do you engage in interest-based bargaining? The answer is to analyze, prepare, and probe. The number one task is to ask a lot of open-ended questions. Find out what the motivations of the other side are. In addition to carefully analyzing your own interests, you need to be an active listener. Watch carefully for communication or cultural problems, which are discussed in the sections that follow. The more prepared you are going into a negotiation, the greater the chances are of achieving your objectives. And because negotiations inevitably involve a great deal of information (facts, issues, positions, strategies, tactics), any comprehensive system for preparation will help you prepare for a negotiation session by organizing pertinent information for later retrieval and sharing. Sharing your strategy and tactics with team members is important if you are trying to sing from the same score.

What does all of this have to do with the management of small and large organizations? In the old days, managers and business owners believed in a military-style command structure. There was a top-down hierarchy and it was expected that everyone functioned on a need-to-know basis. If you had initiative and went out of your "unit," the person would respond, "Have your vice president speak to my vice president." The old-school manager knew that information was power and kept his or her cards close to the chest. Now, with deep managerial layoffs, managers are found running around with lots of responsibilities and little direct authority. Before, the "org chart" ruled. If it failed, bluster and arrogance would win the day.

Today, however, managers have to get the attention and win the cooperation of other managers over whom they have no power. If you ask for cooperation in accomplishing a task, the first question is: "Why do you want to do this?" Then you have to come up with an explanation of how this is good for the other person, the department, *and* the company. This takes a lot of strategy, planning, active listening, good questioning skills, good organization, and solid people skills. If a manager is arrogant, refuses to disclose, refuses to share information, refuses to share credit, and, in short, refuses to be a team player, he won't get the job done. And, in increasing numbers, today's managers agree that getting the right job done is more important than getting the job done right. You need a good perspective on what is important and on how to get others to agree with your perspective—in short, you have to be a good leader, a good persuader, and, when there is disagreement, a good negotiator.

Why Are Negotiations So Hard?

Negotiations are difficult and cause stress for a number of reasons: interpersonal, intrapersonal, process, or analytical. Interpersonal stress comes from the effort to get a united bargaining position within your own team. In fact, many professional negotiators believe that the internal negotiations are the hardest because we expect more from our colleagues, and when they don't agree with us, we are more disappointed than we would be with outsiders. External negotiations are stressful for just as many reasons: the stakes are high; the rules of engagement are vague; the goals change during the negotiation; the negotiators seem difficult or they appear to act difficult for the sake of being difficult; parties hide their true interests and goals; and, if that weren't bad enough, sometimes the parties do not even know what their goals and interests are.

Intrapersonal stress arises from self-doubts. Are you being too soft? Too hard? Not prepared enough? Personal stress comes about from the uncertainty of the outcome on your career and your organization. Also, many people underestimate themselves and overestimate the capabilities of others, especially in cases where they fear a confrontation. The result of having all this stress is that negotiators can get fatigued, have trouble sleeping, become overly defensive, and have difficulty coming up with creative ways around an impasse.

The process of negotiation itself causes stress because, unlike a court case where all the moves are part of a ritual, negotiations do not have a defined form. It is necessary to negotiate the relationship, and then continue to renegotiate the relationship as the negotiation evolves. Newer negotiators feel that negotiations are chaotic. They reason that if they prepare, it will tie their hands and they will not be as agile as if they simply went in prepared for anything.

Surprisingly, even negotiators with years of experience may know little about ways to generate creative negotiating solutions. Instead, they typically employ the competitive strategy, substituting tricks, ploys, and bluster for seeking out stable, creative, and lasting win-win solutions. With the growing popularity of interest-based bargaining, a negotiator on the other side might appear to be following an interest-based bargaining approach, but has only a surface commitment to the process. Then there is the skilled negotiator who appears to be reasonable but defines his or her interests as being as large as a star and yours as being as small as a gnat.

Before you get discouraged, remember that deals are struck all the time between parties that don't like each other, for any number of reasons. A fascinating history of dealmaking in the Middle East is described in *The Secret War Against the Jews: How Western Espionage Betrayed the Jewish People*, by John Loftus and Mark Aarons. The book, gleaned from interviews with aging intelligence agents, shows how negotiators from nations that hated each other were still able to strike durable agreements. Why? Because the agreements satisfied their mutual interests. Meanwhile, other agreements between "friends" were broken because they failed to satisfy everyone's mutual interests.

Underlying the challenges of negotiating is the lack of training in the United States in negotiation skills. There is less rigorous negotiation training here than in the U.K., China, Japan, and elsewhere. In Australia, for example, employers have to set aside 1.5 percent of their payroll for all types of employee training, and negotiation training is commonplace. Surprisingly few business people over the age of 30 have had any exposure to formal negotiation training in general, or interest-based bargaining in particular. Some have heard of *Getting to Yes*, since three million copies of this book have been sold since 1981. But this number pales in comparison to the 12 million managers, six million business owners, three million government managers, over one million CPAs or financial executives, and 750,000 lawyers in the U.S. today. In sum, while everyone negotiates, only a small percentage have been trained to negotiate.

Today, there is a growing body of products that teach negotiation. Video tapes on negotiation and communication skills are available from Conflict Management Incorporated (CMI) of Cambridge, Massachusetts, featuring Roger Fisher and Bruce Patton; the Negotiation Institute of New York City, featuring Gerard Nierenberg; the Nightingale-Conant Corp., featuring Roger Dawson; and others. Videodiscs are also leased by the Educational Technology Department at Harvard Law School of Cambridge, Massachusetts and its representatives. Negotiation software has been developed by Experience In Software of Berkeley, California with its *The Art of Negotiating* featuring the ideas of Gerard Nierenberg, and Wilson Learning of Eden Prairie, Minnesota have developed the *Relate with Ease* and *Keep Your Cool*.

The Importance of People Skills

Besides analytical and preparation skills, people skills come into play in negotiations: jockeying for position; playing to the crowd; appeasing constituencies that need to be heard. Preparation alone is not sufficient to bring success to the negotiator. While negotiators are not therapists, the skill of "reading people" is vital—especially learning how to apply the social lubricants that help people get past the inevitable sticking points. These facilitation skills include active listening, doing favors, and adjusting a deal so that it is desirable to the other side without sacrificing your key interests.

Personalities
Most people think about negotiations strictly in terms of positions or interests, leaving the equally important dimension of personality to chance. Yet *personality* drives some negotiations as much as the issues do. In too many negotiations, differences in style can kill a deal or a potential agreement. Why? Because of underlying personality conflicts. How often do deals fall through because the negotiators don't see eye to eye or cannot communicate? That is a personality problem, not an issues problem.

The interesting tension in all negotiations is that one moment you are working towards forming a partnership, and the next moment you are looking out for your own interests to get a "fair" share of the pie. Sometimes this rapidly shifting process gets out of hand and the negotiation loses the critical balance between creating a bigger pie and claiming your piece of the pie, making it increasingly difficult to reach an agreement. Understanding the personality of the other side can minimize obstacles to effective communication and help maintain the balance between creating and claiming.

Dealing with Difficult People

Using power alone to impose one's will or giving in to the primitive urges of fight or flight are often counterproductive in dealing with a difficult negotiator. Both fight and flight weaken your posture. If you appear to simply give in, the other side is encouraged to ask for the sky. If you bluster, the other side has one more thing to use against you or, worse, they start to bluster back and the negotiation slows to a halt. The trained and prepared negotiator uses his or her training in interest-based bargaining to develop a rich range of options between fight and flight. Professional negotiators often comment that they see the challenge of their job as one of being effective under conditions of stress and frustration. Does this mean that if someone is not well-prepared they cannot do well in a negotiation? No, of course not. But, if you ignore the task of preparation, if you ignore the literature on negotiation, if you expect it to be easy, if you want the difficult people on the other side to only say nice things about you, your team, product, service, knowledge, experience, or the deal in general, then you will inevitably be disappointed.

When someone is being difficult in a negotiation, the two keys to success are (1) to not take anything personally (this is easier said than done!), and (2) to adopt a strategy for conducting the negotiation. One professional negotiator said that "If I am not being frustrated then I am not doing my job—this is what negotiation is all about." If the other side makes disparaging remarks about your position, then of course you will see red and will want to respond in kind. However, it is best to indicate your displeasure without burning bridges. Ury suggests that the angry negotiator pause before responding. He urges a metaphorical step to the balcony to provide perspective and the opportunity to formulate questions and sort out your feelings, or just vent.

Brian Tracy, a leading sales trainer, contends that if the other side is *not* giving you objections, if they are merely nodding when you make your points, then you are not reaching them. He maintains that objections are the core of a major sales interaction because (1) the other side wants to see how you handle such issues, and (2) the other side is raising real concerns that they have. How you deal with the objections is important to building trust so that when other problems come up you will both know how to preserve the relationship. Tracy likens this process to a card game, in which the other side deals you cards with objections on them, and as each objection is revealed you must respond effectively. Gradually you work down to the final card, the last unrevealed objection. If you can find out what that objection is, you have a much better chance at winning the game if it comes out.

Breakthrough Negotiation

A number of ways to handle difficult individuals has been suggested by William Ury in his book *Getting Past No.* He believes a five-step process will lead to what he calls *breakthrough negotiation*:

1. Control your emotional responses and behavior. Instead of immediately overreacting, focus on obtaining your goals. In other words, don't give in to the basic responses of flight or fight. If you do, you lose control in the situation.

2. Help your opponent control his or her negative emotions of defensiveness, fear, suspicion, and hostility. You have to get past the opposition's resistance to reach an efficient, stable agreement.

3. After creating a more positive climate, attempt to get the opponent to stop bargaining over positions and to try exploring options that will satisfy the party's needs.

4. Bridge the gap between the interests of the parties, help your opponent save face, make the outcome a victory for your opponent, and generally make it easy to agree.

5. If the other side thinks he or she can prevail without satisfying your interests, you have to improve their perception of the value of your alternatives and other sources of power. In part, this means identifying your sources of power. Be aware that overdoing this show of power sources may make the other side feel even more defensive. A delicate touch is important. Be sure to put things in a positive, nonjudgmental way to indicate you have other options and they should be aware of them, although you would like to see this negotiation succeed.

Ury notes that his prescription for a breakthrough strategy is counterintuitive in that it has negotiators do the opposite of what their natural feelings suggest. When one party in a negotiation is aggressive, the other tends to be equally tough or to leave. Ury suggests going around the resistance:

Rather than pounding in a new idea from the outside, you encourage him to reach for it from within. Rather than telling him what to do, you let him figure it out. Rather than trying to break down his resistance, you make it easier for him to break through it himself. In short, breakthrough negotiation is the art of letting the other person have *your* way.

International Negotiations

Is the interest-based bargaining approach useful for a negotiation in Mexico or Ghana? The answer is a qualified yes, if you keep in mind that these cultures hold values other than your own. Despite these cultural differences, the evidence suggests that interest-based bargaining works around the world. To better understand a culture, ask yourself these questions suggested by Raymond Cohen in *Negotiating Across Cultures: Communication Obstacles in International Diplomacy*:

➢ Is this an individualistic culture or an interdependent culture where family and patrimony are the dominant forces?

➢ Are roles tied to a hierarchy?

➢ Does truth repose in an individual's search for self-expression, or does it reside in the collective traditions of the group?

➢ Is there a strong collective sense? Are local affiliations more important than national affiliations?

➢ Is saving face (avoiding dishonor) in the eyes of the group more important than carrying out personal desires?

➢ Do people feel guilt or shame for not carrying out a given task?

➢ Are there still feuds—and mechanisms to protect oneself and others from feuds?

➢ Are decisions made on a personal basis, or because of group desires?

The answer to these questions will help shape your analysis of the interests and personalities of, and the impact of culture on, the parties involved.

Further complications can come about in cross-cultural interactions. Since communication is at the heart of negotiation, obstacles to communication will be obstacles to negotiation. Negotiation of issues is not just a simple transfer of and decision about data. There are sensitivities over turf, status, and the like. Negotiation research by Stella Ting-Toomey (in *Negotiating Across Cultures*) provides a framework for the differences in communication styles. It categorizes Japan, Mexico, Indonesia, and the Philippines as "high-context" societies, and contrasts these with "low-context" societies, including the U.S. and its North Atlantic allies (Germany, Canada, England, and France). These differences are outlined in the following table:

Low-Context Cultures (e.g., U.S., Canada)	High-Context Cultures (e.g., Japan, Mexico)
Language is used to share facts and persuade.	Language is used to allude and avoid saying no.
Language is a vehicle used to express individual needs, abilities, and aspirations.	Language is a social lubricant used to express group concerns. The individuals are not very important by themselves.
Language is used to share rights, "facts," and personal opinions; what you are doing is more important than social roles.	Social roles and connections are the most important facts to communicate.
Use of flowery phrases is distracting.	Focus is on the effort to communicate relationships; individual words are not that important.
Avoiding guilt is important—but you can always move to another part of the country.	Avoiding shame is all-important.
Family is very important (except from 9 to 5).	Family is all-important, except to older communal leaders.
More egalitarian.	More authoritarian.
Law has reality of its own. (Tocqueville saw U.S. as a land of laws, but also of violence, kidnapping, and death.)	Most citizens are personally shielded from felonious behaviour by strong social ties.

To successfully conduct cross-cultural negotiations be sure to (1) use only a limited amount of pressure when the other side may feel it is vulnerable, (2) be careful not to rush to an agreement, even if an immediate agreement is mutually beneficial, and (3) emphasize the people-to-people connections— personalize all proposals and never present your proposals as a "strictly commercial deal."

How to Prepare for Business Negotiations: Find and Track the Issues

In most business negotiations, the typical manager has two choices: shoot from the hip or develop a system to keep track of the numerous issues and positions involved. The tendency of the untrained negotiator is to assume that the needs of all the parties are obvious. But this is not usually the case. The solution to the problem of false assumptions is for a negotiator to ask a lot of questions. It is a tactic that would intuitively appear to frustrate all the parties, but in fact it works quite well. This is because (1) few people get enough attention, (2) sometimes you may not accurately hear the other side's concerns, (3) asking questions shows that you are sincerely interested in learning more about the other side's position and concerns, and (4) it helps you reach your goal of getting the best offer from the other side.

However, this tactic still does not solve the problem of how to keep track of what is learned by asking a lot of questions. Aside from questioning skills, effective negotiators need a means of organizing and tracking all the information associated with a negotiation *and* fast access to the accumulated body of knowledge regarding negotiation approaches. When preparing for a negotiation do you have access to the best ideas in the literature? Even the most experienced negotiators stand to benefit from the wisdom of other experts. Only the rare native genius of negotiation does not need books or software. But for the rest of us, a negotiation preparation system should help *organize and track* the issues and positions in a negotiation, *identify* key negotiating tactics, and *offer insights* regarding how to handle a particular tactic or individual negotiating style.

There are a number of questions to ask yourself as you prepare for a negotiation. Note that there will not always be apparent answers to these questions, but they deserve to be taken into consideration. The prepared mind can best seize opportunities that present themselves in the rapidly changing dynamics of a negotiation. The questions listed in the next section have been chosen for this chapter because they are important questions for any negotiation. In this section, we will walk through a hypothetical problem (appearing in italics).

Julia is a partner in an architecture firm and has been assigned to negotiate the extension or termination of a commercial lease for her firm's current offices. Michael is the landlord of her commercial office building. This negotiation is about renewing the lease. Julia's BATNA (best alternative to a negotiated agreement) is to move across the street into another office suite in what appears to be a desirable building where the rent is actually a little less per square foot than her firm has been paying.

Key Questions

When entering a negotiation, the following ten questions should be addressed as part of the prenegotiation preparation process.

Question One: What are the underlying interests of the parties?

Describe in detail the underlying interests of each of the parties—including your own. This is the most important (and difficult) question for every negotiation. It asks for the underlying *needs* of the parties, not just their positions or spoken demands. You can assume you know the interests of the other side, but that approach will lead to missed opportunities and unpleasant surprises.

> As Julia analyzes the interests of both parties to the lease negotiation, she realizes that both parties share certain interests: to have some measure of financial security; to have a well-run business; and to look good to their peers (the other business partners). Michael has mentioned several times that he likes leasing to professional services and would like to see more of them in the building. Julia's firm wants to be associated with similar businesses, which is why she is tempted to move—there is a similar, but larger, architecture firm in the building across the street that might be a future strategic partner.

Question Two: What negotiation styles are going to be involved?

What kind of negotiator is on the other side? If you know the negotiators on the other side(s), you can categorize their personality and negotiation style. If you do not know the other side(s), you can ask other people who have met them previously.

> Julia knows the landlord because her firm has been renting from him for several years. A CPA by training and a detail-oriented person, Michael is an effective cooperative negotiator. Julia feels Michael would probably be happier if he never had to actually talk to his tenants and only had to respond to issues by mail.

Question Three: What are the interests, positions, and standards of each party?

Using only a few words, list the interests of each of the parties to remind yourself of the longer discussion of interests from question one. Then list the proposals (positions), objective standards (objective reasons), and other sources of power that reinforce the positions of each party.

> Michael's interests are financial security, stable tenants, and to get the best possible rent. Julia's interests are financial security, to stay in the current location with adequate improvements, and to pay as little rent as possible. In support of her position, she can point to somewhat lower rents across the street where there are desirable tenants.

Question Four: What are the terms and objective standards supporting the proposals?

What are the "terms" (dollar amounts) and objective standards supporting those terms for each of the parties' proposals? Find objective standards to support everyone's positions (demands). If you cannot find objective standards to buttress your positions, you will have a weaker position—one that cannot easily be supported by an objective standard such as:

> ➤ Trends of recent sales

> ➤ Historical sales patterns

> ➤ Opinion of objective experts

> ➤ Opinion of three arbitrators

The objective standards: Michael offers Julia a rent increase of "only" 5 percent with no leasehold improvements. The objective supporting data is that half of the other commercial rentals in the same building have signed a lease with a 5 percent increase. Julia has done her homework and responds that because of the recession, the average commercial lease rate in this part of town has decreased 10 percent over the last three years, and in fact there is nicer space across the street for rent at 12 percent less. Therefore, she proposes no rent increase and $2,000 worth of improvements to ceiling tiles (which are stained in places) and $3,000 in common area lighting. In other words, she is willing to stay where she is and avoid the costs of moving if the landlord is willing to reduce or keep the rent at its current level and make long-needed improvements to the space.

Question Five: What strategy will you use in the negotiation?

What strategy (overall approach) are you going to select for this negotiation? You can choose among the cooperative, competitive, or principled strategies discussed earlier in this chapter.

Michael is a cooperative negotiator and Julia chooses to be a principled negotiator. Michael is friendly but reluctant to give in on bottom-line issues. However, he will listen to her concerns. She wants him to understand her interests and to accommodate them in a framework of fairness based upon objective data. After Michael and Julia have presented their objective data, he goes back and studies the cost of moving across the street. He figures it will cost Julia's firm approximately $6,000 (a large truck and six movers over two *days). Once Julia's firm is across the street, it will be paying 12 percent less per month and thereby saving approximately $330 monthly, which represents a savings of roughly $10,000 over the period of a three-year lease. Michael estimates that the staff will lose about a week's income in the move (a percentage of the moving notices will be lost in the mail or misplaced). Michael knows that Julia's firm bills about $4,500 a week and has about 7,000 clients—facts Julia has boasted about. Michael estimates that the real cost of moving will be on the order of $18,000 ($6,000 for the move, $3,000 to notify clients, $4,500 in lost billings, and $4,500 in additional expenses). On the other hand, Julia's firm will save $10,000 in rent. What Julia has not revealed is that a move at this time would endanger finishing a large project on time.*

Question Six: What is the setting for the negotiation and what are the ground rules?

What is the setting and ground rules for the negotiation? Where are you going to hold the negotiation sessions? The ground rules generally cover the subject of the negotiation and the manner of handling the negotiation topics. Also, you will need to start negotiating the relationship.

Julia agrees to meet Michael in his office for their first meeting and thereafter to alternate between offices. They agree to discuss the general building atmosphere, rent, and improvements. Julia starts off with the building atmosphere because she knows from past comments that Michael likes her type of business in his building.

Question Seven: How will you open the negotiation?

How will you start the negotiation? What information do you need to obtain from the other side and what information and questions do you have for the other side? Are you willing to make the first offer? Generally it is a good idea to hold off making an offer as long as you can. This has the advantages of allowing you to gather as much information as possible and avoiding a premature offer—an offer that is made before the other side is ready to give it serious consideration.

Julia decides not to make an offer regarding rent. Instead, she asks a lot of questions about when other leases are coming due, how Michael sees the local economy developing, and how he sees Julia's company as a tenant. Michael admits that her firm is ideal and the sort of business he wants to make typical in the building. However, he stresses over and over that he cannot keep up a class A building if he is running the building at a loss. Julia decides to wait until the second session at her office before making her first real offer: that she will stay if he accepts a 5 percent decrease in rent and puts in $4,000 worth of improvements.

Question Eight: What tactics might be useful in the negotiation?

Consider possible tactics and note which you might use. There are two basic tactical approaches: piecemeal approaches, where the issues are addressed one by one, and interconnected (or logrolling) approaches, where trade-offs are made among the issues in order to achieve an overarching agreement. Another tactic is to use a single negotiation text or a document drawn up by either of the parties or by a third party as a starting point. If it is drawn up by a third party, then neither party can be accused of presenting an unacceptable proposal, and both parties can work to make the single negotiation text acceptable. Other tactics include gauging the other side's authority to do the deal and their alternatives.

> *Julia learns that the landlord has a mortgage on the building when he alludes to a banker with ice water in his veins who will blow an ice cube if there is a reduction in the rents of any existing tenants. Michael initially dismisses Julia's request for $4,000 in improvements, but he later suggests that he is willing to take them into consideration.*

Question Nine: How will you close the deal?

How will you close the deal? The typical format for tying down a deal is: "If we do this and this, do we have a deal?" The next step is to translate that verbal agreement into a written agreement as quickly as possible (pick a specific date).

> *Michael admits his embarrassment at the ceiling tile stains and appears convinced that tiles and new lighting would benefit the image of the building as well as the image of Julia's firm. He has done his homework and shows that Julia's firm will gain little by a 12 percent rent decrease if the lost billing time, the cost of the move, the cost of client mailings and lost good will are taken into account. He is also able to show that, according to press releases and general rumor, a number of tenants in the building across the street are actually planning on moving out in the next year. Michael gives Julia a few days to check the rumored moves (which she confirms) and suggests she call midweek after the second meeting. During that call Michael suggests a compromise based on actual rental trends. If Julia's firm will accept the current rent, he will give her a $2,000 budget for site improvements and will replace all the hall lighting by the elevators (a $2,500 value, which he is already planning to do on every floor, but he will start on her floor the day after she signs a five-year lease extension).*

Question Ten: How will you ensure compliance with the deal?

How will you ensure compliance with the deal? Here you want to look for objective and clear milestones that will let all the parties know whether there has been compliance. If the milestones are not clear, then you have to engage in post-settlement negotiations to clear up these points of contention to everyone's satisfaction.

Julia (looking for his best offer) asks Michael if he can do any better on the rent or the improvements, and he appears to be quite firm if not a little warm under the collar. Julia says she will get back to him the next day after she discusses the lease extension terms with her lawyer and accountant—who both feel it is a reasonable deal IF she gets the terms in writing before the end of the week. Michael agrees to send her a lease amendment that confirms the promised start date of the hallway relighting, and he throws in another inducement: he will install a modest kitchen (sink and microwave) in a large utility room on the premises. This is something the space across the street does not have, and it would be useful for Julia's firm to keep the staff on location rather than scattering every day for lunch.

Stages of the Negotiation

Returning to a macro view of the negotiation process, there are six stages or phases of all business negotiations to keep in mind. These stages are outlined next.

Stage One: Prenegotiation

Prenegotiation is a time to assess relationships and determine objectives in light of opportunities and obstacles. If you know the person with whom you are negotiating, it helps to understand the personality profile of both yourself and your counterpart. Doing a profile can help you anticipate some of the obstacles that might appear during the negotiation. Such preparation can lead to greater control over the interaction between you and the other side.

In the commercial lease negotiation described earlier, both parties did their homework, took a close look at the numbers and the personalities involved, the alternatives each party had, and the benefits they would get by doing a deal together. If the parties do not know each other as well, it is a good idea to present a proposal that lays out the potential benefits of coming to an agreement. In the process of presenting such a proposal it is still a good idea to ask whether there are other benefits that are missing from the proposal.

Get in writing all the issues in the negotiation, for your own benefit and for the benefit of others on your team. The easiest way to do this is to create a template of questions that are comprehensive and targeted to your negotiation. A useful system is one with a structured question-and-answer approach to help you look at your own needs and interests as well as those of the other side.

We know Julia prepared for the negotiation using the ten questions discussed earlier from the tenant's perspective, and we assume that the landlord, Michael, has some sort of system for preparation since he is responsible for over 250 commercial rental units, although he seemed a little confused at times because he tried to keep too many of the details in his head.

A good offer is not good until its time has come and the negotiation process has ripened to the point where the other side is ready and the deal is better than everyone's alternatives to no agreement. (This is the BATNA—best alternative to a negotiated agreement.) An important step in preparing for any negotiation is to ask yourself this question: Is what you are offering better than what the person has if they do not agree to the deal? A systematic approach to preparation will anticipate these issues and alert the user to prepare for them.

Stage Two: Entry

Ask a lot of questions—assume you don't know the motivations of the parties. Obtain and listen to high-quality business tapes, read some of the books referenced in this chapter, and use a written template of questions for yourself so you will prepare for all the important issues and not let them slip between the cracks. Double-check your list with other experienced hands. Ask if there have been changes since the last negotiation in political, financial, personnel, or technical variables: "Is there anything I should know about X?" Who is at the bargaining table? Who is not at the table but is concerned about the outcome? Who has authority to deal? What is their budget and time frame for doing this deal? Do you have your constituencies in agreement? Does the other side? What are everyone's alternatives in case the deal does not happen? How can you strengthen your alternatives (BATNA)? Have you brainstormed possible creative and new win-win options? Who will be on your negotiation team and what are their roles?

This is a good time to brainstorm with others on your side. Here you can raise lots of creative ideas without judging the ideas first. Most importantly, ask where the other side is coming from and why. Plumb their thinking, and imagine why they might not like your proposal. This will lead you to envision how they perceive their choices. To succeed in the long run you must change how they perceive their choices.

Entry refers to the initial meeting with the other side where formal presentations are often made. At this early stage of the negotiation, most dealmakers avoid specifics. Instead, work on the relationship and try to sketch out a broad framework of possible agreement in a respectful manner. Be open to suggestions. Don't be afraid to allude to your knowledge, status, and sources of power, but don't overstate the case. Clearly indicate your interest in doing a deal with the other party as well as the fact that you have other options. Likewise, leave all sides a lot of leeway to craft a fair and equitable agreement. If you are abroad, remember that you are the foreigner.

> *In the lease negotiation, Michael held a crucial piece of information: some of the key tenants across the street were planning on moving. When the time was ripe he shared this with Julia. If she hadn't been willing to disclose where she was considering moving to, she could have bluffed, showing only some of her cards, and ended up moving to a building that would have grown increasingly inappropriate to her firm's needs. Michael was able to add to the stability of his building by keeping a good tenant for a five-year extension rather than the typical three-year extension.*

Stage Three: Establishing and Building Relationships with the Other Side

This stage involves creating a foundation of trust and respect, if not rapport. What do you have in common—family, hobby, sports, travel, love of food, mountains, the sea, science, literature, work matters, or something else? If you do disagree, find a way to leave the other side a face-saving means to change its position, and get their constituencies to approve an agreement. Know your weaknesses and those of the other side. If you have a tendency to be irritable or kid people too much, or you have all the latest and greatest information—hold back. If the other negotiators are new and disorganized, give them space to make mistakes and change their minds. At the end of the day, the most important question is whether a deal that should have happened actually did, to the benefit of all parties and better than their BATNA (alternatives).

> *Michael was able to be gracious in their meetings and to convince Julia that he was sincerely interested in keeping her firm as a tenant—the building was right for her firm's needs and offered long-term stability. Julia trusted Michael enough to know that she would get a straight answer to her questions; he was clearly taking time to check the facts. When those facts turned out to be true upon investigation, Julia felt she could trust Michael's assessment of the facts.*

Stage Four: Reformulating Assumptions

This stage enables you to arrive at better proposals to meet the needs of both sides. Use active listening and restate the other side's positions to ensure you are hearing them accurately (e.g., "If I understand your position, you are looking for Y in exchange for X"). Roger Fisher suggests trying to meet the needs of the other side acceptably and your side well. Stuart Nagel suggests trying to find "superoptimal solutions" that are better than what both sides entered the agreement looking to achieve.

Julia indicated that her dream would be for her firm to merge someday with a medium-sized firm in the building across the street. The landlord agreed to do his best to move that firm onto Julia's floor since they are going to move into the building anyway (another piece of information Michael withheld until a critical moment). If the merger comes off and both companies expand, it is clear to Michael that the sum of the pieces will be greater than the individual parts and more space will be needed. Michael created a superoptimal deal when he offered to put in a small kitchen if Julia's firm would agree to a five-year extension.

Stage Five: Bargaining

Bargaining involves the give-and-take part of the negotiation while protecting your bottom line. Note that in some cultures, the give-and-take of U.S. negotiators is seen as inappropriate haggling. Other cultures view bargaining as a sign that proper preparation and research has not occurred. In Japan, it typically takes a long time to reach a position, and it is awkward for negotiators to go back to all the stakeholders (interested managers on the internal team) and once again reach consensus on this new set of demands. In both types of bargaining, any sounding out of the other side needs to be in an informal setting (over drinks or dinner). In both cases, it is better to do the bargaining in the hall, before the other side has come up with its position, since the other side may and not be predisposed to "horse trading" after it reaches its collective position. Where a give-and-take dialogue is possible, seek trade-offs based on asymmetries. Here you look for things you value less than the other side and vice versa. Then you go for the goodies both sides want. This is considered to be the "claiming" part of the negotiation.

Julia asked for somewhat more than she expected the landlord to give. On the other hand, Michael came up with a creative proposal with respect to the leasehold improvements that would keep his rent rolls up (so he would look good for his banker) and still provide the needed improvements for Julia's firm.

Fisher, Ury, and Patton suggest you use reasons, or principles, with objective standards to justify your claims. In addition to using the obvious sources of power to achieve your goals, including objective standards to support your position, try using a combination of other sources of power as they apply to your position: alternative power (walk-away power), referent power (powerful allies you can reference), financial power, location power, issue power, technology power, coercive power, reward power, legitimate power, expert power, moving power, and relationship power.

Both Michael and Julia used research power to come up with objective data in support of their position. Michael used his position as landlord to discover additional information (the pending move of the other architectural firm). As the negotiation proceeded, both parties used their information power to make increasingly trusting disclosures to their mutual benefit.

Stage Six: Reaching Agreement

Reaching agreement involves the use of "yesable" proposals to sound out the willingness of the other side(s) to undertake various action steps. This refers to creating negotiation proposals that are simple and can be agreed to by a yes. The more that emotions, theoretical concepts, organizational pride, resentment, and other higher principles come into play, the harder it is to formulate actions that are yesable. You might want to prepare a public version of your proposal that can be shared with the other side.

Julia put her proposal for rents and improvements into a spreadsheet model she thought Michael would feel comfortable with. This was in effect a yesable proposal that the landlord rejected, but he responded with a yesable counterproposal based on the example set by Julia.

Before the final round is reached and terms agreeable to all parties have become written into a contract, be sure to clarify the exact subjects of agreement since both parties may not have the same frame of reference when it comes to product/service description, shipping terms, quality standards, payment terms, exchange rates and currency, contract milestones, enforcement mechanisms, alternative dispute resolution mechanisms, communication channels, authorized parties, and so forth. Try to have self-enforcing agreements that have clear milestones with clear performance criteria. In trying to ensure compliance, be very careful about having someone from your side available to check on compliance before it is too late to fix the problem. Be sure to evaluate the agreement in light of objective standards and other likely outcomes that are possible.

Julia and Michael moved expeditiously to memorialize their understanding of the deal with a binding letter and a written lease amendment.

The Role of Computers in Negotiations

The factors listed for facilitating negotiations should be sufficiently detailed to be useful and yet not discouraging. While many of the suggestions are of a commonsense variety, applying these concepts to real-world legal negotiations many times comes down to judgment and experience. Using a computer to ask you questions and keep track of all of the above matters is a commonsense idea. As Charles M. Taylor, an experienced business negotiator from Philadelphia has noted, "It might just come down to careful preparation, making some mistakes, and learning what *not* to do the next time." While trial and error is a part of negotiation, important negotiations are facilitated by developing a strategic vision and utilizing a system to achieve that vision. The tasks associated with developing such a vision are shown here with the role of computer assistance indicated in parentheses:

➢ Do not assume you know the other side's interests—ask lots of questions (a negotiation support system in a computer will let you track all your issues, remind you of questions to ask, and save the information you get from the other side).

➢ Do not confuse positions with interests (the computer help glossary or negotiation books will remind you of this distinction).

➢ Use objective data (you can list your arguments supported by objective data and standards in your plan).

➢ Create yesable propositions (these can be created in your plan).

➢ Deal effectively with difficult people (identify personalities, differences in negotiation style, and get advice on how to overcome these obstacles).

No software (or seminar, for that matter) will make a difficult negotiation easy. However, you will have the greatest chance for success if you use good analytical approach and good support tools.

A Walk-Through of Negotiator Pro

Negotiator Pro software is a negotiation support system that helps users create a plan for any negotiation by guiding the user through the key questions every negotiator should address before entering a negotiation and by helping the user profile the negotiating style of the person on the other side. This software is not highly automated and requires an hour or more of concentrated preparation effort. However, the benefit of using Negotiator Pro is that it asks the important questions, creates a negotiation briefing book that can be shared with others, and becomes a repository of data, strategy, and tactics.

An Overview

After you have installed Negotiator Pro from the CD-ROM (see the instructions at the end of this book), go to the Program Manager and double-click the Negotiator Pro icon. After you have launched Negotiator Pro, the first screen you will see is an

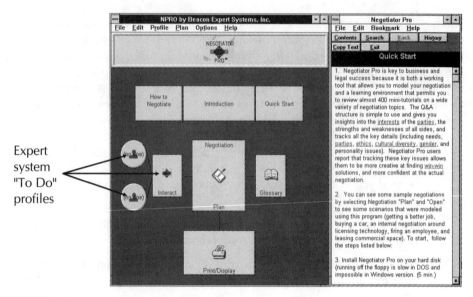

Expert system "To Do" profiles

FIGURE 3-1.   *Negotiator Pro's overview screen*

overview screen (Figure 3-1) that shows the different modules of Negotiator Pro. Three buttons at the top of the screen will enable the user to view text titled "How to Negotiate," "Introduction," and "Quick Start."

> ➢ On the left of the screen is an icon for Negotiator Pro's expert system module. This module is useful to profile the personality and negotiating styles of each of the parties involved in the negotiation. The profiler helps the user determine the right strategies for each of the parties on the other side of the negotiation table—one at a time. (Wait to click the buttons that initially say "No One" until you read the information below on the Profile module.)

> ➢ Summarizing over $3,000 worth of books and articles, the Glossary offers more than 5,000 hypertext connections between 500 minitutorials. This provides the user with an online library of definitions, concepts, and tactics on negotiation theory. You can select the Glossary button from the right section of the overview screen.

> ➢ Negotiator Pro contains a simple-to-use Negotiation Plan template designed to ask the most important questions to help the user define goals, organize thoughts, and map out an overall strategy. With a customizing

option, the question template can be changed to add questions unique to
your industry, field, or company.

➤ A robust library of negotiations is also available from the Negotiation
Plan, which contains examples of actual negotiations, enabling users
to pattern their styles and tactics after successful negotiators, become
aware of various planning strategies, and see the range of issues that
surround a negotiation.

The Profile Module

The Profile module contains questions that help you identify your own negotiation
style and effectiveness and that of the other side. You can also profile and compare
yourself to any number of other negotiators. There are 11 questions that use
forward-chaining expert system technology to make predictions when the user does
not know all the answers about the other negotiator. The system is able to achieve
a minimal level of certainty from the questions that are answered. These
predictions are very useful in a general way.

1. Click on the top "no one" button to enter information on yourself. After you
   have loaded in your profile, the button will show your name. (Alternatively,
   you can select New, then Profile from the File menu at the top of the
   screen to create a profile of any party.)

2. Click on the bottom "no one" button to enter information about the person
   on the other side, if you know him or her. After you have loaded in the
   other side's profile, the button will show his or her name.

   As you are loading in a person's profile, Negotiator Pro will display the
   Export System Report dialog box, shown here:

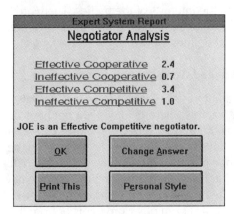

Obviously, if you do not know the key person(s) on the other side, you would skip this module until later.

3. After you have input both your profile and that of the other side, click the Interact button to bring up advice that is fairly detailed about how to relate to different personality types in the negotiation.

Returning to our commercial lease example, Julia had to prepare a profile of both herself and the landlord. She first profiled herself and found that she was moderately effective as a cooperative negotiator and had the personality of an extrovert. To create the profile of Michael, she entered what she knew about him and, despite having to click "Unknown" a few times, the program helped her determine that Michael was also an effective cooperative who had the personality of an "analytic." Julia selected the Interact button and Negotiator Pro made a number of suggestions about how best to communicate with Michael.

The Negotiation Plan Module

The second module of the program is the Negotiation Plan, and it is simply a checklist of questions (10 or 35) that are answered in an edit window on the screen (as shown in Figure 3-2). Whatever the user types into this edit window is the Negotiation Plan, and it can be spell-checked, justified, and shown in bold and italic fonts. The user can also open one of the existing Negotiation Plans that are shipped with the software. These sample negotiations illustrate ways to prepare for typical negotiations.

The standard plan questions link into the hypertext, which explains the terms in depth and offers negotiation hints appropriate to each question. The user can also view an onscreen checklist of issues associated with each question. For instance, question one asks about the interests of the parties. The word "interests" is underlined and displays in green on a color monitor. This indicates it has a hypertext link to text that defines the word.

> ➤   Click the underlined words to view text that defines the term.

A number of typical interests are included in the checklist. This list can help the user brainstorm about possible interests that might not have occurred to him or her otherwise. After reading the hypertext terms, the user can leave open the window containing these definitions or the user can close it to keep the screen less cluttered.

Only words that appear in the edit window (lower left of the screen) will appear in the Negotiation Plan when it is printed. To place new words into the edit window, you can type them into the edit window at the lower left of the screen or insert information or graphics from other programs or from the Glossary into the

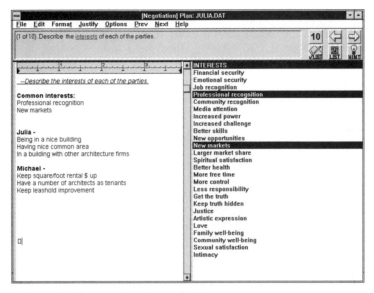

FIGURE 3-2. *The Negotiation Plan module*

edit window, using the Windows clipboard utility (cut and paste). To insert items from the checklist on the right, simply click the term and it will be inserted where the cursor was last positioned. To remove these checklist items from the edit window, just click again on the term on the right.

> *Julia prepared by typing in her plan following the ten-question format. As she worked through the questions, there were several that asked if she wanted Profile information appended to that question. If she clicked on "Yes," the information showed up in that question's window. If Julia chose "No," she would just enter the appropriate information based on the facts of the negotiation at hand and the ideas from the hypertext on different tactics to use with an effective cooperative. To insert the actual text of hypertext topics on "strategies," "tactics," and "impasse," Julia opened the Edit menu, then clicked on Copy to paste the text into the plan question windows, to remind her of the hypertext information. Julia could print out all the information she typed or copied into the plan as part of her briefing book. The briefing book was also useful for her to communicate her negotiation approach to the other principals in her architecture firm.*

When the user is ready to quit the Negotiation Plan, Negotiator Pro does two automatic searches of the information the user has entered into the plan. First, it searches to see if the user has indicated that he or she is dealing with a difficult person. If yes, the program will query the user to see if the related hypertext should be viewed. Then the program does a search and analyzes whether the user has written an adequate amount in six key areas that must be prepared in any major negotiation. These key areas are: interests, BATNA/alternatives, objective standards, yesable proposals, authority, and asymmetries/trade-offs. If the user wants to go back and work on these, the program will take him or her back to the particular questions, or it will allow the user to quit the program.

When Julia was ready to quit after spending about 45 minutes preparing the first draft of her plan, she selected Exit from the File menu, and the small expert system kicked in. It first noticed that she was dealing with someone who was difficult in certain ways (Michael could avoid committing to reasonable proposals by just hemming in the most pleasant manner). The software asked if Julia wanted to read about dealing with difficult people. Julia selected "Yes" and hypertext appeared that discussed a number of issues on this topic. She also looked at the related topics of impasse and acknowledging people, points, and ploys by selecting the appropriately underlined words (hypertext) that led her to other linked negotiation hypertext topics. Julia took a minute to select and view the Bibliography in the Glossary because she wanted to read more on principled negotiation. When Julia wanted to exit, this time she again chose Exit from the File menu, and the small expert system again displayed a dialog box informing her that of six key areas, she had only entered enough information on three and that she might want to go back and add to her analysis of authority, yesable proposals, and compliance.

The Library of Negotiations and Glossary Module

Negotiator Pro comes with a Library of Negotiations, which are sample negotiation plans that provide an idea of what a plan looks like. These sample plans are automatically loaded onto your hard disk when you install Negotiator Pro. There are optional plan libraries (.dat files) for purchasing and financial turnaround negotiations. Use the directions outlined in the lease scenario to view sample plans and to see how to open old plans you may have created previously for review. The Glossary module is a collection of some 500-plus hypertext tutorials on negotiation-related subjects. These tutorials summarize over 200 books and articles. You can click any word or phrase that appears in green on your screen to view the definition of a term. To see the hypertext, select Help and then

Index To Help from the top menu and then click any term in green, or click Search at the top of the hypertext window and move the scroll bar to find a term you wish to see.

Julia has an undergraduate degree in business, but she never took a course in negotiation. In preparation for this negotiation, she spent a few hours casually leafing through the Negotiator Pro Glossary (found in the last 175 pages of the user's manual). After spending a half hour familiarizing herself with the software, she made a point of clicking on the hypertext linked to the questions in the Negotiation Plan module. She found the module by clicking on the Negotiation Plan button (or she could have opened the File menu, selecting Open, then Plan), which brought up a dialog box with all the existing plans listed in it. Julia viewed the sample negotiations by clicking on Plan, Open. This brought up the "Select Plan to Open" dialog box. There she saw the following sample negotiations: Carbuy, Lease, and Jobresp, to name a few. Julia selected Lease and double-clicked on it to view it since it appeared to be similar to the problem at hand.

Customization of Negotiation Plans and Questions

While the basic questions and hints contained in Negotiator Pro are helpful in most situations, the peculiarity of a given negotiation often requires a custom set of questions in the template. Negotiator Pro software addresses this need. Users can customize the plan questions and hints to fit individual needs. The software will adapt to the specific needs of any given industry or type of negotiation.

Julia decided to prepare several custom negotiation templates to assist with routine negotiations she performs for her firm. First she developed a custom template for zoning negotiations by clicking on Plan, and then Create New Template. This brought up a single screen on which she could enter the number of questions to be used in the new template, the name of the questions, the question text, the optional checklist, whether the question was essay only, checklist only, or both checklist and essay, and an almost endless scrolling window to type in text for the hint window.

Application Attachments to Negotiation Plans

Negotiator Pro users have the option of linking text, graphics, and multimedia files to any question in the plan. This feature is a useful alternative when it is necessary to share information among negotiation team members. It also facilitates negotiation preparation by linking Negotiator Pro to helpful applications. A purchasing manager, for instance, could attach prior contracts to appropriate questions within a negotiation plan he or she is developing. A project manager can have an attached graphic or spreadsheet with what-if calculations, or a project management document, or three years of contract language. In general, any sort of file can be attached as long as there is an associated application to operate it.

> *When Julia created her plan (it is a file in the DOS and Windows version called <filename.dat>) she attached another file with the relevant lease language. That way she had easy access to the actual lease and could find it quickly. She also attached relevant state laws about commercial leasing and pictures of lease improvements/lighting that she thought she might incorporate into the lease extension by reference. A notepad called the ActionPad is available from the Options menu. The ActionPad can export files that have the same file format found in most project management software applications. After Julia finished her notes, she printed out a copy of her plan and shared it with her partners. It was a good feeling to be well-prepared and to look forward to her negotiation with Michael.*

Conclusion

Basketball and violin playing require lots of native talent—but everyone agrees that practice and preparation are essential. Even a jazz band that improvises needs a lot of practice. Negotiator Pro is a tool that provides a useful environment for keeping track of interests, positions, personalities, strategies, and tactical moves and countermoves. Negotiator Pro can facilitate one person's thinking or provide a medium for communication within a negotiation team. It provides expert advice that digests the user's input and suggests appropriate strategies. The strength of Negotiator Pro is its ability to offer a supportive environment for creating new templates, doing research on tactics, foreign negotiation styles, and gender differences, and providing ideas that enrich the range of options between fight and flight.

CHAPTER 4

Computer-Aided Thinking for Business

by Roy A. Nierenberg
Experience In Software, Inc.

There is a revolution going on *within* the Information Revolution that challenges all of us. Over the past fifteen years, desktop computers have extended human capabilities in the same way that manufacturing machines did in the Industrial Revolution. This expansion of brain power parallels the expansion of muscle power experienced a hundred years earlier. The revolution *within* the Revolution centers around how we view computers as *enabling* machines, capable of more than simply processing information. The challenge is: are we ready to increase the efficiency and effectiveness of our thinking? And the real question is: what happens if we don't and others do?

Mainstream software programs provide a structured working environment for performing a range of common activities: entering and formatting text (word processing), calculating quantitative and financial data (spreadsheets), and storing and retrieving information (databases). In this albeit limited way, computer programs have exponentially increased our productivity.

Yet many users remain blind to the compelling value of computers to assist our thinking processes. Instead, they continue to view computers as machines—data in and data out. From this perspective, any value added to the data comes from the user's own head, or from the minds of others. While this perspective is largely true—only humans can think creatively about processes and add value to hard data—it fails to acknowledge that many of our thought processes can be systematized and encoded into software using algorithms and logic. Computer software can thus help guide the productivity and quality of our value-added thinking. It can help us efficiently and effectively tap our own intelligences.

A new generation of intelligent computer software is now available to help all of us do just that. An important part of this movement toward intelligent software was the emergence in the mid-1980s of MBA-ware—software tools designed to facilitate higher-level business thinking. These tools provide a virtual dialogue to promote *thinking*, not just a workspace. They deal primarily with *process*, not product, and augment our *preparation and planning* abilities. Drawing on proven business management principles and the insights of experienced management professionals, these programs can improve the user's proficiency in a variety of tasks. Rendering proven management techniques into software makes them more powerful and easier to use. The software provides structure and a template of organization for the user's thinking, and an expert's procedures for a wealth of references.

MBA-ware has been developed for a wide range of managerial tasks, as evidenced by the other chapters in this book. This chapter will survey the needs of managers in typical business situations such as project planning, negotiation preparation, and problem-solving. It will explore commonly used approaches and will illustrate how software can improve and automate the planning processes. Included with this book is a demonstration version of one of the software programs outlined in this chapter: The Idea Generator® Plus. Complete program descriptions and instructions on how to run the demo program can be found near the end of the chapter.

Project Planning in a Corporate Environment

A project is a group of related tasks with a clear beginning, middle, and end. These tasks are not ongoing operations but are goal-oriented, limited-term activities. Projects are often constrained by time and budget, and they involve other people to accomplish them. The difference between projects and ongoing operations is that project tasks tend to be nonrepetitive and all come to an end...at least someday.

Most project frustrations can be traced to underestimating the number and kinds of tasks required to complete the project. To avoid these frustrations and to complete a project on time and within budget, it is useful to develop a comprehensive project plan.

Joseph Fusco, the principal project management consultant of Technical Pathways, a San Francisco-based project management consulting firm whose clients include IBM, AT&T, Microsoft, and Tandem, has seen his share of "no-plan" management: "There is a tremendous cultural barrier in our country to planning if you don't happen to be in a field like construction where it is the norm. I have seen managers that, when asked to pick a new employee insurance benefits package, start by picking up the phone. They try to buy it just like you would buy a suit and all the effort of the organization has to be spent to correct their mistakes afterward."

Fusco says that one of the biggest failures in project management is that people underestimate the number of tasks it takes to complete a project. The shareholder department of another of Fusco's clients recently decided to computerize its shareholder relations. The company had been keeping all its shareholder files in a cumbersome manual filing system. Unfortunately, the company hired a programmer who knew nothing about shareholders. Inevitably, the new system had to be discarded. The company could not go back to its old filing system, because it was now in disarray. The whole department ground to a halt, and Fusco was brought in to resolve the crisis. "When I asked what the goals were behind designing the system, I found out that all that someone had said was: 'automate it,'" says Fusco.

To see the problem more clearly, consider a software programmer who estimates that developing a new software application will require ten days of coding. In his or her mind, the time to complete the project is:

Code program = 10 days

However, the programmer has failed to consider the project as a whole, overlooking several important components on the task list. The real project probably looks something like Table 4-1, and the real timeline is more like 29.5 days.

The travails of project planning used to be the domain of the professional project managers. Today, more and more executives, entrepreneurs, and managers are finding that they are responsible for planning and organizing projects. This is the result of downsizing and job multiplexing common in corporate America. In most industries, planning is not centralized and it is one of many responsibilities for individuals with titles like president, vice president, product manager, marketing manager, or consultant. These professionals possess a great deal of knowledge about how their businesses are run, but few of them have formal training in project planning.

TASK	NUMBER OF DAYS
Determine requirements	2
Develop sample reports	1
Approve walk-through	2
Code program	10
Test and debug	4
Integration	1
Demonstrate program	0.5
Make changes	2
Debug changes	1
Document operations	5
Train users	1
Total	29.5 Days

TABLE 4-1. *Project Tasks for the Software Development Example*

What are they to do? They could ad-lib a plan with pen and paper. This works out better than not planning at all, of course. The fact is, most people have neither the tools nor the training to skillfully plan projects. In addition, people are prone to overlook important tasks in the project. Then there's the procrastination factor. Most people will put off doing something hard until it absolutely has to be done. Then it gets done under pressure. It's hard to clear the decks and come up with a solid plan when one is under stress. In projects, putting off the planning amounts to delaying the project. It's simply not a good idea.

When faced with a skill gap, enterprising individuals typically turn to how-to books for techniques and tricks. In the project management area, there are few books, and they dwell on advanced techniques such as PERT (project evaluation and review technique) and CPM (critical path method) that are suitable chiefly to very large projects.

Another approach is to enroll in a project management seminar, costing hundreds of dollars or more. Seminar attendees typically get some general guidance about the methods of project planning, management, and organization, and there might be a facilitated brainstorming session for a sample project as part of the seminar. But once the seminar is over, people are left to plan their own projects alone.

Yet another option is to hire someone experienced in project management or bring in a consultant. But in a downsized world, it is more likely that the firm's existing personnel must figure out how to do it themselves. Many turn to project management software, but with uneven results.

Project Planning and Project Management by Computer

Numerous software programs are available for project management. The leading programs include Microsoft Project, Symantec's Time Line, and Computer Associates CA-SuperProject. These programs, once believed to be the next "killer app," are powerful tools capable of assisting with the execution of the most demanding projects, such as coordinating reconstruction of the World Trade Center. But when most managers open them up and try to use them, they are confronted by a demanding and confusing process. Many of the applications require that the user become familiar with vacation schedules and salary rates before thinking about the tasks that make up a project. While these applications are great for NASA and Bechtel, they scare the pants off the harried executive who wants only to get the project started and not to become a specialist.

Distinct from these more general project management applications, which focus on project execution, are two software programs designed specifically to assist with project *planning*. Symantec's Guide Line (now bundled with Time Line) was developed to lead the user through a script of questions to delineate project steps in a specified domain, such as going to a trade show. The questions from a Guide ask about the specifics of an area (e.g., How long will the trade show run?). From norms developed over time, the program then generates a project plan with anticipated durations and assignments. Guide Line is most commonly used in a corporate setting. Project KickStart, from Experience In Software of Berkeley, California, was developed to boost the project-planning process, improve organization, strengthen team-building, and help team members achieve a more realistic understanding of the nature of the project's tasks, resources, phases, and goals.

Project KickStart can help anyone lay out a project, define the project's scope, clarify the tasks involved, and decide who will do what and when. It prompts users to identify their project phases and set overall project goals. It then walks users through several steps to generate task items, including looking at the project from different people's perspectives, anticipating problems, and using experience obtained from similar projects. Users can print out a report of their work. Or, with a few key strokes, Project KickStart sends its data to project scheduling applications, such as Microsoft Project for Windows, Time Line, and CA-SuperProject.

Computer-Aided Thinking

Project KickStart is part of a new breed of software called computer-aided thinking (CAT) software. This software doesn't attempt to provide answers. The premise behind CAT is that the basis for solving any problem lies within the user. The trick is getting one's thoughts to flow out in the open, bit by bit, developing organization, and thinking of a problem's implications while planning a strategy. Like a consultant who comes in to help a company, CAT software prompts the user to break down a problem into manageable tasks, to think of possible objections, and to draw lessons from problems solved in the past. All the while, the software collects the ideas the user comes up with. So, the software is like a consultant and a secretary rolled into one. Since the software is interactive and specific to a situation, it is more effective than how-to books and seminars. Project KickStart guards against overlooking important factors by helping the user think through the task list at the outset.

The Idea Generator Plus, Project Kick Start, and The Art of Negotiating each synthesize expert management techniques into simple interactive questions that guide users to their own solutions. The Art of Negotiating and The Idea Generator Plus are discussed in the following sections.

Negotiation Preparation Before Computers

In Chapter 3, Daniel Burnstein describes the difficulties that many people experience when faced with a negotiation. He also describes the tools and techniques that managers used before information technology was applied to negotiation. We'll add a few thoughts to his discussion here.

The two most common pitfalls facing a would-be negotiator are (1) not considering the other side adequately, and (2) approaching the negotiation with rigid positions rather than negotiating alternatives. Abraham Lincoln once said that if he had eight hours to cut down a tree, he would spend six hours sharpening the ax. In negotiation, as in many other endeavors, the key to success is *preparation*. The adage we were told repeatedly as children—"Do your homework!"—applies here as well.

There are many traditional ways to prepare for negotiations. The most common way of boning up for a negotiation is to discuss the matter with family, friends, and colleagues. The benefit of this approach is an increase in ideas and (hopefully) a reduction in anxiety. The problems with this approach are a reliance on amateurs and the lack of a strategic approach to the negotiation.

As with project management, people turn to how-to books, seminars, and tapes on negotiation to get ideas and gain confidence. A good book, seminar, or tape will probably include a chapter and/or a checklist for negotiation preparation. The chapter on negotiation preparation from *The Complete Negotiator*, by Gerard Nierenberg, covers important areas such as: objectives; negotiation (individual vs. team); issues and positions; the meeting site; the meeting; agendas; opposition's maximum position; behavior, and objectives; and long-range training. Readers will get a lot out of the discussion of these areas, many of which will be relevant to the negotiation at hand. But the discussions are abstract and the issues are only tangentially relevant to the reader's specific negotiation. The reader is left with the task of absorbing the concepts and the methods and then trying to apply them to the upcoming negotiation.

Another option is to call in an "expert" consultant, perhaps an attorney, and turn the negotiation over to her or him. Of course, there is the additional expense of hiring an expert, and one never really knows if the right expert has been found. Moreover, a satisfactory outcome is by no means assured.

Negotiation Preparation by Computer

Two leading negotiation software programs are available today: The Art of Negotiating and Negotiator Pro (profiled in Chapter 3). In both programs, the user enters data about a negotiation following a set of structured questions, and then the software guides the user through the preparation process, querying the user for additional information and providing an outline, or briefing book, for the upcoming negotiation. The principal difference between the two programs is that The Art of Negotiating engages the user in more of a dialogue about the negotiation.

The Art of Negotiating software was developed with the full involvement of Gerard Nierenberg, one of the nation's foremost authorities on negotiation and president of the Negotiation Institute, to help the user think through the critical issues. Preparation is divided into seven areas, called modules. A *module* is a series of questions that cover a particular aspect of preparation. Table 4-2 briefly explains what each module covers.

The program's preparation exercises can be used to guide and stimulate group discussion when a team will be conducting the negotiation. Gerard Nierenberg himself uses The Art of Negotiating software during "in-house" negotiation seminars at Fortune 500 companies located all over the world:

> When we conduct an in-house program, we use the actual negotiating needs of the organization as the basis for the course. We take the specific problems and work out solutions on the spot. Many times, I can raise issues that people in the organization would be reluctant to bring up, such as, "What if the product does not work?" or "What if the future two-year effort does not work?" or "What if someone produces a competitive product better and cheaper?"

MODULE	KEY CONCEPTS
Subject Matter	What is being negotiated and all the parties involved
Objectives	The desired results from the negotiation
Issues	The items discussed in the negotiation
Positions	The views each party takes on the issues
Needs	Profiles of both sides' needs
Gambits	Alternative approaches of negotiation
Climates	The feelings created in a negotiation (the climate can facilitate or hamper agreement)
Strategies	Moves that can advance the negotiation and show how, when, and where to use gambits
Agenda	The method and order used to introduce the issues

TABLE 4-2.   *The Art of Negotiating's Preparation Modules*

Well, to cap off our in-house training, we often bring in a laptop computer attached to the LCD screen and challenge the group to see if The Art of Negotiating's structured exercises can help them find solutions to their problems. It gets everybody working together and the solutions that the group comes up with can be pretty amazing.

Recently Mr. Nierenberg used The Art of Negotiating software to help a supplier of automotive pollution control equipment redefine its relationship with General Motors (GM), the company's biggest customer. GM wanted the supplier to use lighter materials in manufacturing and to redesign its equipment to be more effective. At the start of the seminar, the supplier's goal was to get GM to pay more for the new product, but the managers quickly realized that this was a sure way for the company to lose GM as a customer.

"The problem was ultimately redefined as 'how to keep GM as a customer,'" Nierenberg said. "This kind of software makes you think about a problem in a new light so that you make it possible for everyone in the negotiation to win."

Aside from allowing people to redefine their problems, The Art of Negotiating software helps people to generate more alternative negotiating strategies than they would on their own. That way, when they find themselves in the middle of a negotiation and feel one strategy is not working, they are prepared to try another strategy.

Creative Problem-Solving Before Computers

The need for creative solutions to everyday and novel business problems is becoming increasingly clear. Constantly changing customer needs and a competitive market demand creative solutions. In the past, it may have been sufficient for managers and employees to turn to established procedures and technologies to solve their problems. And if they could not come up with a solution, they could talk over the possibilities with their boss or coworker. Today, as competitive pressures increase and companies downsize, fewer resources are available to help. Everyone, even those people in traditional supporting roles, have to make decisions on their own, often under intense time pressure.

Even self-directed, successful people are sometimes caught unprepared by a problem. Very often they end up reacting in knee-jerk, emotional ways. These dysfunctional reactions can take two forms: let's call them the fearful and the frantic. The *fearful* get intimidated as they stare at an empty page or screen. The problems they face suddenly appear too overwhelming and difficult. They draw blanks or simply don't know how to begin. The *frantic* react in just the opposite way. In an effort to give themselves the illusion that they are productive, they immediately start spinning their wheels without thinking about the full scope of the problem they are trying to solve. Employees don't need to suffer from an acute attack of either form of dysfunction for it to slow them down. Wasting just one hour in a panic is enough to hurt a company's productivity.

The problem doesn't end there. Most people will agree that anxiety and creativity are not the best partners. It's hard to see creative solutions under stress. Stress may come from time constraints, personal relationships, monetary needs, or a host of other issues. These all affect our creative problem-solving skills.

And even the best laid plans will go astray if those involved don't share common goals. Sometimes goals are ill-defined or not fully considered in the rush to solve the problem at hand, leaving the solutions incomplete and unsatisfying. We often hear of different departments in a company, such as marketing and engineering, arguing over a project. They are both working to meet the same basic goal of providing a quality product. But marketing's goals may be to beat the competition with a feature-rich product, while engineering's goals may involve lowering production costs and design time. The result of these conflicting goals may be a clash.

In businesses today, the lack of time for productive thinking may be the biggest problem. Sitting at a desk with feet up, thinking, might be hard to justify to the boss. And managers are caught between a rock and a hard place: they want more creative employees, but they can't always afford the money and, more importantly, the time to allow an employee to be away from his or her regular job. So what's the answer?

Problem-Solving: The Cognitive Barriers

In his ground-breaking book, *Conceptual Blockbusting*, James Adams of the Stanford University School of Engineering identifies several major blocks to developing creative solutions to problems, including: the tendency to stereotype novel situations, seeing what one expects to see; difficulties in isolating a problem and breaking it down; and the inability to see a problem from various viewpoints. Overcoming such cognitive barriers can mean the difference between success and failure.

Again, people can try to get new ideas by several standard means: bounce ideas off other people, hold brainstorming sessions, read any of the how-to books on creativity and problem-solving, or attend a creativity seminar. These approaches have the same general benefits and limitations described earlier.

Problem-Solving by Computer

Computers can now help people rationalize the process of problem-solving and overcome their cognitive barriers on the fly?

Four kinds of software packages are available to assist in the problem-solving process. The first category is associative databases—programs such as IdeaFisher, Namer, Headliner, and Writer's Dream—which try to spark the imagination by presenting the user with lists of associations to a word or phrase. For example, typing in the word "blue" in IdeaFisher results in over 300 word associations, including clichés, famous quotes, and word roots.

The second category of problem-solving applications is the outline program, such as MaxThink, More, and Thought Pattern, which helps the user organize his or her thoughts by making it easy to shuffle ideas around. Some of these programs break down ideas into topics and subtopics. Others use graphical tools to "connect" the ideas the user has entered.

Experience In Software's The Idea Generator Plus falls into the third category of creative technique programs, which takes the user through a series of structured mental exercises to help generate ideas for solutions. Mindlink also falls into this category. Finally, the fourth category consists of group technique programs, such as Facilitator and IBM's Team Focus.

The Idea Generator Plus takes the user step by logical step through the problem-solving process. It begins by helping the user describe the problem clearly and concisely and list the elements associated with the problem. Then, once the situation and its components are clear, it guides the user to come up with a list of fresh approaches, using a variety of idea-generation techniques. Finally, it helps the user evaluate these ideas and decide which ones are the most useful.

The structure of The Idea Generator Plus is based on one's own natural problem-solving process. It guides and gently disciplines thinking without restricting it. The program asks questions in a simple, conversational way, always leaving the option to go back and revise the information that has been entered. For example, the user is free at any point to revise the description of the problem if the original focus becomes too narrow or too broad.

Working with The Idea Generator Plus will help the user discover insights that may have been overlooked. Using the program on a new situation results in a collection of new ideas. Even with a familiar problem the program can unblock thinking and offer new perspectives. The Idea Generator Plus enhances the most powerful "expert system" ever devised: one's own mind.

Program Overviews

The following three sections provide more information about each of the Experience In Software applications. A demonstration version of The Idea Generator Plus can be found on the CD-ROM included with this book. Instructions on how to use the demo program can be found in the section describing The Idea Generator Plus.

Project KickStart

Project KickStart provides a quick start for project management and scheduling programs. You can use Project KickStart to develop a task list, assign project responsibilities, describe major project phases, list project goals, anticipate obstacles, organize tasks, and allocate resources. Project KickStart can also be used to determine project feasibility up front, get organized on projects, get started on a marketing campaign, develop a new product, get a manufacturing operation off to a quick start, develop needs assessments, tackle new or difficult projects, get input from persons mandating a project, distribute to-do lists, and develop executive planning skills. In short, you can get your project going. This program was designed to be used by managers, engineers, marketers, financiers, contractors, manufacturers, planners, product developers, consultants, researchers, and anyone else with a large or small project who needs to draw up a comprehensive project plan.

In addition, Project KickStart can be used to enhance the group dynamics involved in planning any team project. The program can be used at project planning meetings with an overhead projector and a data display screen. Co-workers can contribute their project ideas by disk or over a network. Hard copies of generated reports can be circulated for additional editing and comments. Finally, information can be downloaded from Project KickStart into project scheduling programs for setting deadlines and budgets and tracking progress.

Using Project KickStart

Project KickStart begins by asking you to give your project a short descriptive name—a name that you'd like to see at the heading of Project KickStart's reports. Once you have named your project, the program leads the user to the main menu screen (Figure 4-1). The program uses major project elements, such as phases, goals, other people, and obstacles, to help you develop tasks for your project. You're also encouraged to think about how tasks from other projects might fit in.

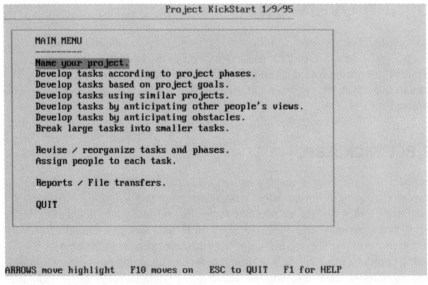

FIGURE 4-1. *Project KickStart's main menu screen*

The other options in the main menu include the following:

➣ **Break Large Tasks into Smaller Tasks** lets you replace larger tasks with more specific action items.

➣ **Revise/Reorganize Tasks and Phases** lets you edit, add, delete, or move tasks and phases. Here is where you can fix up your task list and be sure it's how you want it to look.

➣ **Assign People to Each Task** (resource allocation) lets you figure out who should be assigned to what tasks.

➣ **Reports/File Transfers** lets you print out the task list, assignments, phases, goals, and resources. Or, you can print out assignments (to-do lists) for all team members or for particular people. As an option, the tasks and assignments can be transferred (downloaded) to project management scheduling programs.

Phases, Goals, People, Obstacles, and Notes

Once you have named your project, the next step is to develop a project task list. As you develop your task list, Project KickStart helps identify and develop phases, goals, people, obstacles and notes.

Project Phases   First, Project KickStart encourages you to organize tasks into major time blocks called project phases. Recall the software programming project mentioned earlier in this chapter (see the "Project Planning in a Corporate Environment" section). The project required only 11 tasks over 29.5 days, probably not enough to worry about phases. But what about longer projects that have 100 tasks? Project KickStart would encourage grouping these tasks into: beginning phase, middle phase, and end phase. You can also create phase names that more accurately describe your project, such as: start-up phase, ramp-up phase, development phase, testing phase, and close-out phase.

Project Goals   Project KickStart encourages you to develop goal statements—broader objectives that apply to the entire project. Some examples include:

➣ The project will be completed by July 27.

➣ Development costs should not exceed $30,000.

➣ This project will enhance the reputation and image of our organization.

Goal statements, objectives, or mission statements are global statements that refer to the entire project. For instance, meeting a final deadline, like July 5, is global, whereas getting the go-ahead from a customer might be important but not quite as applicable to the whole project. Once you get a go-ahead, it's behind you. A deadline, however, lasts through the entire project.

People   Project KickStart helps you think through the personnel resource list and assign people to tasks. "People" can mean individuals, like Bill the programmer, as well as entire teams or organizations. Here is an example of how you might assign tasks:

TASK	ASSIGN TO
Determine requirements	Bill, Sue, Pat
Develop sample report	Bill
Approve walk-through	Bill, Sue, Pat
Code program	Bill
Test and debug	Bill, Technical Department
Integration	Bill
Demo program	Bill, Local User Group
Make changes	Bill
Debug changes	Bill, Technical Department
Document operations	Documentation Department
Train users	Bill, Sue

Obstacles   Project KickStart helps you identify obstacles that may hinder the project up front and determine what to do about them. Such obstacles could include:

➤ Lack of dedicated resources due to competition from other projects

➤ Delays due to unproved technology and frequent changes

➤ Lack of financial and management commitment

Notes   Even notes, ideas, or simple reminders, can be included. Thoughts like "Be sure to inform accounting of customer-initiated changes" or "Tell Mike to check this with Ellen" are neither tasks nor goals, but they can always be tracked as project notes. Project notes will be included in your printout.

An experienced Project KickStart user should be able to develop a project plan in only 30 minutes. Even a new user can get through Project KickStart in an hour or so. The program is self-explanatory—everything you need to know is on the screen.

Project KickStart and Other Software

Project KickStart provides a quick start for project management scheduling programs. When you select Reports/File transfers from the main menu, you see a screen to transfer your work to other programs. It lists all of the programs to which you can transfer (export) your tasks, people, and assignments, including:

On Target	Time Line	Microsoft Project
Primavera	Project Scheduler	SuperProject
ProTracs	FasTracs	Lotus Agenda

The Art of Negotiating

The Art of Negotiating software helps you prepare for important negotiations better than you've ever prepared before. It presents a series of questions to focus your thinking on important parts of the negotiation. The answers you provide help you develop plans of action to use in your negotiation.

Your preparation is divided into discrete areas, called modules. You probe each of these areas for your side and for your opposer's side. (We do not refer to the other side as the "opponent," but as "the other side" or "your opposer.") Helping you see things from both sides is an important part of the program and promotes an "everybody wins" approach in your negotiations.

You don't need to be experienced in either negotiation or computers to use this program. The computer asks questions in plain English, and you respond in plain English. Instructions for entering your information and moving through the program are right on the screen.

When you have completed the preparation process, you will have listed and evaluated all the pertinent information from both sides' points of view. You will have established an agenda to use during the negotiation. And all this information will be summarized for you in a printed summary report.

The summary report adds an extra dimension to your preparation. You can use the summary report to review the information, then you can return to the program to revise and refine your answers. Also, the report is a convenient means of communicating your ideas about the negotiation to team members and to management.

Uses of the Program

The Art of Negotiating program can help resolve negotiating problems, improve a relationship, or give insight into the negotiation process. Planning, training, and communications aspects of a negotiation can be approached from a number of different directions. Listed below are just some of the ways you can apply the negotiating program to your business and personal matters.

Planning and Development:

➤ Plan a negotiation as a single negotiator

➤ Plan and coordinate team negotiations

➤ Experiment with creative negotiating approaches

➤ Help with mediation, conciliation, and arbitration

Training:

➤ Train negotiators (purchasing agents, account managers, salespeople) with practice negotiations

➤ Use their summary reports for group discussions

➤ Enhance or refresh negotiating training

Communications:

➤ Bring new members of your team up to speed

➤ Get management approval of negotiating plans before the negotiation begins

The Idea Generator Plus

The Idea Generator Plus is a valuable tool for anyone facing a problem. It can help you to come up with productive ideas about almost any kind of problem you need to solve: writing proposals, developing marketing plans, thinking about a career change, etc. This is a tool for managers, consultants, and other professionals in such varied fields as marketing, sales promotion, quality assurance, research, and education. It can also be used by teams as a catalyst for group creativity.

The program's flexibility and versatility make its uses virtually unlimited. It streamlines such common tasks as goal setting, planning, prioritizing, designing, organizing, and writing. Table 4-3 lists examples of problems that The Idea Generator Plus can help you solve.

The Idea Generator Plus is divided into three major sections, each of which focuses on a particular aspect of the problem-solving process. These sections are shown in Figure 4-2 and are listed here:

> ➤ **Problem Statement** The first step is to describe your problem or situation. Then the program asks you to list your goals and the people involved in the situation.

> ➤ **Idea Generation** In this section, you are encouraged to find solutions to the problem using a variety of techniques that help you look at your situation in fresh and surprising ways.

> ➤ **Evaluation** Finally, you assess your work by rating your ideas, intuitively and in terms of your goals. It also helps you to consider the costs and benefits of each solution and its effects on other people.

A summary report of your work can be printed at any time, including all the ideas you have generated during the session and how you got them. After using The Idea Generator Plus to gain insights into your situation, you can transfer your ideas to your word processor and work out your promotional campaign, you can transfer ideas

USERS	PROBLEMS
Individuals	Developing business plans
	Keeping production quality up and costs down
Groups	Planning a new product introduction
	Developing strategies
	Increasing participation in management groups
Other Users	Planning a career change
	Finding a summer job for a teenager
	Deciding where to go for vacation this year
	Arranging priorities

TABLE 4-3. *Possible Applications for The Idea Generator Plus*

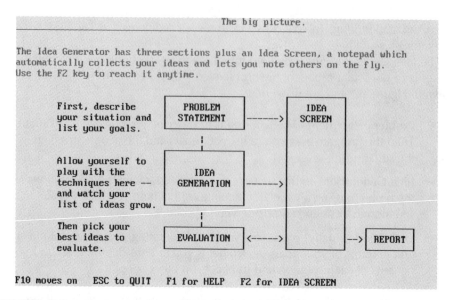

The big picture.

The Idea Generator has three sections plus an Idea Screen, a notepad which automatically collects your ideas and lets you note others on the fly. Use the F2 key to reach it anytime.

First, describe your situation and list your goals.

PROBLEM STATEMENT ------> **IDEA SCREEN**

Allow yourself to play with the techniques here -- and watch your list of ideas grow.

IDEA GENERATION ------>

Then pick your best ideas to evaluate.

EVALUATION <------> --> **REPORT**

F10 moves on   ESC to QUIT   F1 for HELP   F2 for IDEA SCREEN

FIGURE 4-2. *Major sections of The Idea Generator Plus*

to your outliner (ThinkTank, PC Outline, and MaxThink) and refine your book outline, or you can go to your spreadsheet and cost out "What-if" scenarios.

A Walk-Through of The Idea Generator Plus

To run The Idea Generator Plus, first download the demonstration version from the CD-ROM onto your computer, following the instructions found at the back of this book. Once you have done this:

1. Select MS-DOS Prompt from the Windows Program Manager.

2. Type **cd \idea** and press ENTER.

3. Type **DEMO** and press ENTER.

4. Press F10 to proceed. Folow onscreen prompts.

The opening screen of The Idea Generator Plus gives the name and version number of the program. Across the bottom of the screen are some basic instructions on how to use the program.

➤ To advance to the next screen, press F10.

➤ To quit the program at any time, press F6.

➤ To quit what you are doing, press the ESC key until you have returned to the main menu. From here you can begin a new problem-solving process or quit the program by pressing ESC once more.

➤ Press F10.

The first time you use The Idea Generator Plus, the program asks you a series of questions: Can you see colors? Are you using a hard drive? Are you using a laser printer? Answer each question by typing **Y** or **N**. The next question asks you to name a file to use with the demo. You can type in a name or you can leave the space blank, in which case the program automatically names the file IDEA.DTA.

The Problem-Solving Process

The next four screens introduce you to the program and its problem-solving process. Press F10 after you have read each one. The introduction is followed by three screens titled For Your Reference. These orient you to how The Idea Generator Plus works.

1. On the first screen, select "banana" by pressing the DOWN ARROW key two times until "banana" is highlighted. Then press the F10 key.

2. On the second screen, you are asked to select more than one dessert. Move the pointer to a dessert and press the SPACEBAR to highlight it. Use the arrow keys to move to another dessert and highlight it with the SPACEBAR. Press F10.

3. After you read the next screen, press F10. This brings you to the main menu screen (Figure 4-3).

A Sample Problem   The sample problem presented here is how to preserve elephants and get jobs for poachers in Tanzania. To see the sample data:

1. Highlight the first menu item, Use Sample Problem or Pick Your Own Problem. Press F10 to advance to the next screen.

2. At the next screen, press the DOWN ARROW key to highlight the Use The Sample Problem menu item and press F10. You will see a screen confirming your choice of the sample problem. Press F10 again. This returns you to the main menu.

3. Notice that Problem Statement is highlighted in the main menu. Press F10 to proceed with the Problem Statement section.

4. The next screen is the Problem Statement submenu shown in Figure 4-4. Note that the first two items are highlighted. Press F10 again.

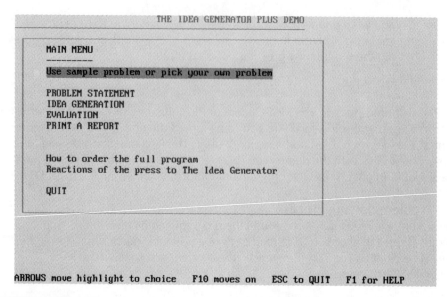

FIGURE 4-3. *The Idea Generator Plus main menu screen*

5. The next screen asks you to describe the situation; it has been filled in with the sample data. Press F10 again to view the next screen for listing your goals.

6. Continue to press F10 to view all the data screens for the Problem Statement section. When you are done, the program returns you to the main menu.

The Idea Generation and Evaluation Processes

The next section of The Idea Generator Plus is the Idea Generation section. Here you are encouraged to find solutions to the problem using a variety of techniques that help you look at your situation in fresh and surprising ways. The Idea Generation, Evaluation, and Print a Report sections of The Idea Generator Plus all work in a similar fashion to that outlined earlier for the Problem Statement section. Feel free to explore the sample data for each of these sections of the program.

Other items on the main menu are How To Order The Full Program, Reactions Of The Press To The Idea Generator (be sure to see the DBMS review), and Quit. These can be viewed by highlighting the selection and pressing F10 to move through the screens. To return to the main menu from anywhere in the program,

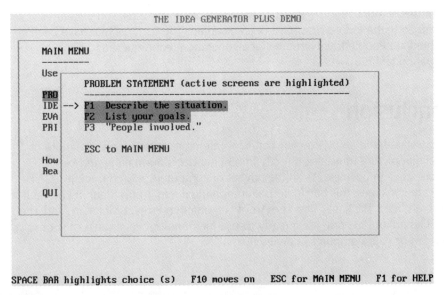

THE IDEA GENERATOR PLUS DEMO

```
MAIN MENU
---------
Use
      PROBLEM STATEMENT (active screens are highlighted)
PRO   -------------------------------------------------
IDE --> P1  Describe the situation.
EVA     P2  List your goals.
PRI     P3  "People involved."

        ESC to MAIN MENU
How
Rea

QUI
```

SPACE BAR highlights choice (s)   F10 moves on   ESC for MAIN MENU   F1 for HELP

FIGURE 4-4.   *The Problem Statement submenu*

simply press the ESC key until the main menu screen reappears. To quit The Idea Generator Plus at any time in the program, press the F6 key, and then press Y to confirm that you want to quit.

Using The Idea Generator Plus to Solve Your Own Problems
To work on your own problem, start from the main menu.

1. Highlight Use Sample Problem or Pick Your Own Problem and press F10.

2. Highlight Pick Your Own Problem and press F10. The program acknowledges that the sample data has been erased. Don't worry, you can always retrieve the original sample problem from the main menu.

3. Press F10 and the program moves you to the Problem Statement section.

Repeat the basic steps outlined above to move through your own problem with The Idea Generator Plus. Begin with the Problem Statement process, and then move on to the Idea Generation and Evaluation processes as needed. You can always go back to a previous section and add or modify information. When you are finished, you can print out The Idea Generator Plus suggestions for your own problem.

In this demonstration version of The Idea Generator Plus, some features contained in the full version have been disabled. The features that have been disabled are People Involved, five idea generation techniques, and two evaluation techniques.

Conclusion

Simply stated, the ability to plan better, create more options, and see more of the bigger picture translates directly into better decision-making and better performance in business. With the advent of computer-assisted thinking (CAT) software packages, this barrier to better individual and group planning has at last been removed. Packages like The Art of Negotiating, Project KickStart, and The Idea Generator Plus provide a ready-to-use methodology regardless of your problem or your computer knowledge.

PART 2

Strategic and
Financial Planning

CHAPTER 5

Industry Structure Analysis and Strategic Business Planning

by Robert Codell with Kirsten Aleo
for Business Resource Software

Planning is essential for any enterprise striving to achieve above-average performance in a competitive situation. This is true for businesses of all sizes, governments and, of course, even athletic teams. Competition permeates our society and rewards those that plan—and act—effectively.

The challenge of business planning—more formally known as strategic planning or strategy development—is to carefully develop and apply a firm's resources and capabilities in the context of its competitive environment. Firm resources and capabilities may include intellectual or other assets, financial resources, production technology, relationships, experience in the marketplace, etc. Effective business planning requires a keen understanding of not only the industries in which a firm competes, but also of its customers' industries, its suppliers' industries, and others.

All competitors face the challenge of an uncertain, interdependent world. To manage complexity, firms use models to capture what are believed to be the essential features and dynamics of the economy under study. Academics and professionals have developed many philosophies, theories, and models that address the operations of industries and firms.

Industry Structure Analysis

In developing a business strategy, one traditionally begins with a study of the nature of the industries in which a firm has a competitive interest. After establishing a framework for the competitive environment, it follows naturally to consider the firm's capabilities and sources of competitive advantage and disadvantage.

Industry structure analysis is the formal name for the study of an industry's components and their dynamic interactions. The dynamics result from the interdependencies and rivalries that exist among customers, suppliers, competitors—even potential competitors sitting on the sideline considering entry into the industry. Much contemporary thinking about how industries are organized and behave is related to the work of Professor Michael Porter of the Harvard Business School. The five forces analysis developed by Porter in *Competitive Strategy: Techniques For Analyzing Industries and Competitors* is a tool used widely in business strategy development. This analysis focuses attention on the five forces that can impact an industry:

- ➢ Rivalry among existing competitors
- ➢ Customers
- ➢ Substitute products from other industries
- ➢ Suppliers
- ➢ Threat of entry of new competitors

Industry structure analysis is concerned with both an industry's structure and its development through time. Each component is considered with respect to present conditions and expectations about future change (or industry evolution). By assessing the influence of these forces on industry competition, one can think more critically about the opportunities and challenges that an industry represents for a firm.

In the discussion that follows, the term *product* is used to describe both traditional products and services. The provision of services is modeled along lines similar to what are often more restrictively termed products.

Industry Definition

The industry definition establishes the boundaries or scope of the analysis. It frequently begins with commonly held beliefs about the marketplace needs and interests presently being met by the firm. Who are the industry's competitors? Who are the customers and what motivates them to purchase? Are there alternative products outside the industry that customers can use instead?

Many firms operate in multiple industries and thus face the task of performing industry structure analyses for each, and, when planning resources permit, for industries having a direct influence on these. It is useful to consider the firm's operations generally first and to develop broad industry definitions that can later be broken down into industry definitions of more limited scope. For instance, a company that manufactures and sells cars may consider itself a competitor in the broad automotive industry, but it may view itself with higher resolution as competing in the truck, van, or small car industries (or subindustries). Using both general and more focused industry definitions permits analysis of both the broad strokes and the finer detail of a firm's competitive environment.

As industries evolve, or new information becomes available about their dynamics, it becomes necessary to revise industry definitions. Defining an industry is, in fact, an ongoing, iterative process. Defining an industry requires describing its components, the definitions of which are largely influenced by the scope of the industry definition. Again, it is best to start with commonly held beliefs about the marketplace. While taking a closer look at industry components (rivalry, customers, suppliers, substitutes, and entry), insights might be realized about a more suitable scope for the industry under study, and its definition can be revised.

Industry Rivalry

In warfare, the intensity of conflict is determined by the combatants' financial and fighting resources and the level of political interest in the conflict's objectives, as well as the combatant's abilities to develop new weapons and tactics. The intensity of rivalry among an industry's competitors is likewise determined by a number of factors:

➢ Competitors' capabilities and interests

➢ Demand for the industry's products in the broader economy

➢ Rate of innovation of an industry's knowledge and technology

➢ Assessing competitor's intentions and capabilities through intelligence gathering

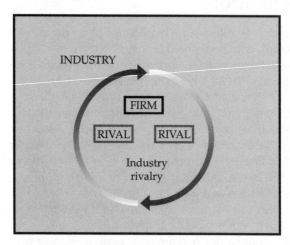

Rival Firms' Capabilities and Interests

Rival firms have differing capabilities in areas relevant to industry competition:

➢ Experience from past participation in the industry or other relevant industries

➢ Ability to conduct research and development that yields marketable innovation

➢ Strength and endurance, determined, for instance, by technical or marketing prowess or access to financial resources

Ultimately, a firm strives to maximize profit (where profit is measured along dimensions important to the firm's owners: financial profit, impact on the community, etc.). A firm's intent in a particular industry may be broader than trying to maximize short-term profit. For instance, a firm may enter an industry with the intention of learning and gaining experience before taking an aggressive course towards industry leadership. Another firm may have a weak commitment to the industry, hoping to reap short-term profits but otherwise is ambivalent about future industry participation. Firms' intentions and interests are as varied as people's intentions are in their personal pursuits: firms can be focused, committed, frightened—even fickle.

Demand for Industry's Output in Broader Economy

The total demand for an industry's products is a primary determinant of net industry profits, the prize for which rivals compete. The size of industry revenues reflects the value placed on industry products by its customers. The greater the level of revenues or the rate of revenue growth, the greater the pressure, or incentive, for rivals to adapt and improve their operations in pursuit of survival and profit. Greater industry revenues also translate into greater industry-wide expenditures for research and development, advertising, employee compensation, etc.—factors that intensify competition. Changes in customer demand for an industry's product represent a change in what is at stake for industry rivals.

Renewal of Industry Knowledge and Technology

Industry knowledge and technology are continually renewed, driven on the one hand by customer demands and, on the other, by advances in the fields of engineering, physical and social sciences, or even mathematics. The firm must continually improve its knowledge and technology as waves of innovation leave obsolescence in their wake. The rate of industry innovation directly affects the risk and uncertainty of the industry's future and the rate at which firms enter, exit, and reposition themselves in an industry.

Competitive Intelligence Gathering

Assessing competitor intentions and capabilities as well as broader economic and technological factors is essential for staying afloat in the turbulence of industry rivalry. Strategy formulation benefits from the ongoing collection of information about competitors and other factors affecting rivalry. This might include knowledge about the distribution of profit in an industry or of the costs of production for industry competitors. It is also valuable to have knowledge of the historical patterns of competition in an industry, and of other industries affecting it, or similar to it in structure or development—just as in football it is valuable to know how a team usually handles third down with a few yards to go.

Competitor intelligence gathering, leading to profiles of rivals and their capabilities and intents, is an important aspect of broader competitive intelligence gathering. Firms need informed strategies for addressing the challenges posed by all industry forces, not just industry rivalry. Staying abreast of developments affecting customers, substitutes, suppliers, and potential new entrants requires proactive competitive intelligence-gathering rather than reliance on common industry knowledge. It is the difference between trying to anticipate an industry's developments and waiting to read about them in the general press.

The Marketplace

The industry marketplace is the arena in which rival firms meet customers to exchange information and incentives (marketing) and to exchange products for financial resources or other forms of value. It is the industry's main stage, and good performance requires many skills. The diverse strategies and operations of a firm are ultimately tested and their value realized in the marketplace.

In Porter's five forces model, customers represent another component of industry structure. Customers are served by an industry's rivalry as well as by substitutes, which are products from other industries that closely substitute for the industry's products from a customer's perspective. The marketplace, comprised of rivalry, customers, and substitutes, may be thought of as a shelf in a store, a catalog, or even a living room, in the case of television programming. Understanding the dynamics of the marketplace requires analysis of both an industry's customers and its substitutes.

Customers

Firms design their products principally with the end user in mind. In many cases, the end user is a person or group desiring to consume the product or put it to use. The end user of an industry's products may be comprised also, or exclusively, of firms desiring to add value to the products for eventual resale in another form. Reaching an industry's end users—both consumers and other producers—is often facilitated by firms that act as market intermediaries.

Market intermediaries include wholesalers or agents that participate in the industry as transitory customers; that is, they sell the product to the eventual end user without any fundamental feature changes—but in a manner that is convenient or otherwise valuable to the end user and producing firm. In-house and direct sales efforts permit firms to reach customers without intermediaries. However, in many industries, intermediaries are dominant (e.g., grocery stores and other stores are the principal distributors of consumer products). Any successful strategy development must include careful analysis of both end users and market intermediaries when addressing the interaction of rivals with customers.

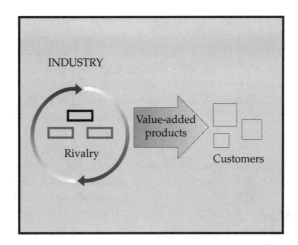

Customers are constantly bargaining with industry rivals for better price and performance. Porter defines *buyer power* as a measure of the bargaining strength of buyers relative to industry rivals. In an industry characterized by low-intensity rivalry (for instance, the U.S. long-distance monopoly in telecommunications before the breakup of AT&T) and strong customer need (long-distance telecommunication is essential to many businesses), the power of buyers would be assessed as low relative to rivalry: customers have no direct market alternative but must accept the stated price. Over time, customers could realize lower prices through regulatory changes, but the dynamics of such change are slow relative to the rapid feedback that occurs in a marketplace with intense rivalry. After deregulation, the long-distance telecommunications industry evolved more rapidly, and its rivalries have become characterized by an intense desire to meet customer needs. The customer, once pauper, is now king—by realizing a higher degree of buyer power.

Customer Analysis and Segmentation

The design, marketing, and distribution of products for customer use are capabilities that are essential to industry success. Effectively delivering value to customers entails carefully understanding their needs, interests, and resources and how these vary by groups within the universe of all customers. Market segmentation is the process of grouping customers according to similarities in their needs, interests, and resources. Those segments deemed favorable or desirable for sales of a firm's products are a firm's market targets. Market segmentation allows an airline, for instance, to study the varied characteristics of first-class, business-class, and coach customers and to serve each or all with these differences in mind.

It is valuable, for instance, to develop segmentation based on price sensitivity. Many customers want a generic, low-cost product instead of product variety or better quality at a higher cost. Grouping customers into segments allows a firm to consider the potential benefits and operational requirements of serving each segment. It may also be useful to segment customers according to their nature (people, businesses, nonprofit groups, government agencies, etc.) or according to size or geography. Customer decision-making attributes, such as degree of product comparison or brand loyalty, are also useful dimensions for segmentation. The challenge is to find market segmentation systems that reveal information about how decisions are made in the marketplace.

Product Attribute Analysis and Design

In addition to understanding the composition of the customer base, it is important to understand the degree to which each customer segment values a product's different attributes. Hedonic attribute analysis is the formal name for determining the value that customers place on each of a product's attributes. For instance, a person purchasing a box of cereal at a convenience store pays a premium for the convenience of not having to go to a larger grocery store, which might require more time or postponement of the purchase. Clearly, a convenience store needs to understand the degree to which this convenience is valued relative to the standard attributes of cereal value (taste, nutrition, brand image) to establish a price.

Customers vary in their preferences for product ease-of-use, durability, technology content, and brand image as well as firm characteristics and stability, among other things. The determination of attribute prices is inexact by nature: the only price that is generally known with certainty is the price paid by the customer for the complete bundle of attributes represented by a product. Managers may use a variety of quantitative tools, such as regression analysis and more sophisticated models of customer decision-making behavior, to determine the prices customers are effectively paying for each of a product's attributes.

Focus groups, interviews, and historical sales information enhance—and can dramatically change—beliefs about customer preferences. Customer preferences are both complex and variable over time. In many cases, it may only be possible to perform a *qualitative* analysis yielding information about the importance of various attributes relative to each other. Analyzing how customers value product attributes allows a firm to design and price a product with greater attention to its ultimate value in the marketplace.

Substitutes

Products from other industries will likely meet some of a customer's requirements in many cases. Identifying substitutes requires detailed knowledge of the customer needs being met by the industry's products. An orchestra promoting its live performances may consider itself in competition with other fine arts performances. An orchestra's customers, however, may be comparing an evening at the symphony not only with an opportunity to attend an upcoming ballet performance, but also with sporting events, movie videos, or even an evening in bed with a good book.

The threat of substitutes is often discounted or overlooked entirely during industry analysis. An otherwise capable firm can be blindsided by unexpected substitution by customers. For example, a store planning a grand opening for the day of the Super Bowl may find, for the first time, that its targeted customers are loyal football fans. Analysis of substitutes, in conjunction with customer segmentation and product attribute analysis, can lead to highly valuable insights about product design, marketing, and pricing. Substitutes force rivals to consider customer needs more broadly and are a catalyst for product innovation.

Suppliers

Suppliers complete the industry's value stream. Suppliers provide the industry with its factors of production, and they include firms that provide raw materials and services as well as people who provide labor services. Classical approaches to industry structure analysis follow the primary flow of value in the industry: upstream suppliers provide factors of production to rival competitors, which provide value-added products to their downstream customers.

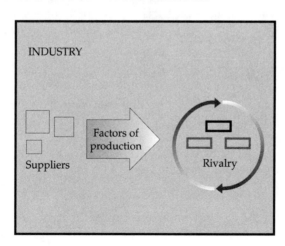

It is important for a firm to understand the role of suppliers in its industry and their role as supplier to other industries. Suppliers benefit from understanding how their products are used by customers to create downstream value for *their* customers by being better able to anticipate downstream trends and to adopt new factor technologies the ultimate user will value. Suppliers were not included in the earlier discussion of the marketplace (comprised of rivals, customers, and substitutes), but they are in fact involved as spectators and recipients of downstream customer purchase criteria through rivals' changing specifications for improved factors of production.

Suppliers find themselves in a bargaining relationship with rivalry just as customers do. Porter defines *supplier power* as a measure of the bargaining strength of suppliers relative to industry rivals. Consider an industry dominated by a small number of large competitors and supplied by a large number of smaller firms. Due in part to their numbers, the smaller firms find themselves in intense competition for the business of the large manufacturers; each manufacturer represents significant market share and is courted carefully.

A manufacturer may have the resources to conduct intensive research that yields accurate estimates of the actual costs incurred by a supplier (its cost structure) and of the rates of profit experienced in the supplier's industries. Accurate estimates of suppliers' financial conditions and expectations increase rivals' ability to negotiate lower prices with suppliers.

Supplier analysis can also help to identify opportunities for a rival to enter a supplier's industry, either as an effort to expand the scope of a firm's value-adding activities or in retreat from an industry's intense competition. When a rival assumes the functions of one of its suppliers (the "make" option in make/buy decisions), whether for in-house use or for broader market acceptance, it is referred to as *reverse integration*. A *forward-integrating* supplier is a supplier that joins an industry's rivalry by marketing its products directly to customers by including in their own operations value-added activities previously left to rivals.

Threat of New Entry

The attractiveness of an industry to a potential new competitor (perhaps a start-up firm or one seeking to diversify) is based on the intensity of the industry's other structural forces (rivalry, customers, substitutes, and suppliers) as well as the rates of profit and levels of risk being realized by existing rivals. Structurally attractive industries encourage new entry into the ranks of industry rivals.

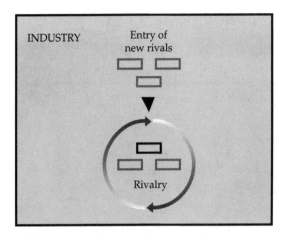

Entering an industry involves first overcoming the industry's barriers to entry, which represent the evolving requirements for effective industry participation. Entering the aerospace industry, for instance, requires large amounts of capital and high-reliability manufacturing experience. Entering a consumer products industry often requires significant investment in product promotion and good relations with distribution channels. Entry into a local taxi industry that operates with a fixed number of taxi medallions is limited by government regulation. Established rivals often strive to erect or strengthen barriers to entry, such as brand recognition, to protect their share of the market prize.

As time passes, however, both entry and exit occur. An unusually high rate of profit for a given level of risk will attract new entrants as a matter of course; unusually low rates of profit and the attrition of intense competition will induce rivals to exit. It is capitalism's course toward greater market efficiency.

As with the threat of substitutes, a firm may overlook or discount the threat of new entry. A future that seemed bright can suddenly become bleak with the introduction of even a single other rival. It is important, therefore, to consider potential competitors in competitive intelligence gathering and to recognize that entry can come from all directions: reverse-integrating customers, forward-integrating suppliers, substitutes that lead to threaten to require broader industry definition, and firms previously on the sideline that intend to get into the game. In some industries (such as health care administration), even the government can be a new entry threat.

Applying the Five Forces Analysis

With the addition of the threat of new entry, Porter's five forces model is complete.

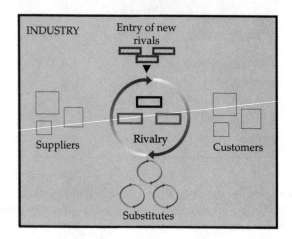

Since it is a cogent view of many complex, interdependent processes, a quick tour of the five forces analysis is useful for identifying key issues and generating tough questions about what is really taking place in an industry.

When applying the five forces analysis, it is useful to assign measures of strength (for instance, high, medium, or low) to each of the forces (rivalry, customers, substitutes, suppliers, and entry), since the relative influence of these forces varies by industry. Then, with an eye to the future development of the industry, one determines how these measures of strength are expected to change. As surfers know, one has to be able to ride waves *and* to see them coming. By studying industry forces and anticipating their flux, one can face an industry's challenges with greater confidence.

Three Generic Strategies

Competitive enterprises generally have different levels at which they are thinking about their company's strategy in a given industry. First, they need to choose a broad strategy. Should the firm try to produce a product of good quality at low cost or a better product at a higher cost? Or should it focus its attention on a particular portion of the industry's customers and try to produce a high-quality product at a relatively low cost? More detailed substrategies concerning actual operations (production, marketing, research and development, etc.) should be developed in a manner consistent with the choice of a broad strategy.

Porter outlined three broad strategies that are stable over time. These generic strategies center on choices that competition forces firms to make, concerning, on the one hand, maintaining a low product cost and, on the other, producing an enhanced product at a higher cost. Porter suggests that a firm cannot, in the long run, be all things to all customers.

The first generic strategy, *cost leadership*, recognizes that price is always a product attribute in which there is customer interest. Some of an industry's customers will demand a product that can get the job done at the lowest possible price without any bells and whistles. Challenges companies face in serving this market segment include tight control on expenses, operational efficiency, acquiring factors of production at low cost, and marketing their products at a low cost.

Differentiation, the second generic strategy, is the provision of a product with unique features, since some customers are less concerned with a product's costs. These customers may demand higher quality or greater product variety. Companies pursuing a differentiation strategy face the challenge of maintaining uniqueness through broad research and development, aggressive marketing, and better customer service. Naturally, these come at a cost that is reflected in a differentiated product's higher price.

The third generic strategy, *focus*, a hybrid of the cost leadership and differentiation strategies, limits the scope of its intended target market. The focus strategy involves competing on both cost and product features but with the intention of serving only a portion of the market.

Attempting to compete on cost and features while serving all customers is an unstable strategy over time. Enhancing product variety and quality usually involves greater increased direct and indirect product costs. These costs put the differentiating firm at a distinct cost disadvantage to the firm trying to serve an industry's most cost-sensitive customers with a product that works adequately. A differentiating firm trying to reach all customers can also find itself at a feature disadvantage to the firm that pursues a strict differentiation strategy without concern for serving the industry's most cost-conscious customers. The firm trying to pursue a mixed cost leadership and differentiation strategy with the intention of serving all customers finds itself, as Porter puts it, "stuck in the middle."

The choice of a broad strategy should be made in the context of a firm's capabilities and the industry's evolution. As time passes, a selection of a broad strategy may change (e.g., a firm may pursue low-cost market penetration while an industry is young, with the intent of pursuing a differentiation or focus strategy during a later stage. It is valuable to consider the firm's ability to pursue each of the three generic strategies before making a broad strategy choice. A broad strategy choice can be changed later, but at a cost, since many decisions about a firm's operations (its substrategies) follow directly from this choice.

Capabilities Analysis

Industry structure analysis is logically followed with a plan for addressing the challenges faced as an industry participant. Judiciously applying a firm's capabilities and resources in pursuit of its stated objectives is the main thrust of strategy formulation. Industry structure analysis describes the competitive landscape. Other analyses address how a firm is to negotiate the terrain.

A firm's capabilities can be modeled in a number of ways. A popular approach, introduced by Michael Porter in *Competitive Advantage: Creating and Sustaining Superior Performance*, takes a cross-sectional look at how a firm creates value (whereas *Competitive Strategy* addresses how industries function). Porter's cross-sectional value chain analysis first covers stages of production common to firms, and secondly, introduces support activities, which influence the primary stages of value creation.

A firm needs to assess its capabilities in each area of its activities in relation to its competitors'. Doing so indicates areas in which the firm may enjoy competitive advantage, or suffer from competitive disadvantage. Comparison to other industry rivals can lead to strategic imperatives for the firm to use and protect its strengths and to avoid or correct its weaknesses.

Primary Value Creation Activities

Porter defines the primary activities, or stages of production, of a firm as:

> ➢ Inbound logistics, or receiving factors of production from suppliers

> ➢ Operations related to transforming these factors into value-added products

> ➢ Marketing and sales

> ➢ Outbound logistics, or delivering products to customers

> ➢ After-sale service and support

Logistics, or distribution activities, whether inbound from suppliers or outbound to customers, affect a firm's production operations along the dimensions of cost, reach, and time. Assuming the roles of one's suppliers by reverse-integrating, if it is strategically viable, may improve a product's cost structure by simplifying logistics activities. Improved logistics can increase access to potential customers and suppliers. Production paradigms, such as just-in-time manufacturing, reduce a firm's inventory costs and reduce the time required to create and deliver products. Similarly, finding lower cost or more customer-amenable means of product distribution are important strategic concerns.

A rival's outbound logistics are its customers' inbound logistics. Therefore, a rival can provide downstream customer value by adapting its outbound logistics to its customers' inbound logistics needs. By linking different firms' value chains in this way, a map can be made (what Porter terms a *value system*) that helps a firm explore the interrelationships in its vast economic environment.

Decisions about a firm's primary value-adding operations should reflect the choice of its broad strategy. Pursuit of a differentiation strategy (where product attributes are nongeneric) requires flexible operations to support variety or careful quality control to provide enhanced product quality. A cost leadership strategy, on the other hand, may require achieving economies of scale as well as limiting product features.

Marketing, sales, and support are activities a firm performs to maintain its relationship with customers and potential customers. Philip Kotler, who has contributed to marketing analysis for over thirty years, developed a complex model of the marketing environment comprised of producers, customers, media channels, and a variety of publics covering virtually all areas of social organization and culture. Analyses for understanding the marketing environment as well as the nature of customer purchase decisions continue to evolve, incorporating increasingly sophisticated mathematics intended to make molehills out of the mountain of marketing.

Marketing, in the view of Kotler, represents the communication of information and the delivery of resources surrounding exchange with customers. This naturally includes efforts by the firm to inform its customers about product benefits and efforts of customers to inform firms of their purchase criteria. In the broadest terms, marketing includes decisions about advertising (developing messages about product appeal and selecting media channels), public relations, sales (allocating efforts between in-house sales, wholesalers, and retail), and other operations important to getting attention in the marketplace. A marketing substrategy must address the many facets of marketing—not just advertising.

Support Activities

Support activities, or secondary activities, are intended to reinforce the firm's capabilities in its primary activities (inbound logistics, operations, marketing, outbound logistics, and service). For instance, each of a firm's primary activities needs to be supported by administrative activities as well as offices, warehouses, and other physical assets (firm infrastructure). Similarly, primary activities are influenced by decisions made in the secondary areas of human resource management, technology, development, and procurement.

The introduction of support activities completes the cross-sectional structure of the value chain analysis. While developing a strategy for a primary activity, it is useful to consider the influence of each support activity. Alternatively, one may focus on a single support activity, such as technology development, and assess its importance to each of a firm's primary activities.

The Role of Computers in Strategic Analysis

The value of strategic analysis depends ultimately on a firm's ability to make decisions and to implement plans that actually prepare the firm for market opportunities and challenges. Since it takes time to tell if plans are succeeding, one must remember that the firm and its competitive environment are dynamic—they change as time passes. The strategic planning process should reflect this by being responsive to change and continuously updated. Many businesses operate in a dynamic environment with a strategy that is mainly static, or unchanging—perhaps with dynamic overtones. There are, however, clear benefits to having an explicit plan based on a detailed understanding of the structure and uncertainty of market opportunities and of the firm's efforts to realize them.

Computers have become an essential part of strategic planning because they can efficiently store, track, and analyze the myriad information needed to perform a dynamic industry structure analysis. Computer models can help an enterprise develop both the broad strokes of its strategies as well as the finer details. By querying users in a structured fashion, storing information and maintaining key relationships among data, and providing the user with meaningful visual results, computers can assist in strategy development. By performing complicated analyses of the marketplace, computers are beginning to take the first steps toward helping managers perform more powerful strategic analysis.

Over the past ten years, a number of computer software products have been developed to assist with strategic analysis and planning in a dynamic industry environment. Several examples of these applications include: Alacrity Strategy by Alacrity, Inc. of Toronto, Ontario; Business Insight by Business Resource Software of Austin, Texas; Competitive Advantage by Strategy Software, Inc. of Los Angeles, California; and MARKSTRAT by Strat*X International of Cambridge, Massachusetts.

Strategic Analysis with Business Insight

Business Insight® is a business factors analysis tool that is used to gather knowledge from the user and to help formulate strategies for business planning. An "expert" software system designed for personal computer users, Business Insight employs a structured set of questions that help the user consider the full spectrum of factors affecting their business and their marketing strategy. Combining an extensive knowledgebase of business concepts with the user's responses, Business Insight generates analyses specific to the user's business. As the user reviews these analyses, the program explains each business concept and how it is influenced by various factors found in the business environment. After walking the user through an analysis of his or her business, Business Insight helps the user develop and test a business strategy suitable for the firm, industry, product, and market.

Business Insight is built around two parts—a knowledgebase and a data collection/analysis program. There are two knowledgebases available: one for manufacturing industries and one for service industries. Users can select either or both of these knowledgebases, depending on their needs. Each knowledgebase includes over 500 factors addressing such nonfinancial concepts as cultural and demographic trends, promotion strategy and experience, pricing strategy, key management experience, status of development technology, conformance to industry standards, suppliers, channels of distribution, the prospective customer, and competitive strength. The strategy analysis component uses a model of competitive industry relationships loosely based on the five forces model described by Michael Porter and Philip Kotler. The analysis program also incorporates insights from the work of over 40 experts in the field of marketing strategy, from the personal experiences of the developers, and from the practical application of Business Insight by users from a wide range of industries.

In addition to the industry-specific knowledgebases and strategy analysis components, Business Insight incorporates a number of other features to facilitate the strategic analysis and planning process.

- ➤ To help users describe their business and their competitive environment, Business Insight offers lists of descriptive terms for various aspects of their industry and allows users to select the position on a range that best describes their competitive situation.

- ➤ Because hundreds of factors are involved in the description of an industry and its environment, Business Insight allows users to rate these factors on a scale of 0 to 100. This enables users to more accurately describe their environment and the factors most important to their particular situation.

- ➤ Where quantitative factors are required, Business Insight provides an integrated spreadsheet manager with templates to itemize details and calculate totals. Spreadsheet information can be imported from other programs, including Lotus 1-2-3 and Microsoft Excel.

- ➤ Business Insight identifies the essential ingredients of a successful enterprise and reflects its influence on a business strategy. Users can review each of these key factors to determine what changes they can make to improve their business strategy.

➤ Business Insight can identify inconsistencies in a business by detecting where key factors are in conflict. In addition to identifying these problem areas, Business Insight can suggest improvements.

➤ Business Insight enables users to compare different strategies, multiple strategies for their business, their strategy versus their competitors', or their strategy versus an "industry standard."

➤ The summary analysis combines all of the analyses into a concise, written review of a business strategy. The major topics of the summary include the business, products or services, prospects, competition, a detailed analysis of the strategy specifically reviewing the potential for a cost leadership, differentiation, or focus strategy, and finally, financial information.

A Hands-on Tutorial for Business Insight

A demonstration version of Business Insight can be found on the CD-ROM included with this book. The demo has had several features disabled—you will not be able to print, create new files, or save your changes. This demo can be downloaded from the CD-ROM following the instructions at the back of the book.

The following hands-on tutorial uses Business Insight's product industry knowledgebase to analyze the process of designing, developing, manufacturing, promoting, and selling a product. To explain the use of Business Insight, we will assume you have an enterprise, HiLight Inc., and you would like to do an analysis of the business factors related to your new product, Smart-Lite.

NOTE
All procedures in Business Insight can be performed with a keyboard—a mouse is not required. However, if you have a mouse installed on your computer system, you may use it to choose commands, to select data, and to scroll window contents. In this tutorial, procedures are given for both the keyboard and the mouse, with the keyboard procedure given first.

The Data Input Process

To start the tutorial, launch Business Insight from your Windows Program Manager.

1. Double-click the Business Insight icon (Business Insight) to open the About Business Insight window on your screen.

2. Press ENTER or click OK. This opens the File Open window:

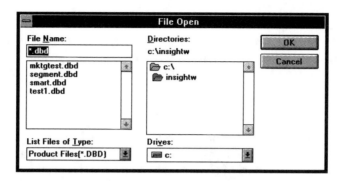

You would normally begin by opening a new analysis, but the Smart-Lite analysis already exists. So, open the existing analysis called SMART.DBD.

3. Select the file named SMART.DBD.

4. Press ENTER or click OK. This opens the Database window:

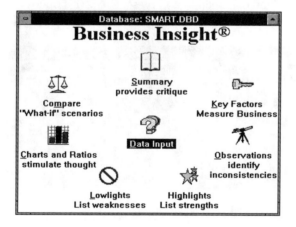

Although data has already been entered for this analysis, we will review the data entry process for familiarization. Note that the center icon in the display is titled Data Input. To initiate the question-and-answer process:

5. Select Data Input by either pressing ENTER (because it is the highlighted icon) or double-clicking on the Data Input icon.

You are now looking at the Data Input window, which contains an outline of several hundred topics, each representing a request for information.

Section A of the outline, which is already highlighted, deals with the most fundamental information, establishing the basis for your analysis.

6. To start the input process, press ENTER.

The display you are now looking at (called a *factor display*) is the introduction to the section, providing a general explanation of the factors to be covered. A factor display screen can be found at the beginning of each section.

NOTE
There are three buttons at the bottom of the display. Pressing ENTER will invoke the action specified by the button that has a bolder outline (the default command button), in this case, the Next-F9 button. You can change which button will act as the default with TAB or SHIFT-TAB.

7. After reading the explanation in the factor display screen, press ENTER or click the Next-F9 button. This moves you to a lower-level section explanation.

8. Again, read the explanation and press ENTER. This opens a *single-value factor display,* shown here, which requests the name of your enterprise.

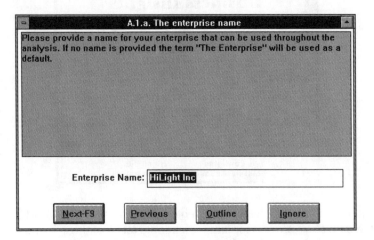

The input process for this type of factor display is to type in the requested information and press ENTER.

9. Type the name **HiLight Inc.** (even though it is already entered) and press ENTER.

You have automatically moved to the next factor display, this one asking for the legal status of your enterprise. This is called a *choices display* and requests that you select the entry best describing your enterprise. In this case, HiLight Inc. is a corporation. You may use the UP ARROW and DOWN ARROW keys or your mouse to select an entry. Select the Corporation entry, as shown here:

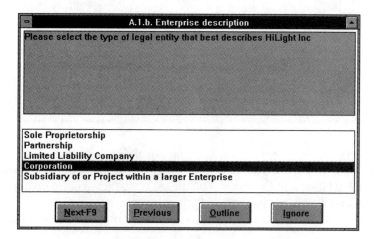

A.1.b. Enterprise description

Please select the type of legal entity that best describes HiLight Inc

Sole Proprietorship
Partnership
Limited Liability Company
Corporation
Subsidiary of or Project within a larger Enterprise

[Next-F9]   [Previous]   [Outline]   [Ignore]

10. Click the Previous button or press ALT-P.

The display moves back to the enterprise name screen. The Previous button will always move you back to the previous factor display in the outline. Pressing ESC on your keyboard will always return you to the previous logical level of Business Insight. The Outline button will automatically return the display to the outline.

11. Click the Outline button or press ALT-O.

The normal data entry process would start with the first factor display, as you just did, and, after entering the requested data, you would then move to the next factor display, again entering data, and so on, until you have responded to all of the requests. You can, however, return to the outline at any time and move your position to any topic by using the UP ARROW and DOWN ARROW keys, PG UP and PG DN, or your mouse.

12. Press the DOWN ARROW key until the topic Commitment To The Industry is highlighted, or click once on the topic, and then press ENTER.

This opens a *scale factor display*, shown next, which deals with how committed you are to keeping the product, Smart-Lite, in the marketplace.

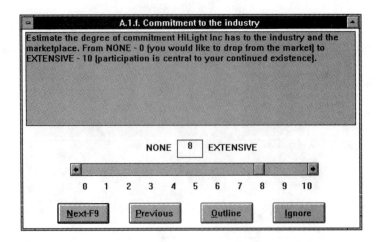

The top window contains the rationale explaining Business Insight's request for information. This factor display provides a scale with the extremes labeled None and Extensive. You are asked to pick a point on the scale that best represents your market commitment.

To set a position on the scale, you can perform one of the following:

➤ Use the LEFT ARROW or RIGHT ARROW key

➤ Position the mouse pointer on either of the scroll bar arrows and click

➤ Position the mouse pointer at the desired location on the scroll bar and click

➤ Position the mouse pointer at the desired location on the scroll bar and double-click

Any of these actions will set the position and move to the next display.

14. Select 8 on the scale—this shows a fairly significant commitment to the market.

Many of the factor displays use the scale concept with the extremes having different values.

15. Press ALT-O or click the Outline button to return to the Data Input outline.

16. Press END twice or use the mouse to scroll to the very end of the outline.

17. Press the UP ARROW key or your mouse to move to the topic entitled 5 Year Revenue Projection and press ENTER.

This opens an *annual display* (see Figure 5-1), which deals with numeric information for a five-year period. For any display dealing with numeric information, you have access to a worksheet. In fact, the data for

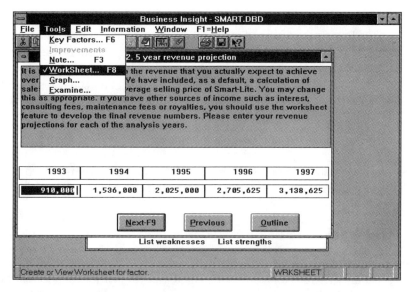

FIGURE 5-1. *The 5 Year Revenue Projection annual display*

this display was entered via a worksheet as indicated on the bottom line of the screen. Let's look at the worksheet used to enter the Smart-Lite data.

18. Press the F8 key or use the mouse to select Worksheet from the Tools menu.
   The worksheet provides most of the functionality of the spreadsheet products common to the market. To better understand these capabilities, let's review the online information.

19. Press F1 to open the Help window.
   Business Insight's online help is context-sensitive, so the information displayed is about the worksheet. For more detail on Business Insight's Help function, press ALT-C or click the Contents button.

20. To leave the Help window and return to the worksheet, press ALT-F and use the DOWN ARROW key to highlight Exit, then press ENTER. Or use the mouse to select Exit from the File menu.
   The numbers that are used as your input to the question are the numbers from the first five numeric columns in the bottom row (Total Revenue $$). In many cases, such as this one, a template (which you can alter) has been provided to help structure your thought processes. In the cases where templates have not been provided, you still have the full power of the worksheet.

21. Press ESC twice to return to the Data Input outline.

   The four types of factor displays that you have seen—single-value, choices, scale, and annual—are the basic forms for all of the input process requests. The questions in the Data Input outline address a range of concepts that are critical to the success of any business venture. You can use the UP and DOWN ARROW keys, PG UP, PG DN, HOME, END, or your mouse to browse through the outline.

22. Press ESC to return to the Database window.

After you have made a first pass at providing the requested information, you can immediately see analysis results, even if you were unable to provide all the information.

The Analysis

A variety of output formats are available in Business Insight, as described in the following sections. There is an icon on the Database window for each format as shown in Table 5-1.

ICON	FORMAT	BUSINESS INSIGHT RESPONSE
	Observations	Applies its knowledge to advise timely actions needed in your business.
	Key Factors	Measures your business against key factors critical to the success of a venture. You can review the conclusions Business Insight has reached, examine the logic used, and alter data you provided for the underlying factors.
	Highlights	Identifies the strongest aspects of your enterprise. You can build your strategy for success around these aspects.
	Low lights	Targets the areas most in need of improvement. Focus efforts here to understand and improve your strategy.
	Charts & Ratios	Provides comprehensive illustrations on strategy, competition, and financials. New ways of looking at your business lead you to new ideas about strategy and operations.
	Summary	Produces a concise, unbiased description of your business. This no-holds-barred description helps you see yourself as others do. Use it to improve your business plan objectively.

TABLE 5-1. *Business Insight Output Formats*

Observations

To begin our analysis of the HiLight corporation, let's review Business Insight's observations.

1. Press ALT-O and then ENTER, or double-click the Observations icon. This opens the Observations outline, which is a dynamic list generated as the result of the information you have supplied. If you change the information in the Data Input section, the observations may change. Normally, you would review all of the observations in detail, but we will look at just one or two. You are sensitive to the fact that you have chosen to price Smart-Lite lower than the competition.

2. Use the DOWN ARROW key or your mouse to highlight Cost Management Key To Low Cost Strategy and press ENTER. Your screen will now look like this:

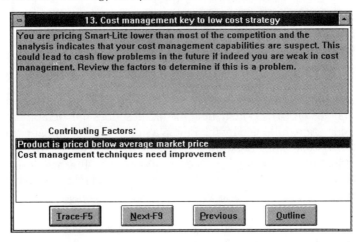

This is the standard display format for an observation. The observation is stated in the top window on the screen and the Contributing Factors that were reviewed in making the observation are displayed in the bottom window.

Notice that a new button (the Trace-F5 button) has been added at the bottom of the screen. This button is used to trace each of the Contributing Factors for your review. Trace is initiated by highlighting the desired Contributing Factor and then either pressing ALT-T, pressing F5, or clicking the Trace button.

In this observation, Business Insight is questioning your enterprise's ability to manage a program with low product costs. To understand how Business Insight arrived at this observation, you need to select the contributing factor, Cost Management Techniques Need Improvement, then trace it.

3. Press the DOWN ARROW key or use your mouse to highlight Cost Management Techniques Need Improvement.

4. Press F5. This opens the Assertion:_Cost Leadership Capacity window:

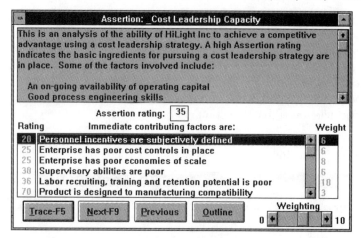

This display, called an *assertion display,* is how Business Insight presents its conclusions. The statement at the top describes the area of consideration, followed by the rating, a numeric value ranging from 0 to 100 (with 100 being the most positive for your enterprise). Below that, the contributing factors are displayed. As you can see, Business Insight has rated your cost controls, your ability to recruit and retain people, and your management capabilities as being quite low. Note that the contributing factors window is scrollable, so there are probably other factors as well. However, the least positive factors are always displayed first, so you know which to concentrate on. You may also choose to assign a weight to one or more contributing factors to adjust the analysis to your specific product and market. You could trace each of the contributing factors in the assertion back to the point of your original input to understand what, specifically, has contributed to the low ratings.

This should improve your understanding of those aspects of your cost leadership strategy that are most vulnerable and in need of improvement. You may also have discovered that you had not fully thought out your responses for some of the requested information or you just didn't have the information at the time. You have the ability to change your responses during your review of the observations or at any time later, which will most likely change the assertion rating.

5. Press ALT-O or click the Outline button to return to the Observations outline.

> Let's look at another observation.

6. Use the arrow keys or your mouse to highlight Support Prospect's Short Decision Process, and press ENTER.

> This observation points out how important promotional literature is to your sales process. It may prompt you to review promotional literature with your marketing personnel.

Each observation addresses a specific aspect of your business endeavor and should be reviewed in detail. You may look at as many observations as you wish, and then press ESC until you are back to the Database window.

Charts & Ratios
Now let's take a look at some of the displays in Charts & Ratios.

1. Press ALT-C and ENTER, or double-click the Charts & Ratios icon. The Charts & Ratios appears:

This outline lists the various displays provided by Business Insight to help you in creating your business strategies. All of the displays listed in the outline can provide you with insights for making your business endeavor a success. However, we will look at only three of them.

2. Highlight the strategy chart in Section A named Generic Strategy Potential, and press ENTER. The Generic Strategy chart appears:

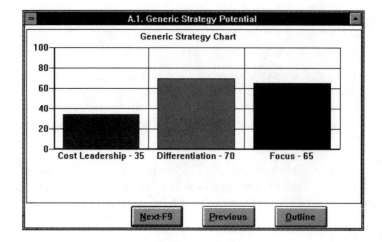

This chart is designed to help you evaluate which of three generic approaches to your strategy is most appropriate. A cost leadership strategy requires that you can produce and offer your products or services more cost effectively than any of your competitors. A differentiation strategy requires that you are able to offer a product or service that is unique enough to justify a higher price than any of the competition. A focus strategy involves defining a market niche, that your enterprise is better qualified to sell to than any of the competition.

➢ If you double-click the bar of the graph, text supporting the analysis logic will be displayed.

➢ If you double-click the strategy rating (i.e., 70 for differentiation) the assertion supporting the analysis will be displayed.

➢ To return back to the chart display from either the text or the assertion, click the Previous button or press ESC.

When you have finished exploring the Generic Strategy Chart, return to the outline by clicking the Outline button or pressing the ESC key.

3. Once you are back at the Charts & Ratios outline, highlight the strategy chart in Section A named Product Positioning Matrix, and press ENTER. The Product Positioning matrix appears:

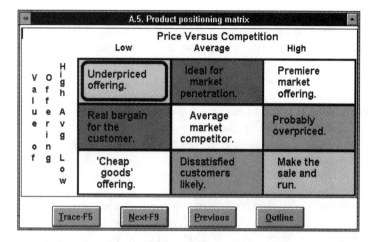

This analysis indicates you are underpricing your offering, in this case the Smart-Lite product. To understand the rationale behind this assessment, you may use the Trace feature to review the influencing factors. After reviewing the factors, click the Outline button or press the ESC key to return to the Charts & Ratios outline.

4. In Section C, highlight the strategy chart named Projected Return On Investment, and press ENTER. The Projected Return On Investment window appears:

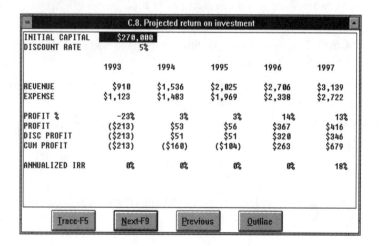

You cannot see the complete display, but you can use the horizontal scroll bar or maximize the display. It is clear that while HiLight Inc. expects to make a profit every year except the first, the return on the original investment of $270,000 is inadequate. Obviously, some more thought needs to go into your business strategy.

You may look at as many of the Charts & Ratios displays as you wish. When you are done, press ESC until you are back to the Database window. Next we will look at the highlights of your strategy as assessed by Business Insight.

Highlights and Lowlights

The Highlights feature of Business Insight helps you to identify the strongest aspects of your business enterprise. The Lowlights are those areas of your business strategy most in need of improvement. You should try to build your strategy around your highlights and focus on trying to understand and improve your weaknesses. Lowlights can be reviewed in the same manner as outlined below for Highlights.

1. Press ALT-G and ENTER, or double-click the Highlights icon to open the Highlights outline window.

    You can review the Highlight entries just as you did those in Observations and in Charts & Ratios. For example, you will find that:

    ➤ _Introduction/Switch Costs will tell you that your buyer can expect a very low cost when switching from their current light switch to Smart-Lite, which is a strong selling point for your enterprise.

    ➤ _Cost Profile will show that Smart-Lite has good potential to reduce the customer's operating costs.

    Again, you can trace each of these back through more detailed levels of analysis to gain insight into your business and strategy.

2. Look at as many Highlights as you wish. When you are finished, press ESC until you are back to the Database window.

Key Factors

The Key Factors represent the factors most critical to the success of a venture. The following is a review of the Key Factors analysis.

1. Press ALT-K and ENTER, or double-click the Key Factors icon to open the Key Factors outline window.

Business Insight considers the factors listed in the outline to be the business aspects most critical for you to understand when establishing your strategies.

2. Highlight THE PRODUCT (Item C) and press ENTER. The Product analysis window appears:

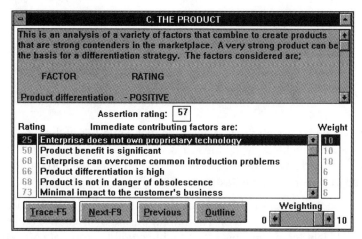

By reviewing this analysis, you will gain more insight into the good and bad aspects of the Smart-Lite product. Similar benefits can be obtained by reviewing each of the other key factors.

3. Review as many of the key factors as you wish, and then press ESC until you are back to the Database window.

Summary

After you have viewed the Observations, Charts & Ratios, Highlights, Lowlights and Key Factors, you can have Business Insight provide you with a descriptive review of HiLight Inc.

1. Press ALT-S and ENTER, or double-click the Summary icon. This displays the Summary outline window.

2. Highlight The Competition (Item E), and press ENTER. The Competition analysis window appears:

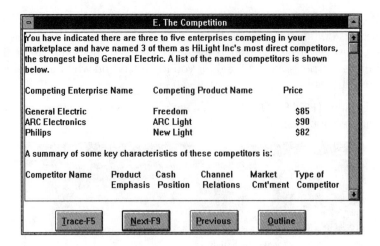

Scroll down through the text and note that a number of the words in the text are highlighted. Using the arrow keys or your mouse, you can move the cursor to any emphasized word and then trace back to the information used in constructing the text.

3. Position the cursor on the emphasized word "credibility" and press F5. Here you see that, based on your input, Business Insight has determined that HiLight Inc. is dealing with a highly credible group of competitors.

4. Press ESC to return to the Competition window.

   When returning from a trace, ESC or the Previous button will return you to the factor display from which the trace was initiated. You may trace other highlighted words if you wish, and then press ESC until you are back to the Database window.

Evaluating Alternative Scenarios

You have reviewed Business Insight's analysis of your enterprise and would now like to make some adjustments to your responses to see how you might improve the results. Because so many aspects of the analysis have the potential to change as the result of one modification of your input, Business Insight provides a way to quickly see the results of a change. The first step is to save your current answers in a form called a *case* using the Save Case command under the File menu. In this instance we have already done this for you by creating a case named SMART1.

(Remember, the demo version cannot save any changes you may have made to the case.)

Using this as a basis for comparison, you can now make a change to the database and compare the results. It is recommended that you change one factor at a time to best understand the implications of the change.

The saved case assumes that you will be the first to the market with a product like Smart-Lite, thus being the pioneer. Suppose you were to wait until others had entered the market and then introduced Smart-Lite? How would that change the analysis?

1. Press ALT-D and ENTER, or double-click the Data Input icon to get to the Data Entry outline.

   Business Insight also includes an outline processor, and you will see some of its power in the next few steps. The outline is quite large, so it would be nice to reduce the number of levels of the outline that were displayed.

2. Open the View menu and select Collapse.

3. Use the DOWN ARROW key to move to the Product Or Product Line topic.

4. Open the View menu and select Isolate.

5. Use the DOWN ARROW key to move to the Strategic Factors topic.

6. Press the RIGHT ARROW key to Isolate again.

7. Use the DOWN ARROW key to move to The Market Life Cycle.

8. Press ENTER.

   The original response to the question was that you would enter the market in the introductory life cycle stage. Now you want to assume that you are waiting until after the introductory stage.

9. Highlight the Rapid Growth choice.

10. Press ALT-O or click the Outline button to return to the outline window.

11. Press ESC to return to the Database window. Now you are ready to compare the analysis results.

12. Press ALT-M and ENTER, or double-click the Compare icon.

13. Highlight the SMART1.CAS case for comparison.

14. Click OK. The Case Comparison window appears:

```
┌─────────────────────────────────────────────────────────────────┐
│ ⊖                      Case Comparison                         ▲ │
│ Changes to Analysis                          Current  Old      ♦ │
│  A.    Enterprise                                                │
│   1.    _Operational differentiation ability      55    56      │
│  B.    Prospect                                                  │
│   1.    Market life cycle stage                                  │
│   2.    _Price vs Value Sensitivity               56    57      │
│   3.    _Knowledge Level                          84    89      │
│   4.    _Comparison Effort                        48    49      │
│   5.    _Quality Assessment Ability               55    56      │
│   6.    _Buyer - Bargaining power                 57    58      │
│   7.    _Market growth                            65    73      │
│  C.    Marketing                                                 │
│   1.    _Full Svc Retail Consistency              59    62      │
│   2.    _Self Svc Retail Consistency              61    60      │
│   3.    _Distribution effectiveness               62    63      │
│   4.    _Advertisability of product               72    77      │
│   5.    _Advertising Importance                   75    76      │
│   6.    _Advertising strength                     55    57    ♦ │
└─────────────────────────────────────────────────────────────────┘
```

The Case Comparison window provides a comparison between your original analysis and the new one. Modified Factors are shown at the top of each section. Assertions and Observations are listed on the left, with the current value shown in the column labeled Current and the value from the case you used for comparison in the column labeled Old. Remember, the higher the rating, the better it is for your enterprise. In this case, it appears that almost every change was for the worse for HiLight Inc.

In the Prospect section, it shows that you changed the Market Life Cycle factor. From this, Business Insight infers that the prospect's knowledge level and quality assessment ability have improved, thus making it a more difficult sale, and therefore the potential for market growth has decreased somewhat. The General Competition section shows more competitive rivalry, and the Competition section indicates that all three competitors are more likely to retaliate when you enter the market. You may position the highlight on any topic and trace it by pressing F5 to better understand the logic behind the rating.

At this point you can return to the Data Input outline, change the Market Life Cycle back to Introductory, and then change some other factor. Alternatively, you can leave the first change and make one or more others to see the results. While it is often best to proceed by changing one factor at a time, sometimes it is not obvious what changes might improve your strategy.

Business Insight offers yet another way to help your analysis process. It is called the Improvements feature. Let's take a look at it.

1. Press ESC until you are back to the Database window.

2. Press ALT-K and ENTER, or double-click the Key Factors icon.

3. Highlight DEVELOPMENT and press ENTER.

The display asserts that your development program rates 70 out of 100. You would like to know what improvements you can make to increase the rating. At your request, Business Insight will review all of the factors that impact this assertion, will show you the maximum rating possible, and will list each of the factors that, if changed, would make a difference. It would seem that you should always be able to improve a rating to 100. However, there are some factors that Business Insight assumes cannot be changed, such as environmental factors and most of the competitive factors. If any of these factors influence a rating, then you may not be able to raise it to 100. Let's see how you might improve HiLight Inc.'s development program.

4. Select Improvements from the Tools menu.

This process will take a few seconds, because Business Insight is analyzing each factor to determine which of its potential values will maximize the Development assertion. The resulting display is once again an outline. The heading states that if you could optimize every factor within your control, you could raise the rating to 100. Each of the topics in the outline is a factor that you can control.

5. To view the path of assertions from the factor up to the Development assertion, select Full View from the View menu.

Topic 1 is for the factor Dev Mgr - Past Experience, and it states that if the factor's value were changed to Extensive, the Development rating could be raised to 75. It is obvious that the only way you could change this factor would be to hire a new development manager. The factors causing a change in the Development rating are listed in order from those having the most impact to those having the least. It is the cumulative effect of changing all of the factors that will raise the Development rating to 100. Review as many of the factors as you desire. You may view any factor or assertion by positioning on the topic and pressing ENTER.

The Improvements feature can be used with any assertion in the analysis to help you determine where improvement may be feasible.

6. When you have finished reviewing areas where improvements might be made, press ESC until you are back to the Database window.

This completes the Business Insight hands-on tutorial. While you have not used all the capabilities of Business Insight, you have done enough to understand the basic concepts and to know how to navigate through the program. Remember, there is a complete Help capability available if you run into problems.

Conclusion

Planning is essential for any enterprise seeking to improve its performance in a competitive environment. The challenge of business planning is to carefully develop and apply a firm's resources and capabilities in the context of an ever-changing marketplace. Effective business planning demands the careful consideration of all the forces affecting an industry and its environment. Once an industry's structure has been thoroughly evaluated, a strategy must be devised that judiciously utilizes the firm's capabilities and resources. The value of developing a strategy ultimately depends on the firm's ability to make and implement plans that actually prepare it for market challenges and opportunities.

The need for strategic planning is common to all firms. With the aid of conceptual models and strategic analysis tools, competitive enterprises—at least some of them—will increase their likelihood of success through effective strategic planning.

CHAPTER 6

Supporting Market-Driven Change

by William B. Rouse and Charles W. Howard
Enterprise Support Systems

Worldwide, many enterprises face the problems and prospects of change. Quite often, companies fail in terms of anticipating, recognizing, and responding to change. An integrated set of software tools, knowledgebases, and databases—an Enterprise Support System (ESS)—can help companies to avoid such failures and to experience change in terms of opportunities rather than crises.

Examples of enterprises struggling to deal with problems associated with change can be found in every industry:

➤ Defense companies of all sizes are facing rapidly declining markets. They need to assess their current and likely future situations and, if necessary, plan for diversification.

➤ Software companies are faced with dramatically declining markets for mainframe computer software. Equally dramatic is the growth in demand for client-server solutions. Companies in these markets need to reposition themselves and develop plans for accomplishing these changes.

➤ Many companies, especially large firms, are reevaluating their internal functions to assure that they explicitly add value to their operating units. Good examples are R&D and information system functions. These organizations have to change to become competitive with outsourcing.

➤ Probably the most compelling illustration is small to midsize companies that want to become larger. To accomplish this goal, these companies have to rigorously assess market situations and develop aggressive plans to achieve growth. At the very least, such assessments and plans are often necessary to attract the investments needed for growth.

This chapter is concerned with understanding the nature of these problems and developing the means to support enterprises dealing with these problems. In particular, the emphasis is on tools that enhance people's abilities and help them overcome their limitations when facing the processes of change in complex organizational systems. These tools focus on helping users answer the following types of questions:

➤ What is my strategic situation in the marketplace and what future situations are possible and likely?

➤ What products and services will delight my customers and provide substantial competitive advantages?

➤ What integrated set of targeted markets and product lines, as well as manufacturing, services, and R&D, will provide me with maximum success potential?

➤ What are the underlying reasons for conflicts about goals, strategies, and plans and how can I resolve these conflicts?

These questions are central to the work of most executives and senior managers, whether they are responsible for whole companies or business units within larger companies.

Why Change Is Difficult

We have found that successfully answering the preceding questions is central to enterprises that find opportunities rather than crises in the process of change. However, most enterprises struggle with the above questions. Why does this happen?

Extensive study of this issue led us to surprisingly simple conclusions. We have identified three central limitations that underlie enterprises' difficulties with change.

The first limitation is that enterprise management simply does not know what to do. They have little if any experience in dealing with major strategic or long-term changes. Their key competencies are usually in the areas of marketing, engineering, manufacturing, or finance. Furthermore, most of their careers have been spent focusing on relatively short-term issues. Consequently, most decision makers fail to recognize when they are being asked to think strategically.

The second limitation is that whenever people attempt to think strategically, it usually takes much time and effort. This is further complicated by the fact that they often have to work within highly bureaucratic organizational structures with many layers of oversight. In both cases, people often grow to resent the time that they are forced to spend in these activities.

The third limitation tends to be totally debilitating: when groups finish such efforts, they often have not produced anything that they value. The resulting plans are filed, shelved, or dutifully completed. Subsequently, life goes on as before—the plans have had no impact.

In developing the Enterprise Support System concept, the goal has been to help people overcome these limitations. In particular, the tools discussed in this chapter focus on helping people know what to do, not take too much time, and produce something that they value. Good plans can develop quickly, and it should be possible to prepare a complete, or nearly complete, plan in about two days.

Enterprise Support Systems

What information and related types of support do enterprises need to deal with change successfully? To answer this question, one should consider enterprises' information requirements in the context of the tasks they perform. By focusing on tasks, one can then determine what information is needed, when it is needed, and how it can best be provided. In a very broad sense, there are three types of tasks that enterprises perform in the process of anticipating, recognizing, and dealing with change:

> **Situation Assessment** Involves answering questions such as "What is happening?" and "What is likely to happen?"

> **Planning and Commitment** Involves generation, evaluation, and selection among alternative courses of action, as well as commitment of resources to the course(s) of action selected.

> **Execution and Monitoring** Involves implementation of plans, observation of consequences, evaluation of deviations from expectations, and selection between acceptance and rejection of these deviations.

These three tasks are usually performed at several levels in an enterprise:

> **Strategic** Involves consideration of an enterprise's mission, goals, strategies, and strategic plans.

> **Tactical** Involves consideration of the objectives specified in strategic plans and is concerned with tactics and tactical plans necessary for achieving these objectives.

> **Operational** Involves consideration of schedules, budgets, and project/production plans.

The purpose of an Enterprise Support System is to support performing the three types of tasks at all three levels of an enterprise.

An overall ESS architecture is shown in Figure 6-1. Note that elements of this diagram may be linked without explicit lines being shown. All elements include inputs labeled "Results," but lines connecting the outputs of all the elements on the right in this figure are not shown, to avoid a very cluttered diagram. In other words, the expected and actual results that flow out of the Situation Assessment, Planning and Commitment, and Execution and Monitoring processes at the Strategic level feed into the opportunites to pursue, and threats to avoid, at the Tactical level. Likewise, the outputs from the Tactical level flow into the Operational level inputs. Conceptually, this model of an Enterprise Support System can be used to map out the decision-making process from the upper-left corner of the diagram, where market trends and events are assessed at the Strategic level, then across the decision-making process at that level and down to the Tactical level. The across-and-down process is then repeated at the Tactical level and ends with the monitoring of the actual and expected results at the Operational level (the lower-right corner).

The process implied by the architecture depicted in Figure 6-1 may seem excessively formalized, and perhaps very rigid. This would be true if this process was used in the linear, hierarchical manner shown. However, note that the flow of connections in the diagram is not exclusively across and down. People and ideas

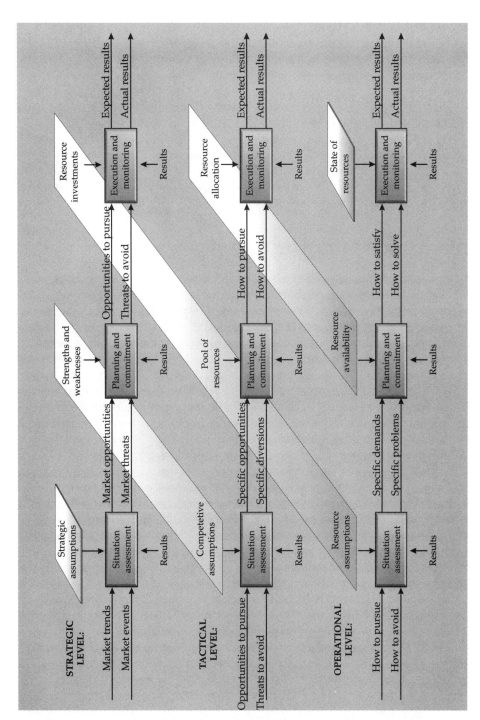

FIGURE 6-1. *Overall architecture of the Enterprise Support System (ESS)*

may cut across an ESS in a much less structured way, entering and exiting at various points in the process, as shown by the diagonals. The strengths and weaknesses that inform the Strategic Planning and Assessment process also inform the competitive assumptions used in the Tactical Situation Assessment. Similarly, Strategic resource assessments influence the pool of resources at the Tactical level and, later, the resource assumptions made at the Operational level. And, of course, today's operational results are tomorrow's market trends and events.

Thus, the process depicted in Figure 6-1 is not a monolithic information system. Instead, this architecture provides a schema for integration of a set of tools, knowledgebases, and databases. From this perspective, an ideal ESS provides uniform and easy access to a wide variety of tools, information sources, and related utilities as discussed in the following section.

Information Infrastructure

It is certainly possible to realize the type of ESS shown in Figure 6-1 without information technology. In other words, all of the tasks depicted in this figure can be performed manually. In our experience, however, these tasks cannot be performed quickly, and are seldom performed well, without the support of information technology. Consequently, in the absence of this support, these tasks are often ignored or given minimal attention. Thus, computer support is needed to create the ideal ESS.

While this ideal has yet to be realized, it is useful to consider the ingredients that are likely to be essential to providing the desired types of support. First, a key element of the ultimate ESS is the information technology infrastructure needed for seamless integration and utilization of data and knowledge. This information technology includes both computer and communications technologies.

At the moment, there are a wealth of these technologies. However, it is difficult to get them all to play together. Nevertheless, the infrastructure necessary for the ideal ESS is emerging. It is quite reasonable to assume that the necessary underpinnings for the ultimate ESS will soon be here. These underpinnings will include low-cost, powerful computers that can communicate anywhere and anytime via wire and wireless networks, as well as standard interfaces and protocols that eliminate the need to patch things together and employ endless access codes and translation packages.

Such accomplishments will not be sufficient to realize the ideal ESS. We also have to be concerned with the applications software that will use this infrastructure. Seamless integration of these applications requires that one move beyond data exchange standards and create compatible knowledge structures and content. This, in turn, requires that developers of applications software employ compatible representations of their problem domains. For example, all of the authors in this book would have to agree to an integrated representation of the related set of problems addressed in their chapters. Such agreement is very difficult to achieve, at least at this stage of the industry's maturity.

A key to gaining a competitive advantage in this process is the ability to lead in setting industry standards. Microsoft is rapidly gaining this advantage for the information infrastructure level of Enterprise Support Systems, based to a great extent on the work of various industry pioneers. However, at the higher levels of knowledge structures and content, many issues remain open. Consequently, there is much competitive advantage yet to be gained.

Component Tools

Beyond information infrastructure itself, there are many tools that access and utilize infrastructure. While the goal is seamless integration across these tools, this goal depends totally on the compatibility of knowledge structures and content. Much progress has yet to be made in these areas of compatibility.

To illustrate, it is useful to discuss several of the component tools within an ESS. Some of these tools are obvious and readily available. The more obvious include packages and systems for word processing, report writing, database access and utilization, spreadsheet modeling, computer-aided design, project management, materials resource planning, process control, order entry and processing, accounting, and forecasting. These types of applications software provide most of the capabilities necessary for the Operational processes found in the lower-right corner of Figure 6-1.

While the levels of integration of these capabilities remain fairly rudimentary, many of the elements are well-defined and evolving toward standardization. Consequently, it is unlikely that new word-processing or spreadsheet packages, for instance, will appear and gain significant market share. These markets are in the midst of, or on the verge of, serious consolidation. Thus, the choices among these types of tools are almost completely defined.

Moving from the Operational realm in the lower-right to the Strategic processes in the upper-left of Figure 6-1, the state of affairs is much more open. This is due to the nature of the processes depicted. While the lower-right is concerned with deducing schedules, milestones, and budgets, as well as comparing actual results to planned results, the upper-left is concerned with the more creative aspects of planning and assessment. These aspects involve issues of what should be pursued and how to pursue it.

Methods and tools that support these higher order tasks are far less numerous than those mentioned to support the more concrete tasks found at the Operational level, and far from being standardized. A variety of such tools—known as MBA-ware—are discussed throughout this book. Enterprise Support Systems, a division of Search Technology, Inc., has been involved in developing three tools (described in this section) that fit into this category. These tools focus on planning new products and services, developing comprehensive business strategies, and preparing for organizational changes.

These three tools are instances of a class of tools called *advisors.* An advisor provides a methodology for supporting problem-solving and decision-making and includes online expert advice and online tutoring in the use of the tools. Advisors also incorporate several of the lower-level tools for word processing, spreadsheet modeling, and project management.

What Users Want

It is useful to discuss the types of support that users need as they engage in the Strategic planning processes depicted in the upper-left of Figure 6-1. They want these types of supports from a variety of tools, not just those discussed in this chapter.

It is important to note that many of these activities are performed in groups. While individuals may prepare background materials and initial analyses, most decisions are made in group settings. In such settings, groups often want a structured process that provides a nominal path for proceeding. People want a clear and straightforward process that can guide their discussions, with a clear mandate to depart from this process whenever they choose.

A second desire expressed by groups involves capturing the information compiled, decisions made, and the linkages between these inputs and outputs. People want such an audit trail so that they can justify decisions and sometimes reconstruct decision processes. Further, since the group may not all be together at the same time, they want group members to be able to access the audit trail asynchronously in order to understand what went on since they were last involved.

A third desire is for facilitation of the group's process. While human facilitation is often a key element in such group settings, computer-based tools can also provide elements of facilitation. For example, large screen displays linked to computer-based tools can present and manage the nominal process, provide prompts in terms of questions, and give advice based on what has transpired thus far. The neutrality of this type of facilitation—the computer has no explicit stake in the proceedings—is often quite compelling. It provides a clear means of short-circuiting tangents and getting back on track.

A fourth desire that people have of such tools is for the tools to tell them something that they do not already know. While structured processes, audit trails, and facilitation are greatly valued, they may involve inputting much information to the computer. This process may result in considerable sharing of information among group members. However, this information is inherently such that at least one of them already knew it. Why should they invest the effort necessary to provide the tool with all this information?

The answer has to be that the tool is able to digest this information, see patterns or trends, and then provide advice or guidance that the group perceives they would not have thought of without the tool. This can be accomplished in a variety of ways. For example, our Product Planning Advisor searches through multidimensional market and product models to provide advice on how best to improve products. Our Business Planning Advisor employs a rule-based expert system to suggest how to best improve the market and technology potential of business plans. Our Consensus Building Advisor deals with conflicts associated with organizational changes by looking for patterns among needs and beliefs underlying these conflicts and prompting groups to focus on key differences. Other examples of similar support tools can be found throughout this book.

The advice and guidance provided by the tool has to be such that it is not viewed as magic. Thus, tools have to be able to explain the sources of their suggestions. People have to be able to explore the basis of the tools' outputs until they can realign their intuitions with these results. Otherwise, they are not likely to accept the advice or guidance.

Note that the types of support that users want can easily be linked to the limitations that make change difficult to deal with. Namely, the four types of support outlined previously can help users know what to do, accomplish things quickly, and create valuable and useful plans in the process.

The remainder of this chapter provides detailed descriptions of how to use Product Planning Advisor. This tool is included on the CD-ROM that accompanies this book. Instructions for downloading Product Planning Advisor can be found at the back of this book.

Features of the Product Planning Advisor

The Product Planning Advisor is based on the book *Design for Success: A Human-Centered Approach to Designing Successful Products and Systems*. The purpose of the Product Planning Advisor is to support you in the creation of products or services that provide substantial competitive advantages.

The first time through the Product Planning Advisor, we recommend that you follow a detailed example called Grocery Buyer's Assistant (GBA). Although this is a fictitious product, there are many things you can learn from it. Feel free to modify the data, add to it, or delete from the GBA example. The GBA example can be found in the GBA.DFS file. In working with this detailed example, you will come to appreciate the value of the Product Planning Advisor.

The Product Planning Advisor helps you to create a plan in either of two ways. In the guided approach, the Product Planning Advisor leads you through the entire product-planning process. You follow this methodology by sequencing through the seven steps shown in the Product Planning Process window. In the free-form approach, you take more direct control over exactly how you go about preparing your plan. You can access the Advisor's capabilities directly through the icons on the tool palette or by opening just the capabilities you want from the Windows menu. Although the Advisor does not actively guide you through your plan in the free-form approach, information and assistance are always available. Also, you can switch back and forth between the guided and free-form approaches easily and at any time.

We recommend using the guided approach until you have developed a bit of expertise, then you can switch to a free-form approach and access all capabilities directly.

Creating a Product Plan

The Product Planning Process window, shown here, is the screen from which navigation in the guided approach begins.

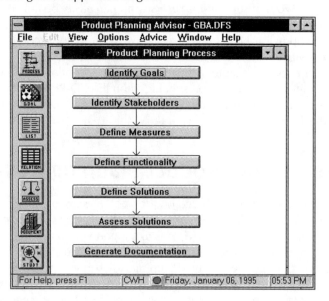

Through this window, you identify goals and stakeholders, develop measures of success, define stakeholder needs and desires, define product functions, identify and assess potential design solutions, and document the design rationale.

To follow the Grocery Buyer's Assistant (GBA) example,

1. Choose Open from under File in the main menu.

2. Double-click on gba.dfs in the File Open dialog box, or highlight the file and click OK.

3. In the Login box, choose any of the available names and click the return button.

From this point on, follow the general instructions in the remainder of this chapter to learn how to use the Product Planning Advisor. You will note that the instructions are written to help you enter your own product ideas. However, the same general steps can be used to explore the Grocery Buyer's Assistant example. You can test each of the program's functions while you walk through the GBA example.

Identify Goals

The first step in a design plan is to describe the product that your plan involves and specify the goals that it will help stakeholders to accomplish.

Goals refer to explicit states or outcomes that designers, users, and other buying influences would like to realize. Goals are often philosophical choices and may be stated qualitatively. Furthermore, there are generally many ways to achieve the same goal. Goals are particularly useful for providing guidance for later design choices.

1. Click Identify Goals in the Product Planning Process window. The Identify Goals window appears, as shown here:

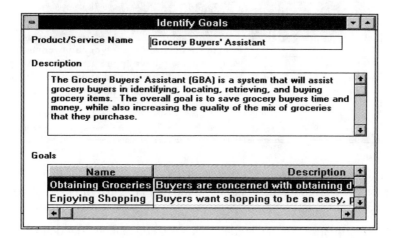

2. Type your product name in the Product/Service Name text box.

3. Type the description of the product in the Description text box.

4. Insert, modify, or delete the goals of the product, using the appropriate command under Edit in the main menu. For example, to insert a goal, follow these steps:

    a. Choose Insert from the Edit menu. The Edit Goal dialog box appears.

    b. To define a goal, enter a name and a short name, and enter a description.

5. To return to the Product Planning Process window after completing these steps, select New Window and Process from the hierarchical menu under the Windows option in the main menu.

Identify Stakeholders

Stakeholders are people who have an interest in the goals of the product, system, or service. Customers and users are obvious stakeholders. Other stakeholders might include product developers, manufacturers, maintainers, product support people, investors, regulators, and so on.

1. Click Identify Stakeholders in the Product Planning Process window. The Stakeholders window appears:

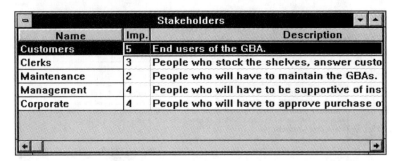

Name	Imp.	Description
Customers	5	End users of the GBA.
Clerks	3	People who stock the shelves, answer custo
Maintenance	2	People who will have to maintain the GBAs.
Management	4	People who will have to be supportive of ins
Corporate	4	People who will have to approve purchase o

2. Insert, modify, or delete the stakeholders of the product, using the appropriate command under Edit in the main menu. For example, to insert a stakeholder, follow these steps:

    a. Choose Insert from the Edit menu. The Edit Stakeholder dialog box appears:

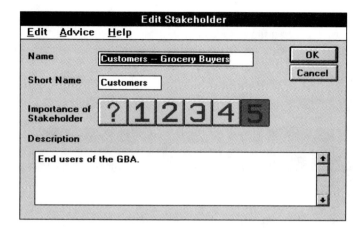

b. To define a stakeholder, enter a name, enter a short name, enter an importance, and enter a description.

Stakeholder importance ranges from 1 to 5, where 1 implies the stakeholder is of little importance to the success of the product while 5 means the stakeholder is very important to its success. Within the GBA example, the users are very important as compared to the maintenance staff. You can view the maintenance stakeholder in the GBA example by selecting it in the Stakeholders window, then clicking on Modify from the Edit menu.

Define Measures

A crucial element in product planning is the measurement structure. This structure defines the factors by which stakeholders will ultimately judge your product—the "scorecard." Its purpose is to support assessing solutions.

> Click Define Measures in the Product Planning Process window. This will produce two sub-steps: Identify Measures and Specify Stakeholder Desires.

Identify Measures

The measurement structure refers to the set of all attributes, measures, and their hierarchical relationships that the marketplace is presumed to apply in judging the worth of your solution. In the Product Planning Advisor, the top node of the measurement structure is always overall utility; viability, acceptability, and validity are the children of this attribute. Each of these three attributes are, in turn, defined by more granular attributes; these must be tailored to different domains. The bottom attributes—leaf attributes—are referred to as *measures*. Measures can be observed and, thus, have units of measurement associated with them, such as dollars, feet per second, or a rating on a subjective scale.

1. Click Identify Measures in the Define Measures window. The Attributes window appears:

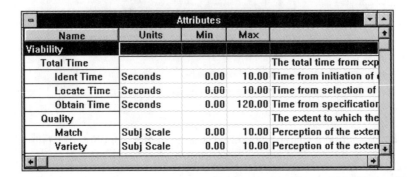

Name	Units	Min	Max	
Viability				
Total Time				The total time from exp
Ident Time	Seconds	0.00	10.00	Time from initiation of
Locate Time	Seconds	0.00	10.00	Time from selection of
Obtain Time	Seconds	0.00	120.00	Time from specificatior
Quality				The extent to which the
Match	Subj Scale	0.00	10.00	Perception of the exten
Variety	Subj Scale	0.00	10.00	Perception of the exten

2. Insert, modify, or delete the measures of the product, using the appropriate command from the Edit menu. For example, to insert a measure, follow these steps:

   a. Choose Insert from the Edit menu. The Edit Attribute dialog box appears:

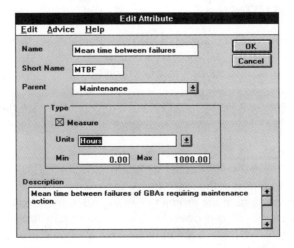

b. To define an attribute, enter a name, enter a short name, enter a description, select a parent attribute, determine whether the attribute is a measure, and if so, enter a unit of measure, a minimum value, and a maximum value.

In the GBA example, one of the measures is Mean Time Between Failures (MTBF). MTBF is measured in hours and has a minimum value of 0 and a maximum value of 1000. You can view the MTBF measure in the GBA example by selecting it in the Attribute Window, then clicking Modify on the Edit menu.

Specify Stakeholder Desires

This window is where you identify the meaningful relationships between Attributes and Stakeholders, otherwise called stakeholder desires. A stakeholder desire defines how changes in the associated measure affect the stakeholder's perceived utility of these changes. For example, the maintenance staff prefers products that have large values for MTBF.

1. Click Specify Stakeholders Desires on the main menu. The Attributes vs. Stakeholders window appears:

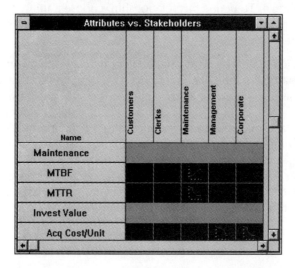

2. Add, modify, or remove stakeholder desires, using the appropriate command from the Edit menu. For example, to add a stakeholder desire, follow these steps:

a. Select the cell corresponding to the measure and the stakeholder for which you want to add a relationship.

b. Choose Add from the Edit menu. The Edit Attribute vs. Stakeholder Relationship dialog box appears:

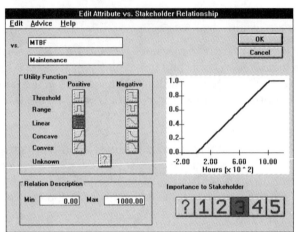

c. Note that the name of the selected attribute measure and stakeholder are shown. To define this relationship, choose a utility function, select an importance to stakeholder value, and set the minimum, maximum, and rate values.

The utility function defines how a stakeholder perceives the worth of a product as it relates to a particular measure. Utility functions can be positive or negative, linear or nonlinear, continuous or discontinuous. The minimum, maximum, and rate values customize the utility function to a particular stakeholder desire. The default minimum and maximum values come from the minimum and maximum values that were entered earlier as part of the definition of the measure.

An example of a stakeholder desire in the GBA occurs between the maintenance staff and MTBF. As the value for MTBF rises, so does the utility value for this product for the maintenance staff. The importance of MTBF to maintenance workers is fairly high, although not as high as Mean Time To Repair (MTTR).

Define Functionality

Functions define *what* a product or system should do, but not *how* it should be done. Functional definitions focus on the product's actions, not on the specific mechanisms that cause those actions. In the Grocery Buyer's Assistant example, one function is "location identification." In other words, determining where in the grocery store the desired product resides.

> Click Define Functionality in the DFS Process Window. This will produce two sub-steps: Identify Functions and Specify Functional Coverage.

Identify Functions

Identifying functions is the first step toward deriving solutions. This window shows all functions that you believe will be needed to meet the market's desires.

1. Click Identify Functions in the DFS Process Window. The Functions window appears.

2. Insert, modify, or delete the functions of the product, using the appropriate command from the Edit menu. For example, to insert a function, follow these steps.

   a. Choose Insert from the Edit menu. An Edit Function dialog box appears.

   b. To define a function, enter a name, enter a short name, and enter a description.

Specify Functional Coverage

In this window, you identify which functions have an impact on which measures. For each relevant pair, you enter a value that indicates both the direction and magnitude of this impact. These data are used in the Assess Solutions step to identify and rank the functions that you can change to improve the marketplace's reaction to your design solutions. For example, the "fault protection" function is positively related to MTBF. As the "fault protection" function is improved, the value for MTBF should improve.

1. Click Specify Functional Coverage in the DFS Process Window. An Attributes vs. Functions window appears:

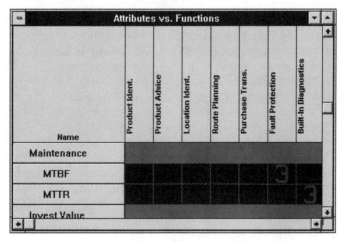

2. Add, modify, or remove an attribute vs. function relationship, using the appropriate command from the Edit menu. For example, to add a functional relationship, follow these steps:

   a. Select the cell corresponding to the attribute and function for which you would like to add a relationship value.

   b. Choose Add from the Edit menu. The Edit Attribute vs. Function dialog box appears. The name of the selected attribute and function are shown.

   c. To define a functional relationship, enter a numerical value and a description. For example, a –3 represents a strong inverse relationship while a +3 represents a strong direct relationship.

Define Solutions

In the Product Planning Advisor, a solution refers to a particular collection of functions that will more or less satisfy the marketplace. A "whole solution" includes all relevant functions from the marketplace's perspective; "partial solutions" include only a subset of the functions. This distinction helps to describe various product development strategies, all of which the Product Planning Advisor will support.

➤ Click Define Solutions in the DFS Process Window. This will produce three sub-steps: Identify Solutions, Specify Solution Functionality, and Specify Solution Measures.

Identify Solutions

A solution refers to a particular collection of functions that will more or less satisfy the marketplace. Solutions can include both your products and competitor's products for comparison purposes. Within the GBA example, some of the solutions are status quo, stationary kiosk, and an in-cart interactive screen.

1. Click Identify Solutions. The Solutions window appears:

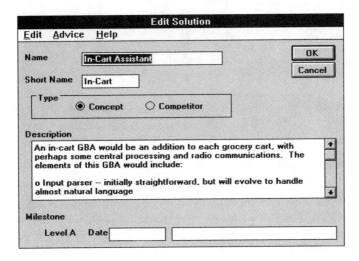

Name	Type	Level	Date	
Status Quo	Concept	Level A		Shopping in the cu
In-Cart	Concept	Level A		An in-cart GBA wou
In Cart	Concept	Level B		Level B includes a
In Cart	Concept	Level C		Level C includes a
Stationary	Concept	Level A		A stationary GBA w
Aisle Phones	Competitor	Level A		This low-cost alter

2. Insert, modify, or delete a conceptual solution or a competitor's solution, using the appropriate command from the Edit menu. (You may want to enter your competitor's products for comparison purposes.) For example, to insert a solution, follow these steps:

a. Choose Insert from the Edit menu. The Edit Solution dialog box appears:

b. To define a solution, enter a name, enter a short name, enter a description, and enter a date and description for each of the three levels; A, B, and C.

Specify Solution Functionality

Your task in this step is to indicate which functions will be included in each solution by placing check marks at the appropriate intersections of the matrix. The status quo solution in the GBA example includes all of the functions except for product advice.

1. Click Specify Solution Functionality. The Solutions vs. Functions window appears:

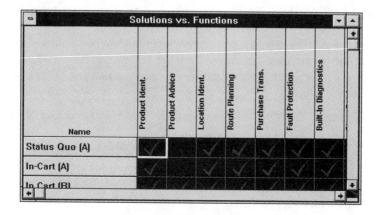

2. Add, modify, or remove a function vs. solution relationship, using the appropriate command from the Edit menu. For example, to add a relationship, follow these steps:

   a. Select the cell corresponding to the function and solution for which you want to add a relationship.

   b. Choose Add from the Edit menu. An Edit Solution vs. Function Relationship dialog box appears. The solution and function names appear in the text boxes. You can enter a note concerning the relationship if you desire. An example note might describe to what degree a function is included in a solution.

Specify Solution Measures

In this window, you indicate the value of the measures for each solution by entering a number in the corresponding cell. In other words, you are defining the solutions in terms of the measures entered earlier. This allows the advisor to calculate the overall utility of each solution and to offer suggestions as to how to best improve it. For example, the estimate for MTBF for the in-cart solution is 250 hours.

1. Click Specify Solution Measures. The Attributes vs. Solutions
window appears:

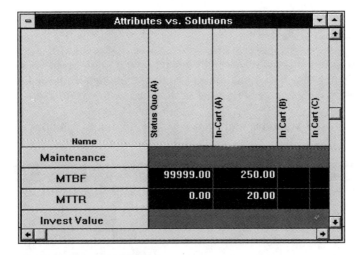

2. Add, modify, or remove an Attribute vs. Solution relationship, using the
appropriate command from the Edit menu. For example, to add a
relationship, follow these steps:

a. Select the cell corresponding to the measure and solution for which
you want to enter a value.

b. Choose Add from the Edit menu. The Edit Attribute vs. Solution dialog
box appears:

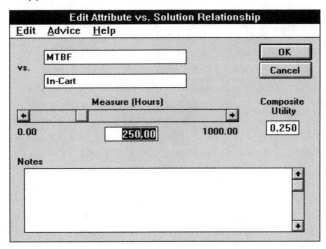

   c. The attribute and solution names appear in the text boxes. To define a solution measurement, enter a measurement.

Assess Solutions

It is useful to assess the market prospects of alternative solutions by, first, comparing them to external benchmarks and to one another and, second, by conducting sensitivity analyses (product evaluations) with the Advisor.

1. Click Assess Solutions in the Main Menu. An Assess Solutions window appears:

Name	Units	Stakeholder	Importance of Stakeholder	Importance to Stakeholder	Status Quo (A)	In-Cart (A)	In-Cart (B)
Overall					0.616	0.592	0.0
+Viability					0.602	0.465	0.0
+Acceptability					0.959	0.535	0.0
+Validity					0.387	0.907	0.0

2. If the circle in the status bar is red, this indicates that information has changed and the assessment needs to be recalculated. From the View menu, choose Recalc.

View the assessment of the overall utility of each of the solutions. In the GBA example, staying with status quo appears to be the best solution since it has the highest overall utility value at .616. Next, peruse the utilities of each of the attributes and measures to understand what is good and bad about each solution. To view the children of an attribute, double-click on that attribute's row in this window. For example, double-click Viability, and then Maintenance. Notice that the in-cart solution appears to have low utility for both "MTBF" and "MTTR" as compared to status quo. Obviously, status quo will have a utility score of 1.0 since the current system (no assistance) cannot break down or be repaired.

From the Advice menu, you can choose How to Improve to get advice on how to best improve the utility value of a solution. Before selecting How to Improve, you must first select the solution you want to evaluate by selecting its column. In our example, click the in-cart column, then select How to Improve in the menu bar. The resulting dialog box, shown here, tells you that if you change "locate time" by 10%, you will improve the overall utility of the in-cart solution from .592 to .602.

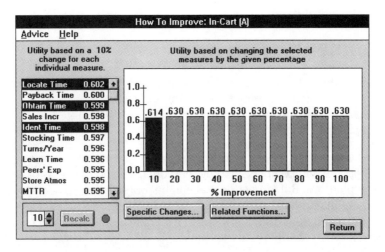

Further down the list, you will notice that if you change the MTTR by 10%, you only get an improvement of .592 to .595. To better understand the full capabilities of this dialog box read the Ask Bill and Ask Chuck help which accompany it.

From the Advice menu, you can choose Ask Bill to get Bill's suggestions on how to perform sensitivity analyses using the Assess Solutions window.

Generate Documentation

The Product Planning Advisor incorporates a full-blown word processor. It automatically generates design documentation for your product which can then be edited in the word processor. First, the Product Planning Advisor can generate an Objectives Document (OD) for each solution. An Objectives Document is a formal product design document which lists the goals, functions, and objectives of your product. Second, the Product Planning Advisor can generate an audit document which alerts you to any missing information, evidence, and/or coverage from your design plan.

1. Click Generate Documentation from the DFS Process Window. The Document window appears.

2. Generate a document by choosing New OD or New Audit from the View menu.

3. After the text is generated, you can edit it in the word processor.

4. Save the text to a file. This file is in a format (rich text format, RTF) which can be read by most word processors including Word and WordPerfect.

Environment

As you navigate through the Product Planning Advisor, you will encounter the following features which are specific to the Advisor itself.

Ask Bill

When you need assistance understanding the principles and concepts of creating your product plan, Ask Bill (an option that can be found in the Advice Menu). Bill Rouse is the originator of the design for success planning process and can give you expert advice gained from his many years of experience in new product development.

Ask Chuck

While Bill can help you with conceptual problems and give you strategic advice, he is not much on details. Ask Chuck (another option in the Advice Menu) if you want to know what to do next or how to do something rather than why you're doing it.

Studies

In the Product Planning Advisor, there is nothing to prevent you from basing decisions about your market, product, and strategy on personal opinion, hunches, and guesses. However, it is often the case that you want greater confidence in your decisions than these informal means can provide. To support this need, the Product Planning Advisor contains a rich set of facilities to define, develop, summarize and apply studies to your decisions. Studies are central to the Design for Success Methodology. They are the means for collecting the evidence that you need to make informed choices about the market and your product. To view or edit studies, choose Study from the tool palette. The Studies window appears:

Studies		
Name	Method	
Shopper Study	Interview	Assess what is important to
Management Study	Interview	Assess store and chain mar
Personnel Study	Interview	Assess store clerks and ma
1st Design Mtg	Design Meeting	Define initial functionality
Shopper Mockup	Mockups	Assess shoppers' reactions
2nd Design Mtg	Design Meeting	Formulation of an evolution;
Shopper Prototype	Prototypes	Assess shoppers' initial us
Competition Study	Magazine and	Determine what products pr

To Insert a Study

1. Choose Insert from the Edit menu. The Edit Study dialog box appears:

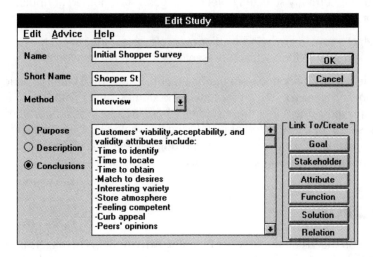

2. To define a study, enter a name, enter a short name, enter a method, enter a purpose, enter a description, and enter a conclusion.

3. When you select Conclusions, a Link To/Create list appears. This list allows you to create an object (e.g., goal, stakeholder, attribute, function or solution) that is supported by the conclusions of the study. You can also link the study to objects that already exist if the study provides further evidence supporting their existence.

Show History

The Show History option on the Edit menu shows you an audit trail of changes to an object.

1. Select a row in any window. For example, select the row in the Stakeholder window that represents the maintenance workers.

2. Select Show History from the Edit menu. The History window appears. This window indicates who created an object (e.g., goal, stakeholder, attribute, function, or solution) and when, as well as who last modified the object and when.

Show Evidence

The Edit menu's Show Evidence option shows you evidence supporting the existence of the currently selected object (e.g., goal, stakeholder, attribute, function, or solution).

1. Select a row in any window. For example, select the row in the Stakeholder Window that represents the maintenance workers.

2. Select Show Evidence from the Edit menu. The Show Evidence dialog box appears. Here you see a list of all of the studies, along with link icons displayed at the left of those studies whose conclusions support the existence of the selected object. Using this dialog box you can add supporting evidence, remove supporting evidence, and view the conclusions of the supporting study.

Conclusion

We have found that using the Product Planning Advisor helps managers and executives to better understand their strategic situation in the marketplace, the products and services that will delight their customers, how to develop products and services targeted to particular markets, and resolve conflicts over goals, strategies, and plans. In short, the Product Planning Advisor can enhance people's abilities and help them overcome their limitations when faced with the processes of change in complex organizational systems.

CHAPTER 7

Integrated Business Planning for Financial Success

by David Davidson, Jack Davidson, and Marshall Mills
Planet Corporation

Timely and accurate financial reports are critical to the success of any business. To start a business, run a more profitable business, or manage a department within a larger organization, it is essential to have access to key financial information about your company or department. This information can take any number of forms, ranging from the usual accounting statements—cash flow, balance sheets, break-even points, profit and loss ratios, etc.—to information specific to a particular business or department—loan documentation, actual costs vs. budgeted costs, product marketing trends, and so on.

Without ready access to accurate financial information, any number of problems can arise. Consider the following:

➤ Your company has just received a large production order, which requires an expansion of your facility and additional production personnel. What financial tools do you need? What format will you present this data in? How fast can the data be assembled and who will provide, assemble, and present it? Will the presentation be the same for a bank as for an investor?

➤ You receive a call from the bank telling you that your checking account lacks sufficient funds to honor your company checks. However, you know that your sales have been doing very well. What financial tools are available to help you recognize and prevent this problem from recurring?

➤ You have a great product, but you don't know how much to sell it for. How could you determine in advance how your pricing decision will affect your financial future?

➤ You want to sell your company and you need to make the best presentation possible to get top dollar. How will you tell potential buyers about your business? What financial data will you need? How should you present this information?

➤ You want to bring shareholders into your business. What can you offer in the way of dividends for their investment? What steps do you need to take to assemble all the information needed to attract and secure investors?

➤ As owner/manager, you want to better understand how your business performs so that you can make informed decisions about what courses of action to take. How can you forecast what affect your decisions will have on your business in a year, or five years from now?

All of the scenarios above are reason enough for the entrepreneur and business manager to purchase, initiate, and utilize an integrated financial reporting system. These scenarios and many more could be played out on a PC with almost instant results. You could plan and adjust your strategies accordingly in these "What-if" analyses to ensure that you make the right business decisions. This would enable you to prepare a better business plan and to execute that plan with greater success.

There are a number of integrated financial planning software packages on the market that could fill your needs. BizPlanBuilder, by JIAN Tools for Sales of Mountain View, California; Business Plan Toolkit, from Palo Alto Software of Eugene, Oregon; Destiny Business Information & Planning System, by Planet Corporation of Worcester, Massachusetts; PFS: Business Plan, from SoftKey International of Cambridge, Massachusetts; and PlanMaker, by PowerSolutions of St. Louis, Missouri, are some of the packages available. Some of these packages, however, are not stand-alone packages—that is, they contain templates, and the user has to provide various formulas in order to set up and use these templates.

Introduction to the Financial Planning Concept

From conception to maturity, the success of a business venture depends to a large degree on the communication of reliable information and the understanding of basic financial principles. Typically, entrepreneurs who start a new business are visionaries who can see money-making opportunities but lack an understanding of important financial skills. If the entrepreneur doesn't acquire these skills, the venture may perform poorly or fail.

Fortunately, there is a tool available to help business owners avoid these pitfalls: the business plan. The plan can guide business owners through a variety of important decisions, including:

➢ New or additional financing

➢ Purchasing another business

➢ Forming an association with another business

➢ Selling a business

➢ Hiring top management

Regardless of the application, if a business plan is required, it will contain financial reports, graphs, and text. This plan should be comprehensively short, usually 20 to 30 pages.

The business plan contains the following financial statements:

➢ Balance sheet

➢ Income statement

➢ Cash flow statement

➢ Break-even

➢ Key Ratios

➢ Highlights

➢ Graphs

➢ Narrative Text

Detailed explanations of each of these financial statements and how they interact would consume many chapters. A thumbnail look at each statement should explain the basics.

Balance Sheet

A balance sheet is used to show the financial condition of a business at a given moment in time (see Figure 7-1). The balance sheet does not show how the business reached that condition, and it does not indicate in what direction (good or bad) the business is heading. It simply states what is happening now.

Destiny Houseware Corporation
Balance Sheet

	Nov-94	Dec-94	....	Oct-95	First Year	....
ASSETS						
Current Assets:						
Cash	2,297,859	743,060	....	2,198,793	2,198,793	....
Accounts Receivable	32,605	76,077	....	206,496	206,496	....
Inventories	286,743	374,359	....	439,833	439,833	....
Other current assets						
Total Current Assets	2,617,207	1,193,496	....	2,845,121	2,845,121	....
Property and Equipment:	1,282,092	1,284,184	....	1,305,104	1,305,104	....
Less Accumulated Depreciation	21,368	42,771	....	258,720	258,720	....
Net Property and Equipment	1,260,724	1,241,413	....	1,046,384	1,046,384	....
Other Assets						
Total Assets	**3,877,931**	**2,434,909**	....	**3,891,506**	**3,891,506**	....
LIABILITIES & EQUITY						
Liabilities:						
Current Liabilities:						
Short-term debt						
Accounts payable	1,650,473	188,740	....	481,375	481,375	....
Other current liabilities						
Total current liabilities	1,650,473	188,740	....	481,375	481,375	....
Long-term debt	2,300,000	2,300,000	....	2,069,900	2,069,900	....
Total Liabilities	3,950,473	2,488,740	....	2,551,275	2,551,275	....
Owners Equity	(72,542)	(53,831)	....	1,340,231	1,340,231	....
Total Liabilities and Equity	**3,877,931**	**2,434,909**	....	**3,891,506**	**3,891,506**	....

FIGURE 7-1. *A sample balance sheet*

As an example, the cash line shows how much cash the business possesses on a certain date, such as at the close of business on January 31, 1995. The dollar value for every other line item shown in the balance sheet must represent the same date. The balance sheet can't show the dollar amount for cash as of January 31, 1995 and the dollar amount for accounts receivable as of February 8, 1995. If the dates used are different, then the balance sheet misrepresents the time frame that is being analyzed and wrong conclusions are drawn. This could have an overlapping effect when analyzing the other financial reports.

The balance sheet sums up the business's assets and subtracts the liabilities (claims by creditors against the assets of the business). The difference is the owner's equity or capital.

Basically, the balance sheet is divided into business assets and business liabilities, which must equal each other. The premise is that the business assets are either claimed by the creditors (such as vendors or banks) or claimed by the owners (who get what is left after the creditors are paid).

If you change any of the line items in the balance sheet, other financial reports such as your income statement (profit and loss statement) are also affected. For instance, increasing the accounts receivable or cash line items on the balance sheet has the effect of increasing the line item revenue in the income statement.

Income Statement

The income statement (see Figure 7-2) is another way of looking at the changes in your business's worth. The income statement summarizes your business's income sources (such as cash and accounts receivable) and expense sources (such as leases and wages).

The income statement and balance sheet are the primary indicators of what is happening with your business. To get an idea of their relationship, think of them in these terms: the balance sheet shows the financial condition of your business as of a specific date; the income statement shows the financial activities of your business over a specific time frame.

Usually, the income statement is created between the dates your balance sheets are created, thus showing the financial activities for this period of time. Any changes in the worth of your business during a specific time frame (usually between two balance sheet reports) have to be explained in your income statement(s).

Make your income statement as detailed as possible—don't bundle items. Detailing creates a clear audit trail when examining your financial reports. To further clarify your income statement, use footnotes. Footnotes help make it clear why, when, how, and where the particular line item and its amount were used.

Destiny Houseware Corporation
Income Statement

	Nov-94	Dec-94	....	Oct-95	First Year	....
Revenues	109,669	219,338	....	520,929	5,264,114	....
Cost of sales	31,860	63,721	....	151,337	1,529,299	....
Gross Profit	77,809	155,617	....	369,592	3,734,815	....
Operating Expenses:						
Fixed expenses	22,812	22,812	....	22,812	273,744	....
Variable expenses	26,966	12,499	....	16,638	190,257	....
Salary expenses	60,010	60,010	....	60,010	720,120	....
Burden expenses						
Bad debt	987	1,974	....	4,688	47,377	....
Depreciation	21,368	21,403	....	21,752	258,720	....
Total Operating Expenses	132,143	118,698	....	125,900	1,490,218	....
Operating Profit	(54,334)	36,919	....	243,692	2,244,597	....
Other Revenue (Expenses):						
Interest income						
Interest expenses	(18,208)	(18,208)	....	(16,690)	(213,944)	....
Gain (Loss) on disposal of assets						
Total Other Income (Expenses)	(18,208)	(18,208	....	(16,690)	(213,944)	....
Profit before income taxes	(72,542)	18,711	....	227,002	2,030,653	....
Provision for income taxes				77,181	690,422	....
Provision for tax refund						
Net Profit	(72,542)	18,711	....	149,821	1,340,231	....

FIGURE 7-2. *A sample income statement*

Cash Flow Statement

Over time your income statement may show significant earnings, while your operating capital (cash) may be nonexistent, especially in the start-up phase of operation. Therefore, the cash flow statement (Figure 7-3) is important to you as the owner and operator of the business. The cash flow statement forecasts what expenses will need to be paid (usually monthly) and how much cash will be

Destiny Houseware Corporation
Cash Flow

	Nov-94	Dec-94	....	Oct-95	First Year	....
Cash Flow From (To) Operations:						
Net Profit	(72,542)	18,711	....	149,821	1,340,231	....
Add depreciation	21,368	21,403	....	21,752	258,720	....
(Gain) Loss on disposal of assets			....			....
Change in operating assets and liabilities:						
Accounts receivable	(32,605)	(43,473)	....		(206,496)	....
Inventory	(286,743)	(87,616)	....	4,726	(439,833)	....
Other current assets						
Accounts payable	1,650,473	(1,461,733)	....	147,883	481,375	....
Other current liabilities						
Net cash flow from (to) operations	1,279,951	(1,552,708)	....	324,182	1,433,997	....
Cash Flow From (To) Investments:						
Additions to property and equipment	(1,282,092)	(2,092)	....	(2,092)	(1,305,104)	....
Proceeds from disposal of assets						
Additions to investments						
Proceeds from investments						
Net cash flow from (to) investments	(1,282,092)	(2,092)	....	(2,092)	(1,305,104)	....
Cash Flow From (To) Financing:						
Proceeds from loans	2,300,000		....			....
Repayment of loans			....	(38,350)	(230,100)	....
Additional capital payments			....			....
Payment of dividends						
Net cash flow from (to) financing	2,300,000		....	(38,350)	2,069,900	....
Net Increase (Decrease) in Cash	2,297,859	(1,554,800)	....	283,740	2,198,793	....
Cash, beginning of period		2,297,859	....	1,915,053	2,198,793	....
Cash, end of period	2,297,859	743,060	....	2,198,793	2,198,793	....

FIGURE 7-3. *A sample cash flow statement*

available to meet those expenses. If there won't be enough cash to handle the expenses, the owner might decide to take a number of actions, including:

➢ Asking suppliers for extended payment terms

➢ Drawing funds from another account (such as savings)

➢ Getting a bank loan depending on what the overall cash flow looks like

You need cash to pay for wages, tools, supplies, utilities, and so forth. Cash is not the same as profits, income, or revenue; cash is the actual money instantly available to the business for the procurement of goods and services to keep your operation going. After you start production, several possibilities may occur:

➢ You sell your product immediately.

➢ Your products have to be inventoried for a period of time.

➢ An error in production causes a throwaway-and-remake situation.

➢ Your product becomes obsolete.

Any of these situations can complicate the registration of a sale and the eventual receipt of cash for that sale. The cash flow statement helps you identify what cash is available to pay projected expenses for a specific time frame.

More often than not, you're going to sell your product(s) and eventually receive cash for your sale. Typically, you grant terms to the buyer of your product(s) or service(s). *Terms* in this context means the temporary extension of time in which the cash payment will be expected by you, the seller. Typically you might extend 30-day terms to the buyer. Therefore, 30 days after the sale is registered in the seller's books, the seller expects full cash payment for the products or services that were bought.

While you are waiting for these payments (accounts receivable), you still need cash to pay for various business expenses that you incur in your daily operations. Thus, you require a cash flow analysis. Basically, the cash flow statement is a projection (based on the terms of your sales agreements) of cash income and cash expenses over a period of time (usually monthly).

In start-up situations, new owners must be very much aware of their projected cash flow so that they can meet company needs and keep production rolling. Typically, in a start-up situation, cash is not available for use immediately. One reason is that businesses often phase in production. Production in the first month might be at 25 percent of capacity, and it will not reach full capacity until after four months. This start-up scenario allows time to phase in equipment and personnel, and it provides time to work out any problems that might occur.

In the phase-in scenario, the cash flow statement becomes very important to the business owner, because maximum cash income won't occur for several months. Unless well funded, this puts a strain on the business owner's pocketbook. The cash flow projection goes a long way toward allowing the owner to be able to plan the way through lean times.

One source of help would be for the new owner to ask a bank for a working capital loan. Working capital is used by the business owner to keep the operation running during periods when cash is short. For example, if your product has seasonal demand, sales will be strong some months and weak others. Another example involves getting through the start-up phase and into the full production phase. Presumably, once full production has been reached, sales will increase and cash income will be received on a consistent basis.

Break-Even

The break-even point simply shows when sales revenue precisely equals expenses. The reasons for wanting to establish the break-even point are:

➤ To set up and establish your company's selling prices

➤ To analyze the impact of various changes in operations

Projected sales are required to offset the costs of creating new products and/or expanding current facilities and personnel. Break-even must include all costs and cost types (fixed and variable). The equation for break-even is:

Sales – (all fixed + variable costs) = $ 0.00.

Break-even information can be displayed to the viewer in either a chart form (see Figure 7-4) or in a graph form (see Figure 7-5). The volumes shown can be stated either in units of sales or in sales dollars. The break-even analysis has to assume that your selling prices, as well as related cost (fixed and variable), will remain constant throughout the year. This assumption is made because both the sales and related cost are each represented by a straight line. The point where the two lines intersect is the break-even point. All points on the graph to the left of the break-even point represent varying degrees of loss, all points to the right of the break-even point represent varying degrees of profit.

Key Ratios

There are a number of key ratios that are important to tracking the financial status of a business. In general, these provide information about the ratio of types of revenues to types of expenses. For example, the Return on Assets ratio shows the

Destiny Houseware Corporation
Break-Even Report
First Year

Percent	Sales	Fixed Expenses	Variable Expenses	Operating Profit
10%	526411	993864	197828	-665280
20%	1052823	993864	395655	-336696
30%	1579234	993864	593483	-8112
40%	**1592231**	**993864**	**598367**	**0 Break Even**
50%	2632057	993864	989138	649055
60%	3158468	993864	1186965	977639
70%	3684880	993864	1384793	1306223
80%	4211291	993864	1582620	1634807
90%	4737703	993864	1780448	1963391
100%	5264114	993864	1978276	2291974
110%	5790525	993864	2176103	2620558
120%	6316937	993864	2373931	2949142
130%	6843348	993864	2571758	3277726
140%	7369760	993864	2769586	3606310
150%	7896171	993864	2967413	3934894
160%	8422582	993864	3165241	4263477
170%	8948994	993864	3363069	4592061
180%	9475405	993864	3560896	4920645
190%	10001817	993864	3758724	5249229
200%	10528228	993864	3956551	5577813

FIGURE 7-4.   *A break-even chart*

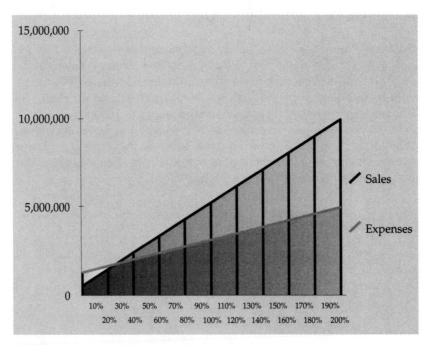

FIGURE 7-5.   *A break-even graph*

net profit divided by total assets. Each ratio is evaluated based on how it compares with other companies in similar types of business. There are five types of ratios used to assess the health of a business: Profitability, Activity, Debt, Liquidity, and Other. In turn, each of these ratios consists of several more specific ratios.

Highlights

Highlights are used to provide a quick overview of your business. The focus of a Highlights report is on five financial summaries: Revenue, Gross profit, Operating expenses and Net profit from the Income Statement and Cash from the Balance Statement. Because it provides a summary of your business at a glance, the Highlights often occupy a prominent place in the business plan, such as the first page.

Graphs

You should include graphs for each of the financial statements that we have discussed. Graphs are pictorial representations of your financial statements that make it visually easier for the reader to see your projected business trends and to spot possible problem areas. Select a financial spreadsheet—pick any one of them. Then bring up your spreadsheet program commands and select the graph option. Basically, the program compiles all the spreadsheet data into graph form. Obviously there is more to it than this, however, the results are the same.

Narrative Text

Typically, the narrative text of your business plan should include the following major topics in its outline: an executive summary; a section about your company, your product(s) and/or service(s) that you'll be offering; your marketing and sales strategy; your management and ownership; your organizational structure and the personnel that staff it; and of course your financial reports and graphs. Remember, you have to write clearly, comprehensively, and concisely. Here is a detailed sample outline that you can use for writing your narrative text portion of your business plan:

BUSINESS PLAN

I. Executive Summary
  a. Purpose of the plan
  b. Summary of market potential
  c. Significant product features
  d. Financial results
II. Company Profile
  a. Company summary
  b. Ownership
  c. History
  d. Locations and facilities
III. Product
  a. Specifications
  b. Applications
  c. Competitive products
IV. Marketing and Sales Strategy
  a. Summary
        1. Description of the industry
        2. Size of the industry
        3. Characteristics of the industry
        4. Customers
        5. Applications of product
        6. Major trends of the industry
  b. Target markets
        1. Major segments
        2. Distribution patterns
  c. Competition
        1. Companies/products
        2. How you compare
        3. Market share
  d. Marketing activities
        1. Marketing strategy
        2. Distribution strategy
        3. Promotion strategy
        4. Pricing strategy
        5. Service and support
        6. Geographical penetration
  e. Selling strategy
        1. Prospect customer identification
        2. Level of selling effort
        3. Commission structure

V. Management and Ownership
   a. Key managers
   b. Compensation of key management
   c. Skills and experience
   d. Board of directors
   e. Current shareholders
VI. Organization and Personnel
   a. People by type
   b. Compensation
   c. Organizational structure
VII. Financial Data
   a. Income statement
   b. Cash flow
   c. Balance sheets
   d. Key Ratios
   e. Break-even
   f. Capital budgets
VIII. Private Placement Disclaimer
   IX. Appendixes
   a. Graphs
   b. Resumes
   c. Pictures of product/prototype
   d. Market studies, articles from journals
   e. Patents

Executive Summary

The executive summary allows you to state clearly and comprehensively what the purpose of your business plan is. You talk about the significant features of your product(s) and/or service(s) that may set them apart from your competition. Discuss the market that you intend to participate in, and its overall projected volume in dollars. What impact on the market do you anticipate your product will have, and how much of the market do you expect to capture? How and when will you start impacting this market with your product(s) and/or service(s)? You need to summarize how your product(s) and marketing strategy will financially impact your business, both in the near term (one year) and in the long term (two through five years).

Company Profile

In the company profile you discuss various facets of your company and show the reader the purpose of your company's existence. You want to summarize the ownership structure, introduce the owners, and give a brief summary of their experience. Then you should summarize (if you have been in business for a while) your company's history: is it privately owned, publicly owned, and for how long? How long has your company been in existence? If you are starting a new operation, you have the opportunity to discuss what kind of growth your business will see in the next year or two, and then you can discuss what kind of growth you want to see in the next three to five years. Don't forget to give the location(s) of your business(es). Also, you may want to briefly discuss what geographical area(s) you would like to expand into in the near future.

Product

In this section you discuss the product(s) and/or service(s) that you'll be offering. Give specifications for each of your products and/or services. Discuss the applications that these products and/or services will have. Summarize your major competitors, who they are, their sales volumes, marketing techniques, and percentage of the market that each has. This allows the reader to get a feel for your products and how they compare to the competition. It also gives the reader a sense of how well the product will (or will not) succeed in the marketplace.

Marketing Plan

The marketing plan is one of the most significant parts of the business plan. This section will tell the reader if you have done your research and homework. If you haven't, this is one area that will stick out like a sore thumb. For example, you may discover that your unit costs (production costs) are too high, which may not allow you to compete as well as you first thought, resulting in a significantly smaller-than-projected market share. This causes you to reevaluate your unit costs (production costs). In this section you want to start by summarizing your marketing and sales strategy. Give an overall assessment of the industry (market) in which you will participate. Then give a monetary assessment about the overall size of the industry. Discuss the major characteristics of your industry.

Next, discuss your target markets, answering the who, what, where, when, and how questions. Talk about what major market segments your product(s) and/or service(s) will impact. What methods of distribution (warehouses, dealerships, distributors, direct sales contacts, sales representatives, etc.) will you employ?

You want to show the reader that you fully understand the market in which you intend to participate, how you intend to break into that market, and what you expect the results of that impact to be on your business as well as your competition's business. For instance, do you expect to pull business away from your competition? If so, how much, when, and where? If not, why not?

Discuss in more detail your competition in the marketplace. Discuss their product specifications. Relate objectively how your products compare to the competition. Discuss in more detail how much of the market each of your competitors share, and rank your eventual position in this market. Make a list and rate your competition as well as yourself. Tell where you place your company on this ratings list and why.

Now describe your marketing activities. Let your reader know the methods you'll use to bring your products successfully into the marketplace. Discuss your marketing strategy, how you will approach this market, and with what type of product(s) and/or service(s). Talk about your methods of promoting your product(s) and/or service(s): newspapers, PR firms, radio, coupons, television. Then get specific about your selling prices and pricing policies. Tell about what types of service and support (direct service staff, warranties, guarantees, service representatives, etc.) you will provide. Wind this section down by discussing your primary demographic reasons (age of population, geographic location, males-to-females, income levels, etc.) for penetrating this market.

Selling Strategy

Discuss how you will select and contact your prospective customers (in-house sales staff, outside sales staff, distributors, etc.). This will let the reader know in detail how you intend to get your product into the marketplace, compete, and gain the upper hand on your competition. Discuss in detail the level of your selling effort (direct sales, sales offices, staff, locations). Conclude by discussing the salaries and commission structure that you will have in place, and what kinds of incentives (trips, tickets, money) you may give your sales staff.

Management and Ownership

The next major section discusses your management and ownership structure. This gives the reader a sense of how well-organized and structured your business is. Also, it shows the strengths of each person and how those strengths will be utilized to make your business a success. Discuss your key managers and summarize their roles in the business. Next discuss what types of compensation (salary, benefits, perks) you plan to give these key managers. Summarize what types of skill and experience your key managers bring to your business and where you will employ this skill and experience. Lastly, give a summary and brief description of each member of your board of directors, and also provide a current list (if this applies) of your current shareholders.

Organization and Personnel

Another major section is your organizational structure and general staffing requirements. Start by discussing what types of personnel are required (skilled, nonskilled, supervisory) and for what areas or departments. Discuss—in summary—the types of compensation (hourly wage, exempt, nonexempt, benefits) that these personnel will receive. Finally, discuss or provide a flowchart of your organizational structure. This gives the reader a visual sense of your company's personnel structure, showing the various departments, who is in charge, overall responsibilities, and the overall company reporting structure.

Financial Data

The last major section—the one that will tell all—comprises the financial statements. This is the "reality check" section. In this section you include the following financial statements: income, balance sheet, cash flow, break-even, and key ratios. Be sure to include graphs for these statements. Capital budget information should also be included if your business is evaluating large capital expenditures for such things as plant expansion, increased research and development for a new or existing product, or a large-scale advertising campaign.

If your company is considering a stock offering or soliciting funds on the side, be sure to include a private placement disclaimer with your business plan to protect the party making the offer. Finally, you should include any and all information that supports your plan in the Appendix. The more information you can provide that supports a proposed plan of action, the more likely it is that you will receive the financing you seek.

Making a business plan requires knowledge, dedication (not stubbornness), long nights, and early mornings. When finished, the business plan will give a clear and comprehensive indication to the banks and/or investors as to what you need, how you will use it, and what the results of their investment(s) will yield for them. Upon receiving approval from your bankers and/or investors, you will be glad you went through all of the work.

Once you have received the funding that you require, you have to set up a means of tracking the "actual" costs incurred while running your operation. You then have to relate this actual cost data to your projected costs (budgeted costs) in your original business plan. Methods of recording this data have to be set up and maintained by you or members of your staff.

Tracking actual vs. budgeted costs and using this information to update your financials is a very essential part of your daily operations. This cost data and subsequent updated financial statements will be required by banks and/or investors to keep them apprised of how you're progressing toward your goals. You want to use this cost information to help you analyze your business operations on a daily basis. It will help you spot potential problems and make decisions on how best to resolve them. Your cost data and updated financial statements will also be required by the Internal Revenue Service.

Writing a Business Plan

To understand what goes into making up a business plan, the entrepreneur might seek help from an accountant, library/bookstore, lawyer, CPA, another business owner, college business school, local chamber of commerce, or any one of a number of business associations. The entrepreneur will soon become frustrated, as most of the materials are written by and for established businesses—not new businesses. Adding to this problem is the fact that very little is written about entrepreneurial finance.

If you write an updated business plan for an established business, the experience will provide a great deal of insight into how and why your business is operating the way it is. You will have the information to make sure that your current goals are the right goals or to determine whether adjustments are needed.

Before you begin to write your business plan, however, your purpose, methods, and goals have to be very clear. You have to sit down and take the time to lay this data all out, digest it, adjust it, think about it, discuss it, sweat over it, lose sleep over it, and then start all over again, until you are certain that everything is crystal clear and no element has been left out. Once you have researched and gathered all of this business plan information, you can use it to generate the necessary financial reports and write a narrative for the plan.

Programs such as Destiny and Ronstadt's Financials by Lord Publishing of Dana Pointe, California automate some of the most difficult and repetitive tasks involved in starting a new business, tracking the actual costs, and comparing those costs to the projected costs shown in your business plan.

Destiny Business Information & Planning System

We will now walk through the setup of a business plan using Destiny Business Information & Planning System software. This software is a fully integrated business planning software and will take you step-by-step through each phase of the business planning process. You will go through the entry of general business information, financial statements, graphs, and finally the outline for the narrative text of your business plan. While this version of the software will not allow you to print or save your work, it will demonstrate the ease of software-based business forecasting.

A Walk-Through of Destiny

To download Destiny from the CD-ROM included with this book, follow the instructions found inside the back cover. Once the program has been installed on your computer, double-click the Destiny icon (shown here) in the appropriate Program Manager group.

Destiny opens to a blank workspace screen with a Quick Help box on the right of the screen. The Quick Help box offers instructions and introductory information useful to the first-time user of Destiny.

To move forward or backward through the Quick Help screens, click the appropriate > and < buttons. To select an item from any of the options presented, click the > button next to the desired topic. To return to the Quick Help main menu from any point, click the Menu button. When you are done, click the Close button. Quick Help can be reopened from any point in Destiny by selecting the Quick Help option under Help in the main menu.

General Information

When you have finished reviewing the information in Quick Help, you can begin your first Destiny planning session by following the steps outlined below.

1. Click Data Entry from the main menu, and select General Information.

2. In the General Information dialog box, click the More button to open the General Information dialog box, shown in Figure 7-6.

   The General Information dialog box allows you to input some very basic information about your business. Destiny uses this information to format the entire business plan, including spreadsheets, graphs, and Destiny text.

3. Next, type in your Company Name and the Initial Year for the first year in which you want to see reports and then select the Initial Month from the pull-down box for the month in which you want planning to begin.

   In the upper-right corner of the General Information dialog box are the Orientation and Inventory fields. The Orientation field has option buttons to select either Cash or Units. Your selection will determine how the Sales Plan data is calculated. The Inventory field requires that you select either Yes or No. If you select Yes, Destiny will know that your business will have an inventory.

   If you select the Cash option in the Orientation field and No in the Inventory field, Destiny will make the following assumptions about your business:

   ➤ All of your invoices are due as they are received.

   ➤ You have no current inventory.

   ➤ You pay taxes quarterly and use the standard IRS tax table.

You now have the option to click OK, to begin entering more specific information and data about your business by selecting Express to enter basic financial information about your company or any one of the more specific

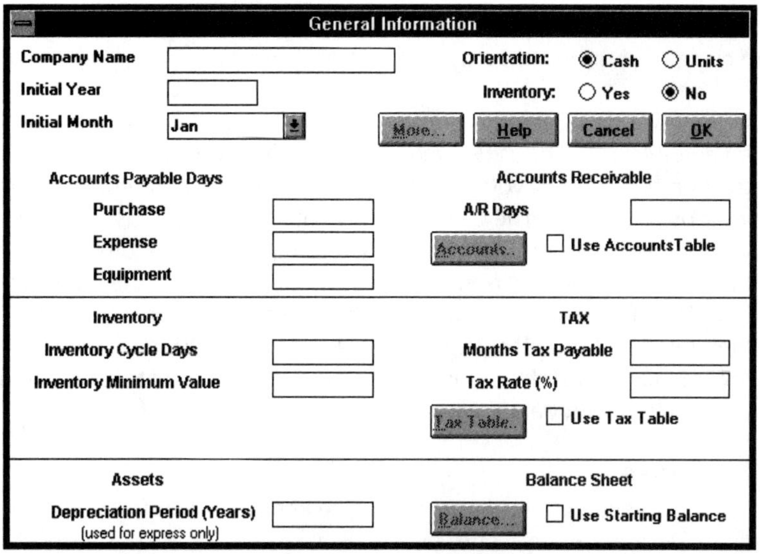

FIGURE 7-6. *The General Information dialog box*

spreadsheets under Data Entry in the main menu. Each of these features will be explained in greater detail later in the chapter. However, if any of the assumptions above are *not* true, you must provide additional information in the General Information dialog box. The rest of the General Information screen is divided into six fields where you can modify the underlying assumptions to meet your needs. These six fields, which are explained next, are: Accounts Payable Days, Inventory, Assets, Accounts Receivable, Tax, and Balance Sheet.

Accounts Payable Days   In the Accounts Payable fields, your input should be in terms of the number of days in an Accounts Payable cycle. An accounts payable cycle is the number of days between when a bill is received and when you are expected to pay it. You can enter any number of days, up to 180.

1. In the Purchase box, enter the number of Accounts Payable (A/P) days for purchases. This entry applies to information in the Cost and Prices spreadsheet and to the Cost of Gross Sales line.

2. In the Expense box, enter the number of A/P days for expenses. This entry applies to the Fixed and Variable Expense lines.

3. In the Equipment box, enter the number of A/P days for equipment. This entry applies to the Equipment Expense line.

Inventory   The information in the Inventory field is used to describe the inventory cycle of your business.

1. In the Inventory Cycle Days box, fill in the number of days in your inventory cycle. This is derived by calculating your "inventory turnover" or the number of times your inventory has been used and replaced during your business year. The calculation is your Cost of Goods Sold divided by the Average Inventory Value. This yields the number of times your inventory will turn over during the year. Next, convert the turnover figure into days. For example, if your inventory turns over three times per year, then divide 12 (months/year) by 3 = 4 (months) × 30 (days/month) = approximately 120 Inventory Cycle Days. This information will be used in conjunction with data entered on the Assets Investment screen.

> **NOTE**
> If you need to use a calculator, select Calculator from Edit in Destiny's main menu, or press F11.

2. The Inventory Minimum Value box is where you enter the dollar amount of the inventory you need to keep on hand. Do not use commas, decimal points, or dollar ($) signs with your entries. Destiny does not use pennies in inventory calculations.

Assets   Use the Depreciation Period (Years) box only if you intend to use the Express data entry feature. Enter the average depreciation in years for your business' equipment.

Accounts Receivable   The default figure for Accounts Receivable (A/R) is 30 days. To change this figure, enter a number in the A/R Days field. For example, if you expect your A/R to be paid up in 60 days, then you would enter **60** in this box.

   To create an A/R table, perform the following steps:

1. Click the Use Accounts Table check box to activate the Accounts button.

2. Click the Accounts button to display the Accounts Receivable Table dialog box, shown here:

3. In the After 1 Month box, enter what percent of your A/R you expect to receive at this time. Repeat this step for the After 2 Months box and After 3 Months box. As

Accounts Receivable Table	
Receivable	Percent From Sales
Cash	100
After 1 month	
After 2 months	
After 3 months	
Percent of Loss Sales:	
Help	Cancel	OK

you enter your data, Destiny will automatically recalculate the Percent From Sales for Cash so that your total will always equal 100 percent.

4. The last box in this table, Percent Of Lost Sales, is where you enter your "estimate" of what percentage of sales will be lost due to bad debt. The figure you enter will be subtracted automatically by Destiny from all noncash (credit) sales, and it will be listed on the Income Statement under the heading Operating Expenses as a line item called Bad Debt.

5. When you have finished entering your information, click OK.
    The entries made in the Accounts Recievable Table apply to information entered on the Sales Plan screen. If you are using Express entry, the information applies to the Sales line.

Tax   Destiny offers the option to customize the tax table or tax rates you use. If you are *not* using a standard IRS tax table, then use this section to create your own customized tax schedule. Just follow the steps outlined here:

1. In the Months Tax Payable box, enter the number of months between tax payments.

2. In the Tax Rate (%) box, enter the number representing the percentage at which you will be taxed. For example, if you will be taxed at 25 percent, you would enter **25**. This information will be used in the Income Statement calculations.

3. If you want to use a more sophisticated tax rate, then click the Use Tax Table check box. An X appears in the check box, and the Tax Table button is activated.

Tax Table			
Over	Up To	Rate	Cumulative
0	50000	15	7500
50000	75000	25	13750
75000	100000	34	22250
100000	335000	39	113900
335000		34	0
Help		Cancel	OK

4. Click the Tax Table button to display the Tax Table dialog box, shown here:

The Tax Table dialog box shows the standard federal tax table. You can modify these default figures to create your own tax table.

5. Once you are satisfied with the entries on the tax table, click OK.

Balance Sheet   Destiny assumes you are starting your business without any assets. If this is *not* the case, follow these steps to enter information about your business' assets.

1. Click the Use Starting Balance check box to activate the Balance button.

2. Click the Balance button to display the Starting Balance Sheet dialog box, shown here: Make sure all entries are in dollars. As we said before, dollar signs, decimal points, and trailing zeros are unnecessary. Entries in the Starting Balance Sheet dialog box may be either current or anticipated. If you make entries in this box, then remember, assets and liabilities must be equal. If they aren't, you won't be able to leave the dialog box when you try to click OK.

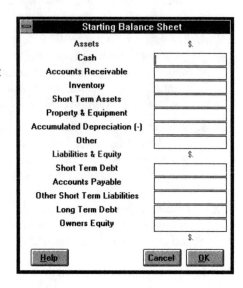

NOTE
Enter Accumulated Depreciation in terms of a positive number. Destiny will automatically make the number a negative in its calculations.

3. When you have entered all the requested information, click OK. This completes the General Information section of your business plan.

4. To exit the General Information dialog box and store your information, click OK.

Now that the General Information dialog box has been completed, it's decision time. Do you want to do a detailed workup of your company's financials, or would you prefer to produce the reports and graphs quickly using Express? If you choose to use Express, you will be able to quickly generate the following reports and graphs: Income statement, Cash flow, Balance sheet, Break-even, Financial ratios (methods to quickly evaluate your financial status), and Highlights.

However, once you have selected Express to develop a particular business plan, none of the other detailed spreadsheet options are available to you (they will be dimmed as options in the main menu). To redo the business plan using the detailed spreadsheets, you will need to begin again with the General Information and create a new business plan using a different file name. How to use the Express feature is outlined in the next section, followed by a discussion of how to use the detailed spreadsheets.

Express

To use the Express datasheet effectively, you need to have an entry in *every* column. All entries must be in dollars—there is no need to use dollar signs, commas, or decimal points. To open Express:

1. Click Data Entry in the main menu and select Express.

    When you open the Express screen, Destiny displays a spreadsheet in which the columns are the months of your company's business year, taken from your entry on the General Information screen. Destiny displays a column for each month of the first business year and a column for the second, third, and fourth years, respectively. Use the scroll arrows at the bottom of the screen to scroll through the columns. To enter information, simply highlight the appropriate cell and type in your entry, using the BACKSPACE or DELETE key to correct any errors. When your entry is correct, press ENTER.

    Now, let's walk through the Express spreadsheet column by column, and briefly discuss what you will enter.

2. In the Sales column, enter the expected gross sales for your business for each month of the first year, and for each of the successive four years.

3. In the Cost of Gross Sales column, enter the costs associated with your gross sales.

4. In the Fixed Expenses column, enter the fixed expenses associated with the operation of your business. These are expenses that don't vary month to month, such as lease, depreciation, etc.

5. In the Variable Expenses column, enter the operational expenses that will vary in amount of costs month to month, such as advertising, office supplies, postage, etc.

6. In the Salaries Expenses column, enter all wages and associated costs, such as salaries, benefits, overtime, etc.

7. In the Equipment Expenses column, enter the costs that you expect to incur from your equipment.

8. In the Owners Equity column, enter the amount that shareholders will be contributing.

9. In the Dividend Payments column, enter how much money the shareholders will draw down from the business.

10. In the Loans Received column, enter the amount of money your business will receive in the way of bank loans or other investment funds.

11. In the Loan Repayments column, enter the amount to be paid out to repay your loans.

12. In the Finance Expenses column, enter all other expenses that you expect to incur from financing your business loan, such as interest.

13. When everything looks good, double-click the minus sign in the Express title bar to close the spreadsheet window.

14. Open the Reports and/or Graphs menu(s), select a report/graph, and generate some impressive visual materials. Alternatively, you can begin working on the text for your business plan by going to the Text dialog box in the Data Entry menu.

Detailed Spreadsheets

If you do not elect to go the Express route, you have several choices for more detailed spreadsheets.

Costs And Prices

One of the selections from the Data Entry menu is Costs And Prices. The Costs And Prices spreadsheet is used for entering your company's products or services and what they cost.

1. Open the Data Entry menu and select Costs And Prices.

When the Costs And Prices spreadsheet window opens, you will not be able to see all the columns. To do so, you can either scroll across the spreadsheet using the scroll arrows at the bottom of the screen or increase the size of the window. You will enter the following information about your company in the Costs And Prices spreadsheet window (Figure 7-7).

2. In the Description column, enter a description of each of your products and/or services.

3. In the Beg. Inventory (Beginning Inventory) column, input the number of units that you have in inventory for each of your products and/or services that you described.

4. In the Unit Cost column, enter the cost for each of your products and/or services that you described in Beginning Inventory. You can use dollars and cents (e.g., 46.89). Your costs should include labor and overhead.

5. In the Unit Price column, enter your unit selling price. Destiny calculates the profit margin on this unit and enters the value in the % Margin column.

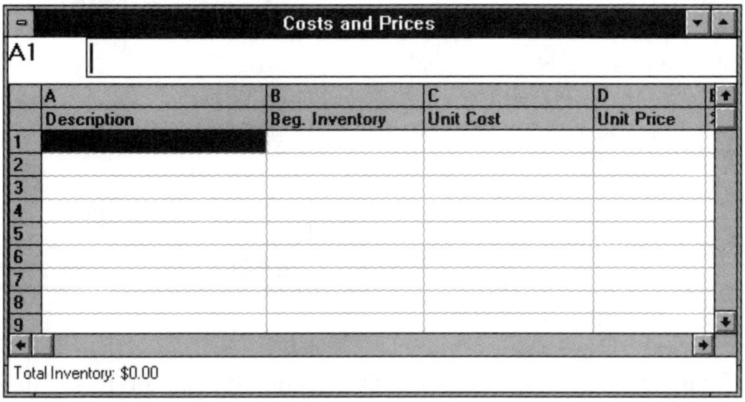

FIGURE 7-7. *The Costs And Prices spreadsheet window*

6. Total Inventory (found at the bottom of the screen) keeps a running total of the number of beginning inventory units times cost: (Total Inventory = Beg. Inventory × Unit Cost). This figure should agree with any entry you have made in the Inventory field of the Balance Sheet.

7. When you have entered the appropriate information, double-click the minus sign in the Cost and Prices title bar to close the spreadsheet window.

Sales Plan

Another spreadsheet selection from the Data Entry menu is the Sales Plan. The Sales Plan spreadsheet is the place to enter your expected gross sales for each item in your inventory. Recall that in the General Information dialog box, you told Destiny whether you would be making entries in cash or units (in the Orientation field). This information is reflected in the title bar of the Sales Plan window, which in this case specifies cash.

1. Open the Data Entry menu and select Sales Plan.

The Sales Plan spreadsheet basically asks for two types of information: Description and Gross Sales. The Description column is automatically filled in, based on the input you made in the Cost and Prices spreadsheet Description column. If you need to make any changes, you must return to the Cost and Prices spreadsheet.

2. In each of the remaining columns, enter your expected gross sales for each inventory item.

3. When you're done entering information, double-click the minus sign in the Sales Plan title bar to close the spreadsheet window.

Expense Structure

If you select Expense Structure from the Data Entry menu, the Expense Structure dialog box will appear, as shown here:

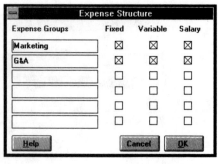

In this dialog box, you select the type and number of expense spreadsheets for your business.

You can have up to six different expense groups in the Expense Structure spreadsheet. Within each group you can have up to three spreadsheets of the following types:

> ➤ **Fixed** This type tracks expenses that occur whether you have sales or not, such as rent.

> ➤ **Variable** This type tracks expenses that vary with sales or the production of goods and/or services, such as advertising.

> ➤ **Salary** This type tracks wages and related costs.

Destiny automatically creates two Expense Structure groups: Marketing and G&A (General and Administrative). Each expense group is also assigned all three types of spreadsheets. You may edit the list by placing an X in or removing the X from the appropriate check box. When you are finished specifying the desired expense groups and their appropriate spreadsheet types, click OK.

Now that you have completed the Expense Structure for your business, it will be reflected in the Expense Groups option in the Data Entry menu.

Expense Groups

If you select Expense Groups from the Data Entry menu, Destiny displays another submenu that lists the types of spreadsheets you have chosen for this group.

In the examples following, you have created two Expense Groups: Marketing and G&A (General and Administrative). When you choose G&A, another submenu displays your previously selected spreadsheets.

Fixed Expense

In the Fixed Expense spreadsheet, list all of your fixed expenses and their costs.

1. Open the Data Entry menu, select Expense Groups, G&A, then Fixed Expense. You are now in the G&A-Fixed Expense spreadsheet window.

2. In the Description column, enter each expense. This would include such items as rent, etc.

3. For each expense listed, enter the associated cost. Here, entries may include decimal points and pennies. If these expenses are the same from month to month, it may be easier to use the Copy Cell option in the Edit menu.

4. When you're done entering information, double-click the minus sign in the Fixed Expenses title bar to close the spreadsheet window.

Variable Expenses

In the Variable Expense spreadsheet, you list all of your variable expenses and their associated costs.

1. Open the Data Entry menu, select Expense Groups, G&A, then Variable Expense. You are now in the G&A-Variable Expense spreadsheet window.

2. In the Description column, enter each expense, such as advertising, office supplies, etc.

3. For each variable expense, enter the associated amounts in each columns. You can enter monthly amounts for each month in the first year, and yearly amounts for each of the next four years.

4. When you're done entering information, double-click the minus sign in the Variable Expense title bar to close the spreadsheet window.

REMEMBER
You must fill out a spreadsheet for each Expense Group that has variable expenses.

Salaries Expense

The Salaries Expense spreadsheet is where you place all the expenses associated with wages for your personnel.

1. Open the Data Entry menu, select Expense Groups, G&A, then Salaries Expense. You are now in the G&A-Salaries Expense spreadsheet window.

2. In the Description column, enter the name of each person or group whose expenses you'll be tracking.

3. In the Burden Rate column, enter the percentage of salary that represents expenses (benefits) associated with each salary, such as payroll taxes, health care, pensions, etc.

4. In the Commissions column, enter the percentage (%) of sales that a person or group will get. If no one will be getting a commission, leave this column blank.

5. In the Yearly Base Salary column, enter the salary for each person or group. You may enter the amount in dollars and cents (e.g., 56629.75). You may leave the Yearly Base Salary column blank and enter monthly salaries for the first year, and annual salaries for each of the next four years.

6. When your Salaries Expense spreadsheet is correctly filled out, double-click the minus sign in the Salaries Expense title bar to close the spreadsheet window.

Assets

The Assets spreadsheet is the place to list your company's assets (equipment) and associated data.

1. Open the Data Entry menu and select Assets. You are now in the Assets spreadsheet window.

2. In the Description column, enter your company's assets. This can be done for each individual asset, or you may list your assets in groups.

3. In the Purchase Date column, enter the date each asset, or asset group was purchased. Format this entry exactly as follows: day/month/year.

4. In the Cost column, enter the total cost associated with each asset or asset group. This figure must be in dollars only.

5. In the Depreciation column, enter the number of years for each asset or asset group that you want the depreciation to be calculated for. The years of depreciation *must* be entered as a whole number.

6. In the Disposal Rate column, enter the date when you plan to sell or dispose of each asset, or asset group. Format this entry exactly as follows: day/month/year.

7. In the Disposal Price column, enter *in dollars* the amount of money you expect to receive for each asset or asset group that you sell. If you just plan to throw the asset or asset group away, then you would enter **0** in the column.

8. When you've completed the Assets spreadsheet, double-click the minus sign in the Assets title bar to close the spreadsheet window.

Finance

When you select Finance from the Data Entry menu, you are presented with three additional choices: Loans, Owners Equity, and Special. Each of these options tracks sources of funds and their related expenses (interest) for your company.

Loans

By using the Loans dialog box, you can track up to ten loans.

1. Open the Data Entry menu, select Finance, then Loans. You are now in the Loans dialog box, shown here:

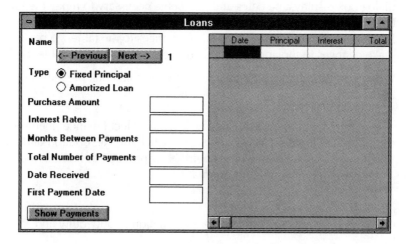

2. In the Name text box, enter the name of the loan. You have a 30-character limit.

3. In Type, click either Fixed Principle (the principal is fixed, but the interest varies according to the outstanding loan balance) or Amortized Loan (the monthly payment includes principal and a fixed interest).

4. In Purchase Amount, enter *in dollars* the amount of your loan's principal (amount you received from the investor).

5. In Interest Rates, enter the annual interest rate of the loan.

6. In Months Between Payments, simply enter the number of months between payments. If your payments are monthly, you would type **1**. If your payments are quarterly, you would type **3**. If your payments are semiannual, you would type **6**.

7. In Total Number Of Payments, enter the total number of payments that you will make. You *must* make an entry in this field.

8. In Date Received, enter the date you received the loan. Format this entry exactly as follows: day/month/year.

9. In First Payment Date, enter the date your first payment is due. Format this entry exactly as follows: day/month/year. The table at the right of the dialog box displays the dates and payments necessary to repay the loan. Destiny automatically calculates this table when you click the Show Payments button. If you want to make changes to the table, go back and make changes to the appropriate fields—do *not* change the table itself.

10. When your Loan data is entered correctly, double-click the minus sign in the Loans title bar to close the dialog box.

To enter another loan, open the Data Entry menu, select Finance, then select Loans. Your previously entered loan is displayed. Click the Next button under the Name text box to display an empty name field. Now proceed as listed in the previous steps to complete your loan information.

Owners Equity

Use the Owners Equity spreadsheet to enter information about equity and dividends.

1. Open the Data Entry menu, select Finance, then Owners Equity. You are now in the Owners Equity spreadsheet window.

2. In the Owners Equity column, enter the amount of money shareholders will be contributing. Entries must be in *dollars*, not dollars and cents. Create an entry for each month of the first year, and yearly for each of the successive four years after that.

3. In the Dividends - Amount column, enter the amount of revenue owners will draw down from the business. Create an entry for each month of the first year, and yearly for each of the successive four years after that.

4. In the Dividends - % column, enter the percentage of net revenue owners will draw down from the business. For example, if the owners will be drawing down 15 percent of net revenue as a dividend, then you would enter **15** in each month's column and yearly for the four years that follow.

5. When the Owners Equity spreadsheet is accurately filled out, double-click the minus sign in the Owners Equity title bar to close the spreadsheet window.

Special Financial Data

The Special Financial Data spreadsheet is the place to put all of the "miscellaneous" financial data that doesn't fit anywhere else.

1. Open the Data Entry menu, select Finance, then Special. You are now in the Special Financial Data spreadsheet window.

2. In the Short-Term Loans Received column, enter nonamortized loans, such as officer's loans.

3. In the Short-Term Principle Repayments column, enter any regularly recurring principle repayments that are due and payable in less than a year.

4. In the Long-Term Loans Received column, enter any long-term loans that are not covered in the Loans spreadsheet.

5. In the Long-Term Principle Repayments column, enter any long-term principle repayments not covered in the Loans spreadsheet.

6. In the Interest Payments column, enter any interest payments not covered in the Loans spreadsheet.

7. In the Interest Income column, enter dividends received from bank accounts and/or any other investments.

8. In the Short-Term Assets(+) column, enter any increase in short-term assets.

9. In the Short-Term Assets(–) column, enter any decrease in short-term assets.

10. In the Other Assets(+) column, enter any increase in nondepreciable long-term assets, investments, or deposits.

11. In the Other Assets(–) column, enter any decrease in nondepreciable long-term assets, investments, or deposits.

12. In the Other Short-Term Liabilities(+) column, enter increases, such as accrued taxes.

13. In the Other Short-Term Liabilities(–) column, enter decreases.

14. In the Depreciation column, enter any other depreciation you want accrued for a specific month.

15. When you have accurately filled out the Special Financial Data spreadsheet, double-click the minus sign in the Special Financial Data title bar to close the spreadsheet window.

Text

Now let's create the text of our first business plan using Destiny. When you enter the Destiny program, you are automatically placed in a new file.

1. Open the Data Entry menu, select Text, then Destiny Text Box. Destiny places you in a business plan outline like that found in Figure 7-8.
    To create your own outline and text, perform the following steps:

2. Select an outline topic and click on it. Destiny activates the Edit button at the bottom of the text box.

3. Click the Edit button. Destiny opens a new text box with your specified topic in the title bar.

4. Enter text exactly as you want it to appear in your business plan; click OK when you are finished. Destiny returns you to the original outline.

5. Repeat the above steps for as many of the topics as you want to include in your business plan.

Using "Word" or "Write"

Alternatively, you can select Using "Write" or Using "Word" to open a copy of Microsoft Write or Microsoft Word. (To do this you must have Microsoft Write or Microsoft Word already loaded into Windows on your computer.) Once selected, Destiny places you in the word processor and opens a copy of a sample business plan, complete with advice and guidelines. Create your text, pasting in the reports and graphs you created in Destiny where appropriate.

The procedure for completing the text of your business plan in a word processor is the same whether you are using Microsoft Word or Microsoft Write.

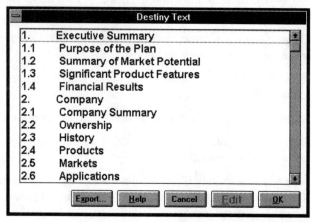

FIGURE 7-8. *A business plan outline in the Destiny Text box*

1. Open the Data Entry menu, select Text, then select either Using "Write" or Using "Word." Destiny opens the selected word processor and then opens a copy of the sample outline for your business plan.

2. Type in the text to your new business plan, using the sample and the advice as guidelines. You can delete the samples and advice once you have finished with them.

3. To import data from Destiny reports, use the Copy As Table option from the Edit menu. Then, use your word processor's Paste option to insert the report into the text of your business plan.

4. To import a graph from Destiny, display the graph, then use the Copy option from the Edit menu. Use the word processor's Paste option to insert the graph in the text of your business plan.

Producing Reports

There are ten types of reports that you can produce with Destiny. To produce a report, follow these steps:

1. Select and display the type of report you want to create.

2. Highlight the section of the report you want to place in the file.

3. Select the Copy As Table option from the Edit menu.

4. Open the word processing file and place the cursor where you want to insert the report.

5. Select the Paste option from the word processor's Edit menu.

6. When you are done, close out the report by performing one of the following steps:

    ➤ Hold down the CTRL key while pressing the F4 key.

    ➤ Double-click the minus sign in the upper-left corner of the report.

    ➤ Place the cursor on the minus sign in the upper-left corner of the report and hold down the left mouse button. When the report's menu is displayed, highlight the Close option and release the mouse button.

Conclusion

A sound business requires a solid business plan. Any good accountant will tell you that formal business planning is essential, not only to raise money or to succeed, but to survive. Plan your work, and then work your plan.

PART 3

Business Process Modeling

CHAPTER 8

Stop Playing What-If and Start Making Decisions

by Chris Dalton, Julia Langel, and Adam Borison
Applied Decision Analysis, Inc.

➢ Your company has a new product almost ready for release. Your competition is rumored to have something special coming out soon. Do you try to beat them to the market, or do you wait to see what they have so you can modify your own product?

➢ You are considering consolidating all operations in one location. The decision will affect many departments and many people. How do you study this decision so that all issues are raised and everyone feels included?

➢ You are considering a large capital expense that will affect your business for at least ten years. How do you strike the right balance between minimizing up-front costs and preserving long-term flexibility?

Making big, risky decisions is one of the most exciting and rewarding components of business. It's also the scariest. Everyone knows that no methodology or computer program can make these decisions easy and foolproof. However, a well-designed process and the right computer tools can harness your knowledge, intuition, and judgment to generate a recommendation that you know is the best possible one, given the resources available to you. This chapter discusses how decision analysis methods can be applied to decisions made in the face of uncertainty. It also outlines how computer software can apply these methods onscreen, thereby simplifying and accelerating the decision analysis process. The chapter concludes with a walk-through of DPL, a decision analysis software program.

Decision Making Is Hard

The most common source of difficulty in making decisions is uncertainty. We would always like to wait until all uncertainties are resolved before taking action. But most decisions involve some degree of chance. You have to decide whether or not to carry an umbrella before you know if it will rain; a product must be introduced before it can sell well or poorly; long-term supply contracts must be signed without benefit of knowing future spot prices.

In addition, many decisions are hard because they involve trade-offs. Getting more of one thing we want may mean getting less of another; what helps in one way may hurt in another. A car buyer might value both brisk acceleration and good fuel economy, but the larger engine that helps acceleration also uses more fuel. A politician deciding whether or not to support a hydroelectric dam project must weigh economic benefit against possible environmental harm. A factory manager wants to cut supply costs, but doing so requires entering into long-term agreements that limit future flexibility.

The simplest of decisions involve choices between two or three clearly defined courses of action. But in the real world, managers must evaluate strategies with many related decisions or contingent decisions that depend on how things unfold in the future. A company ready to introduce a product may have to decide whether to conduct market research, then whether or not to license the product, then how to price the product, with each choice depending on intermediate uncertainties. It would be easier to make the first decision without thinking about the later ones, but this might not result in the best strategy. Sorting it all out and coming to a decision on what to do now may require considering a large number of slightly different scenarios.

With all these problems, decision making is hard enough for an individual—it's even tougher in a business or government environment where a decision maker doesn't act in a vacuum. You may be part of a team charged with making a recommendation. Others in the organization may have important information or expertise that should be consulted. And because the success of the recommended course of action will depend on the people who implement it, it is important to make them feel involved. Each of these individuals brings a unique and valuable set of assumptions, priorities, and viewpoints to the table. It is important that your decision-making process recognize and take full advantage of this pool of expertise.

Decision Analysis Can Help

Decision analysis combines proven management processes with practical tools and techniques to systematically make decisions in the presence of difficulty. Decision analysis helps you to

> ➤ Identify the essential issues relevant to a decision

> ➤ Combine the experience and intuition of experts with empirical data

> ➤ Explicitly consider and manage risk

> ➤ Know when to move from analysis to action

Decision analysis is basically a process for building a mathematical model of a decision. The process provides a systematic and structured way to move from confusion to a clear and well-understood plan of action. The mathematical model enables the determination of a best policy and provides insight into the structure of the problem. The process ensures that the recommendation is not perceived as coming from a mysterious mathematical "black box," but from combining the available information in a logical, understandable, defensible way.

The accent in decision analysis is on decisions, not analysis. The process has been designed to explicitly recognize the fact that real decisions have to be made with limited information and potentially significant uncertainty. Thus, the structure of a decision-analysis model makes it possible to know which assumptions are driving the analysis, which variables it would be worthwhile to investigate further, and when it is time to stop analyzing and start acting.

Developed at Harvard and Stanford, the principles and techniques of decision analysis have been used to solve business planning and public policy decisions for more than 25 years. The approach is general and has been applied to problems in a wide variety of fields including:

> ➤ New product design at a consumer durables manufacturer

> ➤ Research and development planning at a pharmaceutical company

> ➤ Inventory management at an automobile manufacturer

> ➤ Environmental risk assessment for the U.S. Environmental Protection Agency (EPA)

➤ Capital investment analysis for a worldwide oil and gas company

➤ Wastewater treatment strategy for a major domestic municipality

➤ Litigation strategy for a major clothing manufacturer

➤ Market research design for an electronics manufacturer

➤ Supply contract renegotiation at a West Coast electric utility

➤ Water pipe replacement scheduling for a major foreign municipality

➤ Oil field development strategy for a major oil and gas company

A Solid Analytic Foundation

Decision analysis is based on a solid set of logical principles that guide the construction of mathematical models of specific decision problems. These principles, listed as follows, are powerful enough to guarantee consistent, rational, and defensible decision recommendations, but they are also simple enough that anyone can learn enough to start using decision analysis in a couple of days.

➤ The world is full of uncertainty, and a good decision does not guarantee a good outcome.

➤ To make a good decision, you can do no better than to logically combine what you can do (options), what you know (knowledge), and what you want (objectives).

➤ Options are limited to actions, not worries. Focus your analysis on issues for which you have the ability to do something.

➤ Knowledge or lack thereof (uncertainty) should be expressed precisely using probabilities.

➤ Objectives should be expressed using preferences. It may not be possible to achieve all goals completely, so you should be prepared to give up a little of one to achieve more of the other.

These principles lead to some powerful results. A decision-analysis model allows you to look at alternative courses of action, possible scenarios, and trade-offs among objectives. It serves as a logical repository for your understanding of the issues, and this information is readily available for others to understand and discuss.

One of the most powerful contributions a decision-analysis model can make is its explicit recognition of the conditions under which decisions are made: you rarely know what the future will be. Rather than ignoring your uncertainty about the future, or forcing you to make a "prediction," a decision-analysis model includes your uncertainty directly, in the form of probability distributions. For example, although you may not know what sales of your product will be next year, you can define high and low estimates that you feel represent the range of reasonable possibilities. You can also state which end of the range is more likely to occur. You can include all of this information in a decision-analysis model using a probability distribution. You can show how variables affect each other—for example, how competition affects sales. If you specify distributions for several of the variables in your model, you can quickly evaluate many possible scenarios such as high sales/high price/no competition vs. low sales/low price/strong competition, etc. The model will automatically reflect the fact that some scenarios are more likely than others.

Other techniques may allow you to consider scenarios when evaluating a decision. This is sometimes called "What-if" analysis, as in "What if material prices go up by 20 percent?" But you can get into trouble if you simply look at each scenario in turn and determine which decision alternative would perform best in that scenario. If you're lucky, the same alternative is optimal under every scenario. If you're not lucky, you're in trouble. You may try to find the alternative that seems to perform best in the majority of cases, or two that could be merged. Decision analysis expects that the same alternative won't be optimal under every scenario, and it has a solution algorithm to pick the alternative that performs the best, given the fact that you have to act before knowing which scenario you will encounter. Frequently, the best alternative under conditions of uncertainty is not one of the alternatives that performed best under any one scenario—what makes it best is the fact that it can perform adequately under the whole range of scenarios.

By treating uncertainty explicitly, decision analysis is also able to quantify the relationship between uncertainty and information and to calculate the value of information gathering activities, such as product tests, market research, and engineering studies. The value of such information rests in its ability to reduce uncertainty about a specific risk factor, such as sales, which may enable decision-makers to avoid mistakes and eliminate risky plans of action. Thus decision analysis doesn't replace information gathering, but rather it tells the decision maker when and how to use that information.

A Proven Management Process

No matter how solid the mathematical basis of a model is, the fact is that no one will believe, accept, and implement the results of a "black box." What we call the decision-analysis process is the result of academic investigation fine-tuned by years of real-world application. While one goal of the process is to develop a mathematical model, powerful qualitative aspects of the process encourage clear and creative thinking, incorporate the experience and priorities of a diverse group of contributors, and prevent the kinds of surprises that can delay or prevent implementation of the action plan. Every member of the group can examine all the data and assumptions that go into the model and even see how each component affects the outcome.

The decision-analysis process consists of five general phases: structuring the problem, building the model, quantifying the uncertainties or risk factors, evaluating alternative strategies, and communicating the results.

Phase 1: Structuring the Problem

The objective of the problem-structuring phase is to develop a clear statement of the problem and to generate consensus on the nature of the problem and the major issues involved. During this phase, options for solving the problem are identified. One of the most important features of this stage of the decision-analysis process is the opportunity to think creatively and openly about various plans of action.

At this stage, uncertainties affecting the decision problem are also identified. These are the risk factors that might affect the outcome of a particular strategy; that is, the major sources of risk associated with specific plans of action. The goal is to uncover strategies that will work best in a variety of likely scenarios. Often, the best decision is the one that performs well across a mix of potential circumstances and that is least affected by various risk factors.

It is important to include the decision makers and stakeholders in this phase, both to ensure that you understand all facets of the problem and to give everyone a feeling of ownership in the process and, later, the recommendation.

Once you have a statement of the problem and have identified its factors, the next step is to specify measures for judging how the alternative modes of action perform in each possible scenario and how successfully they balance risks and rewards. In business, alternatives are normally judged on the basis of present value of profit, though in some problems other considerations may be involved.

Consider the example of a company that is deciding how to distribute a product its R&D group has developed. The company can either make and sell the product itself or license the technology to another company for a flat fee. If the company decides not to license the product, its profits will depend on the costs and sales of the product, and both of these factors are unknown. The company has a firm offer for the right to use the technology, so the license fee is a known value (not an uncertainty).

Phase 2: Building the Model

During Phase 2, the general results of the problem structuring phase are distilled into a formal model of the problem. Most decision-analysis models combine graphical representations and quantitative models. With this model, you have a visual picture of how your organization thinks about a particular problem, the alternative plans of action, and the risk factors involved.

The most important conceptual tools in decision analysis are influence diagrams and decision trees. Decision-analysis practitioners usually employ one or both of these according to the needs of the problem. It is also common for spreadsheets to be used in constructing the model, either because a trusted spreadsheet already exists or because the problem requires intricate calculations.

Influence Diagrams

An influence diagram represents all the components of a decision problem—decisions, uncertainties, and values succinctly—and the relationships among them. An influence diagram for our simple example is illustrated in Figure 8-1. The nodes in an influence diagram represent decisions, chance events (uncertainties), and values. The arrows between the nodes represent conditioning—the probabilities and values associated with the states of the conditioned event depend on the states of the conditioning event. The specific numbers (probabilities and values) are not shown on the diagram.

Influence diagrams are best for communicating the structure of a problem and showing the relationships among the factors, such as probabilistic and value dependencies. The directional arcs (arrows) between uncertain variables clearly indicate dependence; absence of arcs indicates independence. In Figure 8-1, the arrows from Cost and Sales to Profit indicate that Profit depends on both variables. There is no arrow from to Sales to Cost, so Cost does not depend on Sales.

Decision Trees

A decision tree is both a graphical representation of a decision problem and a framework for its solution. A decision tree for the example mentioned previously is shown in Figure 8-2.

There are two kinds of nodes: decision nodes and chance nodes. The branches emerging to the right from each node represent its states. The states of a decision node are the alternative choices we can make; the states of a chance node are the possible outcomes for the uncertain event. Each branch of a chance node has associated with it the probability of that outcome occurring. Chance and decision node branches can also have values associated with them. In our example, the License branch of the Distribution decision shows 225, meaning that if we sell our technology we will receive $225 million dollars.

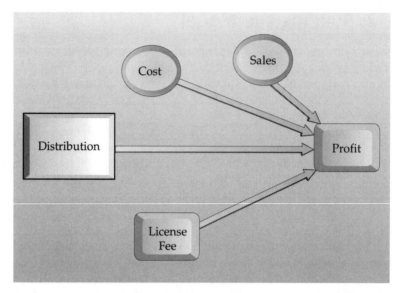

FIGURE 8-1. *A simple influence diagram*

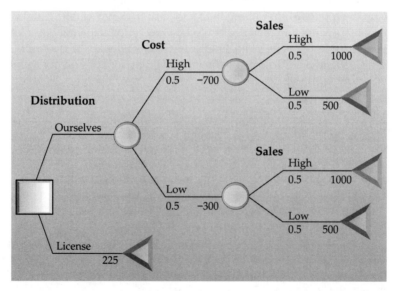

FIGURE 8-2. *A simple decision tree*

A path through the tree, from the first (leftmost) node to an endpoint (triangle), is a combination of specific decision alternatives and chance event outcomes. This path represents a single possible state of the world, or scenario.

An important strength of decision trees is that they clearly specify the chronology of the problem. First we make the Distribution decision, then the Cost uncertainty is resolved. Decision trees also reflect the asymmetry in a problem. In our example it is clear from the tree that Cost and Sales are irrelevant (to us) if we choose to license the product.

The main disadvantage of decision trees is that for real problems they may become too large and cumbersome. If we added a three-state chance node to our tree in such a way that it would be present in every scenario, the tree would have 15 paths instead of 5. If we added three such nodes, it would be too large to draw on a single page. In some contexts, decision trees can be modified to allow them to represent larger problems more concisely.

Spreadsheets

Spreadsheets are often used in decision analysis because they provide a convenient framework for computation. A spreadsheet may exist before decision analysis is applied to the problem; for example, we may have a spreadsheet that tells us what our profits will be when our costs and sales are at known levels. A spreadsheet that tells us the value of our objective when the values of all the other factors are known is often called a *value model*. Such a model can become part of a decision-analysis model when the inputs to the spreadsheet are linked to the decisions and uncertainties. Our example is too simple to require a spreadsheet; however, if we were to expand our scope to include better cost modeling and multiple years, a spreadsheet would be very useful.

Phase 3: Quantifying the Uncertainties

In Phase 3, the major sources of risk associated with specific plans of action are identified and the decision maker assigns probabilities to the critical uncertainties. These probabilities show the likelihood of specific events occurring in the future. These inputs are usually obtained from historical data or from individuals qualified to offer expert opinions. Expert sources are often used when historical data is not available, as in the case of unique or new types of risk factors.

In our example, the probabilities of high and low costs and sales have to be estimated. This has been done already and the numbers can be seen on the branches of Sales and Cost in Figure 8-2. For example, the sales department has estimated that there is a 50 percent chance that sales will be high and a 50 percent chance they will be low.

Phase 4: Evaluating Alternative Strategies

This stage of the decision-analysis process consists of evaluating the range of possible outcomes for each particular strategy. The evaluation phase normally identifies the optimal decision strategy, along with its risk profile or probability distribution. In addition, alternative plans of action and their individual risk profiles are examined. The results not only help solve the current problem, but they provide valuable insights for future decisions.

We start with a decision tree such as the one in Figure 8-2. The process consists of two stages, roll forward and roll back.

Roll Forward

The goal of the roll-forward stage is to obtain two numbers for each endpoint: the probability of reaching that endpoint and the value associated with it. Assume for the moment that we choose to distribute the product ourselves and consider the top endpoint in Figure 8-2. To reach this endpoint we need to have High Cost and High Sales. There is a 50 percent (0.5) chance of getting High Cost, and once we have that there is a 50 percent (0.5) chance of getting High Sales, so the probability of the top endpoint is 0.5*0.5 or 0.25.

To find the value of the top endpoint, we add up the numbers on the branches leading to it. In this case, we pay $700 million at the High branch of Cost and then receive $1,000 million at the High branch of Sales, so we end up with a profit of $300 million. For the second endpoint we lose $200 million. The third and fourth endpoints have values of $700 million and $200 million, respectively.

For the bottom endpoint it is much simpler. If we choose to license the product, there is a 100 percent certainty that we will reach that endpoint, so the probability is 1. The value is $225 million.

Roll Back

Once we have the probabilities and values for each endpoint of the tree, we need to percolate that information up to the branches of the decision node. To do this we use expected values (averages weighted by probabilities). At the upper sales node, we have a 0.5 probability of earning $300 million and a 0.5 probability of losing $200 million, so the expected value is 0.5*300 + 0.5*(–200) = 50. Doing the same with the other sales node, we get 450. We can now forget about Sales and turn our attention to Cost. If Cost is High, our expected value is 50; if it is Low, the number is 450. Combining these we get 0.5*50 + 0.5*450 = 250. So if we decide to distribute the product ourselves, our expected value is $250 million. If we license, then the only possible outcome is that we gain $225 million. So the optimal strategy is to distribute the product ourselves and take our chances with the uncertainties. This information is summarized in Figure 8-3. The darker line indicates the optimal strategy.

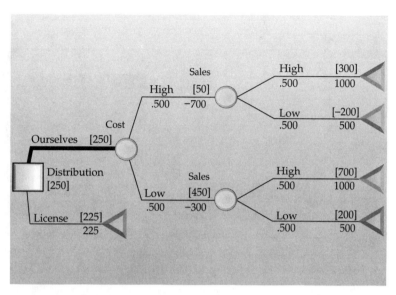

FIGURE 8-3. *The rolled-back tree*

The range of outcomes associated with the optimal strategy can be summarized using a cumulative distribution graph, such as the one shown in Figure 8-4. In the graph, the y-axis represents the cumulative probability of an event while the x-axis represents profit in millions of dollars. We can use the graph to make inferences about the probability of certain outcomes. For example, by following a line from 0 on the x-axis up to the top of the shaded area and then over to the y-axis, we see that there is about a 25 percent chance of losing money. Similarly, there is about a 50 percent chance of making more than $200 million.

Phase 5: Communicating the Results

During Phase 5, the results of the decision-analysis process are presented for review by analysts and managers. This stage provides the foundation for discussions on the results achieved and insights obtained. The model helps answer questions that arise in this phase. For example, if the license fee were negotiable, what is the minimum we should accept? Does the greater expected value in the optimal strategy justify the greater risk? Once these questions are answered, the group is ready to make and implement the decision.

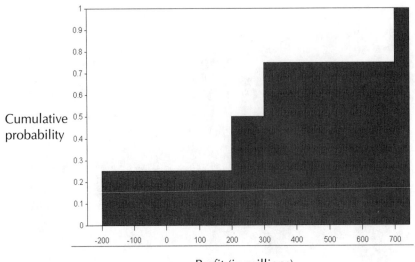

FIGURE 8-4. *The cumulative distribution graph*

Decision Analysis on a Computer

While decision analysis can be done with a pencil and paper, real-world problems are usually too complex for this to be an option. In the example we used, the tree had five paths; most real decision models have hundreds or thousands.

A number of software packages are available to do the computational work in the decision-analysis process and to display the results. Demos and DAVID solve decision problems that are modeled as influence diagrams. DATA and SuperTree work with modified decision trees. DPL can solve either influence diagrams or decision trees, or models that are a combination of the two.

There is also software that deals specifically with risk analysis. Both risk analysis and decision analysis handle uncertainty explicitly, however the former focuses on sensitivity analysis and forecasting rather than on decisions or strategies. Many risk-analysis packages are add-ins to popular spreadsheets. Crystal Ball and @RISK (see Chapter 11) are examples of this type of product.

In addition to doing the basic math, decision-analysis software can help you to better understand a model and the results it produces. A variety of graphical outputs can provide new ways of looking at the model and of checking its logic. A validated computer model also provides a good starting point for future analyses of similar problems.

Decision Analysis in Action

To demonstrate how decision analysis can help focus discussions and provide insights, let's look at our previous example in more detail. This is a fictitious case study based on a real application. If you wish, you may build this model yourself, using the demonstration version of DPL included with this book.

I/O Unlimited (IOU), a manufacturer of computer peripherals, is planning to bring out a new color laser printer. The company already makes a color printer, the SD1000, but its sales are only fair and have been declining sharply as its technology becomes more dated. The new printer will be called the SD2000, and it will retain some design commonality with its predecessor.

DA, Inc. has been asked to lead IOU in a decision analysis for the design and introduction of the SD2000. IOU's CEO is frustrated because so much time has been wasted in meetings that seem to bring them no closer to action. Since this is the computer industry, a delay of a few weeks in bringing a product to market can have serious consequences. The CEO tells DA's analysts that a preliminary strategy has to be ready in one week, so the model needs to be fairly simple.

Phase 1: Structuring the Problem

The DA analysts ask IOU's CEO to call a meeting to discuss plans for the new printer. Those present include the marketing director, the chief financial officer (CFO), the director of engineering for the printer division, and the production manager for the printer plant.

Progress in this phase is swift because the group is only seeking to identify the factors and their relationships, and not trying to produce numbers for them.

The group decides that profit will be the only objective used in evaluating the various strategies. Objectives considered but rejected include public image (IOU started out as a printer company, and producing a high-end printer product bolsters its image as a technology leader) and a desire to maintain high levels of employment.

The first decision facing IOU is how much money to spend on R & D for the new printer. A moderate R & D investment would result in a product similar to the old one, whereas a high R & D investment would allow for an almost total redesign. It is expected that a printer similar to the old one would sell poorly and that a technologically up-to-date printer would have a good chance to lead the market. At the CFO's insistence, spending nothing on R & D and getting out of the business is included as an option.

A second decision identified by the group is whether or not to build a new production plant for the SD2000. While the old plant can be easily modified to produce the new printer, it is clear that it would be unable to keep up with strong demand.

The group considers marketing strategy in the analysis but concludes that this is a lower-level "tactical" issue that would be largely determined by the R & D results.

Profit will depend upon sales revenue, the amount spent on R & D, and the cost of building a new plant if that is done. Other issues include the price charged and the per unit cost of production. The key risk factor affecting this problem is demand. This uncertainty can only be resolved by introducing the product.

The director of engineering and the production manager have prepared rough schedules, and it is apparent that a preproduction version of the printer will be available before the decision on building a new plant must be made. The group decides the R & D result is an uncertainty, and that it contributes to, but does not determine, demand.

At this point the analysts have a good problem statement—they can be fairly confident that if their analysis addresses these issues, a recommendation can be made that IOU can support and implement.

Decision

➤ R & D investment amount

➤ Build new plant

Uncertainties

➤ Demand

➤ R & D result

Objective

➤ Maximize profit

Phase 2: Building the Model

To analyze these decisions, DA's analysts opt to build a model using DPL.

1. In the Windows Program Manager, double-click the DPL icon (DPL 3.1 Standard). DPL starts with a Welcome screen.

2. Click OK. DPL opens into an empty Draw window.

    This window is the control center of DPL—it is where to build models and run analyses. The Draw window starts in an influence diagram view, since this is usually the first thing built in a DPL model.

NOTE
In this and all other DPL windows, if you make a mistake or change your mind after choosing a menu item or icon, press the ESC key.

The first step is to create an influence diagram with the value criterion IOU will use to judge the success of their decision, in this case, Profit.

1. Click the Add Value Node icon ( ).

2. Move the mouse to the right of the screen and click.

3. In the Value dialog box, shown here, type **Profit**, then click OK.

4. Press the ESC key to deselect the node. The blue rounded rectangle indicates that Profit is a value node.
     The next step is to add nodes indicating the factors that are required to compute profit. Profit will be calculated from R&D cost, plant cost, and the sales revenue coming from the new printers.

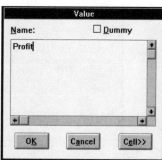

5. Create three value nodes and name them R&D Cost, Plant Cost, and Sales Rev. If you wish the names to appear on two lines, press the ENTER key after entering the first word of each name. Your influence diagram should look like Figure 8-5.

To indicate that these three factors contribute to Profit, we use arrows (arcs) linking the value nodes to the Profit node.

6. Click the Add Influence Arc icon ( ).

7. Click the R&D Cost node, then click the Profit node. This creates an arrow from R&D Cost to Profit.

8. Draw arrows from Plant Cost and Sales Rev to Profit.
     DPL allows the user to have multiple value nodes representing different known or calculated quantities in the model. If these cost and revenue nodes turn out to be uncertainties, it will be a simple matter to convert them later.

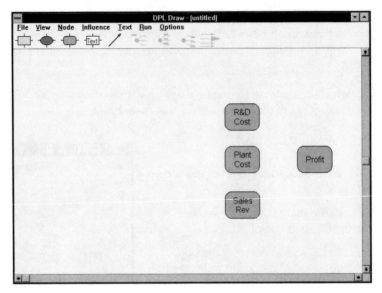

FIGURE 8-5. *The influence diagram with values*

Now you will continue adding value nodes. Sales revenue depends on plant capacity, demand (the number of units sold), unit price, and unit cost. A more complex model might include distribution path (dealer versus direct) or the fact that unit cost decreases with volume, but the IOU group has decided to move forward with a simple model and add to it later if needed. Once a complete model is ready, DA, Inc. can do a sensitivity analysis to determine what the most important factors are, and then concentrate their energies on them.

9. Add these new value nodes to the diagram: Plant Capacity, Demand, Unit Price, and Unit Cost.

10. Draw arrows from the new value nodes to the Sales Rev node. The influence diagram should now look like Figure 8-6.

With only value nodes, the diagram is essentially a graphic equivalent of a deterministic spreadsheet model. To move beyond this deterministic model, it is necessary to add uncertainty. The DA analysts decided to start with IOU's biggest uncertainty: demand.

1. Click the Demand value node.

2. Select Type from the Node menu.

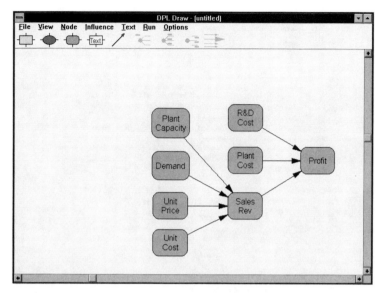

FIGURE 8-6. *The influence diagram with influence arcs*

3. Select Chance in the Type dialog box, and click OK.

DPL prompts for the state names for this new chance node. A state is a possible outcome or scenario for a chance event. DPL provides for up to 32,000 states for each event. However, in this example, we limit ourselves to two or three.

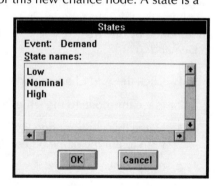

4. Type the state names **Low**, **Nominal**, and **High** in the States dialog box, as shown here, putting them on separate lines by pressing ENTER after each name.

5. When you have entered the state names, click OK.

6. Press the ESC key to deselect the node. The green oval, called a chance node, indicates that the Demand node is now an uncertainty (see Figure 8-7).

The analysts need to be careful when specifying the probability distribution for demand. They were told in Phase 1 that demand is related to R&D. If IOU's engineers design a printer that excels in performance and reliability, it would be

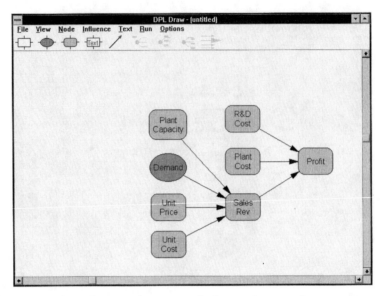

FIGURE 8-7. *The influence diagram with demand uncertainty*

more likely to generate strong demand than if they give us a paper-jamming blotmaker. At this point, the DA analysts will add a new chance node called R&D Result to take this into account. In this chance node, demand depends on, or is conditioned by, the R&D results IOU achieves. So, draw an arrow from R&D Result to Demand.

1. Click the Add Chance Node icon (⬯).

2. Place this node to the left of the Demand node.

3. Name this chance node R&D Result. Press the ENTER key after "R&D" if you wish to put the name on two lines.

4. Click OK.

5. When prompted for state names, define three states by typing **Bad**, **Nominal**, and **Good**.

6. Click OK.

7. Add an arrow from R&D Result to Demand. The influence diagram should look like Figure 8-8.

As stated earlier, the R&D results depend on how much money IOU decides to invest in R&D. Since IOU controls its outcome, the amount of R&D investment will

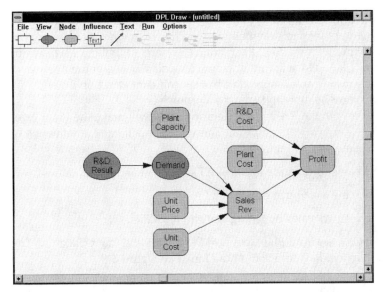

FIGURE 8-8. *The influence diagram with conditional uncertainties*

be added to the model as a decision node. Of course, IOU will make this decision to maximize, not minimize, profit. In addition to affecting R&D Result, this decision will also determine R&D Cost.

1. Click the Add Decision Node icon (⊓), and add a decision node (which appears in the diagram as a yellow rectangle) titled R&D Invest in the Decision dialog box.

2. Place the new decision node above the R&D Result node.

3. Click the Maximize radio button, and click OK.

The DA analysts next consider three possibilities (or states) for the R&D Invest decision: None, Moderate, and High. None would mean getting out of the color printer business, Moderate would be enough investment for an update of the SD1000, and High would allow for a redesign. The director of engineering and the production manager favor High R&D investment, whereas the others have doubts about the payoff of such a move. But at this point the analysts are only laying out the options.

1. Define three states by typing **None**, **Moderate**, and **High**, and click OK.

2. Add arrows from R&D Invest to R&D Result and R&D Cost.

The other decision identified in Phase 1 is whether or not to build a new plant for the SD2000. While there are a number of size options for the new plant, DA will initially consider only one. Later the analysts can determine if this assumption has a significant effect on the recommendation and adjust accordingly.

As with the R&D Invest decision, IOU will make the Plant Invest decision to maximize profit. This decision will have an effect on both Plant Capacity and Plant Cost.

3. Add a decision node and call it Plant Invest.

4. Click the Maximize box. Click OK.

5. Define two states by typing **Yes** and **No**. Click OK.

6. Add arrows from Plant Invest to Plant Cost and Plant Capacity. The influence diagram should now look like Figure 8-9.

NOTE
If the diagram is getting cluttered, move nodes around by double-clicking on them, moving the cursor to a better location, and then clicking once to reposition the node.

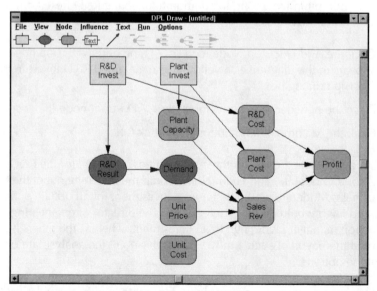

FIGURE 8-9.   *The influence diagram with decisions*

The diagram now contains the essential factors of IOU's decision problem, and the arrows in the diagram show conditioning relationships among decision, chance, and value variables: R&D Result depends on R&D Invest, Plant Capacity depends on Plant Invest. However, the DA analysts have not yet addressed the order in which events will come to pass. They would obviously like to have all the uncertainties (chance nodes) resolved before making any decisions, but this is not feasible. Although they cannot know how successful the R&D effort will be before making the R&D investment decision, IOU is fortunate to be able to examine the new printer before deciding whether to build a new plant.

DA needs to show that the plant investment decision is made only after IOU knows the R&D result. To do so, they will draw an arrow in the model from R&D Result to Plant Invest.

1. Add an arrow from R&D Result to Plant Invest.

In a DPL influence diagram, arrows usually indicate that the probabilities or values for the conditioned event depend on the conditioning event. In the IOU case, the arrow from R&D Invest to Plant Invest is for timing only, and it does not affect any values that might be associated with Plant Invest. This assumes that building a plant to make great printers is no more or less expensive than building one to make mediocre printers.

To indicate that the arrow from R&D Result to Plant Invest is a timing arrow rather than a data conditioning arrow, change the type of arrow between them.

2. Click the arrow between R&D Result and Plant Invest near the arrowhead. The arrowhead will turn magenta, indicating that it is selected.

3. Click the Influence Type icon (⇒).

4. In the Decision Influence Type dialog box, uncheck the box labeled "Separate value expression for each conditioning event state", as shown here, and click OK.

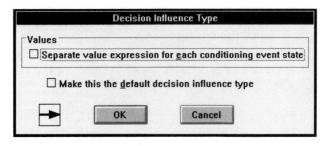

5. Press the ESC key to deselect the arrow. The arrowhead color changes from blue to black.

Arrowhead colors indicate the type of conditioning for each arrow in the diagram. Arrows with black arrowheads indicate timing only.

At this point the DA analysts have finished specifying the structure of their model. One nice thing about influence diagrams is their usefulness for communication. If they put the diagram on a transparency it could be used to concisely explain their thinking about the problem, even to a group not familiar with decision analysis.

DPL is used for specifying and calculating values as well as structuring decision problems. The DA analysts will now use these features to calculate profit for each combination of decision and chance events. First, they will indicate how Profit is calculated. This model will include both numbers and equations.

The analysts need to enter equations for calculating two values, Profit and Sales Rev, from other variables. Start by entering an equation for the Profit node. Profit is determined from sales revenues, R&D cost, and plant cost.

1. Select the Profit node by clicking on it.

2. Click the Node Data icon (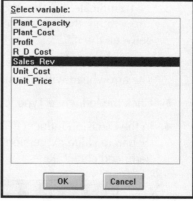).

3. In the Data dialog box, click Variable to open a list of value names, as shown here:

4. Double-click Sales Rev and enter a minus sign (–).

5. Click Variable and add R&D Cost.

6. Enter a minus sign (–).

7. Click Variable and add Plant Cost.

TIP
Notice that DPL enters the name R&D Cost as R_D_Cost. DPL variable names cannot include special characters or spaces, although node names can. If you use the Variable button, DPL will automatically handle this for you.

8. Click OK. The Profit formula will appear in the Data dialog box, as shown here:

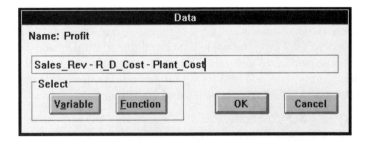

Next, the analysts need to define sales revenue as a function of plant capacity, demand, unit price, and unit cost. IOU will make (Unit Price – Unit Cost) on each printer sold, and will sell either Demand or Plant Capacity, whichever is less.

1. Select the Sales Rev node.

2. Click the Node Data icon.

3. Enter this formula:

   (Unit_Price – Unit_Cost) * (@min(Plant_Capacity,Demand))

   DPL is case-sensitive, so be sure to use the Variable button to get the names of the variables correct. Since no value data has yet been entered for the chance node Demand, the Variable button will not display Demand as a value; type it in, being very careful to spell and capitalize it exactly as you did when naming the node.

4. Click OK. The Data dialog box will display the Sales Revenue formula.

Now that the appropriate equations have been entered into the DPL model for the two calculated values, we need to add data for the other values. First, add the unconditioned value data (fixed model parameters): Unit Price and Unit Cost. The production manager and the director of engineering have come up with a figure of $2,000 for unit cost, based mainly on their experience with the SD1000. In the past these estimates have been accurate, so the group is comfortable using this number. The marketing director believes the unit price will be $10,000. Her estimate for the old printer was right on, but this time IOU's main rival will be introducing a new product a month or so earlier, and if they price aggressively IOU will have to respond. Later a sensitivity analysis will tell us whether this number is key in DA's model, and if it turns out to be, it can be treated as an uncertainty and DA can decide whether to do more research in this area.

To avoid typing zeros, use the following conventions: Plant Capacity and Demand are in thousands of units; Unit Cost and Unit Price are in thousands of dollars; R & D cost, Plant Cost, Sales Rev, and Profit are in millions of dollars.

1. Add data for Unit Price and Unit Cost using the Node Data icon. Unit Price is 10. Unit Cost is 2.

   Next you will add the value data conditioned on decisions: R&D cost, plant cost, and plant capacity. The R&D cost of a redesign will be $20 million, an update will be $10 million, and doing nothing is free. So None, Moderate and High will be 0, 10, and 20, respectively.

2. Select the R&D Cost node, and click the Node Data icon. This opens the Node Data screen shown in Figure 8-10.

3. Enter the data. You can use the arrow keys or the ENTER key to move from branch to branch. If IOU builds the plant, the cost is 100; if they don't, the cost is 0.

4. Add data for Plant Cost by selecting the Plant Cost node and clicking on the Node Data icon. IOU's current plant can produce 5,000 units per year; if they build a new plant, they will be able to produce 50,000 units. So Plant Capacity is 50 if Plant Invest is Yes and 5 if it's No.

5. Add data for Plant Capacity by selecting the Plant Capacity node and clicking the Node Data icon.

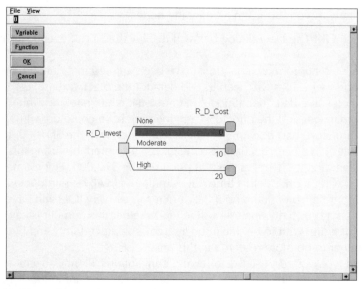

FIGURE 8-10. *The Node Data screen*

Phase 3: Quantifying the Uncertainties

Having added all the deterministic data, DA's analysts can now turn their attention to the sources of uncertainty in their model. They have two chance nodes: R&D Result and Demand.

For R&D Result, they consider three possibilities: Bad, Nominal, and Good. Bad is assumed to be so awful that the SD2000 project would have to be abandoned to save IOU's reputation. The R&D Result node has only probability data, which depend on the R&D investment decision. If IOU makes no R&D investment, the probability of a bad result is 1.0, and the probabilities for nominal or good results are 0. If IOU makes a moderate R&D investment, the probability of a bad result is 0.4, the probability of a nominal result is 0.5, and the probability of a good result is 0.1. If IOU makes the high R&D investment, the probability of a bad result drops to 0.2, the probability of a nominal result is 0.5 and the probability of a good result increases to 0.3. There are no values associated with the states of R&D Result.

1. Enter data for R&D Result. For each branch, the dialog box will prompt for both a probability and a value (in thousands of units), as shown in Figure 8-11. Since we aren't entering values, press the ENTER key twice after entering each probability to move to the next probability field.

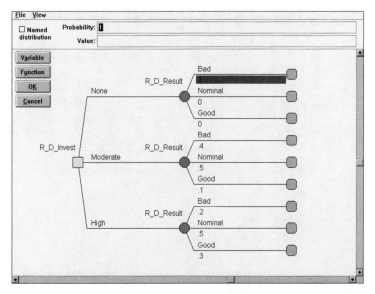

FIGURE 8-11. *The Node Data screen for a conditioned chance node*

In this case, the probability and value data are conditioned on the R&D result outcome. If IOU gets a bad R&D result, demand will always be 0. The probabilities don't matter much, so use 0.25 for low, 0.5 for nominal, and 0.25 for high.

With everyone having some input, the IOU decision group agrees to the following set of numbers for demand in the nominal and good cases. If they get a nominal R&D result, IOU will get a low demand of 5 with 0.25 probability, nominal demand of 10 with 0.5 probability, and a high demand of 20 with 0.25 probability.

If IOU gets a good R&D result, they can expect a low demand of 10 with 0.25 probability, a nominal demand of 20 with 0.5 probability, and a high demand of 40 with 0.25 probability.

2. Enter data for Demand.

Now that all the data has been entered (we won't enter directly any value data for the two decision nodes), the influence diagram is complete. DPL has automatically created a decision tree to accompany this influence diagram. By including the timing information in the influence diagram, DPL can develop the correct decision tree for this situation. The tree shows the sequence of events and the Profit value criterion.

3. Press the TAB key to activate Decision Tree view, shown in Figure 8-12.

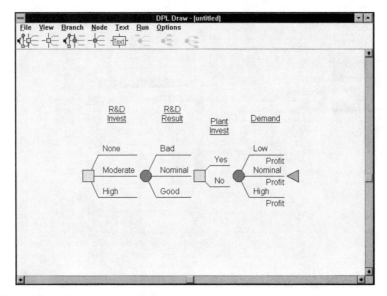

FIGURE 8-12. *Decision Tree view*

The decision tree is symmetric, which means that every path through it consists of the same sequence of events. Because of this symmetry, there is no need to show every path explicitly. Instead, it just shows the sequence of events. This notation is called "schematic" notation and allows us to reduce the size of the displayed tree without losing modeling detail. Notice also that the tree has no numbers. The probabilities and values were defined in the influence diagram and don't need to be repeated; in fact, if they were to be displayed on the tree, we couldn't use the schematic notation and the tree would be much larger.

The variable name "Profit" attached to the final branches is called a "Get/Pay" expression, and indicates that as each branch is evaluated, the appropriate value Profit should be calculated for that branch. Because Profit was defined in the influence diagram with a formula that depends on the individual states of the decision and chance events, the profit value that gets calculated for each path will depend on the path itself.

Phase 4: Evaluating Alternative Strategies

This model is now complete. The structure and data of the decision model were specified in the influence diagram, and the decision tree has been constructed. Now we are ready to conduct a decision analysis using this model.

1. Open the Run menu from the main menu bar and select Decision Analysis. The Decision Analysis Options dialog box will appear.

2. Click More. In the box labeled "Number of levels for gathering decision policy," enter **5**; this ensures that the full decision policy will be available for display. The Decision Analysis Options box will now look like this:

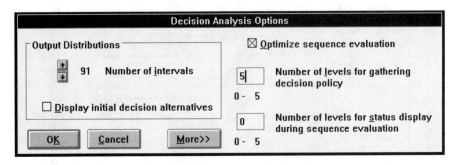

3. Click OK. DPL evaluates the model and displays the expected value of $24 million for the optimal policy.

4. Click OK. By default, DPL opens two windows with decision-analysis results: the Decision Policy window and the Distributions window.

The Decision Policy window (Figure 8-13) displays the full policy tree, including probabilities and values. The heavier lines indicate the optimal policy based on maximizing expected profit. The numbers in brackets indicate the expected value at each node and endpoint.

5. Maximize the Decision Policy window by clicking on the arrow pointing up at the upper right corner of the window.

6. Click the right mouse button to redraw the tree so that it fits in the window.

This decision policy recommends committing to the highest R&D level, then waiting for the R & D results before committing to a plant investment alternative. If the R & D results are bad or nominal, IOU should not make the plant investment. They should make the plant investment only if the results are good. The expected profit is $24 million, compared to $18 million for the next best alternative. This view of the policy shows only enough of the tree to see all the decisions on the optimal path. The rest of the tree information is available, if we wish to see it.

1. Double-click the green chance nodes to expand the policy tree.

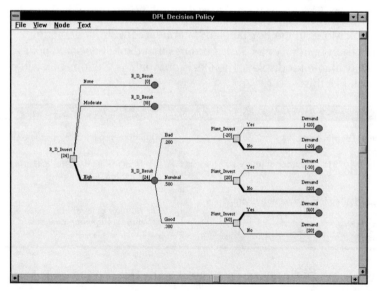

FIGURE 8-13. *The Decision Policy window*

2. Click the right mouse button to redraw the policy tree so it fits in the window.

3. Close the Decision Policy window. The Distributions window (Figure 8-14) displays the risk profile, a cumulative probability distribution of outcomes (in this case, profit) for the optimal policy.

As you can see, even the optimal policy, the high level of R&D investment, is fairly risky; the possible outcomes range from losing about $40 million to making about $200 million.

4. Close the Distributions window.

The DA analysts can now develop their recommended actions based on the input model and data, but how robust is this answer? In Phase 2 IOU assumed a unit price of $10,000, but there was some concern about competition forcing it down. What if IOU knew that their rival would bring out a similar product priced at $7,000 and that they would have to match this price? How would this affect IOU's profits? Would it change their strategy? To answer these questions, run a sensitivity analysis on Unit Price.

5. Open the Run menu on the main menu bar and select Value Sensitivity Analysis, then Rainbow Diagram.

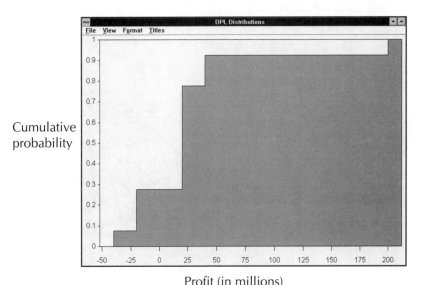

FIGURE 8-14.   *The Distributions window*

6. Double-click Unit Price; the current value of 10 will appear in the dialog box. Enter **5** for the starting value, **12** for the ending value, and an increment of **1**. You can use the TAB key to move from field to field.

The dialog box will now look like this:

7. Click OK. DPL will run the sensitivity analysis and open a rainbow diagram window.

8. Click OK to remove the information message, and the window will look like Figure 8-15.

What does this window tell us? The graph shows how the expected profit changes as the unit price varies. The expected profit varies from $0 to over $40 million. The

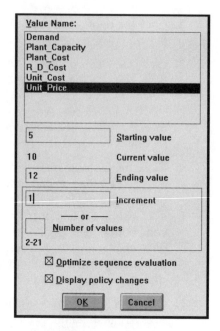

color changes indicate that the optimal policy changes as unit price is varied as well. The policy changes occur between $5,000 and $6,000,

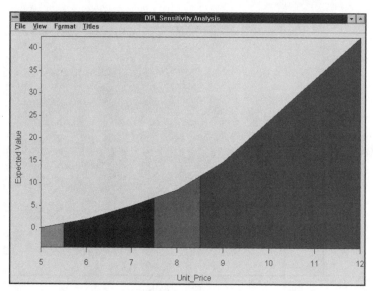

FIGURE 8-15. *The Sensitivity Analysis window*

between $7,000 and $8,000, and between $8,000 and $9,000 per unit. This means that if there is a significant chance that unit price will drop below its nominal value of 10, the assumption that it is certain is a dangerous one and we should model it probabilistically. We would do this by defining scenarios (e.g., high, low) and assigning each a probability and a price.

9. Close the Sensitivity Analysis window.

Phase 5: Communicating the Results

One of the advantages of using DPL is that in the process of solving a problem we generate material that can be used in presenting our results. The influence diagram, decision tree, decision policy, and distribution graphics are all ready for presentation. In our example, all the people involved are on board and doing modeling from the beginning, which is the best way to make group decisions. When this isn't possible, the DPL graphical outputs can be easily pasted into word processing or presentation software for persuasive reports and presentations.

The DA recommendation to the CEO was that he make the high R&D investment and wait for the results before taking further action. Time was limited, so DA developed a strategy that is based on the best information available. DA also has a list of things like unit price that they would analyze if more time were available. With this information, the CEO can decide whether to act now or extend the analysis. If he gives us more time, the DA analysts can revisit each phase, extending and enhancing the model using their current analysis as a framework.

Conclusion

Decision analysis is a collection of quantitative tools and techniques together with a practical process for putting them to work on real-world problems. If you've read through the case study you know that in it our attention remained focused on the decision at hand, not on computational details. DPL is simple and intuitive enough that it can be used in the conference room as the decision is being formulated, and its graphics make explaining the results easy.

Decision makers as diverse as politicians and businesspersons find decision analysis helpful in making hard decisions. Decision analysis helps focus attention on the factors that really matter, so time isn't wasted on side issues. It provides a systematic way of combining hard data with the intuition and experience of experts. Risk is considered explicitly, making it possible to make a good decision without pretending to predict the future. It can even tell the participants when enough analysis has been done and it's time to take action.

The disc accompanying this book contains other sample files that you may wish to examine. In our case study, we only needed the basic features of DPL; you may want to go through the menus and explore some of the other options.

CHAPTER 9

Strategic Reengineering to Create High-Performance Organizations

by Barry Richmond, L. Philip Odence, and Paul Kucera
High Performance Systems, Inc.

It would be surprising to thumb through a business magazine or to scan the list of management best-sellers without encountering at least one reference to how breakthrough improvements in performance can be achieved by applying some new technique to the problem of business process reengineering (BPR). But truth be told, a lot of what is labeled reengineering really isn't. And, a good chunk of what is reengineering has not produced breakthrough improvements at all. Instead, it has generated painful and costly failures.

However, beneath all the hype surrounding reengineering, a profound change is underway in the fundamentals of how business is done. Reengineering is an important manifestation of this change, but far less important than the change itself. The change is the result of a paradigm shift in both the way we view our organizations and in the way we view the nature of our work. To reap the benefits of reengineering, it is essential to understand that reengineering is not just a new way to play the game, but also a way of winning the game.

A New Business Paradigm

Sometime during the early 1970s, a quality-based approach to doing business began to seep out of Japan. The approach first made itself felt in the more traditional heavy manufacturing industries. It then swept rapidly over the entire business landscape, and it has now penetrated even the most service-based of service organizations. Quality and the pursuit thereof, i.e., total quality management (TQM), has since become the dominant business ethos.

The basic business equation, which had been written using "ors" (cost or quality, price or functionality) has been rewritten using "ands." Customers are no longer willing to accept trade-offs among quality, service, functionality, price, and other product attributes. Instead, they are demanding it all—and getting it. To succeed in this new, customer-is-king, no-trade-off environment, businesses have had to shift from a product (thing) orientation to a process (relationship) orientation.

From a *product* orientation, things are delivered to customers. These things are seen as the results of the combined contributions made by each of a set of essentially independent functions, e.g., R&D, Manufacturing, and Sales. According to this view, the path to delivering better things is in increasing the excellence of each function.

In contrast, those adopting a *process* orientation consider what is being delivered to customers not to be things, but rather an ongoing relationship—a relationship that must be continually nourished if customer satisfaction is to be maintained. The process orientation holds that relationships with customers must be created and sustained through the seamless execution of a set of cross-functional and cross-organizational business processes. These processes run horizontally through the organization, as shown in Figure 9-1, and in so doing explicitly violate the heretofore sacrosanct boundaries that had defined functional fiefdoms within the organization. The processes also pierce the boundaries of the organization itself, subsuming suppliers, customers, the community, and often even competitors. Interdependence, rather than independence, is the watchword.

According to a process orientation, the way to improve what is being delivered to customers is to improve the workings of the business processes themselves. And, unlike products (which are things, and hence discrete packages), the processes that

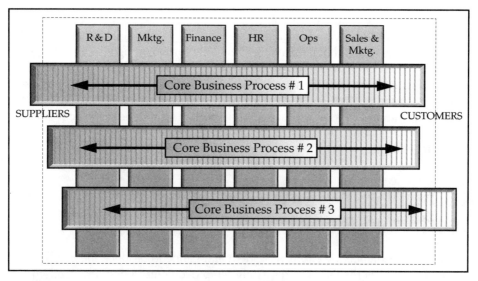

FIGURE 9-1. *The cross-functional organization*

yield products are always in motion. Their very nature is dynamic. Hence, improving processes is a never-ending quest—you don't just achieve it, then declare victory.

And so, the major revolution in business, which has been unfolding over the last decade or so, has been a shift from a product/functional view to a relationship/process view. The shift has brought interdependency to the forefront and caused people to extend their time horizons in order to embrace the commitment to ongoing process improvement.

BPR and TQM

When the process revolution first began, the name of the game was continuous incremental improvement. The TQM methodology stressed setting performance targets for each process, gauging performance relative to these targets, then feeding back performance discrepancies in order to stimulate corrective actions (which in turn would cause process outputs to continuously home in on established performance targets). This highly focused and disciplined approach has yielded, and will continue to yield, some impressive performance gains.

Recently, a more radical group has arisen from within the quality movement. Under the unofficial leadership of Michael Hammer and James Champy, this group advocates revolution before evolution under the ethos of business process reengineering (BPR). They argue against making incremental improvements in processes that are in need of radical redesign (i.e., don't rearrange deck chairs on the Titanic). Their credo: Begin anew, question all the old assumptions, jettison all previous dogma. If the process is fundamentally broken, don't try to fix it—redesign it from the ground up. Rethink, *then* reengineer. Afterward, they argue, you can incrementally improve the new process. It's important to add the last piece: BPR does not displace TQM. TQM just becomes a second phase within the process improvement cycle.

Reengineering: Silver Bullet or Overhyped Blank?

A majority of reengineering efforts miss the mark, failing to produce the much ballyhooed and eagerly anticipated quantum improvements in performance. Truth be known, many of these efforts not only fail to achieve quantum improvement, but they also actually leave process performance virtually unchanged—or worse, cause it to degrade. Such results, in many cases after millions of dollars have been spent and vast amounts of precious time and energy have been consumed, have seriously tarnished the image of reengineering as a silver bullet. But before dismissing reengineering as just another overhyped blank, let's consider both why such results are being achieved and what organizations might do to increase the likelihood of achieving dramatic performance improvements.

The root cause of the inability to achieve the anticipated improvements from reengineering efforts is a failure to view these efforts in a proper perspective. Reengineering efforts are too often viewed as mechanical in nature. You simply wipe the slate clean, then logically redesign the process infrastructure. But organizations are not silicon chips. You never have a blank slate in reality. People's power, self-esteem, self-confidence, and sense of security are tied up with the way things are.

True reengineering implies dramatic organizational change. Reengineering efforts fundamentally change the way a business works. Why is it so difficult to make organizational change happen? Simple. Because any change is inherently threatening. The more fundamental the change, the more threatening. And, when people feel threatened by a change, they resist it. If enough of them resist, change grinds to a halt—often accompanied by a loud screeching sound and lots of thick smoke. Even if things are not going well within a process, process residents often have little confidence that reengineering outsiders actually can crack the code on how to make things work any better. Finally, even a great reengineering solution and low initial levels of resistance to change do not ensure success. A failure to adequately understand, and hence a failure to appropriately set expectations for, what will unfold in the transition from "as is" to "to be" can ultimately fuel I-told-you-so resistance when the inevitable transition hiccups occur.

So, basically, it is not easy to succeed at reengineering. A fundamental problem lies in the assumption that it should be easy. However, it is possible to achieve the promise of large improvements in process performance through reengineering. And software tools are available that can go a long way toward helping you realize this promise. Before we look at how these tools can help reengineering efforts succeed, let's look a bit more closely at what it takes to reduce resistance to change.

Reducing Resistance to Change

Some resistance to change should be expected in any organizational setting. In fact, some experts argue that resistance to change is essential in order to ensure a measure of organizational stability. However, it is possible to significantly reduce the dysfunctional resistance that can arise throughout the life cycle of a reengineering effort. Understanding how to reduce resistance begins by having a clear picture of why such resistance arises in the first place. Resistance is a coping mechanism people use to counter the perceived threats and resulting fears that are created by the prospects of change. Fear is an extremely powerful motivator. It can cause people either to cling to their seats or to strap on their parachutes. The former occurs when the "as is" appears preferable to the "to be." The latter occurs when remaining with the "as is" looks more uncertain than leaping into the "as yet untried." Reducing the perceived threat is a three-step process.

Step One: Develop and Communicate a Compelling Case for Change
The first step in inspiring people to embrace change is to develop a compelling case for why change must occur. For reengineering initiatives, this means first showing clearly that if the existing process(es) remain as they are, performance will continue to be poor and may degrade further. Next, people must see that the structure of the process itself—and not, say, senior management, another process or function, particular personalities, or some other external factor—is the fundamental cause of poor performance. Seeing these two things is an intellectual endeavor. However, the appeal to rationality is usually not enough to inspire a reach for parachutes. Complementing the rational arguments with an appeal that strikes an emotional chord, inspiring fear, usually finishes the job. With fear as a motivator, people are more willing to assess where they are, what is wrong, and where they should be headed. In short, they are ready to strap on their parachutes.

Step Two: Paint a Clear Picture of Where the Change Will Lead
With parachutes strapped on, next it is essential to give the leapers a clear sense of where it is they will be leaping to. Ideally, people will understand how their best interests are to be served by embracing the change. To accomplish this, it is

important to show people how change will help achieve their personal interests within the organization and the larger interests of the organization itself. The purpose of helping people to see how change is in their best interest is to reduce the number of clouds obscuring where it is they will land. The more clouds between the leaping and landing points, the less willing people will be to take the plunge. The deeper the appreciation for change—where it will lead, and what it will look and feel like once on the new ground—the lower the resistance to leaping.

Step Three: Illuminate a Clear Pathway for Getting There

Once the need to leap has been clearly understood, and the landing zone is in sharp focus, the final step is to illuminate the pathway from here to there. This step is often given short shrift in reengineering efforts. Reengineers are so eager to wipe the slate clean and begin anew, they forget that no matter where it is you want to get to, you are starting from somewhere else. And, a straight line is often not the best way to get from here to there. Sometimes it is essential to do things in the short run that are off the straight-line pathway. In addition, while "there" may ultimately be a better place to be, abandoning "here" may cause things to become worse for a while. Transitions can be painful. For people to stay the course, it's important that they know what pain to expect and how long to expect it to endure. Such knowledge greatly increases the chances of a reengineering initiative coming to full fruition.

Tools for Business Process Reengineering

To the extent that organizations have paid attention to the steps in reducing resistance to business process reengineering, they have typically not relied on tools per se. Approaches like working with organizational development consultants, conducting awareness training, and providing strong leadership have been the "tools" that have most often been employed to move organizations forward.

Still, there has been some application of software tools to business process reengineering. The first tool to mention is our old friend the spreadsheet. Projected financial statements under alternative scenarios can be used to make a case for change, both to illustrate a perilous future and to illustrate a better alternative. Tying organizational change to bottom-line numbers makes a good deal of sense—in business the bottom line is...the bottom line. However, part of the reason why so many change efforts fail is that this kind of analysis is insufficient.

While it may satisfy the analytical left side of the brain, the highly artificial approach taken with financial spreadsheets speaks very little to people's emotional side. As described in the previous section, resistance to change is rooted deeply in the human psyche. Looking at numbers cooked up by someone else does little to alleviate fear of the unknown.

Moreover, while the numbers purport to show that the "to be" is a nicer place than the "as is," it is difficult for recipients of the argument to understand why. The logic that connects the process to the numbers is buried behind the spreadsheet's output. The leap of faith necessary to believe a matrix of numbers and to believe that they reasonably reflect the performance of a new process is usually a stretch. When you look at a spreadsheet, you simply don't see the process.

There is nothing wrong with spreadsheets—they are the tool of choice for many tasks—but their inability to show processes has led to the advent of maps and mapping tools. Included in this class are everything from general-purpose graphics packages like MacDraw™, to idea organizers like Inspiration™, to full-blown mapping tools like Design™ or MacFlow™. The maps these tools can produce can reasonably communicate what a process does or what it will look like. They are easier for people to relate to than spreadsheets, and to some extent they speak to people's emotions. In a sense, it enables them to see where they fit in the larger scheme of things.

While there is great value in a map, there are limitations as well. The static view of a process in a map in no way suggests how a process will perform. Just as spreadsheets show performance without process, maps show process without performance. Neither shows the connection between the structure of a process and its performance. And maps, because of their static nature, certainly do not show how a process will feel. Feelings require experience. You cannot experience a map; all you can do is look at it.

To effectively aid in reducing resistance to change, what is needed are tools that show the structure of the process, tie the structure to performance, and enable people to experience the process. What is needed is a dynamic mapping tool that combines the outputs of spreadsheets and the visual cues of maps to produce more understandable "as is" models and "to be" alternatives. There are a handful of such dynamic modeling tools currently available for use in any computer. Some examples include ithink™ by High Performance Systems of Hanover, New Hampshire; Extend™ by Imagine That, Inc. of San Jose, California (see Chapter 10); and Process™ by Process Research Group of Gresham, Oregon.

The Role of Dynamic Modeling Software

Dynamic modeling software has been applied to reengineering in a wide variety of business processes within industries ranging from services to heavy manufacturing. Though the contexts are quite different, the basic reengineering principles and process are quite similar. Modeling and simulation can play a vital role in each step of the three-step process as outlined earlier in the "Reducing Resistance to Change" section.

In Step 1 (developing and communicating a compelling case for change), software can be used to replicate the performance problems associated with the "as is" process. Rising cycle-times, spiraling costs, poor quality, and whatever other performance barometers are signaling the need for reengineering, can be created in a model. And, if the model is equipped with a Flight Simulator interface, in which users "fly" the process model as if making the appropriate decisions in real time, then people can have the experience of creating the performance difficulties through their own stream of decisions—ruling out any it's-being-done-to-us arguments. To varying degrees, dynamic modeling packages enable the creation of models that are visual and comprehensible. Such models let people develop an understanding of precisely how the structure of the existing process is creating the performance difficulties that are being experienced. This understanding in turn paves the way for embracing the reengineering solution.

Step 2 of the process—reducing resistance to change—is to paint a clear picture of the "to be." Dynamic modeling is equally applicable in this realm. The easier-to-use packages enable virtually anyone to use the software and become involved in mapping possible reengineering process designs. And, the greater the involvement in the mapping process, the more buy-in that is achieved to the ultimate reengineering solution. What's more, because a dynamic model can be simulated, proposed solutions can be quickly tested to see if they can indeed yield the results promised by proponents. In addition, a simulation of the "to be" can be an extremely useful vehicle by which those who will operate within the process can gain some preimplementation experience. Such experience builds confidence in process players so they will be able to make the reengineered process hum.

Step 3, in reducing resistance to reengineering process changes, is to clearly illuminate the pathway from "as is" to "to be." Using simulation, it's possible to develop a good feeling for how long the transition is likely to take and also for what hiccups are likely to occur along the way. Appropriately setting expectations increases the likelihood of being able to stay the course and see the reengineering effort through to completion.

Overview of the ithink
Operating Environment

To better understand how the ithink software can be used in the context of BPR and other types of analyses, let's review how the management of visual (and model) complexity is handled within the software. Figure 9-2 provides an overview of the ithink operating environment. It is a multilevel, hierarchical environment for constructing and interacting with models. The environment consists of two major layers: the High-Level Mapping & I/O (input/output) layer, and the Model Construction layer. The High-Level Mapping & I/O layer gives the user a compact

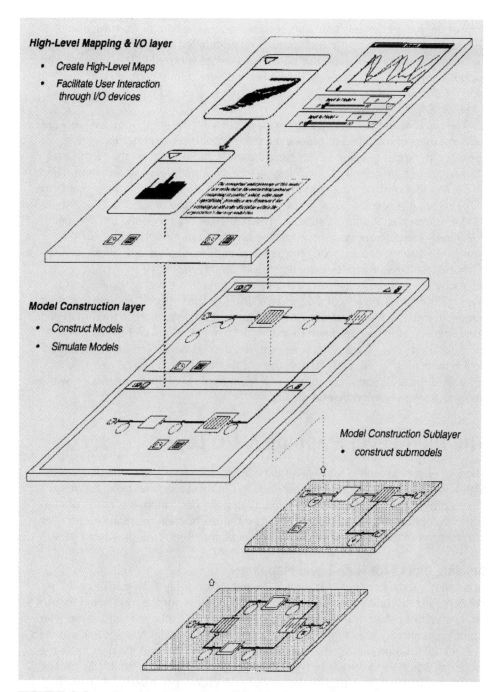

FIGURE 9-2. *Graphical overview of the ithink operating environment*

view of the main elements contained in the model. The Model Construction or Diagramming layer gives the user a much more detailed view of the model. Within the Model Construction layer, it is possible to create submodels that operate within various elements of the larger model. Submodels are tightly coupled with the Model Construction layer, which, in turn, is tightly coupled with the High-Level Mapping & I/O layer.

The purpose of the layering is to manage complexity—both for producers and for consumers of models. For producers, the environment fosters a top-down approach to model development. Using the tools and objects on the High-Level Mapping & I/O layer toolbar, modelers can create a high-level system map. Then, on the Model Construction layer, they can develop a more detailed representation of the relevant processes. Finally, the microlevel structure of specific processes can be represented within submodels. The net result is a modeling environment that allows seamless movement across the layers of the model and facilitates conceptualization, construction, analysis and communication activities.

For consumers of a model, the benefits of the layered environment are even more obvious. Model consumers can begin on the High-Level Mapping & I/O layer, gaining an overview of the model's structure and interacting with the model through the use of input and output authoring features. Working at their own pace, consumers can then move down to the Model Construction layer to work with a more detailed view of the system. As required, they can go even further into the details by exploring submodels. Because of layering, details can be revealed at a controlled pace. As such, consumers will learn the lessons from the model, without becoming overwhelmed by complexity.

The High-Level Mapping & I/O Layer

The High-Level Mapping & I/O layer was designed to facilitate conceptualization, high-level mapping, and model input/output. On this layer, the use of building blocks provides a visual aid for conceptualizing the basic elements of the model and developing a high-level map. Objects provide concrete mechanisms for user interaction with the model. These building blocks and objects are shown in Figure 9-3.

Building Blocks for High-Level Mapping

At present, model conceptualization is largely an art rather than a science. In the conceptualization stage, the modeler defines a purpose for the model and focuses on a pattern of behavior over time that the model is to explain. Then the modeler simplifies reality by selecting and aggregating those interrelationships that are seen as essential for representing these patterns of behavior. To help the user focus the modeling effort, the software provides three high-level mapping tools: the process frame, the bundled flow, and the bundled connector. Since these higher-level building blocks are less detailed than the basic stock and flow building blocks, they

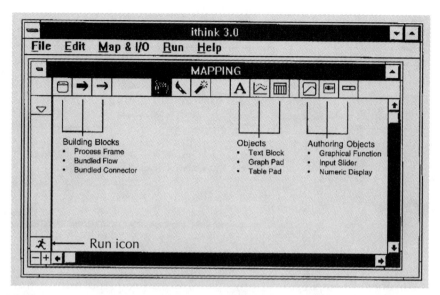

FIGURE 9-3. *The High-Level Mapping and I/O layer*

provide a conceptual bridge between the mental model (how people understand a process) and the formal model (how that understanding is represented in the simulation tool). The resulting map—consisting of key system processes, as well as the material and informational flows between them—can make it easier for a novice to understand the overall structure of the model. A simple high-level map is shown in Figure 9-4.

It's important to note that the high-level map is more than simply a static picture of the system. As one creates a high-level map using the process frame, the bundled flow, and the bundled connector, sector frames are created automatically to help organize the model logically. These sector frames appear on the model construction layer (explained in greater detail later in the chapter). These frames will house the stock and flow structure of the process under investigation. Navigational controls allow users to drill down to the details of a specific model sector. Finally, as material flow and information connections are made between sectors on the model construction layer, the high-level map will be updated automatically to reflect these connections. The high-level map thus will always be in sync with the underlying detailed representation.

Nonabstract Objects for Input and Output

The second salient feature of the High-Level Mapping & I/O layer is its collection of objects. In the first set of objects, the text block enables one to use text to name

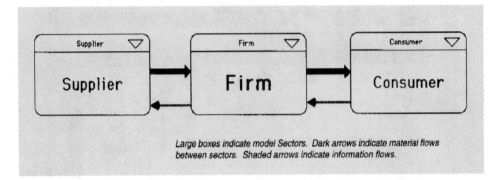

Large boxes indicate model Sectors. Dark arrows indicate material flows between sectors. Shaded arrows indicate information flows.

FIGURE 9-4. *A high-level map*

and describe the map as desired. The table pad and graph pad facilitate the collection of model output as tables and graphs. The second set of high-level objects are available only in the authoring version of the software. The graphical function input and display (GFID), input slider, and numeric display devices provide compelling, nonabstract mechanisms for users to interact with a model. These objects are illustrated in Figure 9-5.

The authoring objects make it possible to develop learning environments and management practice fields in which users can enhance their mental models by interacting directly with a formal model. The graphical function input and display (GFID) device, for example, makes it possible for model consumers to sketch a

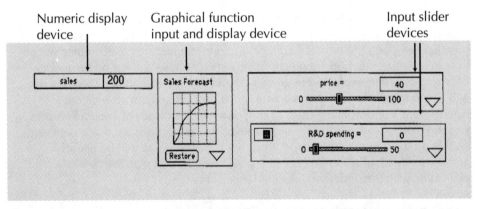

FIGURE 9-5. *Using mapping objects to create a simple control panel*

model relationship without requiring them to work with the detailed structure of the formal model. The slider enables consumers to change input parameters, either while a model simulation is paused or while it is running, and to override the model's equation logic. This makes it possible for consumers to compare the results of their own decision rules against the output of decision rules that have been embedded in the model. Finally, the numeric display reports the current value of selected model variables, providing consumers with a sense for the current state of the system as the model simulation progresses.

The Model Construction Layer

The graphical approach to construction and analysis extends down to the Model Construction layer. On this layer, a modeler will use a set of modeling building blocks to construct the formal model. Again, a collection of objects facilitates analysis and interaction with the model. These building blocks and objects are shown in Figure 9-6.

Building Blocks for Model Construction

The stock, flow, converter, and connector are the structural building blocks that the modeler uses to construct a formal model. Once selected from the toolbar, each building block is positioned within the diagram, and then hooked together with other elements as desired to reflect the structural relationships under investigation. Associated with each building block is a set of structural and procedural rules.

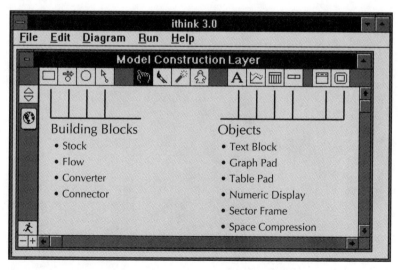

FIGURE 9-6.   *The model construction layer*

These rules prevent the user from making typographical and syntactic mistakes. They also remove much of the technical tedium traditionally encountered in constructing a formal model.

For example, as the user creates a structural map using stocks and flows, the software infers the difference equation structure required for simulation. This equation structure is available as a separate window for user examination. However, there is never a need to write a difference equation. Instead, the user can spend time in the graphical domain, representing the relationships that govern particular flow processes.

The user adds flesh to this structural skeleton by using converters and connectors. Converters represent constants, time series inputs, and algebraic conversions of other model variables. In addition, converters are used to represent graphical functions—graphically constructed table lookup functions. Connectors indicate logical or causal connections between model elements. Only realistic connections are allowed. For example, the software will not allow the user to connect converters only to form a feedback loop—an intermediary stock is required. Similarly, the software will not allow the user to drag a connector into a stock—stocks can only change through the movement of their associated flows.

Once a stock and flow map has been developed, it's possible to drill down to another level of detail by creating submodels. A simple submodel is shown in Figure 9-7. As this figure illustrates, submodels can be selectively displayed to enable modelers to manage the visual complexity associated with a formal model.

Within each stock, flow, and converter are repositories for storing equation logic and for documenting assumptions. The user accesses these repositories by

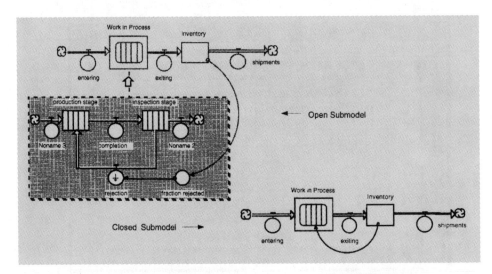

FIGURE 9-7. *A simple submodel*

double-clicking on an element. Defining an equation simply requires pointing and clicking with the mouse (there is no need to type variable names, and hence no chance for typographical errors). A sample equation dialog is shown in Figure 9-8.

There are several aspects of this dialog to consider. First, the user defines the equation using the list of required inputs. These inputs are required, because they have been indicated on the model diagram as being required to define the associated construct. The software thus enforces a one-to-one correspondence between the structural map and the equation logic that drives the simulation. Second, the equation is defined in isolation. The user can focus on the specifics of a particular process, without being distracted by other aspects of the model. Third, special built-in functions (steps, ramps, Boolean operations, distributions, etc.) are available from within the dialog. The user can simply choose from among these as needed. Finally, space for documenting each relationship is available. Documentation may be left visible within the dialog or may be hidden from view. In either case, the verbal description is available to both the producer and the consumer of the model in a context-sensitive manner.

With this high-level overview under our belts, we're ready to get on with building a working model.

A Walk-Through and Tutorial of ithink Software

On the CD-ROM accompanying this book, you will find a Windows demonstration version of the ithink software (ithink is also available in a Macintosh version). This

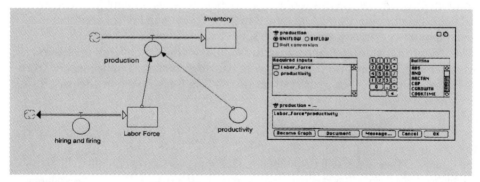

FIGURE 9-8.   *A sample equation dialog*

is a full-featured version of the authoring product; the only limitation is that you will be unable to save any models you modify or create. In addition to the application, you will also find several prebuilt models or learning environments. Many of these will be used during the tutorial that follows, which is designed to guide you through a hands-on experience with model conceptualization and development, interface construction, and management flight-simulator testing of the hypotheses underlying the model structure. The disc also includes a game called "Start-up, Inc.," in which you can try to succeed in a start-up business by making a variety of decisions over a two-year period.

Working with a Management Flight Simulator

The ithink software is designed to help people build a deeper understanding of how their business works and of how to make it work better. In what follows, you will find an example of a management flight simulator, built with the authoring version of ithink, which is based on a simple ithink model of a service business (like a consulting company). We encourage you to spend some time "flying" this business using ithink. In the second section of the tutorial, we will take you step-by-step through the process of building a portion of the engine that powers the flight simulator. After completing this exercise, we will give you an opportunity to extend the model, or you can construct a model of your own.

Flight Simulator Context

Maintaining a smooth, high-quality workflow is a challenge in any business. In this flight simulator, you will be asked to try your hand at balancing headcount and work backlog in a consulting organization known for its high-quality work. The organization is gaining clients at a rapid rate and is aware of the tendency for consulting companies to grow too quickly, only to have their client base collapse. When this occurs, companies are forced to lay off large numbers of consultants and, more often than not, are unable to survive the collapse.

In trying to understand (and avoid) the rapid-growth-and-collapse mode, you will examine the relationships among work backlogs, quality, and headcount. Your basic decision will be how many new consultants to bring online in any period. Each new consultant must go through a six-month training process during which time they are assumed to function at half the work-completion productivity of fully experienced consultants. As the backlog of work swells, each consultant will need to work longer hours to increase throughput. And since long hours take their toll, the quality of their work will begin to slip. Declining quality eventually will cause clients to defect as well as reduce word-of-mouth advertising. Finding the balance between headcount, work backlog, and quality, while not violating budget constraints, will be the challenge you'll face while trying to fly this firm.

First you will need to download the ithink demo from the CD-ROM, following the instructions at the back of the book. The demo will initially open to a blank high-level mapping page.

1. Close the default window by selecting Close Window under the File menu.

2. Now use the Open command under File to open the model called SERVICE.ITM in the Tutorial subdirectory of the ithink demo. You will see the high-level map shown in Figure 9-9.

Notice the arrows linking the process frames in the high-level map. These indicate that one or more relationships exist between the various major elements of the underlying model.

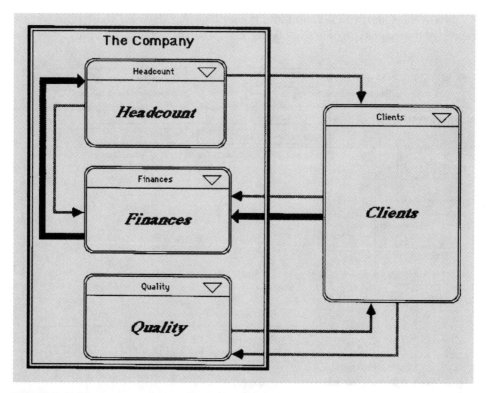

FIGURE 9-9. *Service model high-level map*

Flight Simulator Overview

After opening the model, scroll down the page until your screen looks like the one in Figure 9-10. This is the cockpit, and it is from here that you will fly the company and test your hypotheses about the underlying structure of the system and your decisions about how to control the company's growth.

At the top of the screen are two slider input devices. These devices are directly linked to a corresponding model variable and will allow you to change the values of these variables while you're flying.

1. Click and hold the Hiring slider, and slide it back and forth. As you slide, notice that the value of the slider changes—in this case, changing the current number of people hired per month. Alternately, you can type a number into the box that displays the current value of the slider.

2. Set the value of Hiring back to 10 when you have finished testing the slider.

Below the sliders you will find four numeric display devices. These displays represent the magnitude of active clients, cash reserves, rookies, and pros. They

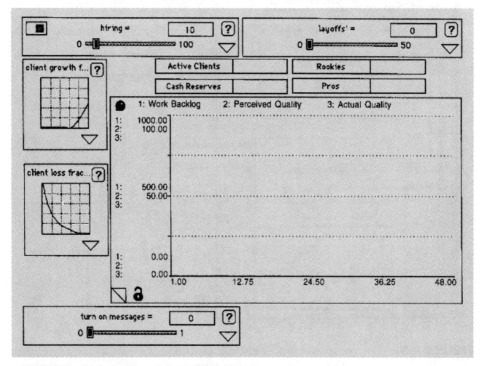

FIGURE 9-10. *Service model cockpit*

will allow you to see the current value of each variable throughout the flight. Below the numeric displays, you see a graph pad that is set up to show you the trend traced by work backlog, actual quality, and perceived quality as the simulation unfolds. Notice the pushpin in the top-left corner of the graph. If you click once on the pin, the graph pad will unpin and become a separate window. While it is unpinned, you can reposition it or resize it (using the resize box in the bottom-right corner).

Be sure to pin the graph pad back down before clicking elsewhere, or it will move behind the active window. (If this does happen, double-click the small square icon labeled Graph Output on the control panel, and the graph will reappear.) Tables and graphs provide the most frequently used ways to view the output of a model. Other alternatives include the numeric display, diagram animation, and QuickTime™ movies. (QuickTime is currently available on the Macintosh only.)

The final devices, on the left side next to the graph, are the graphical function input and display (GFID) devices. These devices show the effect of perceived quality on the fraction of new clients generated by word of mouth and the number of active clients who are lost each month. We will go into more detail about these relationships in a moment.

Simulating the Base Case

Now you are ready to run your first simulation. Make sure all the sliders, the numeric displays, and the graph pad are showing on your screen and be sure the graph pad is pinned.

1. Select Restore under the Map & I/O menu, and then select All Devices. This ensures that the model is set up with a clean slate.

2. Click the Run icon in the lower-left corner of the screen. The Run Controller box shown next will appear. (To move the Run Controller box, click on the top border and then move it to the desired location.)

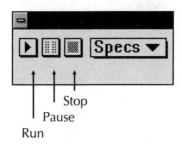

3. Click the Run button in the Run Controller box (or you can choose Run from the Run Menu).

As the model runs, you will see the simulation time below the buttons. The graph will show the pattern that work backlog traces in response to increased customer demand, as well as the perceived quality and actual quality. The graph should appear as in Figure 9-11.

4. Click the box in the top-left corner of the Run Controller to close it.

As the number of active clients increases (one of the numeric displays), work backlog also increases. This leads to increased work hours, which begins to take its toll on the quality of work. The model shows that client perception of quality is generally out of sync with actual quality. As actual quality falls, it takes a while for clients to adjust their perceptions of quality. As the clients' perception of quality declines, the rate at which active clients are lost increases.

The same relationship holds as quality increases. Clients delay in accepting that quality has improved. As their perception of quality improves, the rate at which word of mouth generates new clients slowly increases. ithink is designed expressly to incorporate these types of closed-loop interdependencies. The relationship between these three factors (work backlog, actual quality, and perceived quality) is reflected in the graphical output of the model.

The strength of these interdependencies can be modified in the GFIDs on the left side of the cockpit control panel.

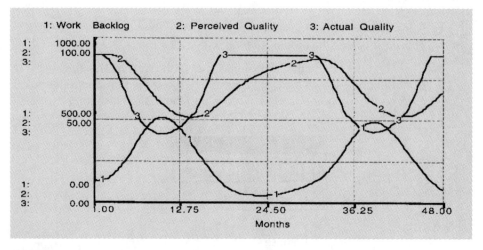

FIGURE 9-11. *Work backlog changes over time*

1. Double-click anywhere on the Client Growth Fraction GFID. A dialog box opens, revealing a curve that shows the assumed relationship between perceived quality, on the x-axis, and client growth fraction, on the y-axis.

   The model calculates the level of perceived quality during the current month. This value then determines the corresponding client growth fraction value for that month. To change the strength of the interdependency, and thus the client growth fraction:

2. Place the cursor inside the grid (the arrow will turn into a cross hair).

3. Click and hold, then move the cursor around. The curve will follow the movements of the cursor (the active points on the grid are on the vertical lines).

4. When you've got the curve you like, click OK.

5. Then run the model again by clicking the Run button in the Run Controller box (or choosing Run from the Run Menu).

   What effect does the change you made in the perceived quality/client growth fraction relationship have on the model behavior? How does a steeper or flatter curve impact the dynamics of work backlog? Try the same experiments with the client loss fraction. When you have completed your experiments,

6. Select Restore from the Map & I/O menu, then select All Devices to restore the original graphical function relationships.

Flying the Company

Now is your chance to try your hand at flying the company. Your goal is to maintain a steady growth in active clients while remaining financially solvent. Use the two sliders to implement your stream of hiring/layoff decisions:

1. Set Hiring to the number of people you want to hire each month.

   All new hires start as rookies and go through a six-month training program. (Keep in mind that there is continuous attrition among pros, so you must hire some each month to replace those who leave—unless you want to reduce headcount.)

2. Set Layoffs to the number of people you want to lay off. This slider resets to 0 after each month.

   If you have any questions about what each slider represents, click on the **?** button near the slider. This opens up a document field that will give you additional information. You will find these **?** buttons on many of the elements on the cockpit control panel, so make full use of them.

REMINDER
Your challenge is to fly the hiring process in such a way as to establish and maintain balanced growth with high quality for the company. In doing so, you should try to understand what is creating the problem. Don't just react! See how well you can do at achieving balanced growth. Good luck!

Before you try your hand at improving things, let's make two quick changes in the way the model runs.

3. First, set the Turn On Messages slider to equal 1. This will enable the software to send you some warnings while you are flying.

4. Second, select Specs on the Run menu, then choose Time Specs. Change the value of the pause interval from INF to 4. This will cause the model to automatically pause every four months, allowing you to make the changes you think will bring the system into balance. (You can pause anytime you want by clicking on the Pause button on the Run Controller, by choosing Pause under the Run menu, or by clicking and holding a slider.)

5. Click OK.

6. Set Hiring and Layoffs to the initial values you desire.

7. Click the Run button to begin the simulation. When the model pauses, make any changes you wish to the values of the sliders.

8. When you have finished making your changes, click on the Run button in the Run Controller box (or choose Resume from the Run menu).

A Last Look from the High-Level Map

Let's take one last look from the high level. Use the scroll bar on the right side of the page to take you up to the very top, so you see the map in Figure 9-9.

1. Click once on the down arrow button on the top-right side of the Clients process frame.

You've now figuratively lifted the hood and you are looking at the engine that has powered your flights. Scroll around and explore the model. In the next section, we are going to show you how to create some of the pieces of this engine. If you want to go back up to the high level,

2. Click the arrow on the sector header (it looks like the one you clicked to get down here except it points upward) and you are there. Alternatively, you can click the up arrow on the left border, and you will be presented with the high-level view.

Once you have completed your experiments with this flight simulator, move on to the next section. There you will learn how to build a model, such as the one used in this exercise.

Building a Model

At the beginning of every modeling effort, it is important to focus your efforts by concentrating on the most important aspects of the system you are interested in understanding. The most important aspects of the management consulting system you experimented with in the previous section are clients, headcount, finance, and quality. We will begin by laying out a high-level map showing these pieces. Then, we will navigate to the diagram layer to build a portion of the related model.

If you still have ithink open to the Service model from the previous exercise:

> Choose Close Model from the File menu, then choose New from the File menu.

Or, if you are just starting:

> Double-click the ithink program icon to open a blank high-level page.

Mapping: The High Level

Using the Process Frame building block (the far-left icon on the toolbar), begin by creating the high-level map shown in Figure 9-12.

1. To place a building block, click on the desired icon in the toolbar and then move the cursor into the worksheet and click again.

HINT
If you hold down the ALT key, the last building block, tool, or object you used will be retained. So, if you hold down the ALT key after placing your first process frame on the screen, you can put down the three remaining process frames without having to return to the toolbar each time. If you make a mistake, use the dynamite tool or choose Clear from the Edit menu.

2. To name the process frames (Headcount, Finances, Quality, and Clients), double-click anywhere in the frame and type the desired name in the Sector Name box.

Now let's explore two aspects of the consulting organization in more detail.

3. Click on the down arrow in the header of the Clients process frame.

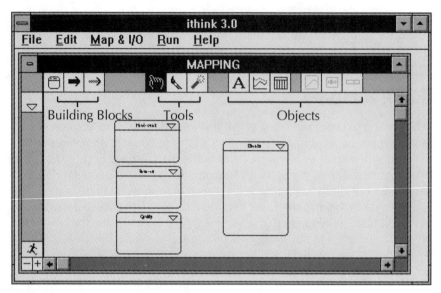

FIGURE 9-12. *The high-level map*

You are now in the model construction or diagramming layer and you are looking at the Clients sector frame, the correspondent diagram-level structure to the high-level Clients process frame. Inside this frame, we will put all of the parts of the model that relate to Clients.

Mapping: The Diagramming Level
Using the building blocks at the far-left side of the diagram-level toolbar, begin creating the map shown in Figure 9-13.

> To move a sector frame, click and hold on the header, then move it to a new position.

> To resize a sector frame, click once to select it (notice the handles that appear at the corners of the frame), then click and hold one of the handles and drag. The sector will resize.

NOTE
Make sure your flow is connected to the stock (there should be only one "cloud") and that you use two connectors. You will know that a flow is connected to another block when the target block is highlighted.

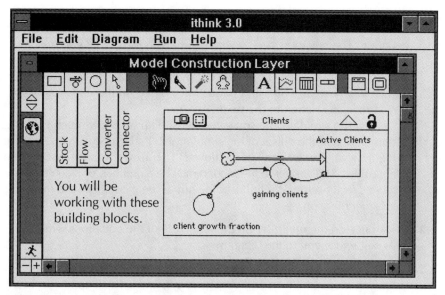

FIGURE 9-13. *Creating a Clients sector*

Modeling: Round 1

Once you've created the simple Clients map, we'll next want to bring the map to life through simulation and animation. To do so, we'll need to enter a few numbers and some relationships. But first, you should note that the ithink software already has given you a big head start in this process. The software automatically creates the equation framework needed to do the basic accounting for whatever system you lay out. This framework is generic, and thus the software can automatically create it for any system—no matter what the context. To take a look at the framework:

1. Click once on the down arrow located just above the Globe icon on the left border of the diagram frame. You should see the equations shown here:

Clients

[?] Active_Clients(t) = Active_Clients(t − dt) + (gaining_clients) * dt
INIT Active_Clients = { Place initial value here... }
INFLOWS:
　　🐟 gaining_clients = { Place right hand side of equation here... }
(?) client_growth_fraction = { Place right hand side of equation here... }

For each accumulation, represented by a stock (a rectangle), and the associated set of flows (pipes with arrows), the software creates a generic equation. The equation says: "What you have now is what you had an instant ago (i.e., 1 unit of time in the past), plus whatever flowed in over the instant minus whatever flowed out over the instant." The software automatically assigns plus and minus signs based on the direction of the flow arrows in relation to the stock.

In order to simulate, the software needs to know "How much is in each accumulation at the outset of the simulation?" It also needs to know "What is the flow volume for each of the flows?" The answer to the first question is a number. The answer to the second may be a number, or it could be an algebraic relationship. We'll illustrate both as we move from the mapping to the modeling phase.

2. Click once on the up arrow on the left frame of the equations window. This will return you to the diagram.

3. Then, click once on the Globe icon. Doing so will shift you into the modeling mode (the icon will change to χ^2), and a **?** will appear in each icon on the diagram. The **?**s indicate the need for information to enable the model to be simulated.

Let's begin by thinking about the dynamics of active client levels. This company has depended almost solely on word of mouth for the generation of new clients. Therefore, an increase in active clients will cause a further increase in active clients. In order to show this dependency in the map, we used the connector to link Active Clients to its own inflow, Gaining Clients.

4. Double-click the Gaining Clients flow regulator (the circle attached to the pipe).

5. Click in the equation (Active Clients * Client Growth Fraction) by clicking on the respective variables in the Required Inputs list. Don't type in the variable names (you might make an error in typing, and ithink makes it unnecessary to do repeat typing, since you've already done it once).

6. Click in the * sign linking the two variables from the Calculator keypad in the dialog box; alternatively, you can type the * sign from your keyboard.

7. When you've established the correct equation, click OK to exit the dialog box. Notice that the **?** no longer appears on the gaining clients flow regulator.

Next, we need to determine an initial value for Active Clients at the beginning of the simulation. Make it 100.

8. Double-click on Active Clients and click in (or type) **100**.

9. Click OK.

Now, to define the client growth fraction let's assume that there are two new clients for every 10 active clients in the stock or a growth fraction of .2.

10. Double-click the Client Growth Fraction converter and click in (or type) **.2**.

11. Click OK to exit the Client Growth Fraction dialog box.

Simulating: Round 1

Now, before we run a simulation of this simple model, we will need a way to view the results. So, let's create a graph. To do so:

1. Click the Run icon to open the Run Controller.

2. Select the Graph Pad icon from the Objects palette on the toolbar.

3. Click once on the diagram to deposit a graph pad in that spot, and then double-click on the resulting blank graph pad page.

4. Since Active Clients is the variable that we want to track, move Active Clients from the Allowable list to the Selected list by highlighting Active Clients and then clicking on the >> arrows between the two lists. Click OK.

5. Click the Run button on the Run Controller (or choose Run from the Run Menu) and watch the graph of Active Clients unfold over time. (If your graph has disappeared behind the diagram, double-click on the Graph 1 icon to bring it forward again.)

The scale for Active Clients should run from 100 to 1040.13. This is not a very clean scale to display your results. So, let's specify a scale for the graph, rather than letting the software automatically set it for us.

1. Double-click anywhere on the graph.

2. Click once on Active Clients in the Selected list.

3. While Active Clients is selected (it should be highlighted), click once on the two-headed arrow to the right of Active Clients.

Horizontal lines will appear above and below the arrow. These lines indicate that you are about to set a local scale (i.e., a floor and ceiling) for the variable. Local means that the scale applies to this graph only. (It is also possible to set a global scale for a variable that will apply to all graphs in the document.) Notice the scale boxes below can now be edited.

4. Type **0** in the Min box and **1500** in the Max box.

5. Click the Set button.

6. Click OK to exit the dialog box—you now should have a new scale for your graph.

If you would like to see a numeric output, you can create a table.

1. Double-click the close box in the upper left corner of the graph pad page to put the graph pad page away.

2. Select the Table Pad icon from the Objects palette. Set it down next to the Graph Pad icon.

3. Double-click the resulting page and enter the Gaining Clients flow and Active Clients stock into the Selected list.

4. Click OK, and click the Run button.

The Table results should show you how ithink is calculating the values for the entities you selected. Close the table when you are finished with the run.

Before we move to the next step in the modeling process, let's take a quick look at the animation capability of the software. There are two types of animation available in ithink. The first is animation of diagram icons. The second is the use of QuickTime movies (available on Macintosh only). We will take a peek at diagram animation here.

1. Choose Diagram Prefs (the last item) under the Diagram menu. Under the word "Animate," you will see three icons.

2. Click each icon once; a square will be drawn around each item successively to indicate animation has been turned on for that particular construct. Before clicking OK, peruse the dialog box. This is where you can add more pages to the diagram, change diagram font types, etc.

3. Click OK.

4. Run the model and watch the diagram elements.

You'll see that the Active Clients accumulation will fill over time. Little needles (like a speedometer) will indicate the volume of flow in the flow regulator associated with gaining clients and the converter called client growth fraction. Icon animation is a good way to get a visual sense for the dynamics of a system.

Modeling: Round 2

Remember the rapid-growth-and-collapse dynamic we are seeking to represent? The graph and table results definitely suggest that there is something missing from this picture. Active Clients is growing exponentially, but there is nothing to check its progress. As a result, there is no collapse to the pattern. In order to generate a collapse, we will need to have some check on active client growth. One obvious check on the growth dynamics is losing clients. Add a Losing Clients flow and a Client Loss fraction with the associated connectors to the diagram to make it look like the map shown in Figure 9-14.

NOTE
To enlarge the sector frame, move the hand over the header until it turns into an arrow. Click once. Notice the handles that appear in the corners. Click and hold any one of the handles and the sector will resize according to where you drag the cursor.

Next we will define the two new entities (losing clients and client loss fraction).

1. Open the losing clients flow and click in Active Clients from the Required Inputs list.

2. Click OK. You will receive a message telling you that you have not used one of the required inputs: Client Loss Fraction.
   With ithink, what you see is what you get. If you have shown a relationship in your map, then the relationship must be included in your equation.

3. Position your cursor in the equation box after Active Clients and click in ***client loss fraction**.

4. Then type + **inventory**.

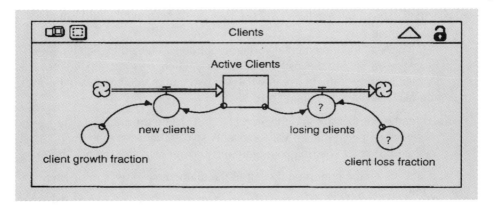

FIGURE 9-14. *The Clients sector*

5. Click OK. You should get another message telling you that inventory is not an object on the diagram.

   It is also true in ithink that what you don't see, you don't get. If you haven't shown the relationship in the map, you can't use it in the equation.

6. Delete "+ inventory." Losing Clients should now equal Active Clients *Client Loss Fraction. Click OK.

7. Set Client Loss Fraction to .02.

Simulating: Round 2

How do you think the addition of a losing clients outflow will alter the pattern traced by Active Clients? To find out, run the model and observe the new behavior on the graph. What you should have seen is that Active Clients continues to grow in an exponential pattern. Even though we have slowed the growth, we have yet to stop it, or to produce the collapse we are seeking.

Perhaps the problem is that the value of client loss fraction that we've chosen is too small. Suppose we want to test various values for client loss fraction to see how they affect the pattern traced by Active Clients. Sensitivity Analysis is ideal for conducting such tests. Sensitivity Analysis enables you to examine the sensitivity of model performance to variations in model parameter values.

1. Choose Sensi Specs from the Run menu.

2. Enter **client loss fraction** into the Selected list within the dialog box.

3. Next, replace the 3 with a 4 in the box labeled # of Runs (in the middle-left side of the dialog box).

4. Click once to select Client Loss Fraction in the Selected list (it should be highlighted).

   Note that the Incremental variation option is selected by default. The incremental option means that, in this case, client loss fraction will be varied incrementally between whatever two values you enter into the Start and End boxes in the dialog box.

5. Enter the number **.02** into the Start box and **.1** into the End box. The software will determine 4 values, evenly spaced between (and including) .02 and .1. After entering your Start and End values, click the Set button.

6. Click the Graph button on the left in the dialog box so we can set up a comparative graph.

7. Enter **Active Clients** into the Selected list within the Graph dialog box. (Note that the Comparative option is checked for Graph Type.)

8. Click OK.

Run the model and watch the four simulations play out on the comparative graph. If you would like to see the parameter values that were used to produce the four curves, click the **?** on the lower left of the graph pad page.

Modeling: Round 3

Still no collapse. So, the problem is not client loss fraction. How can we get our stock of clients to collapse? The answer is that we need to include a relationship, not just change a number. The relationship must either cause the client loss fraction to rise (during the simulation) to exceed the client growth fraction, or cause the client growth fraction to fall to a level below the client loss fraction.

The sensitivity runs indicate that the closer to .1 the client loss fraction came, the less rapidly Active Clients grew. Suppose our model allowed the client loss fraction to increase as the stock of Active Clients increased. Doing so would proxy the effect of a growing client workload on consultants. ithink provides a vehicle for including such relationships. That vehicle is called a "graphical function." Let's incorporate the client/client loss fraction relationship into our model using a graphical function.

1. Draw a connector from Active Clients to Client Loss Fraction.

2. Double-click on Client Loss Fraction.

3. Click once on Active Clients in the Required Inputs list, and then click once on the Become Graph button. A blank grid will appear.

4. Change the default ranges on the x and y axes of the grid to reflect the numbers in the graphical function shown in Figure 9-15. Place your cursor inside the blank grid until it turns into a cross hair. Then, click and hold and drag the mouse around the grid.

A curve will be traced by following your movements. You can try your hand at sketching in the curve you see in Figure 9-15, or alternatively, you can type the numbers into the Output column (use the TAB key to progress through the column). There is no need to reproduce the exact numbers shown in the illustration. Just capture the shape of the relationship.

Simulating: Round 3

Now that you have incorporated the client/client loss fraction relationship into the model using a graphical function, you are ready to run another simulation.

1. When you have entered your Client Loss Fraction curve (remember, this relationship is an input, not a graph of output), click OK.

2. Under the Run menu, choose Sensi Specs. You will get a message telling you the current setup has been changed.

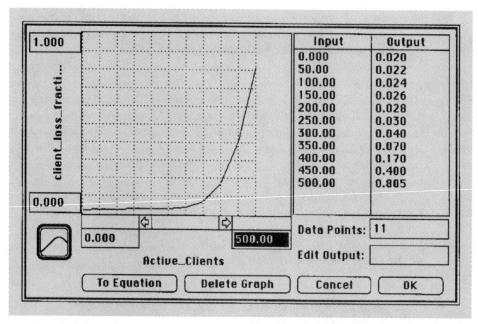

FIGURE 9-15. *Client Loss Fraction as a function of Active Clients*

3. Click OK, then click Cancel in the resulting dialog box.

4. Double-click Graph 1 to open it and run the model.

Active Clients no longer grows forever. However, we have yet to achieve collapse. Instead we have generated a common growth pattern in business: S-shaped growth. To produce this pattern, Client Loss Fraction had to become a variable. You may wish to experiment with alternate patterns for Client Loss Fraction to see if you can cause the system to collapse.

The graphical function enables you to capture complex nonlinear relationships without the need for much mathematical expertise. Many interesting processes in business contain nonlinear relationships. Thus far, we have discovered the relationships that create two growth patterns, but we have yet to produce a collapse. At this point, can you suggest what we need to do to the model in order to generate such a pattern?

What we need to do is cause the client loss fraction to increase above the value of the client growth fraction—not just to rise up and equal it. In order for this to happen, the client loss fraction must depend on some variable other than active clients. In reality, this would be true. Clients are not leaving because of the size of the client base, but because the client base has become too large for the firm to offer quality work given its resources. The client's perception that the quality of your work is low will cause them to go elsewhere for the services you offer. Let's add this quality element to the model.

Modeling: Round 4

To incorporate quality into our model, we need to add more structure to the diagram. Find the sector frame called Quality. It will be on your diagram because we put a corresponding process frame on the high-level mapping layer in the first part of this section.

1. Move the Hand icon over the header until it turns into an arrow.

2. Click and drag the sector over until it is below the Client sector.

Add to your model to make it look like the map shown in Figure 9-16. Make sure you add all the new connectors and delete the connector between Active Clients and Client Loss Fraction.

Now the map tells us that there are two places where there is feedback between clients and quality. The first is that as Active Clients grows, actual quality will be affected. The other feedback relationship is between perceived quality and client loss fraction. In this case, as the perception of quality goes down, clients will

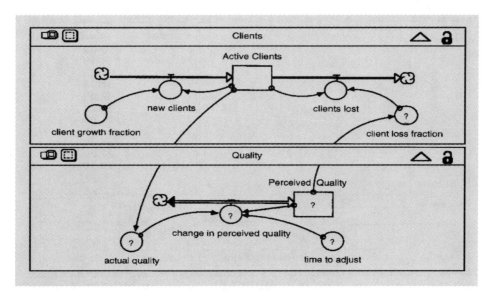

FIGURE 9-16.   *Adding feedback relationships*

leave at a higher rate, and as the perception of quality goes up, clients will leave at a lower rate. Let's take a look at these two feedback relationships.

Notice the connector drawn from Active Clients to Actual Quality. As the number of clients rises, actual quality will go down. This is a great place to use a graphical function to show this relationship.

1. Double-click on Actual Quality and click once on Active Clients from the Required Inputs list.

2. Click once on the Become Graph button and set up the axes and curve to look like the example shown in Figure 9-17. Click OK when you are finished.

The other point of feedback between the sectors is the one from Perceived Quality to Client Loss Fraction. The relationship we want to show in this case is that as the clients' perception of quality decreases, they will begin to leave our stock of Active Clients at a higher rate.

1. Double-click on Client Loss Fraction. Replace Active Clients with Perceived Quality from the Required Inputs list.

2. Click once on the To Graph button. Set up the axes and curve to look like the one in Figure 9-18.

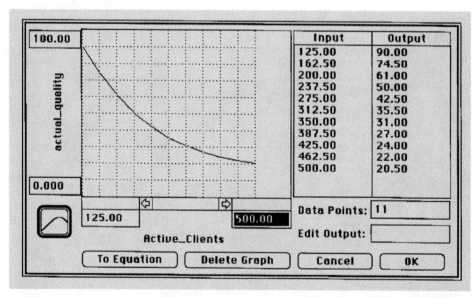

FIGURE 9-17. *A graphical relationship between active clients and actual quality*

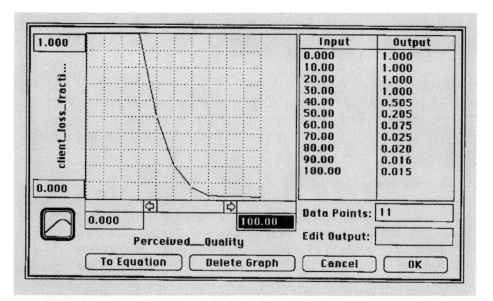

FIGURE 9-18. *A graphical relationship between perceived quality and client loss fraction*

Now let's look at the time to adjust converter. When the quality of your work slips, it will take a while for clients to realize that quality is lower. Conversely, when you improve your quality, it will take clients time to realize it and trust your quality again. To capture that delay in the adjustment of Perceived Quality, we have included the variable time to adjust.

1. Double-click on Time to adjust and set it equal to 5. This means that it takes five months for clients to adjust their perceptions of quality to match actual quality.

2. Double-click on Perceived Quality and set it equal to 90.

3. Now, double-click on the Change In Perceived Quality flow. Look at the Required Inputs list. There should be three things on the list: Perceived Quality, Actual Quality, and Time To Adjust. Enter this equation:

   ((actual quality–Perceived Quality) / time to adjust)

   The first part of the equation will give the difference between actual quality and the clients' perception of quality. Then, by dividing it by Time To Adjust, we will only make a portion of the adjustment between the two each month. This creates a delay in the adjustment.

4. Before you click OK, click the button next to BIFLOW in the top-left corner. This will allow the flow to put quality into the stock, as well as to take it out (or take on a negative value).

Simulating: Round 4

Now we are ready to run the model. Open your graph pad and examine the behavior of Active Clients. Voilà! The collapse! Can you explain why this pattern occurs? You may find it useful to create a graph with other variables on the model to see how they interact.

A Last Look at the High Level

Let's take one last look at the high-level map. Click on the up arrow on the Clients sector to navigate to the high level. Notice that the software has automatically created the bundled connectors (the arrows between process frames) that correspond with the structure we put into the model on the diagram layer. To rearrange them:

1. Click and hold on one of the connectors and drag it to a new location.

2. Double-click on one of the connectors. You will see a list of the connectors between the two process frames that correspond with the direction of the arrow in the bundled connector (in this case there is only one). If we had flows between the sectors, corresponding bundled flows would appear on the high level as well.

From this point, you can expand the model to incorporate Headcount, Finances, or whatever your needs or interests dictate. With a few name changes, this same model could be used to represent many other processes within your business. The experiments that are possible with even a simple model, such as the one explored in this tutorial, are limited only by your imagination and creativity.

When you have finished your experiments with this model, move to the next section where you will be exposed to another interesting feature of ithink: submodels. Submodels allow you to compress model detail to limit visual complexity of the diagram.

Creating Submodels

Submodels allow you to drill down and view additional model structure while maintaining a simple, clean diagram. We will use this method of managing diagram complexity to add detail to the headcount we saw in the first section of this tutorial.

1. If you still have the clients and quality model open on your machine, close it and choose New from the File menu.

2. Click on the down arrow located on the left border of the high-level mapping layer. Doing so will transport you to the diagram layer. Now build the simple headcount map shown here:

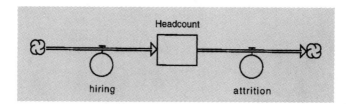

3. Click on the Globe icon to shift into Modeling mode.

4. Double-click on Headcount. Notice the choices along the top border of the dialog box: Reservoir, Conveyor, Queue, Oven. Each of these represents a different type of stock.

5. Click once on the Conveyor button.

6. Click the Submodel check box.

7. Finally, click OK.

What you now see is the Submodel icon with an open submodel space; this is where we will put the drill-down detail associated with Headcount.

Before you add the detail, let's look at a few issues related to having a submodel open on your diagram. First, notice how the items on the diagram have become grayed-out. This has happened because when a submodel is open, you are no longer able to directly interact with items on the diagram. In fact, if you move the cursor to a point outside of the submodel space, it turns into the international prohibition symbol ($\oslash$) to remind you that you are out of bounds.

You can build within the submodel space using the building blocks in the same way that you did on the diagram. However, if you want to perform operations on the standard diagram, you must hold down the CTRL key in order to do so. If you need more room in the submodel space, move the Hand until it is over the border of the submodel space. When it turns into an arrow, click once. Handles will appear in each of the corners of the space so you can resize it to whatever size you desire. If you need to move it, click and hold on the border, then drag to move the entire space.

With the submodel space open, use building blocks to create a map that looks like the one shown in Figure 9-19.

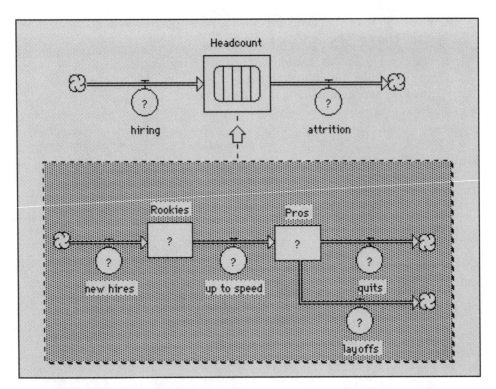

FIGURE 9-19. *A Headcount submodel*

To define the parts of this model, let's review the hiring process for this business. Anytime we hire someone, we put them through a six-month training process. When they complete the training, they become pros. Pros leave the company, either by quitting or by being laid off. One stock type that we can choose is the conveyor. The conveyor works just like the name suggests: things get on it, travel for a period of time, and then get off the other end. Let's use the conveyor to represent the training time for rookies.

1. Double-click on the Rookies stock and click the Conveyor button at the top of the dialog box. Now we have several choices of how to configure the conveyor.

2. Enter **6** into the Transit Time and **60** for the Initial Value. This means that stuff (in this case, employees) will get on and travel for six time periods (in this case, months). The Initial Value will be spread evenly over the six months of the process (ten in each month).

3. Click OK. Notice that the icon has changed to look like a conveyor.

4. Set the initial value of Pros to **100**; set quits equal to **10**; and set layoffs equal to **0**.

Now we need to set up the relationship between the stocks and flows within the submodel and the Submodel icon and flows on the diagram level. First, let's identify the chain of stocks that will "roll up" into the submodel.

1. Hold down the CTRL key and double-click the Submodel icon inside the Headcount stock in the diagram layer. Here you see a list of all the possible choices for roll-up. In our case, there is only one.

2. Click once on the Rookies+Pros line. When the software calculates values for Headcount it will add these two stocks together to yield the number for Headcount.

3. Click OK.

Now for the flows. We need to tell the software what flow rolls down from the Submodel icon inflow into new hires.

1. Double-click on New Hires. Notice that hiring is the only allowable input for this inflow. This is because Hiring is the only inflow to the Submodel icon.

2. Click once on Hiring. Then click OK. A special symbol has been added to the Submodel inflow and its name has been changed to Hiring to show that it is equal to the Hiring inflow which appears on the diagram layer.
Now we need to determine what outflows on the submodel layer roll-up into the outflow called Attrition on the diagram layer. In this case, there are two roll-up outflows: Quits and Layoffs.

3. Hold down the CTRL key and double-click on the Attrition outflow on the diagram layer. Notice that both Quits and Layoffs appear on the Allowable Inputs list. (If they don't appear on this list, check to be sure the flows are connected to the stocks.)

4. Click once on each of them—now they are rolled-up into the Attrition outflow from Headcount.

5. Click OK. Notice that the names have changed in the submodel.

Did you notice that when we changed Rookies to a conveyor, the **?** in the up-to-speed flow was extinguished? This is because the flow will equal the amount getting off the conveyor each month. You have no control over this.

That leaves only the hiring flow to define. Let's assume that we will replace each person who quits by hiring a new person.

1. Draw a connector from the Attrition flow that was quits in the submodel space to hiring on the diagram level. You won't have to hold down the CTRL key to do this.

2. Hold down the CTRL key, double-click on the Hiring flow, click once on Attrition from the Required Inputs list.

3. Click OK.

4. To close the submodel space, click once on the up arrow below the Submodel icon. This will retract the space. To open it up again, double-click the Submodel icon.

Simulating

Now create a graph and table of Headcount and run a simulation. We set this model up in "steady-state," so you should see a very flat Headcount. There is another way to see the numbers of the diagram entities as the model runs without a full table. Let's use the numeric display device to do this.

With the submodel closed:

1. Click once on the Numeric Display device in the Objects palette.

2. Click again to place the display below the Headcount submodel icon (click and hold to move it around after you deposit it).

3. Double-click on the numeric display and a dialog box will appear that will have a list of all entities in the model. Move Headcount from the Allowable list to the Selected list using the >> button.

4. Click the box next to Show Name to deselect it. This way you will only see the number, not the entity name.

5. Click OK and create any other numeric displays you are interested in seeing.

6. Run the model. Now you can verify that the model is in steady state.

Next, we'll send a shock through the system and see how it will respond.

1. Open the submodel and then double-click on the Attrition flow that was Quits.

2. Click once after the 10 in the equation box and click in a + sign.

3. Now, scroll down the Built-ins list on the right side of the dialog box until you see STEP. (These built-ins are similar to the functions you would find in a spreadsheet.) Click once on STEP.

4. Click OK. Along the bottom of the dialog box you will get online help to tell you what information you need to enter into the STEP built-in.

5. Type or click in **STEP(5,4)** in the equation box. This means that Quits will step up by five at month four. The whole equation should read:

   10+STEP(5,4).

6. Click OK. Create a new page on the graph with Pros on it.

Before you run the simulation, make a guess as to how you think the stock of Pros will respond to the step-increase in attrition. Then you can go on to run your own experiments using the model.

NOTE
Each entity on the diagram level has two locations—one when any submodel is open, and one when all submodels are closed. ithink permits a second position so that you can move diagram entities around so they won't lie directly under a submodel space. Try putting some new structure on the diagram where the submodel space will fall when opened. Then, open the submodel. With the submodel open, hold down the CTRL key, and click and hold on the new structure. Then move it out from under the submodel mat. Now, click on the roll-up arrow at the top of the submodel space. When the submodel is closed, all the diagram entities you moved while it was open, should return to where they were before you opened the submodel.

Another method of managing diagram complexity is the space compression object. If you want to compress a portion of the model structure, click once on the space compression object in the objects palette, then click on the diagram to deposit it. The result will be an object that looks similar to the Submodel icon. The space compression object works just like the submodel, and is useful when you don't have any flows to roll-up and roll-down.

Conclusion

The ithink software facilitates a shift from a down-in-the-weeds perspective to a stepped-back perspective that enables participants involved in examinations of business systems to view those systems as parts of a larger whole. Since locally implemented process change usually creates problems elsewhere within the system, any reengineering change must consider impacts on the entire system in order to be effective.

The higher-level perspective supported by ithink also facilitates top-down analysis. This approach, contrasted with a bottom-up approach implicit in many reengineering methodologies, maximizes the resources applied to a reengineering effort. The systems perspective helps reengineering teams to discover high-leverage intervention points within the system by focusing initial effort on understanding the entire, end-to-end system. Only where analysis suggests additional information is required will the team apply resources to drilling down into the details.

Whether staying at the high level or selectively proceeding down to a lower level, the ithink software gives reengineering team members a framework or a language with which to articulate their understanding of how the system under study really works. The process of articulating that understanding promotes a valuable dialogue among stakeholders from across the enterprise. That communication, facilitated by the software itself, enhances the understanding of the underlying structural relationships that drive the system. This understanding is essential before engaging the enterprise in a reengineering initiative.

Used as part of the three-step approach to successful reengineering outlined earlier in the chapter, ithink can help in creating an experience of why change is needed, what the nature of the change will be, and how to best get from where you are to where you want to be. The ability to create "What-if" scenarios and engage in improvement initiatives with relatively low risk not only enables users to increase organizational learning, but it also contributes to the overall success of a reengineering effort.

CHAPTER 10

Beyond Guesswork and Speculation: Dynamic Modeling for Reengineering

by Pat Diamond
Imagine That, Inc.

Your company's future depends on finding ways to get new products to market more quickly and at less cost while increasing customer satisfaction with your existing products and services. Yet cost reduction and quality improvement are not sufficient to achieve greater market share. To be successful, your organization must also be able to quickly develop and provide innovative new products and services.

One of the major factors keeping companies from being innovative and optimally productive is the outdated and duplicative state of their business processes. Few companies take full advantage of the technological innovations of the past 20 years, and most business processes reflect that. Where technology has been implemented, redundant processes have often been left in place without meaningful change. As Michael Hammer and James Champy assert in *Reengineering the Corporation*, "America's business problem is that it is entering the twenty-first century with companies designed during the nineteenth century." This results in higher production costs, excessive delays in converting sales orders into cash receipts, increased customer dissatisfaction, and a slower response to changing market conditions.

Given the need to make informed decisions and the drive to optimize operations, business managers, analysts, and consultants can benefit from technologically advanced computer tools and structured methods to analyze and redesign processes. This is commonly known as business process reengineering or BPR. One of the primary tools for reengineering business processes is dynamic modeling, which provides the framework and structured approach needed to determine *what* should be changed and *how* it should be changed.

Dynamic modeling allows you to capture the essence of very complicated systems in a computer model, then play "What-if" games to compare alternative futures (system performance under various scenarios) and measure the effect of the decisions you make. It points out areas most in need of change and encourages the prioritization of improvement possibilities. It lets employees see their ideas in action and makes it easier to demonstrate to managers the impact of proposed changes. Dynamic modeling is most commonly used when exploring alternatives for systems and processes that are complex, involve uncertainty, and have limited resources. Since most business processes meet that profile, dynamic modeling is the tool of choice for examining the results of proposed changes when improving or redesigning business processes.

This chapter is organized into three sections. The first section tells why business processes need to be analyzed and reengineered and discusses current practices, tools, and requirements. The second section shows how to use the dynamic modeling tool Extend+BPR. The final section provides examples of business applications using Extend+BPR.

The Need for Change

The challenge to every business is that in order to succeed, it must improve. There are many definitions of what improvement for a business might be: growth in income, increased profits, reduction of debt, or any other measurement factor. Since the need for improvement is so pervasive, one might assume it is a given. The reality is that determining *how* to improve a business is the subject of endless debate in management circles. The main thrust of corporate management has traditionally been to increase profits through piecemeal changes in operations. More recently, an emphasis has been put on such concepts as continuous improvement, total quality management, systems thinking, and the development of people within the organization. But these are philosophical approaches to the problem, and business philosophies have changed constantly in response to their failure to resolve the underlying problems.

In their quest for improvement, organizations are faced with such questions as:

> ➤ Should we automate?

> ➤ Can we improve the way we do business?

> ➤ How much do our processes actually cost?

> ➤ How can we reduce time-to-market?

Considering the rapidly changing global economy and the struggle to remain competitive, the answers to these questions and others like them are more important than ever. These answers cannot be found through philosophical methods. If they could, we would have stopped seeing new theories of management long ago.

Recently, attention has focused on redesigning business processes to make them more efficient and to serve as a basis for the insertion of new technology. Business processes provide an excellent opportunity for organizations to improve, since improvements in process throughput and productivity can add considerably to a company's bottom line.

Business Processes, Events, and Elements

Although businesses have traditionally been discussed in terms of functional units (for example, accounting, manufacturing, or human resources), they are actually composed of processes. *Business processes* are a series of logically related tasks undertaken to achieve a specified outcome, typically either a product or a service. Processes represent how organizations actually work. They are complete cycles, such as:

> ➤ New product development (concept origination, research, and prototype creation)

> ➤ Product flow (purchasing, receiving, and manufacturing)

> ➤ Customer acquisition (marketing, customer inquiry, and resolution)

> ➤ Product turnover (order entry, delivery, and billing)

> ➤ Employee acquisition (hiring, training/promotion, and firing)

In business, most processes are organized around events, such as the receipt of an order, a request to purchase equipment, or an idea for a new product. Events occur at random but somewhat predictable intervals. They can be economic or noneconomic. Events drive the business.

Each process is a combination of elements (people, procedures, technology, materials, equipment, information, space, and energy) involved in an activity to achieve a goal. Business processes therefore represent the utilization and flow of elements, driven by events. Some examples of business processes, a typical event that might drive them, and an element that flows through or is consumed by the process are shown in Table 10-1.

Current Practices

While an exact analysis of the state of business processes is difficult to come by, recent work performed by the Software Engineering Institute (SEI) at Carnegie Mellon University provides some insight. The SEI has determined that software development processes can be categorized into one of five levels of maturity depending on their effectiveness, with "chaos" being level 1 and "optimized" being level 5. A study of software development processes conducted by the SEI over a four-year period indicated that, of the organizations studied, 81 percent were at process maturity level 1, while another 12 percent were at process maturity level 2.

In level 1, processes have evolved through the addition of components, procedures are not documented, participants lack an overall understanding of the process, results are variable, and the mechanisms used to create a product or provide a service change frequently. In such a situation, the quality of the end product, time to completion, and costs of production are likely to be volatile.

PROCESS	EVENT	ELEMENT
Developing a new product	A new product idea	Prototype
Creating a marketing plan	New product is being planned	Marketing plan
Processing an insurance claim	Claim is received	Claim
Hiring and training employees	Company wins contract	Employees
Providing customer support	Customer contacts company	Customer inquiry
Writing a proposal for a contract	Request for proposal is received	Proposal
Approving a loan	Customer submits application	Credit application

TABLE 10-1. *Business Processes, Events, and Elements*

In level 2, processes are repeatable, procedures are documented, and the quality of products produced is predictable. However, processes have not been defined enough to show how the process flows or the conditions under which certain process paths are taken, and the quality of the product is probably not high.

This means that a total of 93 percent of the companies in the SEI study conducted their main business in an environment where tasks and processes had not been formally defined or documented and where participants in process tasks lacked an understanding of how their tasks related to the overall process.

Extrapolating these results to businesses in general indicates that business processes in most organizations are not optimized and in fact are probably hindering the organization's achievement of its goals. The concept of "Do it right the first time or it will take twice as long to get it right the second time" applies as well to business processes as it does to engineering systems. In fact, for optimization and efficiency, the processes of a business should be analyzed and engineered in much the same manner as the products that the business was created to sell. Once processes have been optimized, the organization will have the structures in place to achieve its goals.

Why Not Just Automate?

Automating processes using information technology is known as *technology insertion.* For example, electronic funds transfer, imaging systems, client/server networking, electronic data exchange, and E-mail are examples of how technology is used to automate processes. Technology insertion can be a cure for poor process performance. However, there are two problems with how most organizations apply technology: the insertion of technology is often done in a vacuum, without sufficient data to support whether the automation will improve the process or not; and automating a process may not speed up the system as a whole. In other words, even if automation is the correct way to improve a particular process, it may have little effect if the entire system is not improved to account for those changes. For an example, see the "Documentation Revision Model" later in this chapter.

Technology applied to ineffective processes will be ineffective. The current Information Age has not had the expected impact on business operations, since applying technology has typically meant merely automating or speeding up *existing* processes rather than improving them. It has been estimated that of the $3 trillion U.S. corporations have spent on information technology in the past decade, about $1 trillion has been wasted since it has not had the desired effect. To be improved, processes need to be analyzed and redesigned, rather than just automated.

Why Continuous Improvement Isn't Enough

Most business processes were developed before modern computers and communication systems existed. As the Industrial Age progressed, systems and rules (both documented and undocumented) changed in response to the situations encountered. Instead of being designed using a structured, engineered approach, processes have mutated.

Change does not always equal improvement. And changing a process, while it might improve the process, may not improve overall performance. Continuously improving existing processes means that companies are often doing better what should never have been done at all (to paraphrase Peter Drucker). The problem is that while processes might be improved, they were never engineered in the first place.

Continuous improvement is only appropriate for processes that are already operating reasonably effectively in a stable environment. Inefficient processes, processes that are ad hoc or that have mutated to a point where procedures are performed because "that's the way we do it," must be redesigned from the ground up. To optimize processes, to make them as efficient and effective as they can be, means that the processes have to be *reengineered*, not just improved. This is the core of business process reengineering.

Business Process Reengineering

Although business process reengineering (BPR) is a fairly new term (first coined by Hammer in 1990), it is not a new practice. The term BPR encapsulates the structured, analytical practices that have been used by many companies to redesign their processes to eliminate built-up redundancy and take advantage of current technology. BPR is the analysis and redesign of business processes. Organizations that are reengineering their processes need to answer questions about how they do work: what they do, why they do it, what it costs, how it can be changed, and what the effects of changes will be.

What BPR Isn't

As mentioned earlier, reengineering is not just automating and it is not continuous improvement. It is also not restructuring or downsizing. Downsizing is a current response to current conditions. According to Hammer and Champy, "Downsizing and restructuring only mean doing less with less. Reengineering, by contrast, means doing *more* with less." Reengineering is not the same as reorganizing or flattening the organization, since reengineering deals with *process* structure, not with organizational structures.

Total quality management (TQM) is not the same as reengineering. Quality programs are based on a company's existing processes, and TQM seeks improvement in quality through continuous incremental improvement. Reengineering, on the other hand, seeks to redesign processes from the ground up.

BPR is also not Systems Thinking. According to Peter Senge, Systems Thinking is the "fifth discipline" that integrates the disciplines of working with mental models, building a shared vision, team learning, and personal mastery. Systems Thinking utilizes Systems Dynamics, a modeling methodology developed by Jay Forrester approximately 35 years ago as a method of examining public policy issues. While Systems Thinking can be an adjunct to the reengineering process (for example, to help identify goals and set policies), it works only at the highest levels (the "bird's-eye view"). Process reengineering requires that processes be redesigned from the ground up. Before you implement changes in a process, you need to evaluate the quality of those changes and their impact on the process. You have to be able to drill down into the system components and look at the detail of the individual interactions of the process elements. Only then can you evaluate the effects of implementing policies and determine staffing levels, equipment justifications, and whether automation would benefit the process.

BPR is not a philosophy, it is not a talking solution, nor is it a quick fix. While communication is an important aspect of BPR, talking about processes and process changes is not the solution. BPR requires more than just talk, it requires *work*. At its most basic level, BPR is about starting over—discarding existing processes and replacing them with new ones. BPR requires the use of tools and techniques, combined with enabling technologies such as automation, to make changes throughout an organization. And it takes time and commitment: The successful procurement process reengineering efforts at Ford are often cited, but seldom mentioned is the fact that it took approximately five years to implement the associated changes.

Steps in the Reengineering Process

To reengineer its processes, an organization should follow these steps:

1. **Develop a Business Vision and Objective** Prioritize objectives and evaluate the organization's capacity for change.

2. **Understand the Existing Process** Dynamically model and measure the current system to provide a baseline and determine where problems lie.

3. **Identify Processes to Redesign** Focus on areas that are critical and have the most possibility for change.

4. **Identify Information Technology Opportunities** Brainstorm and simulate to determine where automation can appropriately be inserted.

5. **Design and Prototype a New Process** Redesign and streamline operations so that processes are integrated and workflow is simplified and accelerated. Then dynamically model the new process to determine its effects on performance measurements.

Process Reengineering Goals

As indicated earlier, business process reengineering is a structured approach that relies on dynamic modeling and performance measurement to determine which processes should be reengineered and to determine if proposed changes will have a productive impact.

The key performance goals, which measure whether processes are optimized, are:

➢ Decrease cycle-time to bring it into alignment with customers' needs

➢ Decrease costs and increase profits

➢ Manage throughput based on customer requirements

➢ Increase productivity and utilization of resources

Meeting these performance goals can result in significant changes in a company's financial picture.

To achieve their goals, organizations need to change their existing processes to:

➢ Eliminate nonessential steps

➢ Implement and insert technology where appropriate

➢ Improve workflow to emphasize value-adding functions

➢ Provide measurements and metrics for meaningful analysis and strategic planning

Traditional Process Reengineering Tools

The greatest opportunity a manager gets to establish a process that works correctly and efficiently occurs when the process is being designed or reengineered. At those stages, features can be evaluated to determine which process design is best in terms of functionality, cost, simplicity, and so forth. When making decisions regarding process design and changes, managers and analysts have traditionally relied on mental models, process mapping, and spreadsheet models.

Mental Models

Mental models are adequate only when proposed changes are minimal or when the impact of any change is obvious. However, most business processes are too complex and too strategic to be analyzed just by thinking about them. For instance, while a process with two variables will have four possible change scenarios, a process with three variables has at least eight scenarios. And a process with ten variables has 1,024 possible outcomes! Given those numbers, an attempt to mentally explore all alternatives is bound to fail.

As an example of how mental models are inadequate, consider this question: If a customer comes into a bank every 2 minutes on the average, and if it takes an average of 1.9 minutes for one teller to process each customer's transaction, what is the expected length of the waiting line at the end of an eight-hour day? (The answer can be found at the end of this section.)

Process Mapping

Process maps and flowcharts pictorially show process components and flows. They are fine for identifying the factors that influence a process and for giving a general idea of how a process flows, but they are not reliable as the primary mechanism for investigating changes to processes. Process maps cannot show the results of constraints on resources or the savings in throughput time caused by parallel processing. Moreover, when you make changes to a process, you affect how the process works, but this will not necessarily affect what the process flow looks like.

For example, hiring another order entry clerk should increase the number of orders processed, but it will not alter the physical flow of paperwork from mail room to order entry department. The behavioral view of a process (how it works) is much more important than the functional view (what the flow looks like) for predicting the effects of changes, and process maps do not show the underlying behaviors of their components.

Figure 10-1 shows two flow diagrams, each showing a process that consists of four tasks, pictured in sequence from left to right. Each task takes an average of 2 minutes, with a buffer or queue between two of the tasks. Which is the most efficient process in terms of throughput? (The answer can be found at the end of this section.)

Spreadsheets

Spreadsheets are useful for predicting possible outcomes based on initial conditions and percentage of expected change. But spreadsheet predictions are static and linear, and the future is never just an extrapolation of the past. Spreadsheets do not deal adequately with business complexities, such as circular relationships, feedback loops, resource constraints, or nonlinear interdependencies. In particular, spreadsheets cannot reflect time-based events: spreadsheets show a snapshot of a

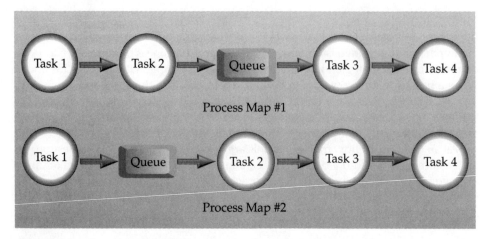

FIGURE 10-1. *Process maps*

process at one point in time when what is really needed is a movie showing how the process responds to changing conditions.

Recently, hybrid tools that combine the functionality of spreadsheets with the visual representation of flowcharts have appeared. While they may be important in the future, these tools have not yet reached maturity. Although their visual paradigm is an improvement over spreadsheets by themselves, hybrid tools still retain the shortcomings of process maps and spreadsheets: they do not adequately reflect resource limitations, parallel process effects, or the effect of changes over time when there is feedback.

Mental models, process maps, and spreadsheets provide a basis for understanding processes but by themselves are not fully adequate for designing or reengineering business processes.

Modeling and Simulation

Business process reengineering requires companies to look at their fundamental operations from a cross-functional perspective and ask "Why?" and "What if?" The objective is to simplify workflow so that the functions within each process are optimized.

Reengineering is a complex undertaking, and sophisticated tools are needed to analyze, visualize, redesign, and document business processes. For most classes of

Answers to the Mental Model and Process Map Questions Posed Earlier

Mental Model Answer

The expected length of the line at the end of the day is approximately 11. If we hadn't implied that there was a line, wouldn't you have guessed that there would be no line? However, the question specified that the times given were <u>averages</u>. The results should be calculated not by using 2 minutes and 1.9 minutes as the exact times, but by using them as the average or mean of a random distribution. The actual line length of 11 can be determined by dynamically modeling the process for a simulated 8 hours using exponential distributions with means of 2 and 1.9 for the arrival and process times, respectively.

Process Map Answer

The most efficient system is process number 1. The throughput of any process is dependent on the slowest task in the process. Because there is no space for items to accumulate between tasks, a higher number of closely-coupled tasks in a segment will be less efficient. The queue acts as a separator between task segments. By putting the queue between the second and third tasks, the process is effectively divided into two task segments each containing two coupled tasks. If the queue were placed between the first and second tasks, the resulting system could be viewed as a single task followed by three closely-coupled tasks. Three closely-coupled tasks will operate less efficiently than two closely-coupled tasks.

business problems, dynamic modeling is required to model both the "as is" and "to be" scenarios and to provide the metrics for effective decision making.

Modeling Defined

A model is a representation of a system. Instead of interacting with the real system, you can create a model that corresponds to it in certain aspects. For example, the board game "Monopoly" is a model of a real system—the hotels and facilities of Atlantic City. You might use modeling to:

> Predict the course and results of alternative courses of action

> Understand why observed events occur

➤ Pinpoint problem areas before implementing changes

➤ Evaluate ideas and identify inefficiencies

➤ Gain insight and stimulate creative thinking

➤ Communicate the integrity and feasibility of plans

Models enable you to test hypotheses at a fraction of the cost of actually undertaking the activities that the models represent. For example, modeling is usually a lot less expensive and less time-consuming than building a pilot process. In addition, the modeling process itself is beneficial: it is generally acknowledged that about 50 percent of the benefit of a modeling project derives from the efforts expended before modeling begins (gathering data, posing questions, understanding processes, etc.).

Models are typically either static or dynamic. *Static models* describe a system mathematically, in terms of equations, where the potential effect of each alternative is ascertained by a single computation of the equation. The variables used in the computations are averages and the performance of the system is determined by summing individual effects. Static models assume linearity and ignore time-based variances. For example, they cannot be used to determine the impact of *when* something occurs in relation to other incidents. Also, static models do not take into account the synergy of the components of the system, where the actions of separate elements can have a different effect on the total system than the sum of their individual effects would indicate.

Dynamic modeling (also known as *simulation*) is a software representation of the dynamic or time-based behavior of a system. Andy Siprelle has defined a dynamic model as

> ... a conceptual "black box" which consists of a structure and various inputs and outputs. The inputs consist of one or more initial conditions, accounting relationships, decision rules, variables, and random numbers. When the dynamic model is run (simulated) it produces output data for analysis.

Where a static model involves a single computation of an equation, dynamic modeling is iterative, causing the equations to be computed over and over based on time.

Dynamic Modeling

Dynamic models provide the intelligence and consistency necessary for an effective reengineering effort. Dynamic modeling can predict the outcomes of possible courses of action and can account for the effects of variances or randomness. You cannot control the occurrence of random events; you can, however, use dynamic modeling to predict the likelihood and the consequences of their occurring.

A good dynamic modeling tool is flexible enough that models can be tailored to fit a specific industry, company, or project. It should provide benchmark figures for comparing current "as is" processes to future "to be" processes, allow you to explore alternative approaches, and help you determine how resources can be prudently used and how non value-added tasks can be eliminated.

There are many dynamic modeling programs, ranging from general purpose to specialized applications (such as for control systems modeling). Dynamic modeling tools are typically classified as either continuous, discrete event, or combined.

Continuous Models

A continuous model views a system as an uninterrupted flow of homogeneous "stuff." For example, a constant stream of fluid passing in a pipe, the raising or lowering of water temperature in a lake, or a chemical conversion are continuous flows. Continuous models involve a rate of change over time (delta time, or dt). In continuous models, values change based directly on changes in time and time changes in fixed and equal increments. Some examples of popular continuous modeling software applications are: Dynamo, TUTSIM, and VisSim (distributed by Pugh-Roberts Associates, Inc., Tutsim Products, and Visual Solutions, respectively). Systems Dynamics, discussed earlier, is a subset of continuous modeling that uses differential equations and a stock-flow-converter paradigm to represent continuous systems. PowerSim and ithink (distributed by MicroWorlds, Inc. and High Performance Systems, Inc., respectively) are typical Systems Dynamics software applications.

Discrete Event Models

Discrete event modeling differs from continuous modeling both in how it represents time (in discrete increments, not continuously) and in how it deals with what is being modeled (individual items, not homogeneous stuff). For example, orders arriving, parts being assembled, and customers calling are examples of discrete events. In discrete event models, things happen in the model only when an event occurs. Since events happen at random intervals, the time between events is not equal. Discrete event modeling also considers its elements to be individual, discrete entities. This means that you can specify the experience level of different groups of employees, track parts by type, or route sales orders to specific departments depending on whether the customer wants custom or standard products. Some well-known discrete event modeling software applications are GPSS/H, SERVICE MODEL, and SIMSCRIPT II.5 (distributed by Wolverine Software Corporation, Promodel Corporation, and CACI, respectively).

Combined Models

Combined discrete event and continuous applications can model systems either discretely or continuously. These hybrid applications combine all the features of continuous and discrete event modeling. This is an important advantage, since some systems lend themselves more easily to one type of modeling than the other. Some combined modeling applications are: Extend, Siman, and SLAMSystem (by Imagine That, Inc., Systems Modeling Corporation, and Pritsker Corporation, respectively).

Characteristics of a Dynamic Modeling BPR Tool

A useful dynamic model has a high correlation with and a strong relationship to both business objectives and business processes. The model should help you make decisions that will result in a better quality product at a lower cost or faster service with fewer complaints. Usually, this correlation is indicated by a specific measurable goal, such as increased throughput or cost reduction. For example, consider a dynamic model of orders arriving and being processed by workers who are interrupted by the telephone. The model can show you what might happen if you were to have fewer or more people to process the orders, if there were more telephone lines to answer, or if the workers could do other tasks when there were no orders to process and the phones were not busy. By examining the throughput (the number of orders processed), you can determine which strategy works best.

To be an effective BPR tool, a dynamic modeling application should offer the following capabilities and features.

Visual Paradigm with a Behavioral Approach

A dynamic modeling tool should have a customizable iconic interface. This provides a functional view of the process, graphically showing where the process flows, what is happening, and what is being produced. The more customizable the interface, the better, since communication of ideas is greatly enhanced if viewers can directly relate to what they see. The tool should also integrate process behavior with the iconic view. An example is a block-diagram approach, where the icon of the block looks like a process component and the block behaves the way the process or process component behaves.

Process Animation and Reporting

The modeling tool should enable visualization of workflows and automatically provide process information. It should visually and numerically identify bottlenecks, trace paths, and interactively report "out of tolerance" conditions. Ideally, the tool should support visual comparisons between "as is" and "to be" model parameters.

Hierarchy

Hierarchy, or the ability to nest subprocesses within higher-level processes, is essential for communication. Processes are composed of a series of logically related tasks, all of which must be represented in the model. To be effective as communication tools, business models should support the hiding and revealing of model complexities.

Sensitivity Analysis

It is essential that the tool have the capability to compare and contrast multiple scenarios to determine how a change in one parameter affects the system as a whole. This sensitivity analysis feature must include the ability to explicitly specify individual parameters that should be changed and to provide a menu of methods for changing them.

Ability to Uniquely Specify Process Elements

An effective tool must be able to uniquely identify process elements (people, procedures, materials, equipment, etc.). In addition, there must be a mechanism for attaching characteristics such as priorities, costs, types, and other values (collectively known as *attributes*) to the various process elements. Attributes are essential in order to specify, route, and track individual elements as they move through the process. This allows the model to examine the characteristics and history of each element and make decisions based on that. For example, you may need to be able to classify workers by type or experience level, characterize a procedure by level of difficulty, or select equipment based on particular capabilities. Since this information is often required throughout the model, allocating a percentage using random values is not sufficient.

Representation of Activities, Queues, and Batching

Business processes are a combination of elements (people, procedures, materials, equipment, information, space, and energy) involved in an activity to achieve a goal. It is important that a BPR tool show elements involved in activities, queued in waiting lines, combining with other elements, and being delayed.

Timing That Corresponds to Real-World Events

In business, most processes are organized around events, such as the receipt of an order, a request to purchase equipment, or an idea for a new product. Although somewhat predictable, events seldom occur at regular intervals; instead, the time between events is most often random and unequal. Moreover, processes take variable amounts of time, from fractions of seconds to months or years. It is important to be able to represent unequal time intervals and noninteger processing times.

Interruptible Processes That Run in Parallel or Serially

One of the major methods used to reengineer processes is to design processes to run in parallel to speed up the end result. Moreover, since the processes involved are usually dependent on some resource, a BPR tool must be able to simulate the situation where a process is interrupted if sufficient resources are not available.

Connectivity

An effective BPR tool must be able to get data from outside the application and send data to other applications. Due to the speed limitations of importing and exporting, the ability to read and write data files is a must.

Object Orientation

An object-oriented tool should be modular, extensible, and reusable:

> ➤ A *modular* approach makes model building easier, since users can start with a small approximation of a system, then add to it to expand and refine the model. Modularity allows for "smart process" blocks—modules that have preprogrammed behavior corresponding to how processes and process elements actually work. This makes model building easier since there is no need to enter equations or to program.

> ➤ A tool should provide all of the necessary components to model most business processes. For situations that fall outside of the usual, the tool must be capable of being *extended*, either through an internal language or through calls to external code, but preferably through both. The tool should have an open architecture that allows for the modification of block icons, behavior, and input/output channels.

> ➤ Once something has been designed, completed, and tested, it makes sense to want to use it again in a similar situation. An object-oriented tool supports the *reuse* of its components.

A dynamic modeling application that offers the capabilities and features outlined earlier represents an effective BPR tool that will allow the user to concentrate on modeling and modifying business processes rather than trying to apply the most recent business philosophy to existing practices.

Extend+BPR

Extend+BPR provides an object-oriented environment for dynamically modeling, analyzing, reengineering, and documenting business processes. Its iconic building-block paradigm facilitates communication and is designed to allow users to concentrate on the *process* rather than on any particular methodology.

Since most business systems are composed of real-world elements that interact when specific events occur, Extend+BPR simulates those systems using blocks that mimic business processes and timing that represents the actual occurrence of events. The Extend+BPR blocks directly correspond to the activities, queues, delays, and transformations that comprise business processes. BPR blocks also incorporate high-level reengineering concepts such as batching, cycle timing, and conditional routing.

Extend+BPR can help answer questions about business processes. You can use it to state the questions, build a model using familiar flowcharting icons, run the simulation over time, and analyze the results. Then you can change aspects of the model and run it again to perform "What-if" analysis. This modeling allows you to predict the value, effectiveness, and cost of implementing proposed changes, and it serves as a basis for developing a strategy that will get your organization "from here to there."

Features of Extend+BPR

By comparing Extend+BPR's features to the requirements discussed in the section "Characteristics of a Dynamic Modeling BPR Tool," you will see that it provides the industrial-strength capabilities a dynamic BPR modeling application should offer:

➤ A built-in library of "smart process" blocks which provide an easily recognizable general process model yet can be customized to resemble any specific process.

➤ Customizable animation and reporting, including automatic calculation of critical measurements. Extend's integrated authoring environment includes interactive controls and the ability to prompt users based on a wide range of factors.

➤ Hierarchical modeling in multiple layers "from the ground up" or "top down". Users can easily add custom icons and animation to hierarchical blocks.

➤ Menu-driven sensitivity analysis for investigating the effects of changes in a structured, controlled manner. Output is to graphs, tables, and customized reports.

➤ Extend views each process element as a unique entity (called an *item* in Extend), which can be separately identified and routed. Attributes can be attached to any item in the system, tracked throughout the model, and interrogated at any point.

➤ Blocks that directly correspond to the activities, queues, delays, and transformations that comprise business processes. Support for *and* conditions (batching), such as a purchase request requiring both a supervisor's *and* a manager's approval.

➤ Timing that advances automatically according to when events occur. Processing times can be statistically or dynamically set to any value to correspond to real-world operations.

➤ Because elements in Extend+BPR are unique entities, they can run in parallel or serially, with dramatically different results (corresponding to the real world). In addition, processes are interruptible either interactively or based on model conditions.

➤ Full connectivity with other applications, including communication with spreadsheets, word processing applications, and text files.

➤ An object-oriented framework utilizing "smart process" blocks. Extend's built-in language and dialog editor provide for full extensibility and modularity.

About the Demo Version of Extend+BPR

A demonstration version of Extend+BPR can be found in Section III on the CD-ROM included with this book. When you select the "Demo" button in the Extend+BPR product section of the CD-ROM, the installer will install an Extend program group. The demo comes with a library of iconic blocks so you can try your hand at building your own process models. The demo also includes several prebuilt models that you can examine and run; these models are explained in the section "Extend+BPR Application Areas" later in this chapter. The demo version is limited in three ways: printing has been disabled; your work cannot be saved; and the new models you build can use no more than 25 blocks.

Building a Dynamic Process Model

The most important technique to remember when building a model is to start small, test the model against known or hypothetical data, refine the model, and validate it. Extend provides numerous tools for measuring, testing, and validating models, from readout and timer blocks that can be inserted at any point in the model, to the ability to step through a model while it animates or displays messages.

As discussed in greater detail in the following sections, the steps in building a model are as follows:

1. Start Extend and open a library.

2. Select blocks from the library and place them on the model window.

3. Connect the blocks with the mouse to indicate the flow.

4. Enter the appropriate data.

5. Run the simulation and view the output.

6. Prepare the model for presentation.

As an example, the next section will show you how to build a portion of the bank queuing model described earlier in the "Traditional Process Reengineering Tools" section of this chapter. As you may recall, that mental model exercise stated that customers arrived every 2 minutes on the average and that the teller took an average of 1.9 minutes to process each transaction.

NOTE
The completed Bank Line model (BANKLINE.MOX) is included with the Extend demonstration files on the CD-ROM packaged with this book. To build or view this model, you need to install the Extend demo from the CD-ROM.

Starting Extend and Opening a Library

1. Double-click the ExtendDemo icon ( ) in the ExtendDemo group in the Program Manager window. Click once when Extend's startup screen appears to cause the application to continue; an empty model window (MODEL-1.MOX) opens.

2. Once Extend is open, select Open Library under Extend's Library menu.

3. In the Open Library dialog box, select DEMO.LIX and click OK. This opens the Demo library so that it is listed at the bottom of the Library menu.

Putting a Block on the Model Window

The next step in building a model is to select a block from the library and place it on the model window. There are two ways to add a library block to a model:

➤ The first method is to select directly from the Library menu. Click in the Library menu and drag down to the DEMO.LIX library. When the DEMO.LIX library is selected, the names of the blocks appear to the right. Drag down the list until the name of the block you want is selected, then let go. The block will appear at the upper-left corner of the model window.

➤ Another method is to drag blocks from the Library window to the model worksheet. At the top of the list of blocks in the DEMO.LIX menu is the Open Library Window command. When you select this command, the DEMO.LIX Library window opens, showing block icons as well as names. You can click on any block in the list with a mouse and drag the block to the worksheet.

For example, to add a block to the model using the second method, choose the Open Library Window command as discussed earlier, then:

1. Click on the Import block in the DEMO.LIX window at the left.

2. Drag the block to the model window on the right.

3. Drag a Stack block onto the model window following the same procedure (if necessary, use the Window menu to bring the DEMO.LIX Library window to the front again.) Your screen should look like this:

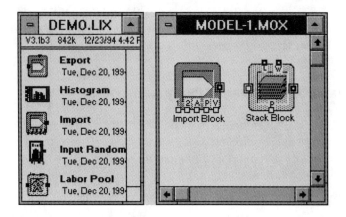

Each Extend block is a combination of an icon, a dialog box, and scripted behavior. The *icon* is the picture that represents the function of the block. The *dialog box* (which you access by double-clicking on the icon) is for entering data and obtaining measurements specific to the block. The *script* determines how the block behaves in the model. For example, the Import block represents an arrival of items into the model, as indicated by the arrow on its icon. Items can be any process element, such as people, materials, tasks, orders, etc.; in the Bank Line model, the Import block represents customers arriving at the bank. As you will see later in the "Entering Data" section, the Import block's dialog box allows you to specify how often customers arrive. The Stack block's function is very different from the Import block; as you can see from its icon and dialog box, the Stack block represents various types of queues or waiting lines.

Connecting the Blocks

Most blocks in Extend have input and output connectors. (These are the small squares attached to each side of the block.) As you might expect, information flows into a block at input connectors and out of the block at output connectors.

Connecting lines are used to hook blocks together in the model window. These connections show the flow of information from block to block throughout the model. You need to use a mouse to make the connection from one block to another, in this case from the output of the Import block to the input of the Stack block. To draw a connection from the Import block to the Stack block in the model window,

1. Move the cursor to the output connector on the right side of the Import block. When the cursor is positioned over the connector, it changes from an arrow to the head of a drawing pen.

2. Click in the output connector, then drag the pen to the input connector on the left side of the Stack block.

3. When the connection has been made, the line you are drawing will thicken. At this point release the mouse button. If the connection has not been made properly, the line will be dotted rather than solid. In that case, you can delete the connection by selecting the line and pressing DELETE or BACKSPACE and start over. The completed connection looks like this:

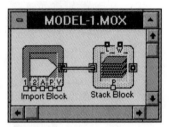

Once the connection line has been made, customers will automatically flow from the Import block to the Stack block. (It should be noted that if the Import block were connected to two Stack blocks, the flow would go to one or the other Stack block, *but not to both at the same time.* This automatic routing feature is important, since routing is common in business processes.)

Entering Data

Each block in Extend has a unique function. Extend blocks are *smart process* blocks, which means that BPR practitioners can build models without the need to write software programs. Because blocks have their behavior already programmed in, there is usually no need to enter equations or formulas. This means less work when constructing a model.

To enter data,

➣ Double-click a block's icon to access its dialog box.

➣ Once you are in an icon's dialog box, click the appropriate buttons or type the required information directly into the appropriate field.

For this model,

1. Click the FIFO button in the Stack block's dialog box to specify that you want a first-in, first-out queue.

2. In the Import dialog box, click the Exponential distribution button to select a randomly distributed arrival rate, then enter a Mean of 2 as the average or mean time between arrivals and click OK. When you do this, the Import block will be set so that customers arrive randomly approximately every two minutes:

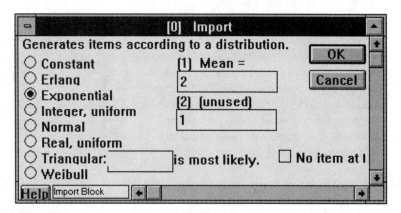

Once the rate of arrival is set in the dialog box, the block will generate customers arriving at that rate for the entire simulation run. If you want, you can also connect other blocks to the Import block to cause the rate of arrival to change based on the time of day, model conditions, and so forth.

Now that you've seen how a model is built, rather than walk through the entire process of building the Bank Line model, the next step proceeds directly to the prebuilt model.

Running the Bank Line Model and Obtaining the Results

The completed Bank Line model (BANKLINE.MOX) is included on the CD-ROM that comes with this book. To open the existing Bank Line model,

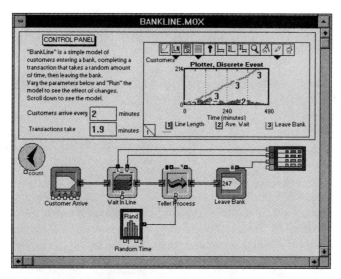

FIGURE 10-2. *The Bank Line model*

1. Select Open under the File menu.

2. In the Open dialog box, double-click BANKLINE.MOX.

When the model opens, you will see a control panel and graph. (These authoring features are discussed later, in the section "Preparing for Presentations.") Scroll down the window or resize it in order to view the entire Bank Line model. Note that the block labels have been changed to indicate the function of the blocks. The finished Bank Line model looks like Figure 10-2.

Once the model is built, it is time to run the simulation. To do this, you first need to specify the ending time for the simulation run in the Simulation Setup dialog box.

1. To open the Simulation Setup dialog box, choose Simulation Setup under the Run menu.

2. For this model, you would set the end time to 480 minutes (8 hours) as shown here:

End simulation at time	480
Start simulation at time	0

3. Click Run Now to see the simulation run.

When you choose to run the simulation, Extend automatically handles the timing of events based on the data you have entered in the block dialog boxes. In this case, the model takes only a couple of seconds to run in real time, but simulates 480 minutes, or eight hours, of model time. If this simulation were run 500 times (to be statistically significant), you would see that the average length of the line at the end of the day varies from 10 to 12.

Simulations can be run with or without animation (animation can be turned on or off by selecting Show Animation under the Run menu). When a simulation runs, model information is automatically calculated and reported. Depending on how you design your model and the blocks you use in building it, you can choose the output in the form of graphs, tables of data, or customized reports. You can also run multiple scenarios using Extend's built-in sensitivity analysis feature. For example, when you ran this model a graph of the number of customers who have finished their transactions (line 1), the number who are waiting at each point in time (line 2), and their average wait time (line 3) was generated as shown here:

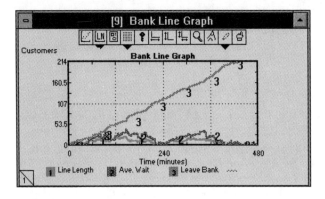

Important statistics about the line of customers (as determined by the Stack block named Wait in Line) are automatically calculated and could be presented in a table:

Row	Block	Block Name	Ave Length	Max Length	Ave Wait	Max Wait
0	Wait In Line	Stack	5.2038128601356	18	11.000019268384	31.167540351883

Preparing for Presentations

At the simplest level, an Extend model is a window containing iconic blocks connected together with data entered in their dialog boxes. If you left all your models at that point of development, they would of course provide the information you need. But those models might not be as comprehensible to others as you would like.

Extend's built-in authoring environment lets you organize and present your models in a form that is aesthetically pleasing and very comprehensible. This is especially important if your models are going to be presented to or used by nonmodelers. In addition to the features described earlier, Extend offers several additional features that help make models easier to use and understand, including:

> **Text and drawing tools** to help the user document and customize model segments

> **Customizable animation** including QuickTime movies and pictures

> **Hierarchy and notebooks** that provide an "executive interface," serving as control panels and reporting windows

> **Control blocks** for interactive control over model parameters

> **Cloned dialog items** that let the user drag and drop important parameters anywhere: on the model worksheet, into Notebooks, or into hierarchical blocks

> **User messages** that alert the user to model conditions or prompt for inputs

> **A built-in dialog editor and compiled language** for creating custom blocks and dialogs

Notebooks, the model window, and hierarchical blocks can serve as control panels or a flight simulator interface, providing a unique and accessible front-end to models. These windows can contain text, pictures, tables, graphs, controls, and so forth. You can use them for documenting model assumptions, controlling model inputs, and reporting model output from one location. For example, the Bank Line model (BANKLINE.MOX) that comes with the Extend demonstration files on the CD-ROM uses cloned dialog items and drawing tools to reserve a portion of the model window as a small "control panel." Having a high-level interface may not seem important for small models like the Bank Line model, but for large models it is essential. For instance, the top hierarchical level of a communication company's operations model is shown in Figure 10-3.

This view provides system-level visualization of company operations. It uses Extend's hierarchical architecture to nest layers of submodels and provides natural ways of viewing processes and their linkages. For example, a person approaching this model for the first time can learn about the customer order process by opening the "Customers" block and clicking on buttons to follow the flow laterally to other affected units or downstream to the increasingly detailed submodels. (Due to the 25 block limit of the Extend demo, this model is not included on the CD-ROM.)

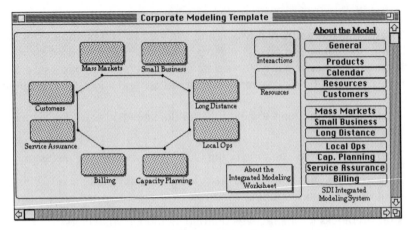

FIGURE 10-3. *A top-level view of the company-wide model*

Extend+BPR Application Areas

Extend+BPR is not just a business process reengineering tool. As illustrated by the following applications, Extend+BPR is a tool for modeling business processes, whether for reengineering purposes, for training about existing procedures, or for ISO 9000 documentation and quality assurance.

Where possible, the following sample models are included with the demonstration version of Extend+BPR on the CD-ROM included with this book. The models can be opened using the same procedure that was described for opening the BANKLINE.MOX model.

Performance Measurement

With Extend+BPR, performance measurement is an integrated part of the model. Unlike process maps or data flow diagrams, which only show a pictorial representation, Extend+BPR dynamically models business operations. The measurements obtained by simulating a process tell you how effective the process is, gives data for comparing it with other processes, and provides an objective basis for making strategic reengineering and improvement decisions.

There are three main reasons to measure performance:

> Measurement gives you an objective basis for decision making.

> Systems that get measured are more likely to get improved.

> Any measurement is superior to not measuring at all.

Measuring operations in a structured manner is the key for companies who want to optimize processes. Typically, industry and government focus solely on productivity and quality measures, a perspective reinforced by practically all TQM and continuous improvement philosophies. However, the number of products produced or the percentage of products considered defective provides only a small perspective on the overall dynamics. Other parameters to consider include: time to completion for each task and the overall process, input inventory levels at each step, productivity of workers, and conditions that determine the paths a process follows.

The Support Services Model   The Support Services model (SUPPSERV.MOX), shown in Figure 10-4, was used to reengineer a technical support process consisting of technicians who responded to customers' telephone, fax, and E-mail inquiries.

The modeling process itself provides a structured framework for measuring performance. For instance, the Support Services model makes some assumptions about how often telephone calls and written reports arrive and how long it takes to do the support. When building a model, users can gather data and use the actual parameters, then compare model output to the real-world situation.

The model shows how one process (On-Line Support) interrupts another process (Off-Line Support) resulting in fewer total problems being resolved. This model also automatically provides measurements that can be used for decision making. For instance, the queue blocks (labeled Probs Wait and Calls Wait) calculate and display the average time to process a report and how many

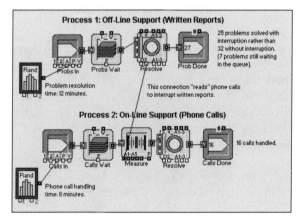

FIGURE 10-4.   *The Support Services model*

telephone calls were received, respectively. The utilization calculations in the two blocks labeled Resolve automatically tell how productive the workers are. By using Extend's customizable reporting features, this information can be presented in a report or output to another application for further analysis.

Cycle-Time

One of the most important business process factors to measure and improve is cycle-time. Cycle-time is a measurement of the time an item remains in a process, either in the entire process or in a specific part of it. Another way to look at cycle-time is that it tells how long an item takes to get from point A to point B. For instance, the cycle-time for an order in the entire order turnover process starts when the order is received and ends when the customer receives and pays for the goods. In the order entry segment of that process, the cycle-time for the order is the time from when the order is received until it is input into the computer.

Cycle-time is not the same as processing time, productivity, or utilization:

> **Processing time** is the time it takes to perform a task or activity; this is also called *task time* or *delay time.* For instance, the processing time for an order entry task is the actual time it takes to enter the order into the computer.

> **Productivity** is the ratio of the outputs to the inputs that produce them. For instance, a measurement of productivity could be products produced per employee, dollar revenues per store, customers served per payroll dollar, and so forth. In some cases, productivity is based on how many items can be output in a particular segment of time. For example, if 100 orders are entered into the computer in one day of labor, productivity is 100 per labor day.

> **Utilization** is the ratio of the time spent processing compared to the entire amount of time available for processing. The *idle time* percentage is the complement of the utilization amount (1-utilization). Continuing the preceding example, if it takes four minutes to enter each of the 100 orders (for a total of 400 minutes of work), the order entry utilization ratio is 83 percent based on a 480-minute day. This is calculated as 400/480. The idle time percentage would then be 17 percent.

Note that although a process is composed of one or more tasks, cycle-time is not the same as the sum of each task's processing times; in fact, it is almost always greater. In any process or subprocess, cycle-time is the sum of:

> The preprocessing times (the sum of the times the item waits until it can be processed by the next task)

➢ The processing times (the sum of the actual task times)

➢ The post-processing times (the sum of the times required for the processed item to wait for the next step)

For example, although an order entry clerk can input an order in minutes, the cycle-time for each order may be days if orders arrive faster than they are processed or if they are held up in the mail room.

In addition, an improvement in cycle-time may not have an impact on productivity. If workers are already working at full utilization, for example, a decrease in cycle-time may not increase the number of items output for the specified time period.

The Invoice Approval Model   The Invoice Approval model (INVOICE.MOX) illustrates a two-task process in which invoices are approved and checks are generated. Invoices arrive approximately every 6 minutes and take 7.25 minutes to process. It takes 0.25 minutes to print and mail checks once invoices are approved, and there are 6 invoices waiting approval when the model starts. The purpose of the model is to calculate cycle-time for the process.

The question is, how long is the cycle-time? If you guessed, you probably estimated seven or eight minutes. If so, you have not considered the cumulative effect of having the processing time be slightly more than the arrival rate.

When you run the model, the plotter shows not only the cycle-time for each invoice, but also the trend. As seen in this model, the trend is that cycle-time continuously increases. Although it takes 7.5 minutes to process each invoice, the cycle-time increases so that invoices arriving at the end of the day have a cycle-time of *over 150 minutes* as shown on line 1 of this graph:

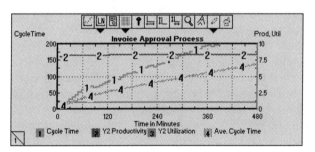

Here, the cycle-time is plotted on the left axis while both the utilization for the approval task and the productivity of the entire process are plotted on the right (Y2) axis. As seen earlier, productivity at the end of the day is about eight invoices approved per hour (line 2) and the utilization (line 3, at the bottom of the graph) is 1, indicating that the approval task is always completely busy.

Technology Insertion

Technology insertion, or the substitution of computer technology for manual processes, is a common business process reengineering technique. As discussed in the earlier section "Why Not Just Automate?" the promise of technology insertion is that process performance will be enhanced by changing a time-consuming manual process into an instantaneous or nearly instantaneous computer transaction.

When you consider implementing technology, it is important to realize that any process is part of a larger process, and changes to a portion of a process may not improve the overall performance. Time to completion is regulated by the slowest task in any process, so speeding up a couple of tasks in a multitask process may have no effect on the overall process.

The Documentation Revision Model

A government agency supported its flight control software through a sophisticated technical documentation process where changes in the software resulted in the revision of the technical manuals. The revision process consisted of modifications to documentation, review of the modifications, and printing of the final documents (represented in the model by the hierarchical blocks Software Engineer's Review, Reviewer Changes, and Print Changes, respectively). The agency determined that it took approximately 65 days to revise 30 documents. They suspected that cycle-time could be reduced by the installation of an automated document management system, changing from a manual process to an automated process.

In the manual process, three software engineers took between two and three days each to modify each document while the mail took one day to travel from the software engineers to the reviewer and from the reviewer to the printer. The automated system was expected to decrease each engineer's modification time to one day and eliminate the need for interoffice mail.

The Documentation Revision model (DOCUMENT.MOX) was used to model both the manual and automated processes. By simply changing a couple of parameters from the manual process settings, the model showed the effect that automation had on the system as a whole. Using the model, the agency determined that the time to complete the first task in the process (Software Engineer's Review) decreased from approximately 29 days to 10, a 300 percent improvement. They expected corresponding time savings throughout the process with automation. However, as shown by the following results, there was no significant improvement in cycle-time for the process as a whole:

Manual Process

New Process

The problem was that the planned application of technology reduced the time to perform tasks early in the process, but it did not reduce the time for all the tasks.

Since the tasks occurred in sequence, the printing task dictated the overall timing of the process. Unless the printing task was automated, there would be no net improvement over the old process.

Workflow

Workflow tools are used to model business processes prior to creating customized applications that will automate them. Before building information systems and databases, it is common to specify types of data or items, show how data and items are routed, and monitor their status.

The inherent discrete item methodology, coupled with extensive routing capabilities, makes Extend+BPR the ideal tool for workflow modeling. Model items can move sequentially (when one person or operation is done with an item it automatically goes to the next step) or on parallel tracks (items are "cloned" and sent on to two or more different but noncontradictory steps). Routing can also be affected by the following conditions:

- ➤ Rules (if the requisition is $500 or more, route it to A; otherwise route it to B)

- ➤ Events (if A's In box reaches a specified level, route incoming items to B)

- ➤ Time (if A hasn't signed the paperwork after three days, route it to B)

The Order Processing Model   The Order Processing model (ORDERS.MOX) shown in Figure 10-5 shows the flow of work in an order entry department. Incoming orders are classified by type (new customer or existing customer) by attaching "order type" attributes to each order. Kathi processes new customer orders, which take longer because of the credit check. Joe processes orders for existing customers. Based on type, the orders are processed by either Kathi or Joe, then sent to production.

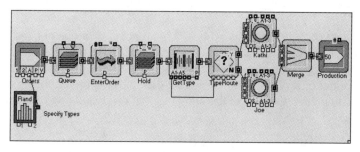

FIGURE 10-5.   *The Order Processing model*

Activity-Based Costing

Extend+BPR makes it convenient to track the accumulated costs of processes and activities, providing management with valid bases for making decisions about providing services or producing products.

The limitations of traditional cost accounting systems are becoming apparent. World-class manufacturing, TQM, cycle-time reduction, and continuous improvement techniques require that expenditure allocations be realistic and informative. However, current cost accounting systems are obsolete and provide distorted information to management. Since this information is the basis for strategic decisions regarding capital investment, product pricing, and so forth, inaccurate information directly impacts a company's ability to compete.

Traditional cost accounting systems assign overhead to products and services based on direct labor hours. However, direct labor is steadily declining as a percentage of product content. Using direct labor as a basis for allocating indirect labor and other overhead expenditures causes the costs of complex or low-volume products to be understated. The result is that companies can produce products that consume resources but provide little or no economic benefit.

Activity-based costing (ABC) assigns costs to the final product or service (also called the *cost object*) based on the use of resources by the processes (called *activity centers*) that produce the cost object. Resources are the economic elements directed to the performance of the activity, such as workers, parts, or information systems. Resources are consumed or utilized by the activity centers at a rate that is based on variables called activity drivers. These drivers are simply the typical occurrences in any business process, such as the number of insurance claims received, the number of telephone calls in a support center, or how many parts are required for a product. The costs of providing resources to an activity include such items as salaries, office space rents, costs of information systems, outside consulting expenses, and indirect costs such as electricity and telephone.

Allocating the cost of resource utilization to a process gives companies the ability to determine the actual cost impact of improving processes. Continuous improvement and reengineering programs can then use ABC as their basis for analysis rather than relying on inaccurate information or faith alone.

The Activity Costing Model   The cost of an activity can be derived from a number of factors, such as material cost, labor, processing time, and so forth. Extend+BPR provides the capability to define those factors as attributes that travel with the product or service. By interrogating the values of the attributes when the product is completed, the cost of the activities that produced that product can be obtained.

The Activity Costing model (ABC.MOX) calculates the costs of three types of tasks in hierarchical blocks: Type 1, Type 2, and Type 3. Using the model information, you can determine the activity cost for each type of task, as seen in the following graph:

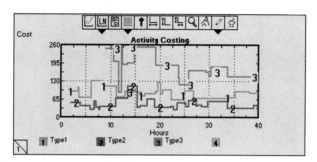

Implementing Strategic Plans

Managers and planners need a tool with which they can interpret their organization's strategic directions, identify tactical areas, and explore alternatives. It is not sufficient merely to specify strategic plans: the plans have to be implemented, the implementation must be consistent with how the organization works, and the results of the implementation must be weighed against the organization's strategic objectives.

Operational planning is the process of translating top management's focus and strategy into guidelines that are meaningful in the context of the organization's daily operations. For example, operational planning investigates how many people should be added to the sales force of an organization, so that management's goal of increased market share can be realized. Here are some other operational considerations:

➢ What should we spend on advertising and marketing?

➢ How long should this R&D project be funded?

➢ Where should we build a new plant?

➢ How do we fund major equipment purchases?

Traditional planning methods have not been particularly successful. The continuing jolts of a precipitous future turning into reality have made a shambles of many a plan, no matter how coherent and logical these plans were when originally conceived. This is often due to the delays between stages in the traditional planning process, which is shown in the following diagram:

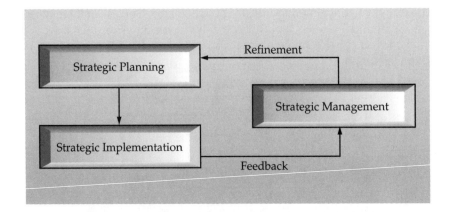

In the traditional method, plans are either implemented directly (faster but dangerous) or implemented in stages through pilot projects (safer but takes longer). Both methods result in excessive delays in obtaining feedback and therefore in refining the plan. It is not unusual to have a three- to five-year delay from plan creation to plan refinement. Given the current economic and competitive environment, this is totally unacceptable. Furthermore, these delays have caused many managers to abandon formal planning. As a consequence, organizations often are reacting to change rather than anticipating it.

In contrast, dynamic modeling allows for the continual evaluation and refinement of how strategic plans are implemented. Instead of implementing the plans directly or in the form of pilot projects, managers use models to aid in strategic thinking and to obtain the information necessary for plan refinement. This collapses the planning cycle to an acceptable time period and assures that strategic plans are consistent with the operational and tactical workings of the organization. The planning cycle incorporating dynamic modeling looks like this:

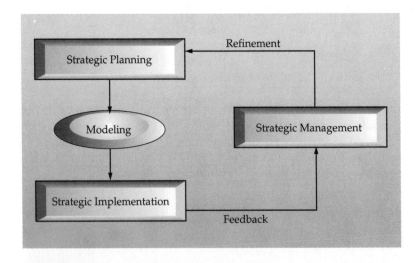

The Support Planning Model   A software company needed to plan how many customer support representatives to hire over the next two years. In order to forecast hiring requirements, the company first modeled how it does business. Specifically, the company modeled how customers evaluate and purchase software and how many users are expected to be active, requiring technical support.

The planning manager determined that there were four types of potential customers, each with its own evaluation, purchasing, and usage patterns: corporate users, small businesses, other users, and people who had no intention of buying the software. Based on this information, the manager built the Support Planning model, the middle portion of which is shown in Figure 10-6. (Note: Due to model size constraints, this model is not included on the CD-ROM).

This model considers such questions as "What percentage of contacts ask for evaluation copies?" "How many evaluators decide to purchase?" and "How often will the purchaser buy multiple copies?"

ISO 9000/EN 29000

Extend+BPR is the perfect tool for facilitating all aspects of a company's ISO 9000/EN 29000 certification process, from documentation of quality procedures to assurance of compliance. You can also use Extend, and especially its many third-party libraries, for more detailed analyses of specific subprocesses, such as engineering product design, calibration, or control systems analysis.

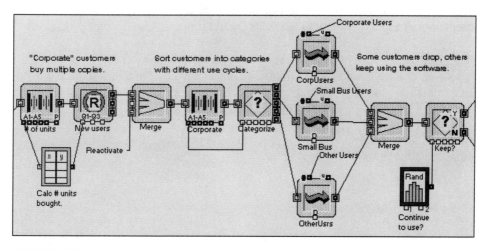

FIGURE 10-6.   *The Support Planning model*

Assessment and certification of a company's quality management system is rapidly becoming a prerequisite for all manufacturing and service industries that trade internationally. The International Organization for Standardization (ISO) and the European Committee for Standardization (ECN) have developed the ISO 9000/EN 29000 series of quality standards. ISO 9000 and EN 29000 provide guidelines for implementing a quality management system that will ensure customer satisfaction with the goods and services companies provide. These standards are the benchmarks for quality in any organization.

The ISO 9000/EN 29000 certification process is rigorous and ongoing. The operation of the company's quality assurance process must be documented in a Quality Manual that addresses what must be done, who is to do it, when it is to be done, and how it is to be done. Then the Quality Management System is assessed for compliance with the ISO 9000/EN 29000 model (9001, 9002, or 9003) appropriate to the company's scope of operations. After certification, companies must continuously assess and assure compliance through internal and external audits that verify that the actual activities comply with planned arrangements, determine the effectiveness of the quality management system, and provide objective data for review by management and the auditors.

Extend+BPR provides a rigorous and objective methodology for assessing operations, documenting the quality manual, and demonstrating compliance. You can use Extend+BPR to model and document quality assurance procedures, improve procedures to bring them into compliance, and continuously assess compliance by comparing actual performance to model performance. Extend+BPR's high ratio of one-to-one conformity with real-world operations facilitates all aspects of the ISO 9000/EN 29000 process.

The Testing Process Model　　Whether you manufacture a product or provide a service, quality should be an important component of what you sell. One way to determine and document that your quality assurance process is in control is to simulate it. The Testing Process model (TESTING.MOX) shown in Figure 10-7 documents the final inspection of software packages before shipment. After a period of time, the inspector determines that the packages are acceptable, unacceptable, or require repackaging.

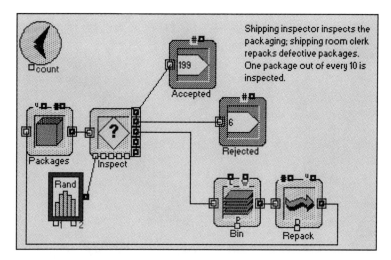

FIGURE 10-7. *The Testing Process model*

Conclusion

Extend+BPR was developed to augment the philosophical approaches of TQM and continuous improvement by applying systems analysis techniques to process improvement and reengineering efforts. The BPR library is a collection of modeling functions designed specifically to help business people make informed decisions about the way they do business. Use it to look at business processes from a global view, or use it to get a detailed picture of how processes function. Whether you are in industry or government, using the Extend+BPR package will save you time and money by reducing the risk of counterproductive and nonproductive changes while maximizing your process reengineering efforts.

PART 4

Sales and Financial Forecasting

CHAPTER 11

Risk Analysis for Business Decision Support

by Joseph Prisco, Palisade Corporation
and Wayne L. Winston, Indiana University

Everyone knows that risk affects the gambler about to roll the dice, the wildcatter about to drill an oil well, or the tightrope walker taking that first big step. The concept of risk comes from our recognition that the future is uncertain: we do not know what the future will bring in response to a given action today. Risk implies that a given action has more than one possible outcome.

In this simple sense, every action is "risky," from crossing the street to building a dam. The term is usually reserved, however, for situations where the range of possible outcomes to a given action is in some way significant. Common actions like crossing the street usually aren't risky, while building a dam can involve significant risk. Somewhere in between, actions pass from being nonrisky to risky.

This distinction, although vague, is important—if you judge that a situation is risky, risk becomes one criterion for deciding what course of action you should pursue. At that point, some form of risk analysis becomes viable.

Risk analysis, in a broad sense, is any method—qualitative and/or quantitative—for assessing the impacts of risk on decision situations. A myriad of techniques are used that blend both qualitative and quantitative techniques. The goal of any of these methods is to help the decision maker choose a course of action, given a better understanding of the possible outcomes that could occur. In order to focus in on this, we need to take a closer look at risk.

Characteristics of Risk

Risk derives from our inability to see into the future, and it indicates a degree of uncertainty that is significant enough to make us notice it. This somewhat vague definition takes more shape by mentioning several important characteristics of risk.

First, risk can be either objective or subjective. Flipping a coin is an objective risk because the odds are well known. Even though the outcome is uncertain, an objective risk can be described precisely based on theory, experiment, or common sense. Everyone agrees with the description of an objective risk. Describing the odds for rain next Thursday is not so clear cut and represents a subjective risk. Given the same information, theory, computer models, etc., weatherman A may think the odds of rain are 30 percent while weatherman B may think the odds are 65 percent. Neither is wrong. Describing a subjective risk is open-ended in the sense that you could always refine your assessment with new information, further study, or by giving weight to the opinion of others. Most risks are subjective, and this has important implications for anyone analyzing risk or making decisions based on a risk analysis.

Second, deciding that something is risky requires personal judgment, even for objective risks. For example, imagine flipping a coin—you win one dollar for heads and you lose one dollar for tails. The range between winning one dollar and losing one dollar would not be overly significant to most people. If the stake were $100,000, however, most people would find the situation to be quite risky (there might be a wealthy few who would not find this range of outcomes to be significant).

Third, risky actions, and therefore risk, are things that we often can choose or avoid. Individuals differ in the amount of risk they willingly accept. For example, two individuals of equal net worth may react quite differently to a $100 coin flip bet—one may accept it, another may refuse it. Their personal preferences for risk could differ.

The Need for Risk Analysis

The first step in risk analysis and modeling is recognizing the risk and the need to analyze it. Is there significant risk involved in the situation you are interested in? Here are a few examples that might help you evaluate your own situation for the presence of significant risk:

> ➤ **Risks for New Product Development and Marketing** Will the R&D department solve the technical problems involved? Will a competitor get to market first or with a better product? Will government regulations and approvals delay product introduction? How much impact will the proposed advertising campaign have on sales levels? Will production costs be as forecast? Will the proposed sales price have to be changed to reflect unanticipated demand levels for the product?

> ➤ **Risks for Securities Analysis and Asset Management** How will a tentative purchase affect portfolio value? Will a new management team affect market price? Will an acquired firm add earnings as forecast? How will a market correction impact a given industry sector?

> ➤ **Risks for Operations Management and Planning** Will a given inventory level suffice for unpredictable demand levels? Will labor costs rise significantly with upcoming union contract negotiations? How will pending environmental legislation impact production costs? How will political and market events affect overseas suppliers in terms of exchange rates, trade barriers, and delivery schedules?

> ➤ **Risks for Design and Construction of a Structure (building, bridge, etc.)** Will the cost of construction materials and labor be as forecast? Will a labor strike affect the construction schedule? Will the levels of stress placed on the structure by peak load crowds and nature be as forecast? Will the structure ever be stressed to the point of failure?

> ➤ **Risks for Policy Planning** If the policy is subject to legislative approval, will it be approved? Will the level of compliance with any policy directives be complete or partial? Will the costs of implementation be as forecast? Will the level of benefits be what you projected?

Assessing and Quantifying Risk

How do you quantify the risk you have identified for a given uncertain situation? Quantifying risk means determining all the possible values a risky variable could take and determining the relative likelihood of each value. Suppose your uncertain situation is the outcome from the flip of a coin. You could repeat the flip a large number of times until you had established the fact that half of the times it comes up tails and half of the times heads. Alternatively, you could mathematically calculate this result from a basic understanding of probability and statistics.

In most real-life situations, you can't perform an experiment to calculate your risk the way you can for the flip of a coin. How could you calculate the probable learning curve associated with introducing new equipment? You may be able to reflect on past experiences, but once you have introduced the equipment, the uncertainty is gone. There is no mathematical formula that you can solve to get the risk associated with the possible outcomes. You have to estimate the risk using the best information you have available.

If you can calculate the risks of your situation the way you would for a coin flip, the risk is objective. This means that everyone would agree that you quantified the risk correctly. Most risk quantification, however, involves your best judgment. There may not be complete information available about the situation, the situation may not be repeatable like a coin flip, or it just may be too complex to come up with an unequivocal answer. Such risk quantification is subjective, which means that someone might disagree with your evaluation.

Your subjective assessments of risk are likely to change when you get more information on the situation. If you have subjectively derived a risk assessment, you must always ask yourself whether additional information is available that would help you make a better assessment. If it is available, how hard and how expensive would it be to obtain?

Modeling and Simulation vs. "What-if" Analysis

Realizing that you have a risky situation in need of analysis is the first step in any risk analysis. The next step is creating a model. *Modeling* is a catchall term that usually means any type of activity in which you are trying to create some kind of representation of a real-life situation. Your representation, or model, can be used to examine the situation and, hopefully, to help you understand what the future might bring. You probably have already created several models using spreadsheets. Spreadsheet files are in fact models of real-life situations. If you've ever played "What-if" games with your project by changing the values of various entries to see how the outcome changes, you are well on your way to understanding the importance of uncertainty in a modeling situation.

There are two basic approaches to quantitative risk analysis. Both have the same goal—to describe the range of possible outcomes of an uncertain situation—and both generate valid results. The first approach is simulation. This approach relies on the ability of the computer to do a great deal of work very quickly, such as solving a spreadsheet repeatedly using a large number of possible combinations of input variable values. Simulation is discussed in greater detail in the next section.

The second approach to risk analysis is an analytical approach. Analytical methods require that all uncertain variables in a model be described mathematically. Then the equations for these distributions are combined mathematically to derive another equation, which describes the probability distribution of all possible outcomes. This approach is not practical for most uses and users. It is not a simple task to describe distributions as equations, and it is even more difficult to combine distributions analytically given even a moderate level of complexity in the model. Furthermore, most people interested in using risk analysis do not possess the mathematical skills necessary to implement the analytical techniques required.

If you have quantified risk—determined outcomes and probabilities of occurrence—you can summarize this risk using a probability distribution. A *probability distribution* is a device for presenting the quantified risk for a variable. There are many forms and types of probability distributions, each of which describes a range of possible values and their likelihood of occurrence. Most people have heard of a normal distribution—the traditional "bell curve." But there are a wide variety of distribution types ranging from uniform and triangular distributions to more complex forms such as gamma and weibull.

The Need for Simulation

Models enable you to determine the optimal course of action. In many situations where uncertainty is present, it is difficult (or impossible) to build a tractable mathematical model that will yield useful information. For example, queuing models are often used to model a situation where people wait in line. An analytic model adequately describes the situation of a bank in which all customers wait in a "snake" or single line for the first available teller. This model can be used to predict customer waiting times and to evaluate how adding additional tellers will reduce the waiting times. At present, however, no queuing models can adequately model a supermarket that has express lines, where customers may freely jockey between lines. Simulation is used in situations like this where no tractable mathematical model exists.

In most instances, a simulation model is a computer model that imitates a real-life situation. Often the simulation model can provide a decision maker with important information. For our supermarket illustration, a simulation model might help us answer questions such as:

> ➤ If an additional express lane were added, how much would the average waiting time of a customer decrease?

➢ Currently baggers help people load their groceries into their car. How much would the average waiting time of a customer decrease if we eliminated this practice?

➢ How does the number of checkout counters needed to provide adequate service vary during the day? This information would be a great aid in scheduling employees.

A simulation can be used to determine how sensitive a system is to changes in operating conditions. For example, if the store experiences a 20 percent increase in business, what will happen to the average time customers must wait for service?

A simulation model also allows the user to determine an "optimal" operating policy. For example, the supermarket could use simulation to determine the relationship between the number of open registers and the expected time a customer spends waiting in line. Then this relationship (along with the cost of opening a register) could be used to determine the number of registers corresponding to all possible arrival rates.

The Limitations of "What-if" Analysis

You may be asking, "Why do I need to use simulation? I can simply enter different values into my spreadsheet model and see what results I get." This is called "What-if" analysis. Most people will look at a spreadsheet, pick two or three important factors (or variables), determine their best and worst values, and enter in combinations of these to come up with several possible outcomes.

There are two major problems with this approach to "What-if" analysis. First, it is not rigorous. You are only considering a few variables, but in most models, many more variables need to be considered. Trying all the best and worst values for a large number of variables is time-consuming. Second, it does not take into account intermediate values. How often do the best-case and worst-case values actually come up in real life? Not very often. Usually the values that occur are somewhere in between your best and worst estimates. If you are going to apply "What-if" analysis to a spreadsheet, you really should look at these intermediate values. Also, in most cases, these intermediate values are not going to be equally likely to occur. A truly rigorous analysis should take this important factor into account as well.

Let's consider the following scenario. Suppose your company is going to be marketing a new product, and you've been told to come up with projections for net cash flow and net present value (NPV) with a 10 percent discount rate for the next ten years. You create a spreadsheet model that is based on information about the price of production, volume of sales, design costs, sales price, overhead, and many other factors whose values are based on experience and research. You must also take into account the possibility that a competitor may come out with a similar product and how that will affect sales.

The problem is that most of the values in this model are actually variables. You cannot make solid predictions for many key factors in your model. For example, your company has determined that the price of the product with a competitor in the market could have a minimum value of $30, a maximum value of $80, and a most likely value of $50. R&D has told you that after looking at past projects, it has determined that the design cost for this project could fall anywhere in a normal distribution with a mean of $50,000 and a standard deviation of $10,000. Several other departments have given you similarly uncertain values for key factors. You need to provide a rigorous analysis of this model, but there are so many variables and so many possible values for each variable that even with a spreadsheet you would be at this problem for weeks.

You could simply provide the best and worst case for all variables, and maybe try a few intermediate values, but how many intermediate values are enough? How long must you work until your answers are valid and useful? We will return to this scenario throughout this chapter and in the tutorials that follow.

Corporate Use of Simulation

A *Fortune* magazine article, "A New Tool to Help Managers" (May 30, 1994), illustrates the use of simulation in corporate finance. The article describes a simulation model referred to as a Monte Carlo model. (It is described in greater detail in the next section.) This model was used by Merck (the world's largest drug company) to determine whether Merck should pay $6.6 billion to acquire Medco, a mail-order drug company. The model contained inputs concerning the following four aspects of the acquisition decision:

➢ Possible scenarios for the future of the U.S. health care system, such as a single-payer system, universal coverage, etc.

➢ Possible future changes in the mix of generic and brand name drugs

➢ A probability distribution of profit margins for each product

➢ Assumptions about how competitors would behave after a merger with Medco

The Merck model contained thousands of equations. A simulation was performed to see how the merger would perform under various scenarios. Merck's model indicated that the merger with Medco would benefit Merck no matter what type of health insurance plan is enacted by the federal government. As Merck's CFO, Judy Lewent, noted, "Monte Carlo techniques are a very, very powerful tool to get a more intelligent look at a range of outcomes. It's almost never useful in this kind of environment to build a single-bullet forecast."

The results that you get from risk analysis must be interpreted by you as an individual. The same results given to different individuals may be interpreted differently and may lead to different courses of action. This is not a weakness in the technique but a direct result of the fact that different individuals have different preferences with regard to possible choices, timing, and risk acceptance. You might feel that the shape of the output distribution shows that the chances of an undesirable outcome far outweigh the chances of a desirable outcome. A colleague who is less risk-averse might come to the opposite conclusion.

Monte Carlo Simulation and Computers

The type of quantitative simulation we have been discussing is known as Monte Carlo simulation. The name Monte Carlo comes from a World War II project in which scientists used this technique during the development of the atomic bomb. Inputs in a model that have uncertainty are represented by probability distributions. The results you are interested in are your outputs. The distribution of possible outcomes is generated by letting a computer recalculate your model over and over again, each time using different randomly selected sets of values for the probability distributions. In effect, the computer is trying all valid combinations of the values of input variables to simulate all possible outcomes. This is just as if you ran hundreds or thousands of "What-if" analyses on your model, all in one sitting. The results are distributions of values for your outputs that you can use to determine the probabilities of certain outcomes happening.

It's important to note that Monte Carlo simulation does not calculate *every* possible outcome that can occur in a model. Just one input that can take on any value from 0 to 1 has an infinite number of possible outcomes. What Monte Carlo simulation does is test hundreds or thousands of different combinations of inputs to create a distribution that comes close to representing all possible outcomes. The more times you recalculate your model, the more accurate your results will be. Usually a few thousand recalculations will provide good results. In the amount of time it would take you to try a handful of best and worst case combinations, a computer can produce hundreds or thousands of Monte Carlo values, giving you a more complete picture of possible outcomes.

A recent development in Monte Carlo simulation is Latin Hypercube sampling, which more accurately samples from a distribution. As a result, you can produce good results with fewer recalculations of your model. The simulation method is still called Monte Carlo when Latin Hypercube sampling is being used.

Monte Carlo simulation has been implemented on mainframes, minicomputers, and, most recently, on personal computers. The first PC program to do Monte Carlo simulation was PRISM, a stand-alone package. Monte Carlo simulation moved into spreadsheet software, such as Lotus 1-2-3 and Microsoft Excel, shortly thereafter. The reasoning behind this was that most people use spreadsheet software, and most people have, as mentioned earlier, already created models using spreadsheet software. @RISK was the first spreadsheet add-in program to implement Monte Carlo simulation and complete Latin Hypercube sampling. Other products have come out in recent years that also implement Monte Carlo simulation in spreadsheets, such as Crystal Ball by Decisioneering of Denver, Colorado.

Implementing Monte Carlo simulation using a spreadsheet add-in program is fairly easy, following the four basic steps of quantitative risk analysis. First, develop a model by creating a worksheet. Second, identify uncertainty in your model and represent this with probability distributions in your worksheet and by selecting output variables. Third, run a simulation and generate distributions of possible outcomes for all output variables. Fourth, make a decision based on the results, analysis provided by the add-in, and your own personal preferences.

@RISK for Windows

@RISK is Palisade Corporation's risk analysis and simulation add-in software, utilizing Monte Carlo simulation methods as described above to add risk analysis to either Lotus 1-2-3 for Windows or Microsoft Excel. You can use it to analyze the risk in any spreadsheet model, no matter how complex or simple by adding uncertainty using a set of @RISK probability distribution functions. When a simulation is run, random values are sampled from each @RISK function, and the spreadsheet is recalculated. Values you are interested in (such as profits) are recorded as outputs. When the simulation is over, you can view the results in the form of graphs or detailed statistics. You can then perform various analyses of this output data to determine probabilities of events, sensitivity analysis, and much more.

Let's say you're working in Excel, and you are modeling the new product release scenario we described earlier. You want to represent product price uncertainty when a competitor has also entered the market. Recall that your product's minimum price is $30, the most likely price is $50, and the maximum price is $80. With @RISK, all you need to enter is =RiskTriang(30,50,80) in an appropriate cell or formula to represent the distribution; @RISK handles all the necessary Monte Carlo calculations.

@RISK for Windows also utilizes an extensive set of high-resolution graphics to display information. You can select any output in @RISK and generate a variety of understandable graphics, from histograms to Tornado diagrams, displayed as a range of possible outcomes and the likelihood of each outcome occurring. All the graphs are in standard formats; just drop them into a spreadsheet, export them to your word processor, or print them immediately.

@RISK for Windows includes a number of additional features:

➢ **Toolbar Interface** @RISK's main functions are controlled by a toolbar interface, as shown here, which allows users to access most major functions by pressing a single button. (Toolbar buttons are not labeled in the spreadsheet.)

➢ **True Add-In Functions** @RISK adds uncertainty to your spreadsheet software by adding new spreadsheet functions to represent statistical distributions. These functions can be entered and used just like any other Excel or Lotus function. @RISK for Windows keeps track of all input distributions in an inputs and outputs list for easy reference.

➢ **Sensitivity Analysis** @RISK for Windows performs two types of sensitivity analysis (multivariate stepwise regression and Spearman rank-order correlation) to determine which of your inputs have the most impact on your outputs and in what way. The results can also be viewed graphically, using simple-to-interpret Tornado diagrams. Sensitivity analysis is an important starting point in an iterative risk analysis process that can save you both time and money.

➢ **Target Values** @RISK calculates the probabilities of achieving certain goals. Just enter in the value you would like an output to attain, and @RISK returns the probability of getting that value or less. Or enter in a percentile, and @RISK will return the value from the distribution at that percentile.

➢ **Scenario Analysis** Scenario Analysis identifies combinations of input variables that are the most important in causing a given output to achieve a user-specified target. For example, suppose a decision maker wants to identify the factors that might cause a project's costs to exceed a given level. There might be many possible variables, but @RISK's Scenario Analysis can isolate the most significant factors that drive costs above the target using what's known as a conditional median analysis to generate its scenarios. Scenario Analysis also tells you the values for these significant factors.

➢ **Convergence Monitoring** @RISK for Windows monitors the output distributions as they are generated. When they become "stable" (when changes in mean, standard deviation, and percentiles falls within tolerance you specify), @RISK stops running iterations, providing good results in less time.

➤ **Macros** @RISK for Windows contains a complete macro language, with a macro for each @RISK command. These macro commands can be used directly in your Excel or Lotus macro language allowing you to automate your risk analysis to any degree you desire. @RISK for Windows allows you to run macros before a simulation, before or after each iteration, or after a simulation, giving you complete control of your application.

➤ **Online Help** @RISK for Windows has complete online help to answer any question about @RISK functionality, including a PDF (Probability Density Function) Help, which contains all the information about distributions from the Appendix of the @RISK manual.

An @RISK Tutorial

This section contains a tutorial, which will lead you step-by-step through the features of @RISK, using the new product release scenario described earlier. The tutorial assumes a working knowledge of Excel or 1-2-3 commands, formulas, and menus. If you are not familiar with Excel or 1-2-3, please consult your Excel or 1-2-3 system documentation. It also assumes the user is familiar with basic mouse operations. The user should know how to perform the following mouse functions: Click, Double-click, and Drag.

The figures that accompany the chapter will show you what you should be seeing on your display as you complete the actions. There may be minor differences between your display and the one shown, depending on whether you are using Microsoft Excel or Lotus 1-2-3.

The tutorial covers the following topics:

➤ Starting @RISK and loading the sample model

➤ Looking at uncertainty in cell values

➤ Inputs and outputs for an @RISK simulation

➤ Simulation settings, running a simulation, and simulation results

➤ Viewing simulation results graphically

➤ Statistics on simulation results

➤ Cumulative curve

Starting @RISK and Loading the Sample Model

Prior to starting the tutorial, you will need to install @RISK onto your computer's hard drive from the accompanying CD-ROM according to the instructions found at the back of this book. To launch @RISK:

1. **Double-click on the @RISK icon in the Windows Program Manager.** The new product release scenario we discussed previously is included in the version of @RISK that accompanies this book. This model represents net cash flow and NPV (10 percent) for a potential new product that a company considered launching in 1993. To load this model, use the standard Excel or 1-2-3 File Open command.

2. **Select the Open command on the File menu.**

3. **Double-click the EXAMPLE file directory (a subdirectory beneath your @RISK directory).**

4. **Double-click FINANCE to open the worksheet.**

The onscreen @RISK toolbar contains all the commands necessary to set up and run a simulation on an Excel or 1-2-3 worksheet. Opening the FINANCE worksheet also automatically loads the simulation data for FINANCE that was distributed with your copy of @RISK. When you run and save your own simulations, the saved data will be reloaded each time you open a simulated worksheet.

Looking at Uncertainty in Cell Values

The @RISK demonstration model, FINANCE, looks just like a typical Excel or 1-2-3 worksheet (see Figure 11-1). In this financial model, worksheet columns are labeled

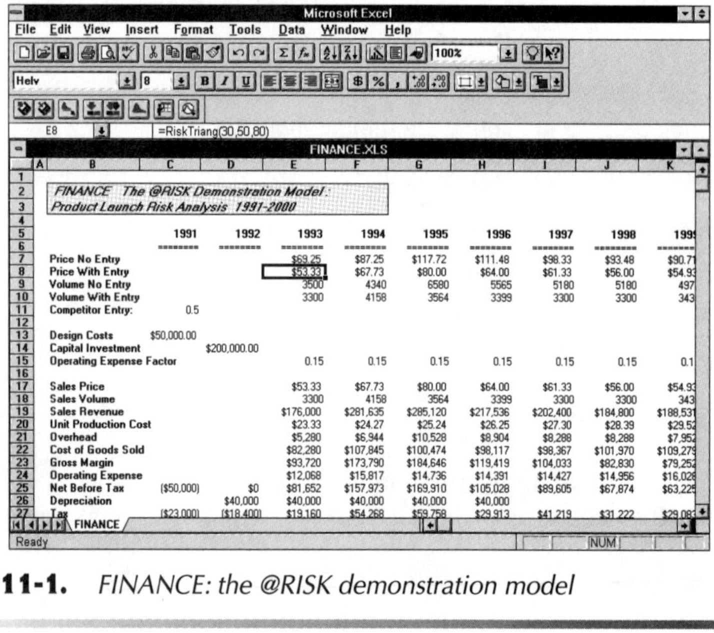

FIGURE 11-1. *FINANCE: the @RISK demonstration model*

as years and row headings show the variables. All cells show single entered or calculated values. To find @RISK and the uncertain cell values it uses:

> ➤ Click on cell E8.

The cursor is now positioned on the worksheet row labeled Price With Entry in the column for year 1993. Look up at the contents of cell E8 shown in the menu bar. Notice anything unusual? Cell E8 has the contents =RiskTriang(30,50,80) in Excel and @<<RISK>>TRIANG(30,50,80) in Lotus 1-2-3. TRIANG is not an Excel or 1-2-3 function—it is an @RISK function for a probability distribution. The function specifies that the values possible for this cell are described by a probability distribution that is triangular in shape. The distribution has a minimum value of 30, a most likely value of 50, and a maximum value of 80.

When you enter a distribution function in a worksheet cell, you specify a range of possible values for that cell. @RISK samples possible values for this cell from across the range of this distribution. In each iteration of the simulation, a new possible value will be sampled from the triangular distribution and placed in the worksheet cell.

What Is the Value Shown in a Cell?   The value shown in the worksheet for cell E8 is 53.33. What is this value and how was it calculated by @RISK? It is the expected value for a triangular distribution that has a minimum value of 30, a most likely value of 50, and a maximum value of 80. The expected value is also known as the mean of the distribution. This mean value is used when you recalculate your model using Excel or 1-2-3. By placing the expected value for distribution functions in worksheet cells, @RISK allows you to use Excel or 1-2-3 as you always have, with single, fixed cell values. However, with distribution functions, you can also use the simulation capabilities of @RISK to sample cell values from a range of possible values.

Other Distributions for Worksheet Cells   Let's look at some other examples of @RISK distribution functions.

1. Click on cell E9.

    Worksheet cell E9 specifies a normal distribution for cell values using the NORMAL function. This normal distribution has a mean of 3,500 and a standard deviation of 300. During a simulation, @RISK will sample a value for this cell from the entered normal distribution. Again, the cell value shown on the worksheet is the expected value for the distribution 3,500.

2. Click on cell E21.

    Distribution functions in @RISK can be used just like any Excel or 1-2-3 function. They may be included in a cell formula and may have arguments that are expressions and references to other worksheet cells. In Figure 11-2, the uniform distribution in cell E21 takes its minimum and maximum values from cell E18.

A wide variety of distribution types are available in @RISK. They are displayed under the Formula menu (Excel Version 4.0) or the Insert menu (Version 5.0) the Paste Function dialog box for easy entry into your formulas. By using the available distribution types, you can model nearly any type of uncertainty present in your worksheet models.

What Is an Output Range?   The worksheet cells that make up an output range specify the locations in the worksheet for which you would like to see simulation results. A simulation result is a probability distribution of the possible values that could occur for a worksheet cell. This distribution tells you the range of values possible for the cell and their relative likelihood of occurrence. The distribution also tells you the chance of achieving any value in the range of the distribution, i.e., what is the chance of a result of at least one million?

Typically, your simulation outputs will be the same cells that hold your worksheet results: profit, bottom line, etc. But any cell anywhere in the worksheet may be selected as an output.

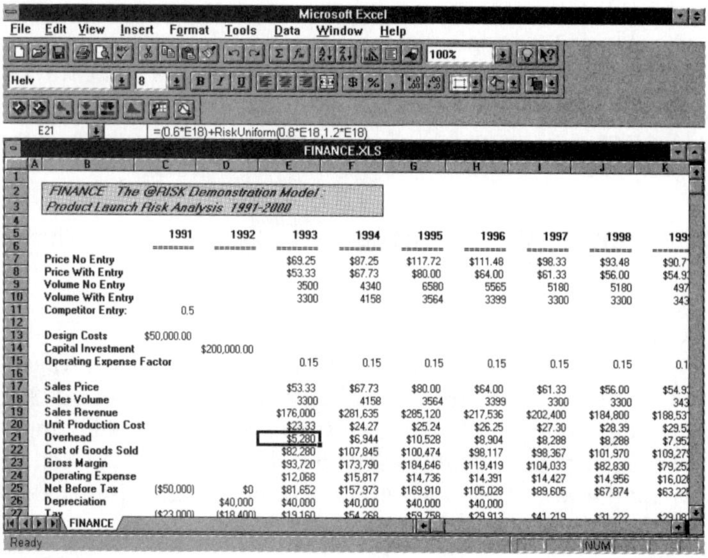

FIGURE 11-2.   *Use of @RISK functions within formulas*

Selecting Outputs for an @RISK Simulation
Let's select some outputs for the sample model FINANCE.

1. Click on cell C32 in the FINANCE worksheet.

2. Click the +Output icon on the @RISK toolbar.

3. Click and hold on cell C31 and drag the pointer across to highlight the range C31 to L31.

4. Click the +Output icon again. A black "Adding Output C32" box will appear on the screen while @RISK is preparing the spreadsheet for a simulation.

Inputs and Outputs for an @RISK Simulation
We've looked at how @RISK allows you to enter ranges of values in a single worksheet cell and select outputs for a simulation. But where is @RISK and how do you run a simulation with it?

1. Click the List icon on the @RISK toolbar. The Inputs By Output table, shown here, now appears in the @RISK window.

			Inputs By Output			
Outputs			**Inputs**			
Cell	**Name**	**Curren**	**Cell**	**Name**	**Current**	**Worksheet**
C32	NPV 10%	$115,070	E7	Price No Entry / 1993	Histogrm(50,90,{10,2,30,40,20,10})	FINANCE.XLS
C31	Net Cash Flow	($50,000)	E8	Price With Entry / 1993	Triang(30,50,80)	FINANCE.XLS
D31	Net Cash Flow	($200,000)	E9	Volume No Entry / 1993	Normal(3500,300)	FINANCE.XLS
E31	Net Cash Flow	$81,652	C11	Competitor Entry / 1991	Discrete({0,1},{50,50})	FINANCE.XLS
F31	Net Cash Flow	$125,945	C13	Design Costs / 1991	Normal(50000,10000)	FINANCE.XLS
G31	Net Cash Flow	$110,151	D14	Capital Investment / 1992	Normal(200000,30000)	FINANCE.XLS

Delete Output | **Fix/ Vary** | **Correlate** | **Hide List**

Outputs are ranges of cells in your worksheet for which you want to get simulation results. We already selected the outputs for the FINANCE worksheet. These ranges are listed in the Outputs portion of the window: the NPV 10 percent cell and the net cash flow cells. @RISK will automatically try to create a name for each input and output distribution cell. These names are created by scanning the spreadsheet around the cell where the input or output is located.

The Inputs portion of the table lists the cells that contain @RISK distribution functions.

2. Click the Hide icon to return to the FINANCE spreadsheet.

Simulation Settings

The @RISK toolbar invokes the commands necessary for executing a simulation on your worksheet model.

Let's take a look at the settings for the simulation of the FINANCE worksheet.

1. Click the Sim Sett icon on the @RISK toolbar. The Simulation Settings dialog box, shown here, appears on your screen.

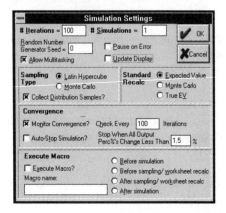

Notice the different setting options available in the Simulation Settings dialog box. Sampling Type controls how each distribution function in your worksheet will be sampled. The sampling type set here is Latin Hypercube. This option gives you the best simulation results in the least amount of time and is the default value for sampling type. The additional setting options are used to control different aspects of @RISK, such as seeding the random number generator, specifying the values displayed by distribution functions during a standard Excel or 1-2-3 recalculation, and others. For now, let's change just one of the default settings for running a simulation.

2. Click the Update Display check box to select it (if it is not already marked with an X).

Let's look at another important setting that is used in @RISK simulations.

Iterations An @RISK simulation works by repetitively recalculating a worksheet, each time using a new set of values sampled from each of the distribution functions contained in the worksheet. The number of iterations performed by a simulation can be any value. The default value, shown in the Simulation Settings dialog box, is 100. You usually will want to run your simulations with more than 100 iterations—300 to 500 is typical. We'll stick with 100 iterations in the tutorial to save time.

➤ Click OK to close the Simulation Settings dialog box and return to the FINANCE worksheet.

Running a Simulation

The @RISK Simulate icon starts a simulation of the FINANCE worksheet.

1. Click the Simulate icon on the @RISK toolbar.

2. Click No in the message box when asked to Save Current Simulation Results. (Remember, opening the FINANCE model opened the previously saved simulation data that was distributed with @RISK.)

Once the Simulate icon has been selected, the simulation of the FINANCE worksheet begins, as shown in Figure 11-3. With each iteration, @RISK draws a new sample from each distribution function in the worksheet and recalculates the entire worksheet using the new values.

For all analyses, if you want to see @RISK "animate" its operation during the simulation, click the Sim Sett icon on the @RISK toolbar and then click in the Update Display check box in the Simulation Settings dialog box or press the NUM LOCK key during the simulation. @RISK will then show you how it changes your spreadsheet iteration by iteration and generates results.

The sampled values combine to generate a range of possible results for your selected output cells. Each recalculation represents a new "What-if" scenario—a possible combination of values that could be encountered. With each iteration, @RISK collects the new calculated results from each cell in your selected output ranges as well as your input distributions. These values are stored on disk for use in creating and analyzing your output probability distributions.

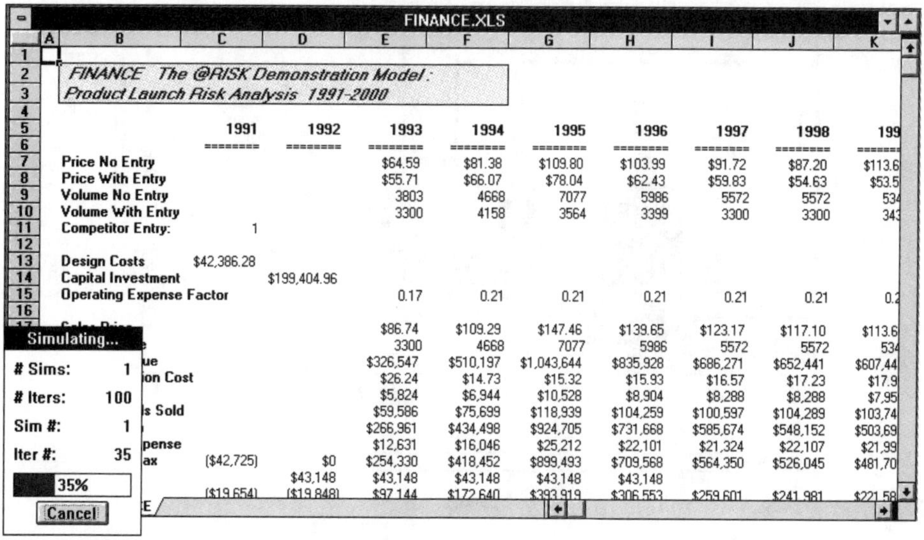

FIGURE 11-3. *Running a simulation*

Simulation Results

When the simulation is complete, @RISK displays your results in the @RISK window, in the form of Results and Simulation Statistics. The left side of Results displays a summary of the simulation that was executed, including the worksheet simulated, the number of iterations, the number of simulations, the number of input distributions, the number of output cells, sampling type, and simulation run time. The Summary of Results list shows the minimum, mean, and maximum values calculated for all output cells and input distributions that were sampled.

Simulation Statistics, displayed on the bottom half of the screen, gives detailed statistics on the same output cells and input distributions. These reports are useful for calculating target values across different output cells. To see simulation statistics for other output cells, click on the scroll bar at the right of the Summary of Results list.

Viewing Simulation Results Graphically

Numeric reports are nice, but often a graph better displays the distribution of possible results for a cell. To view simulation results graphically:

> Click the Graph icon on the @RISK toolbar. This generates a graph of the first highlighted entry in the Summary of Results list (NPV 10 percent), as shown in Figure 11-4.

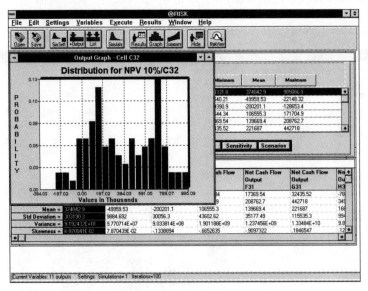

FIGURE 11-4.   *Graphing results in @RISK*

The Graph icon allows you to graph the simulation results for the cells in the outputs you entered earlier. The Summary of Results shown in the Results display lists each of the output cells for the simulation. The first cell listed, NPV at 10 percent, is the single cell in the NPV at 10 percent output range. The graph on the screen shows the distribution of the possible values for cell C32. The distribution is a graphic display of the uncertainty inherent in the results for this cell.

Your distribution may not be exactly the same as the one we show. Remember, each iteration randomly samples a new set of possible values from the distribution functions in the worksheet, and new results are calculated. Thus, different results were used in creating your distribution for NPV at 10 percent in cell C32 than were used for our distribution. If we had run a large number of iterations, say 1,000, then the results would be very similar from one simulation to another. Keep the graph for cell C32 on the screen for an upcoming graphing example.

Statistics on Simulation Results

Along with graphics, @RISK generates statistics for the output distributions from a simulation. Let's look at the statistics for cell C32.

1. To increase the size of the Simulation Statistics window, either press the maximize window button in the upper right-hand corner or double-click on the Simulation Statistics title.

    The statistics for all the output and input cells are displayed in this worksheet (see Figure 11-5). Listed below the minimum, maximum, and mean are additional statistics on the distribution, including the Standard Deviation, Variance, Skewness, and Kurtosis calculations.

NOTE
Your statistics will be slightly different from the ones in Figure 11-5 since you have slightly different simulation results.

2. Click the Restore command under the Control menu (under the minus sign in the upper left-hand corner) to return the sheet to normal size.

Percentiles   A probability distribution can be divided into equal probability increments called percentiles. @RISK calculates the percentiles of every output distribution generated by your simulations. The percentile values for NPV at 10 percent in cell C32 are shown in the displayed statistics report. A percentile value indicates the percentage of the generated results that are less than or equal to the associated value.

	NPV 10%	Net Cash Flow	Net Cash Flow	Net Cash Flow	Net Cash Flow	Net Cash Flow	Net C
Name							
Description	Output	Output	Output	Output	Output	Output	Outpu
Cell	C32	C31	D31	E31	F31	G31	H31
Minimum =	-244331.8	-73640.21	-289390.9	-11644.34	17369.54	32435.52	-7816.
Maximum =	985086.1	-22148.32	-128653.4	171704.9	208762.7	442718	34960
Mean =	374042.9	-49959.53	-200201.1	106555.3	139669.4	221687	16651
Std Deviation =	303190.3	9884.692	30056.3	43602.62	35177.49	115535.3	99412
Variance =	9.192432E+10	9.770714E+07	9.033814E+08	1.901188E+09	1.237456E+09	1.33484E+10	9.8829
Skewness =	6.070841E-02	7.870439E-02	-.1338894	-.6652635	-.9097322	.1846547	.12092
Kurtosis =	1.890587	2.83848	3.012898	2.60189	4.288673	1.508613	1.5250
Errors Calculated =	0	0	0	0	0	0	0
Mode =	708467.1	-51756.16	-205003.7	139618.8	165699.3	104235	72602
5% Perc =	-78862.8	-66518.84	-249460.8	19274.08	67546.34	80423.81	30360
10% Perc =	-3211.806	-63159.62	-238872.3	44038.85	96490.04	84217.8	48094
15% Perc =	28071.53	-60374.53	-232050.5	49784.45	107739	94884.98	57489
20% Perc =	107428.4	-58449.34	-225663.6	66908.48	119170.9	108298.6	70996
25% Perc =	123299.9	-56950.77	-220558.7	81313.53	121205	113491.2	77000
30% Perc =	153908.9	-55434.67	-216106.9	84560.2	124418.5	119023.1	82254
35% Perc =	179446.4	-54100.54	-212124.5	93244.98	130581.2	128951.1	91034
40% Perc =	210869.7	-52633.2	-208315.4	97517.23	133841.3	144208.8	10177
45% Perc =	282749.2	-51472.3	-204513.3	105338.7	137363.2	158903.5	11800
50% Perc =	312662.5	-50141.7	-200372.1	110557.1	141564.5	191225.8	14038
55% Perc =	427435.2	-48783.91	-196783.9	121868.8	148345	255559	20043
60% Perc =	487901.3	-47694.45	-192617.1	130986.3	152293.8	269285.1	20813
65% Perc =	535141.3	-46372.53	-188644.5	135589.9	156337.4	299368.4	23296
70% Perc =	610913	-44930.43	-184983.9	137804.4	160212.5	322092.1	25345
75% Perc =	665143.1	-43356.99	-179900.3	141919.2	164645	336596.7	26580
80% Perc =	691950.4	-41698.66	-175008.9	145078.1	167052.8	345547.5	27334
85% Perc =	723468.2	-40015.92	-169746.3	150924.5	172178.7	353984.6	28061
90% Perc =	751362	-37410.47	-162984.3	156098.6	177282.6	372652.9	29426
95% Perc =	803197.9	-34422.48	-151073	158528.3	189194.3	395236.6	31392
Filter Minimum =							
Filter Maximum =							
Type (1 or 2) =							

FIGURE 11-5. *Detailed statistics in @RISK*

Cumulative Curve

A distribution of possible values for a worksheet cell also can be displayed as a cumulative probability distribution.

1. Click the Output Graph - Cell C32 entry on the Window menu.

2. Click the right mouse button on the graph window to get a new submenu.

3. Select Type from the submenu. The Type dialog box displays the available options for the type of graph that is displayed. The graph for cell C32 is currently displayed as a histogram with bars. The histogram is divided into 20 classes or bars, as reflected in the #Classes/Points field of the Type dialog box. Let's change the settings to display an ascending cumulative curve in area graph format.

4. Click the Cumulative Ascending option button in the Type field.

5. Click the Area Graph option button in the Display Using field. The Type dialog box should now look like this:

6. Click OK.

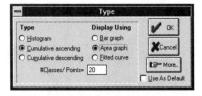

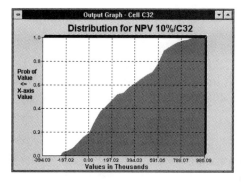

The graph of the distribution of possible values for NPV at 10 percent in cell C32 is now shown as a cumulative probability curve, as you can see here.

The ascending cumulative curve shows the chance of a result less than or equal to any value in the range of the distribution. You can see that there is a 0 percent probability that NPV at 10 percent in cell C32 will be less than –215,000 and a 100 percent probability that the value will be less than approximately 1,000,000.

REMEMBER
Due to the random nature of simulation and the small number of iterations run, your results may be slightly different than those shown in the illustration above. We have more simulation results to look at, as there were other output ranges selected in @RISK.

7. Double-click the control menu box in the upper-left corner of the graph window to close it.

The Summary of Results lists each of the cells in each output range for the simulation. The second cell listed, C31 Net Cash Flow, is the first cell in the net cash flow output range.

8. Select the second entry in the Summary of Results list (C31 Net Cash Flow).

9. Click the Summary icon on the @RISK toolbar. A summary graph is generated for the net cash flow output range, as shown here.

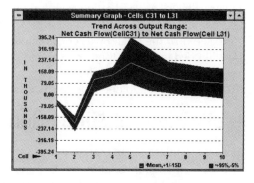

Summary Graph   The graph displayed for the net cash flow output range is a summary graph. During the simulation, a probability distribution was generated for each cell in the output range—a total of ten cells and ten distributions. This graph summarizes the ten distributions generated for the cells in the net cash flow output range.

The center line represents the trend in the expected value of the distributions. The bands surrounding the trend represent (from bottom to top) the 10th percentile to the 90th percentile, respectively. The summary graph is very useful for looking at how values change across the selected output range. For example, this graph shows how the expected value for net cash flow goes negative then positive over the first three cells in the range (the first three years of the model). The band around the trend widens or spreads in cell #5 in the range. This means that the risk or variability in results increases. An individual probability distribution can be viewed for any cell in the output range as we did with the NPV.

We're done for now, so let's exit @RISK.

1. Click the Hide icon on the @RISK toolbar.

2. Select Exit on the File menu to exit Excel or 1-2-3.

3. Click No when prompted to save the FINANCE worksheet.

@RISK Summary

In just a few steps, you've used @RISK to perform a powerful risk analysis. You have gotten a look at how uncertainty is specified for cell values in @RISK. You've run a simulation on the sample model and seen the execution displayed on the screen. And you've looked at the results of a simulation. We saw probable values for the NPV and cash flows for the next ten years.

Another @RISK Example

Now that you've been introduced to @RISK for Windows, let's have an expert show you how to produce some great results with very basic spreadsheet models. Wayne L. Winston (Ph.D., Yale University), the author of the following example and text, is a professor of decision and information systems at Indiana University, where he has won numerous awards for teaching excellence. He is the author of numerous textbooks and articles, including *Operations Research: Applications and Algorithms*, 3rd ed., and *Introduction to Mathematical Programming*, 2nd ed.

To see how the model was constructed, as described in the rest of this section, you will need to launch the @RISK demo program and load the sample model as described earlier in the chapter. The sample files mentioned are included with the @RISK software in a folder called WINSTON.

Applications of Simulation to Finance

Many companies use simulation in their capital budgeting and financial planning processes. Simulation can be used to model the uncertainty associated with future cash flows. Simulation can be used to answer questions such as:

> What is the mean and variance of a project's net present value (NPV)?

➤ What is the probability that a project will have a negative NPV?

➤ What are the mean and variance of a company's profit during the next fiscal year?

➤ What is the probability that during the next year a company will have to borrow more than $2 million?

The following example illustrates how simulation can be used to compare investment opportunities.

General Ford Auto Corporation (GF) is trying to determine what type of compact car to develop. There are two models under consideration. Each model is assumed to generate sales for ten years. In order to determine which model should be built, information about the following quantities has been gathered through focus groups with the marketing and engineering departments.

➤ **Fixed Cost of Developing Car** This cost is assumed to be incurred at the beginning of year 1 (or end of year 0), before any sales are recorded.

➤ **Variable Production Cost** The variable cost incurred in producing a car.

➤ **Sales Price** Assumed to be $10,000 for each model.

➤ **Sales of Car During Each of Next Ten Years** For simplicity we will assume that all sales occur at the end of each year.

➤ **Interest Rate** It is assumed that cash flows are discounted at 10 percent. This means that a cash outflow of one dollar at the beginning of year 1 is equivalent to a cash outflow of $1.10 at the end of year 1.

Fixed and variable costs and annual sales are not known with certainty. The views of marketing and engineering about these quantities are summarized in Tables 11-1, 11-2, and 11-3.

FIXED COST FOR MODEL 1		FIXED COST FOR MODEL 2	
Probability	Value	Probability	Value
.50	$6 billion	.25	$4 billion
.50	$8 billion	.50	$5 billion
		.25	$16 billion

TABLE 11-1. *Fixed Costs for Models 1 and 2*

VARIABLE COST FOR MODEL 1		VARIABLE COST FOR MODEL 2	
Probability	**Value**	**Probability**	**Value**
.50	$4,600	.50	$2,000
.50	$5,400	.50	$6,000

TABLE 11-2. *Variable Costs for Models 1 and 2*

Of course, if a car sells well the first year, it probably will sell well in subsequent years. GF models this belief using the following relationship:

Expected Year t Sales for a Model = Actual Year $t-1$ Sales

Then GF assumes that

Actual Year $t-1$ Sales for a Model = Expected Year t Sales + Error Term

The error term models the variability of each model's sales about the expected sales for each year. For model 1, we assume that the error term is normally distributed with a mean of 0 and standard deviation of 20,000. For model 2, we assume that the error term is normally distributed with a mean of 0 and a standard deviation of 30,000.

For simplicity, we assume that the variable cost for each year's production is the same. This ignores inflation. How do we use simulation to compare the merits of the two proposed models?

Figure 11-6 (file NPV1.WK4 or NPV1.XLS) contains the spreadsheet used to simulate the NPV for model 1. We will describe the development of the spreadsheet for model 1 and leave model 2 to the reader.

YEAR 1 UNIT SALES FOR MODEL 1 (NUMBER OF CARS)		YEAR 1 UNIT SALES FOR MODEL 2 (NUMBER OF CARS)	
Probability	**Value**	**Probability**	**Value**
.25	230,000	.25	80,000
.50	250,000	.50	220,000
.25	270,000	.25	390,000

TABLE 11-3. *Projected First-Year Sales for Model 1 and Model 2*

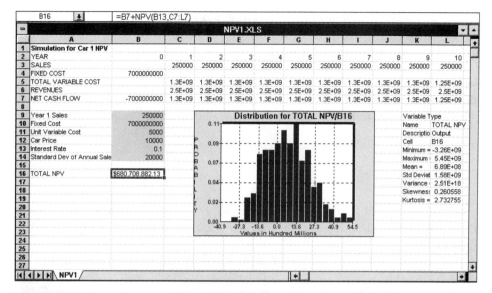

| B16 | ⬇ | =B7+NPV(B13,C7:L7) |

NPV1.XLS

	A	B	C	D	E	F	G	H	I	J	K	L
1	Simulation for Car 1 NPV											
2	YEAR	0	1	2	3	4	5	6	7	8	9	10
3	SALES		250000	250000	250000	250000	250000	250000	250000	250000	250000	250000
4	FIXED COST	7000000000										
5	TOTAL VARIABLE COST		1.3E+09	1.3E+09	1.3E+09	1.3E+09	1.3E+09	1.3E+09	1.3E+09	1.3E+09	1.3E+09	1.25E+09
6	REVENUES		2.5E+09	2.5E+09	2.5E+09	2.5E+09	2.5E+09	2.5E+09	2.5E+09	2.5E+09	2.5E+09	2.5E+09
7	NET CASH FLOW	-7000000000	1.3E+09	1.3E+09	1.3E+09	1.3E+09	1.3E+09	1.3E+09	1.3E+09	1.3E+09	1.3E+09	1.25E+09
8												
9	Year 1 Sales	250000										
10	Fixed Cost	7000000000										
11	Unit Variable Cost	5000										
12	Car Price	10000										
13	Interest Rate	0.1										
14	Standard Dev of Annual Sale	20000										
15												
16	TOTAL NPV	$680,708,882.13										
17												

Distribution for TOTAL NPV/B16

Variable Type
Name   TOTAL NPV
Descriptio Output
Cell   B16
Minimum = -3.26E+09
Maximum : 5.45E+09
Mean =   6.89E+08
Std Deviat 1.58E+09
Variance : 2.51E+18
Skewness 0.260558
Kurtosis = 2.732755

NPV1

FIGURE 11-6. *The spreadsheet for model 1 with @RISK results*

The following describes how the spreadsheet was built. We began by entering the inputs for our simulation in the cell range B9-B14. In cell B9 of Figure 11-6, we generated year 1 sales by entering the following formula:

[1-2-3] @RiskDiscrete(230000,250000,270000,.25,.5,.25)

[Excel] =RiskDiscrete({230000,250000,270000},{.25,.5,.25})

In cell B11, we generated the variable cost for each car by entering the following statement:

[1-2-3] @RiskDiscrete(4600,5400,.5,.5)

[Excel] =RiskDiscrete({4600,5400},{.5,.5})

This ensures that there is an equal chance that the variable cost of each car will be $4,600 or $5,400.

In cell B10 we generated the fixed cost associated with model 1 by entering this statement:

[1-2-3] @RiskDiscrete(6000000000,8000000000,.5,.5)

[Excel] =RiskDiscrete({6000000000,8000000000},{.5,.5})

This ensures that fixed cost is equally likely to be 6 or 8 billion dollars.

In cell B12 we entered the sales price ($10,000) for each car. Then in cell B13 we entered the interest rate (.1 or 10%). Finally, in cell B14 we entered the standard deviation (20,000 cars) of annual unit sales about last year's actual sales.

In cell C3 we entered the year 1 sales generated in cell B9 with this formula:

[1-2-3] +B9

[Excel] =B9

Recall that actual year sales $(t-1)$ equals expected year sales (t) plus the error term. Using this relationship and the error term determined above:

Year 2 Sales = Year 1 Sales + (Normal random variable with mean 0 and $\sigma = 20,000$)

To model this relationship, we generated year 2 sales by entering into cell D3 the formula:

[1-2-3] +C3+@RiskNormal(0,$B14)

[Excel] =C3+RiskNormal(0,$B14)

Copying this formula from cell D3 to E3..L3 generates sales for years 3-10.

In cell B4 we reentered the fixed cost (assumed to be incurred in year 0, before the sales of any cars occur) with this formula:

[1-2-3] +B10

[Excel] =B10

In cell C5 we determined that Year 1 Total Variable Cost = (Variable Cost per car)*(Year 1 Sales) by entering:

[1-2-3] +C3*$B11

[Excel] =C3*$B11

Copying this formula to the range D5..L5 generates the total variable cost incurred during each year.

In cell C6 we computed Year 1 Revenues = (Car Price)*(Year 1 Sales) by entering this formula:

[1-2-3] +$B12*C3

[Excel] =$B12*C3

Copying this formula to the range D6..L6 generates sales revenue received during years 2-10.

In cell B7 we computed Year 0 Net Cash Flow = -(Fixed Cost) by entering:

[1-2-3] -B4

[Excel] =-B4

In cell C7 we generated Year 1 Net Cash Flow = Year 1 Revenues - Year 1 Variable Costs by entering:

[1-2-3] +C6-C5

[Excel] =C6-C5

Copying this formula to the range D7..L7 generates net cash flow for years 2-10. In cell B16 we determined the NPV of all cash flows by entering the statement:

[1-2-3] +B7 + @NPV(B13,C7..L7) *or* (1+B13)*@NPV(B7..L7)

[Excel] =B7 + NPV(B13,C7:L7) *or* =(1+B13)*NPV(B7:L7)

This statement computes the NPV for years 1 through 10 according to the following formula, which is the NPV of all cash flows:

$$\text{Net Cash Flow Year } 0 + \frac{\text{Net Cash Flow Year } 1}{(1+.1)} + \frac{\text{Net Cash Flow Year } 2}{(1+.1)^2} + \ldots + \frac{\text{Net Cash Flow Year } 10}{(1+.1)^{10}}$$

Next we selected cell B16 as our output cell using the Add Outputs button and ran a 400 iterations simulation with @RISK. See Figure 11-6 for the results of the simulation. A histogram of the NPVs for the 400 iterations is given in Figure 11-6. After running 400 iterations of model 2 we obtained the results in Table 11-4. Note that to simulate model 2 we need only change our inputs for model 1 in cells B9, B10, B11, and B14.

	MODEL 1	MODEL 2
Average NPV	$682 million	$990 million
Standard Deviation	1.47 billion	7.40 billion
Probability NPV<0	34.25%	43.38%
Probability NPV<−1 billion	12.8%	35.67%

TABLE 11-4. *Results for Car Simulation*

Table 11-4 indicates that model 1 has a lower expected NPV than model 2. Model 1 also has a much lower standard deviation than model 2. This indicates that on the average, model 2 yields a higher NPV, but that model 2 is a much riskier proposition than model 1. This is confirmed by the fact that for our simulation, model 1 has only a 15.6 percent chance of losing more than $1 billion (in NPV terms), while model 2 has a 35.67 percent chance of losing more than $1 billion. If your company is strongly risk-averse, then model 1 is the way to go.

The NPV probabilities were obtained by calculating Target values. If you scroll down in the Simulation Statistics window, you will come to a section with row labels "Target#1 (Value)," "Target#1 (Perc%)," and so on. Here you can find the probability of a value occuring or the value attained at any given probability level for any input or output. To calculate the probability that the NPV will be less than 0, select the "Target #1 (Value)" cell under "TOTAL NPV," type 0 and press ENTER. A probability will appear in the "Target#1 (Perc%)" cell close to 34%. Similarly, you can enter a probability percent and get the value whose cumulative probability is the one entered. You can calculate up to ten Target values at one time.

Using the Triangular Distribution to Model Sales
It is unrealistic to assume that year 1 sales must always equal 230,000, 250,000, or 270,000 cars. A more realistic model would allow car sales for year 1 to assume any value between 230,000 and 270,000. To model this possibility, we enter into cell B9 the statement:

[1-2-3] @RiskTriang(230000,250000,270000)

[Excel] =RiskTriang(230000,250000,270000)

This ensures that year 1 sales are drawn from the distribution pictured in Figure 11-7.
For obvious reasons this is called a *triangular distribution.* The first input to the RiskTriang statement is the smallest value (most pessimistic) the random variable can assume, the second input is the most likely value the random variable can assume, and the final input is the largest value (most optimistic outcome) the

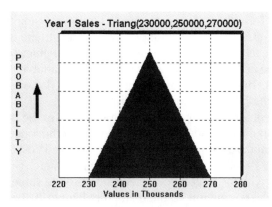

FIGURE 11-7. *Triangular Distribution for Year 1 Sales*

random variable can assume. It is useful to model a random variable by a triangular distribution when you have a good guess at the best case, worst case, and most likely scenarios.

To get an idea of the probabilities implied by a triangular distribution, recall that probabilities of interest for any continuous random variable can be found by finding the area under the density function. For example, Figure 11-7 implies that the probability that year 1 sales are at most 240,000 cars equals

.5*(240,000-230,000)*(.000025) =.125

and the probability that year 2 sales are between 240,000 and 250,000 cars equals

.5*(250,000-240,000)*(.00005 + .000025) = .375.

NOTE
In our triangular distribution, the most pessimistic and most optimistic outcomes are the same distance from the most likely outcome. It is unnecessary to make this assumption.

Sensitivity Analysis with Tornado Graphs
A question of natural interest is which inputs to the simulation have the most effect on our output (NPV). We can answer this question using the Tornado graph shown in Figure 11-8. The Tornado graph was generated by clicking on the Sensitivity button in the Results window and then clicking the Graph button and selecting either Correlation or Regression in the dialog box.

The regression Tornado graph was created as follows. Using the results of our 400 iterations as data, @RISK ran a multiple regression with the dependent variable being the NPV for each iteration and the independent variables being the values for each iteration of the cells that are "random" (fixed cost, variable cost per unit, and sales for each year). Then @RISK graphed the standardized regression (or beta) coefficients for each of the independent variables.

A beta coefficient for an independent variable indicates the number of standard deviations by which the dependent variable increases if the independent variable increases by one standard deviation. Thus, increasing fixed cost by one standard deviation will decrease NPV by .636 standard deviations, etc. The most influential variables are those with the largest coefficients (in absolute value) in the Tornado graph. Thus, from the correlation Tornado graph in Figure 11-8, we find that fixed cost and variable cost per car are the most influential variables on NPV, with year 2 and year 3 sales right behind.

The correlation Tornado graph plots the correlation between any cell that is "random" and the output cell (NPV). The variables having the most influence on the dependent variable are those with the largest (in absolute value) correlation with the dependent variable. From the correlation Tornado graph in Figure 11-8, we find that fixed cost and unit variable cost are again the most influential variables, followed by year 2 sales and year 1 sales.

Sensitivity Analysis with Scenarios

You can also use the @RISK Scenarios command to do sensitivity analysis. For each output cell you can enter up to three scenarios. To do this, move to the bottom of the statistics results. The default scenarios are the 10th, 75th, and 90th percentile for the output cell. For each scenario, @RISK will look at those iterations that "meet" the scenario and identify any "random" cell whose median value for

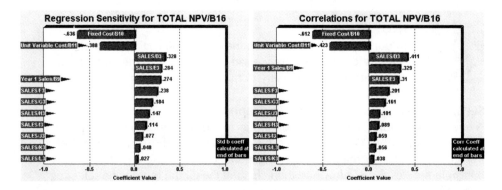

FIGURE 11-8.   *Tornado diagrams for the NPV*

iterations meeting the scenario differs by .5 standard deviations or more from its overall median. Click on the Scenarios button to access Scenarios.

If you highlight the cell(s) in the top part of the scenario report, you will obtain a more detailed analysis in the bottom half of the screen. @RISK will identify random cells whose values appear to be atypical when a scenario is met. In a particular simulation (the NPV>75% scenario), @RISK identifies cell E3 (year 3 sales) as being .5 standard deviations above average. This means that for the iterations in which NPV was in the top 25 percent of all iterations, the median of year 3 sales were .5 standard deviations above the median for all iterations.

For the NPV>90% scenario, @RISK identified cell D3 (year 2 sales) as having a median value of .65 standard deviations above the overall median for iterations in which NPV was in top 10 percent of all iterations. @RISK also identified cell E3 (year 3 sales) as having a median value of .62 standard deviations above the overall median for iterations in which NPV was in the top 10 percent of all iterations.

For the NPV<25% scenario, @RISK identified cells B11 (unit variable cost) and B10 (unit fixed cost) as both having a median value two standard deviations above the overall median for iterations in which NPV was in bottom 25 percent of all iterations. Thus we see that the Scenarios command allows us to zero in on variables that assume atypical values when a particular scenario occurs. For example, we see that when NPV is very low both fixed and variable costs tend to be much higher than average. When NPV is very high, sales during years 2 and 3 tend to be much higher than average.

NOTE
If you plan to create a Tornado graph or a Scenario Analysis, you must turn on the Collect Distributions Sample setting in the Simulations Settings dialog box.

Conclusion

Risk analysis is an important process that allows you to minimize any hazards you may face. One type of risk analysis, simulation, takes you beyond basic "What-if" analysis by allowing you to take into account ranges of possible outcomes as opposed to just best- and worst-case scenarios. @RISK adds the power of risk analysis to a familiar workspace—your spreadsheet. We've seen in this chapter the kinds of financial analysis @RISK can perform. But @RISK can do more than just predict your NPV. *Any* spreadsheet you have that contains values you are uncertain of can undergo risk analysis using @RISK. It is a powerful tool in your quest for answers in an uncertain world.

CHAPTER 12

Making Informed Decisions with Statistical Forecasting

by Eric Stellwagen, Robert Goodrich, and Kathleen Heming
Business Forecast Systems, Inc.

According to the *Oxford English Dictionary,* to *forecast* is to "estimate or calculate beforehand." Since every corporation plans for its future, every organization must forecast, although not all of them formalize the process.

The purpose of forecasting is to improve decision making. Accurately forecasting the demand for products or services allows a corporation to better meet that demand while maintaining lower inventories or staffing levels. Thus the forecast's contribution to the management process is, or should be, measured in dollars.

With today's emphasis on global competitiveness and concepts such as just-in-time production, there is increasing pressure on corporations to improve the accuracy of their forecasts. This has spawned a growing demand for easy-to-use forecasting software that is accessible to the average businessperson and integrates easily with the corporate IS environment.

This chapter will survey the forecasting needs of a typical corporation and discuss some of the issues facing the corporate forecaster. It will explore commonly used statistical forecasting methodology and illustrate how the use of intelligent software can improve and automate the forecasting process, saving both time and money. The chapter will conclude with a hands-on demonstration allowing the reader to use the Forecast Pro for Windows software to generate forecasts for a variety of business data.

Forecasting in a Corporate Environment

In a typical corporation, forecasts are often generated in several different departments and are used for different purposes.

To plan production and to control inventories, forecasts must be generated at the lowest level of aggregation. A widget manufacturer, for example, needs to know how many blue widgets to produce in size 5, style B. Often there are thousands of such SKUs (stock keeping units) to forecast. At this level, the forecasts drive thousands of relatively minor decisions made on a daily basis (e.g., materials movements across a network of factories, warehouses, and local distribution facilities). The pace of the decision making is fast and time horizons are short, but no single decision is crucial to the organization. The forecasting process must be nearly automatic and fully computerized in order to handle such large volumes of data. Forecasting is usually just one component of a larger information system.

In the marketing or revenue planning department, the forecaster typically deals with higher levels of aggregation. A product manager, for instance, may submit periodic sales projections at the brand level for different markets. These forecasts may be disseminated upward to support revenue projections or to plan corporate strategy, or downward to plan procurement or production. Managers at this level often rely on statistical forecasting models based on historical sales figures. At times they will judgmentally adjust the statistical forecasts to incorporate their knowledge or beliefs of future events (e.g., advance orders, upcoming price changes, etc.). They produce their forecasts on their desktops working with interactive forecasting software and strive to understand issues such as the impact of promotions, product cannibalizations, position in the product line, etc.

In the boardroom, corporate planners integrate forecasts of revenues, cash flows, market share, and other crucial variables into the plans that steer the corporation. Although the forecasts are usually judgmental, they are based on objective summary data, including forecasts that have percolated upward through the corporation. Few decisions are made, but each one is crucial to the corporation, perhaps for years to come. Individuals at this level are unlikely to use forecasting or other analytic products on their own desktops.

Judgment vs. Statistics

Some industries, such as electric power, telecommunications, and finance, employ professionals whose primary responsibility is forecasting. These individuals tend to have training in either statistics or econometrics and are comfortable using statistical models to prepare forecasts.

In most industries, however, preparing forecasts is not centralized and is one of many responsibilities for individuals with titles like product manager, marketing analyst, production planner or materials manager. These professionals possess a great deal of knowledge about how their business is run, but few of them have formal training in statistics or econometrics. As a result, when faced with the task of preparing forecasts, these individuals rely on either judgment, simple quantitative representations or algorithms (e.g., moving averages, percentage growth, best-fit line, etc.), or highly automated forecasting software.

We cannot unequivocally identify statistical (quantitative) methods as superior or inferior to judgmental methods except in particular cases. Ideally, any comprehensive forecasting system, be it automated or not, should incorporate both. The following list compares some of the features of the two approaches.

> ➤ The advantage most frequently cited for judgmental forecasting is that the user can incorporate nonquantitative information or knowledge of events that are likely to occur in the future. Humans can sometimes recognize data patterns that are missed in pure statistical analysis. Unfortunately, humans can also often "recognize" patterns that do not exist.

> ➤ Judgmental forecasts are always subjective and often biased as a consequence of wishful thinking, conformity to the group, conformity to goals, etc.

> ➤ Judgmental forecasts are neither consistently more accurate nor less accurate than quantitative. Their relative accuracy depends upon the interplay of many factors.

> ➤ Judgmental forecasting is much more expensive than quantitative forecasting because of the high cost of human time. Judgmental methods are not suitable for forecasting large numbers of items.

> ➤ Quantitative methods are supported by statistical computer software and can usually be made nearly automatic.

➤ Statistical forecasts include confidence limits as well as point forecasts. Production and inventory control planning use the confidence limits to set stocking levels. At a more strategic level, confidence limits can be used to assess risk.

➤ Quantitative forecasts can be repeated and lend themselves well to performance tuning. Judgmental forecasts are much more volatile and harder to incorporate in a forecasting system.

As the need for quantitative forecasting grows in the business world, businesspeople look for resources to support expanded forecasting activity. Many businesspeople recognize the potential benefits of quantitative forecasting but do not have the statistical background to implement it. For the most part, rather than turning to the professional societies or literature to learn statistics, they acquire software packages that incorporate the forecasting expertise that they need. Although academics have expressed some concern over this trend, most businesspeople see it simply as a solution.

"Intelligent" forecasting software gives businesspeople access to statistical forecasting techniques regardless of their quantitative analysis skills. The software embodies a "statistical strategy" that enables it to automatically make analytical decisions that would otherwise require human expertise. In a sense, when a corporation purchases a highly automated forecasting package, what they receive is as much a service as a product. They acquire the services of an expert forecasting consultant, safely packaged as a software product.

Forecasting Software

Most forecasting software falls into one of three categories: general statistics packages, business forecasting packages, or batch forecasters (forecasting engines).

General statistics packages are designed for statisticians. They tend to offer a wide range of analytical tools. Forecasting is almost always available, usually as an optional (extra cost) module. These packages assume a strong quantitative background on the part of the user and require that all model building and validation decisions be made by the user. Examples of popular general statistical packages include SAS and SPSS.

Business forecasting software is designed for businesspeople. These packages tend to be fairly narrow in scope, offering only forecasting and concentrating on the forecasting models most relevant to business (exponential smoothing, Box-Jenkins, and dynamic regression). The software usually offers an automatic mode, in which the software can make all of the modeling decisions, and an interactive mode, in which the user maintains control. Examples of popular business forecasting packages are Forecast Pro, featured in this chapter,

SmartForecasts by Smart Software, Inc. of Belmont, MA (see Chapter 13), and Autocast, from Delphus, Inc. of Morristown, NJ.

Batch forecasting packages are designed to forecast large numbers (hundreds or thousands) of items automatically. Although they can be operated independently, they are usually integrated with other software such as production planning or inventory control systems. Most business forecasting software packages, including all of the ones listed above, offer batch versions, and many production planning and inventory control systems include their own forecasting engines.

Creating Statistically Based Forecasts

Preparing statistically based forecasts requires that the forecaster execute the following four steps.

1. Collect a database of historic values for the item to be forecast.

2. Identify the form of a statistical model that is likely to fit the data.

3. Fit the parameters of the model to the historical data.

4. Use the equations of the fitted statistical model to extrapolate (forecast) from the historical data.

Forecasting software packages vary greatly in the forecasting techniques they provide and the amount to which the user is responsible for performing the above steps.

Data Collection

Forecasting packages work with time series. A *time series* is a set of measurements for a variable evenly spaced in time (e.g., monthly sales figures or inventory levels for the last four years). Preparing the forecasting database is usually accomplished by exporting a file of historical records from the corporate database and formatting it for input into the forecasting package. If you plan to use any associated explanatory variables (advertising budgets, economic indicators, etc.), that data also needs to be included.

Selecting a Forecasting Model

Most software packages offer a variety of forecasting techniques to accommodate different types of data. The methods most useful for business applications include these four: moving averages, exponential smoothing models, and Box-Jenkins for univariate forecasting (univariate techniques forecast based solely upon the past history of the forecast variable); and dynamic regression for multivariate forecasting (multivariate techniques forecast based on the historical relationships among several variables).

The moving average is an extremely simple forecasting technique that averages the values of the variable's recent history. For example, to prepare a forecast for next month's widget sales using a three-month moving average, you would add together the widget sales figures for the most recent three months and divide by three. Moving averages are incapable of forecasting trends or seasonal patterns and should only be used when the data are extremely short or extremely volatile.

Exponential smoothing models are the most widely used of the statistical models and are found in most forecasting software. They work by identifying features found in the historical data, such as trends and seasonal patterns, and projecting them into the future. Their ability to adapt to change and to smooth over volatile data makes them ideal for most univariate product-oriented forecasting.

The Box-Jenkins technique extrapolates correlations of the data from the past to the future. If these correlations are strong, homogeneous, and stable, then Box-Jenkins is likely to yield more accurate forecasts than exponential smoothing. However, if the data are highly irregular, or if the correlations are changing over time, Box-Jenkins may perform poorly. In these cases, it sometimes extrapolates data correlations that do not really exist.

Dynamic regression allows you to model relationships between the variable you wish to forecast (the dependent variable) and explanatory variables such as promotional schedules, advertising budgets, demographic information, and economic indicators (independent variables). Dynamic regression produces an equation that captures the behavioral relationship of a dependent variable to its own past and that of the explanatory variables. You should use regression only when (1) the data are long and stable enough to support a correlational model, (2) reliable forecasts for the explanatory variable(s) are available, and (3) the model outperforms univariate techniques.

General statistics packages place the burden of selecting an appropriate model for a given data set entirely on the user's shoulders. Most business forecasting packages offer both automatic and manual model selection. A few batch forecasting packages offer automatic model selection; however, many limit the available models to exponential smoothing and simple techniques (moving averages, percentage growth, same as last month, etc.) and force the user to select the same technique for all time series.

Approaching the Data

In the next section ("Forecast Pro's Statistical Strategy") we will explore one approach to automatic model selection. Before we do this, let's look at a specific example and consider how a human forecaster might approach the same problem.

Often, the first step in modeling an unfamiliar time series is to examine it graphically. This enables you to make some general conclusions about the major characteristics of the data.

Figure 12-1 depicts the time series INWARD, which represents monthly installations of residential telephones. We do not have any explanatory variables for this data set, so we will only consider univariate techniques. As you examine the data, ask yourself the following questions: Is the data trended? Is the data seasonal? Is the data highly irregular?

The first two questions are easy. The overall positive trend is obvious. The consistently high Septembers and repetitive annual pattern indicate strong seasonal factors.

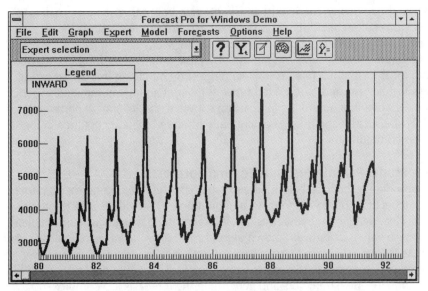

FIGURE 12-1. *A graph of residential telephone installations*

The forecaster's own knowledge of the data (*domain knowledge*) can also help to answer these questions. A telecommunications forecaster familiar with this data set would know that the strong September peaks are caused by new connections for returning college students and that the overall trend is caused by improvements in the local economy or by population increases.

The third question is harder to answer but very important. There are three univariate techniques under consideration: simple moving averages, exponential smoothing, and Box-Jenkins. Simple moving average is ruled out, because it can account for neither trending nor seasonal changes. Exponential smoothing and Box-Jenkins can both account for these features, but exponential smoothing usually works better for irregular or volatile data.

You can see some evidence of unstable, or volatile, behavior in the data. The seasonal patterns vary from year to year, and 1983 seems to be unusually strong. From this, some forecasters might conclude that exponential smoothing will outperform Box-Jenkins—others would disagree.

After selecting the model family (in this case, exponential smoothing or Box-Jenkins), the practitioner still must select a specific model for the data. Most forecasting packages offer a variety of exponential smoothing models (usually between three and nine) that differ in the way they forecast trend and seasonal changes. Theoretically, there exist an infinite number of Box-Jenkins models to choose from. Often deciding upon the specific form of the model is more challenging than deciding upon the model family.

Manual model selection is a highly subjective process requiring knowledge of both the data and the forecasting techniques. By replacing human judgment with statistical tests and hard-coded rules, software can fully automate this process. Before the advent of automatic forecasting software, the level of expertise required to apply statistical techniques to data greatly hindered their acceptance in the business community.

Fitting Model Parameters and Creating Forecasts

After a model has been selected, the next step is to set the parameters. *Parameters* are numbers that go into the forecasting equations. Their values affect both the fit to the historical data and the forecasts. Most forecasting packages will automatically select these values using well-known algorithms. Some packages require the user to set the values—this should be avoided. Once the parameters have been set, the final step is to generate the forecasts using the resulting equations.

Optimizing the parameters and generating the forecasts are complex, calculation-intensive operations. One would not want to attempt them by hand or on a spreadsheet. Fortunately, they are exactly the kind of procedures that a software program can easily automate.

Forecast Pro's Statistical Strategy

Forecast Pro™ is a time-series forecasting package designed for the business forecaster. This section will outline Forecast Pro's approach to automating statistical forecasting.

The Forecast Pro product line consists of three products: Forecast Pro, Forecast Pro XE (extended edition), and Forecast Pro Batch Edition. The software that accompanies this book is a limited version of Forecast Pro XE. The primary limitation is that data cannot be read from, nor saved to, external sources (e.g., spreadsheets, ASCII files, etc.).

Forecast Pro includes a wide variety of techniques to accommodate different types of data. These include moving averages, exponential smoothing models, Box-Jenkins, and dynamic regression. Extensions of exponential smoothing are available to accommodate event modeling (forecasting promotions or other periodic events) and to perform multiple-level reconciliation (generating consistent forecasts across a hierarchy).

The user can either specify a particular technique or allow Forecast Pro's expert system to determine the best model automatically. The expert system tests data properties such as length, volatility, the presence of trend, the presence of seasonal change, and correlation to explanatory variables. If the findings are conclusive, the expert system recommends an appropriate forecasting technique; if they are not, the program performs an out-of-sample evaluation.

To perform the out-of-sample evaluation, Forecast Pro withholds data from the end of the time series (e.g., the last 12 months) and prepares forecasts for this "hold-out" period using the techniques under consideration. Each technique's performance is measured by comparing the forecasts against the actual (withheld) values. Thus the out-of-sample evaluation allows you to answer the question "Which method would have been most accurate if I were preparing forecasts last year?" Although a technique's past superiority cannot guarantee its future superiority, the procedure is quite logical and tends to work extremely well.

The next step is to fit the model's parameters to the historical data. This is done automatically using maximum likelihood estimation or, in the case of exponential smoothing, using a nonlinear search algorithm to arrive at values that minimize the squared error over the historic fit set. Once the model is selected and the parameters are fit to the data, the final step is to generate the forecasts using the resulting equations.

A Walk-Through of Forecast Pro

The remainder of this chapter will acquaint you with Forecast Pro and work through several real-world problems that illustrate the challenges facing the corporate forecaster. All of the examples use sample data provided with the program. The data are not "cooked up"—they come from actual corporations that use the software on a daily basis. The diagnostics from some of the statistical models fall short of perfection, as is often the case for real-world data.

A Sample Forecasting Session

In this first exercise, you will analyze and forecast the time series INWARD, the monthly telephone data we considered earlier. The objective is to acquaint you with the basic operation of the program—to illustrate how to choose a univariate forecasting technique and to explore the univariate models.

To install the Forecast Pro demo on your computer, follow the instructions for downloading programs from the CD-ROM found inside the back cover of the book. To start the Forecast Pro demo,

> ➤ Double-click on the Forecast Pro icon in the Program Manager. After the program has been launched, you will see a display like Figure 12-2.

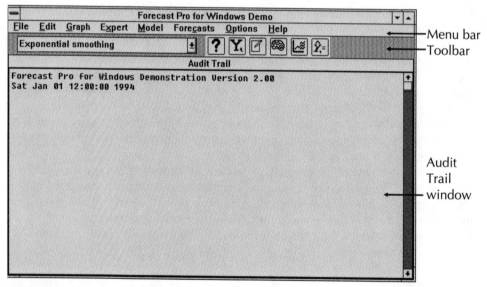

FIGURE 12-2. *The main menu*

The main window, titled Forecast Pro For Windows Demo, consists of a menu bar, a toolbar, and a nested window titled Audit Trail. The Audit Trail window is one of three specialized windows you will see in this portion of the display. The other two are the Data Tableau and the Graph windows.

The menu bar provides access to all the forecasting procedures. The most commonly used procedures can also be accessed instantly via the icons on the toolbar. The model selection box on the toolbar displays the current forecasting mode and allows you to change it.

The nested window currently displays the Audit Trail file, which maintains a running record of your forecasting session. You can edit this record to add notes or comments and may save it to disk at any time.

The Main Menu

Before we proceed further, let's consider each of the menus on the menu bar.

- The File menu provides access to all data and printing options and allows you to exit the program. You will not be able to read or write your own data files with this limited version of Forecast Pro. Instead, you will have to use the sample data provided.

- The Edit menu provides access to standard editing tools, dynamic data exchange (DDE) link options, and the data editor.

- The Graph menu lets you plot your data and forecasts. You cannot access the graph options until you have read some data into memory.

- The Expert menu also requires data before you can select it to execute expert system analysis. The expert system analyzes your data and suggests an appropriate forecasting technique.

- The Model menu provides access to all of the different forecasting techniques and model diagnostics.

- The Forecast menu options allow you to view your current forecast, save it to memory, retrieve previous forecasts, generate forecast reports, and specify the components to be included in your forecast output file.

- The Options menu allows you to set various defaults, which we will discuss in more detail next.

- The Help menu provides access to Forecast Pro's hypertext help system, which we will discuss in more detail next.

Forecast Pro Options   By clicking Options, you will be placed in the Options dialog box shown, here:

Set FPW Options	
Data directory	A:

File format
- ○ .WK1 file ...
- ○ .XLS file ...
- ● .UNV file
- ○ .MLT file ...
- ○ DDE links

Output orientation
- ● Vertical
- ○ Horizontal

OK

Cancel

Help

☐ Cumulative forecasts

Upper confidence limit	97.5
Lower confidence limit	2.5
Forecast horizon	12
Decimal places	3

Missing values
- ● Truncate data
- ○ Interpolate
- ○ Set to zero

The Data Directory and File Format options allow you to specify the location and format of your data files. These options are disabled in the limited version found on the CD-ROM. Forecast Pro accepts data from a variety of sources, including ASCII files, Lotus or Excel spreadsheets, and DDE links. (Future releases will also support object-linking and embedding [OLE] and open database connectivity [ODBC], allowing direct links to all major databases.) The remaining options allow you to set the confidence limits, length of forecast (forecast horizon), number of decimal places, and treatment of missing values.

The Forecast Pro Help System   When you open the Help menu, you have access to Forecast Pro's hypertext help system, Microsoft's Help on help (Windows Help), and the Business Forecast Systems' copyright notice. You can also access the Forecast Pro help system by clicking the Help icon (**?**) on the toolbar.

In addition, many of the Forecast Pro dialog boxes and all of the error messages contain a context-specific Help button.

NOTE
If you receive the error message "Cannot open help file," you will need to open the file manually. To do this, click OK to clear the message, select Open from under File in the Windows Help menu, select FPW.HLP from the subdirectory containing the Forecast Pro demo files, and click OK. This extra step is due to the way the limited edition is installed.

When you open the help system, you first see an index of help topics. The How Do I... and Road Map To Forecast Pro For Windows topics are particularly useful for new or infrequent users of Forecast Pro. Take a few minutes to browse through the help system. When you wish to exit, just select File Exit from the Help menu.

Selecting a Time Series

Our first step will be to select the variable we wish to forecast.

1. Click the Data icon ($\boxed{\text{Y}}$) on the toolbar. Notice that the Data Tableau (Figure 12-4) replaces the Audit Trail window.

   The Data Tableau is used to list the variables you want to forecast or analyze. The variable list box located on the right side of the screen displays the historic data that is available. You can type the variable names directly into the Data Tableau, one to a line, or you can double-click variables displayed in the list box. The latter technique inserts the variable at the current insertion point (i.e., cursor location).

2. Scroll the variable list box until INWARD is visible.

3. Double-click on the series INWARD to insert it on the first line of the Tableau, as shown in Figure 12-3.

4. Click Process to tell the program you have finished entering variables.

5. Click OK to accept the default starting and ending points of the series.

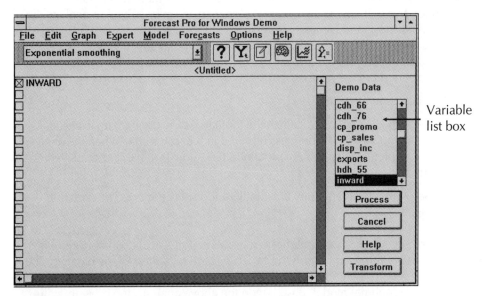

FIGURE 12-3. *The Data Tableau with the INWARD series selected*

Analyzing the Data

The INWARD series is now selected and read into your computer's RAM.

1. Click the Graph icon ( ) on the toolbar. A graph of INWARD appears. You can scroll the graph using the horizontal scroll bar.

2. Select Graph on the menu bar.
    The Graph menu contains options that allow you to customize the display in several ways. Options that appear with check marks to the left are activated. You can toggle any option on or off by clicking it.

3. Toggle on the ALL option by clicking it. Forecast Pro redraws the INWARD display to show the entire time series in a single nonscrollable window, as was shown in Figure 12-1.

Preparing the Forecasts

In our previous discussion of this data set, we concluded that selecting a forecasting model via visual examination was a highly subjective and difficult process. By analyzing the data quantitatively and performing an out-of-sample evaluation of the different models, the expert system can usually make a better judgment about volatility and the appropriate forecast method than a human practitioner. We will now use Forecast Pro's expert selection option to analyze the data, build a model, and create the forecasts.

1. Click the drop-down arrow ( ) on the toolbar to open the Model Selection box.

2. Click Expert Selection.

3. Click the Model icon ( ) on the toolbar. As the program analyzes the data, you will see its progress reported in the status box. When the analysis is complete, the results are written to the Audit Trail file and displayed on the screen.

4. Scroll the Audit Trail upwards until your display matches the screen in Figure 12-4.

   The first section of the output (basic statistics and classical decomposition) is calculated every time you consult the expert system, regardless of the data set. The next section reports the findings of additional tests that are performed as needed to close in on the optimal model. Based upon the above analysis, the program will recommend a model.

   Notice that the expert system acts in much the same way as an expert statistical analyst. It performs a series of statistical tests, interprets the results, performs more tests if necessary, and finally makes recommendations based upon the results. The

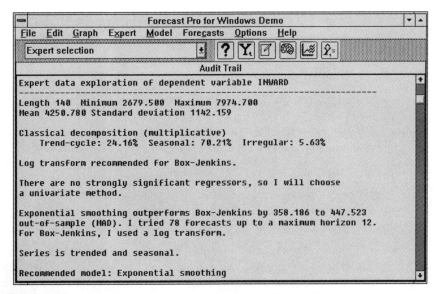

FIGURE 12-4. *The Expert system analysis of the INWARD series*

expert system embodies the statistical strategy of its designer, Dr. Robert Goodrich, who received his Ph.D. from Harvard University in stochastic systems theory and has over twenty-five years of experience in the forecasting field.

For this data set, the expert system selected exponential smoothing over the other techniques because the data are trended and seasonal and because out-of-sample testing favored exponential smoothing over Box-Jenkins.

In addition to the expert system analysis, a description of the selected model, including model parameters and diagnostics, is included in the Audit Trail. You may view additional diagnostics via the Diagnose option under the Model menu. Although this information may not be of interest to everyone, it is always available to support your forecasts. If you wish, you can continue to scroll down the Audit Trail to examine the model and standard diagnostics.

Viewing the Forecasts

There are several ways to examine the forecasts for the current model.

1. Open the Forecasts menu on the menu bar.

2. Select View. The numerical values of the forecast and confidence limits are placed into the Audit Trail.

3. Click the Graph icon on the toolbar. The graph displays the historic data, forecasts, and confidence limits. To add the historical fitted values to the graph:

4. Open the Graph menu on the menu bar.

5. Select Fitted Values. The historic fitted values are one-step forecasts that Forecast Pro made while fitting the model to the data. Notice how closely the fitted values overlay the historic data and that the forecasts reflect the trend and seasonal pattern. To view a forecast report:

6. Open the Forecasts menu on the menu bar.

7. Select Report. The check boxes select or deselect report elements. In this case, make sure every box is checked, so that you will obtain the fullest possible report. Let the column width remain at its default value of 12.

8. Click OK to view the report. The report is written to the Windows Notepad. Notepad gives you printing and formatting options to make a presentable report. In commercial editions of Forecast Pro, you can redirect the report to the editor or word processor of your choice rather than Notepad.

9. Select File Exit from the Notepad menu to close Notepad and return to Forecast Pro.

The commercial versions of Forecast Pro also allow you to save the forecasts to ASCII or spreadsheet files. This allows you to easily use the forecast values in other applications or to prepare custom reports and graphs.

Adjusting the Forecasts

You will sometimes want to adjust your forecasts or historic data. For instance, if you know of a large incoming order or a data entry error, you may need to change a number or two. Forecast Pro allows you to quickly and easily make adjustments directly on the graph.

1. Open the Graph menu on the menu bar.

2. Click All to toggle off the option.

3. Open the Graph menu on the menu bar.

4. Toggle on Peek And Poke by clicking it. Notice that the display now includes a Peek And Poke view box listing a date and the values of the graph variables at that date. You will also see one or more cross hairs positioned at that date (Figure 12-5).

5. Click December 1990 on the INWARD graph. (The months are marked along the X-axis; longer tick marks represent Januarys.) Notice that the

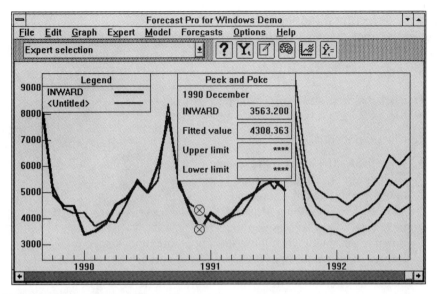

FIGURE 12-5. *The Peek And Poke utility*

cross hairs have moved to the new location and the data in the Peek And Poke box have been updated.

6. Go to edit the December historic value you can either drag the appropriate cross hair to the new value on the graph or edit the value in the view box. Try the first method to raise December's value to the mid-7,000 range. To restore the original value:

7. Open the Graph menu on the menu bar.

8. Click Undo.

You can also edit the data in the Peek And Poke box directly. Click the box that displays the value you want to change. Edit the value as you want and press ENTER. The change will then take effect.

When you adjust data, the changes are immediately applied to data in memory, but not on disk. Thus, you will be using the adjusted data during your current session, but you will only alter the data file if you explicitly save it. Your last few changes are recorded so that you can undo them. However, once you leave the Graph window, you lose your ability to undo the changes without rereading the data file. Another way to edit data and forecasts is to use the Forecast Pro data editor. This is particularly convenient if you need to make numerous changes or add additional data points.

Manually Selecting a Model

In our first example, we used expert selection mode to automatically select and build the forecast model. At times, you may want to make the model selection yourself. In this section, we will take a look at how this is accomplished.

1. Click the drop-down arrow to open the Model Selection box.

2. Click Exponential smoothing.

3. Click the Model icon on the toolbar.
   Forecast Pro supports a total of nine different exponential smoothing models. The Smoothing Model dialog box, shown here, allows you to let the program automatically choose the smoothing model, specify one of the three standard models, or build a custom model.

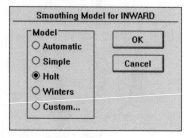

4. Select the Holt model from the Smoothing Model dialog box.

5. Click OK. Forecast Pro builds the specified model and writes the model description and diagnostics to the Audit Trail. All of the graphical, diagnostic, and reporting features we saw for the first model are now available for the current model.

6. Click the Graph icon on the toolbar.

7. Open the Graph menu on the menu bar.

8. Toggle off Peek And Poke by clicking it.

9. Open the Graph menu on the menu bar.

10. Toggle on All by clicking it.
    As you can see from the graph in Figure 12-6, the Holt model is a nonseasonal model and is thus not appropriate for this data set.

11. Click the drop-down arrow to open the Model Selection box.

12. Click Box-Jenkins.

13. Click the Model icon on the toolbar.
    The Box-Jenkins dialog box has two options, Automatic and Custom. The program identifies the model in automatic mode. The custom option allows you to specify the form of the model. For practitioners familiar with the Box-Jenkins identification procedure, the Identify option under Model on the main menu accesses the autocorrelation function and the partial autocorrelation function.

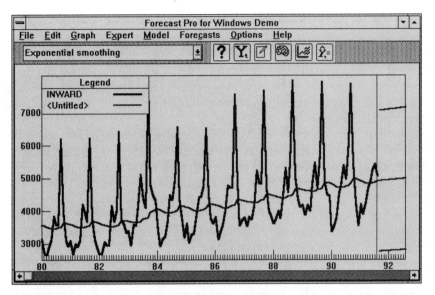

FIGURE 12-6.   *Forecast results using the Holt model*

14. Select Automatic identification mode in the Box-Jenkins dialog box.

15. Click OK.

16. After the model is built and you examine the Audit Trail, click the Graph icon on the toolbar to view the results.

Except for dynamic regression (covered later in this chapter), each model has its own dialog box allowing you to specify the form of the model you wish to build. Whenever possible, the dialog box includes an automatic option.

This concludes the first exercise. To exit Forecast Pro:

1. Open the File menu on the menu bar and select Exit.

2. When the Save Forecasts dialog box appears, click No.

3. When the Audit Trail dialog box appears, click Discard.

Event Adjustment Models

In the preceding exercise, the best model for the telephone connection data turned out to be a Winters exponential smoothing model. As you recall from the earlier discussion, exponential smoothing models estimate the trend and seasonal patterns in the data and extrapolate these features into the future. While exponential smoothing works well under a wide range of circumstances, many data sets contain features other than trend and seasonal change. For example, sales promotions, worker strikes, acts of God, or an unusually large one-time order may dramatically impact the data and forecasts but they cannot be explained as part of the trend or seasonal pattern. Event adjustment models extend exponential smoothing by allowing you to adjust for these types of events.

Event adjustment models work almost the same as seasonal index models. In a seasonal index model, each month gets its own index, which is updated each time that month recurs. In an event adjustment model, each event type gets *its* own index, which is updated each time an event of that particular type recurs. The difference is that while January recurs every 12 months, an event of type 1 usually recurs irregularly. For an event adjustment model, the forecaster must tell the program when events of each type occur, including future events when these are known in advance (e.g., upcoming sales promotions).

Before building an event adjustment model, the user constructs an event variable that classifies each period by event type (0 = no event, 1 = event of type 1, 2 = event of type 2, etc.). The format is the same as that for any other historic data record, except that its entries are small integers. The event variable must be defined for each period in the historic record. If you want to forecast the effects of future known events, you must include these future periods as well.

In this example, you will use an event model to capture the relationship between sales of a consumer product and promotions. The example will conclude with a discussion of more involved uses for event models.

Forecasting the Response to Promotions

If you have already installed Forecast Pro on your computer following the instructions inside the back cover of the book, all you need to do to start Forecast Pro is double-click on the Forecast Pro icon in the appropriate Program Manager group. The next step is to read and graph the data.

1. Click the Data icon ($\boxed{Y_i}$) on the toolbar.

2. Double-click CP_SALES in the variable list box. (This places the variable on the first line of the Data Tableau.)

3. Click Process and then click OK to accept the dates.

4. Click the Graph icon ($\boxed{\cong}$) on the toolbar.

5. Open the Graph menu on the menu bar and toggle on the ALL option by clicking it.

   CP_SALES represents the monthly sales of a nationally advertised consumer product. The prominent peaks in Figure 12-7 are not due to seasonal patterns—they are the result of price promotions.

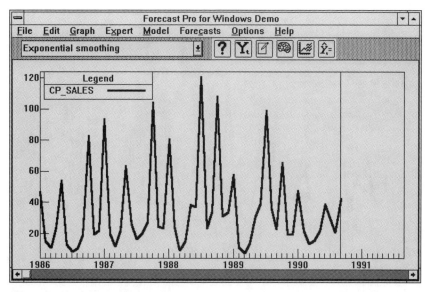

FIGURE 12-7. *A graph of nationally advertised consumer product*

Let's begin by modeling CP_SALES using a standard smoothing model.

6. Click the drop-down arrow (⬍) to open the Model Selection box and select Exponential smoothing.

7. Click the Model icon (𝒴̂ₜ₌) on the toolbar.

8. Select Automatic and click OK. A seasonal model is selected, and the adjusted R-square is 0.49. (This indicates that the model is only explaining 49 percent of the variation in the data.)

Exponential smoothing recognizes the effects of the promotions as a form of irregular seasonal change. The forecasts from such a model tend to repeat the promotional pattern of the last year of historic data. If, as is usually the case, your future promotions are patterned differently, the forecasts may be very bad.

9. Click the Graph icon on the toolbar.

10. Open the Graph menu on the menu bar and toggle on Fitted values by clicking it.

Notice that the model predicted several peaks that did not occur, and missed several peaks that did occur, as shown in Figure 12-8. The model is trying to

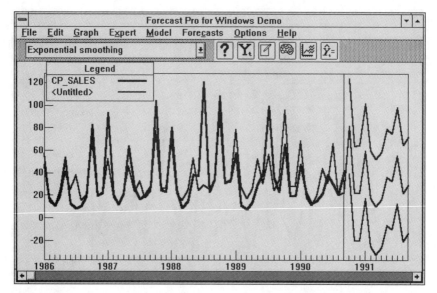

FIGURE 12-8. *A graph of CP_SALES forecast without event adjustments*

capture the peaks as part of the seasonal pattern. However, the promotions that caused these peaks did not always fall in the same months and thus cannot be modeled using seasonal indexes.

Building an Event Model

We will now return to the Data Tableau and specify that we wish to build an event model.

1. Click the Data icon on the toolbar.

2. Position the cursor after CP_SALES in the Data Tableau and type **\EVENT=CP_PROMO**.

3. Position the cursor on the second line of the Data Tableau by pressing the DOWN ARROW key.

4. Double-click CP_PROMO in the variable list box to add it to the second line. Your Data Tableau should now be identical to the one in Figure 12-9.

   CP_PROMO is an event variable. The first line on the Tableau indicates that if a smoothing model is built for CP_SALES it should include event indexes based on CP_PROMO. The second line is included so we can graph CP_PROMO.

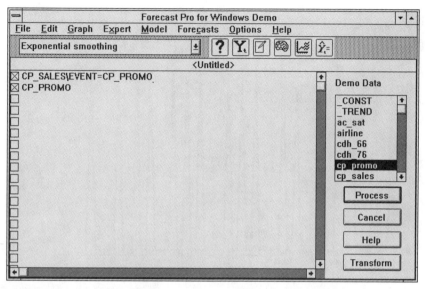

FIGURE 12-9.   *Setting up the Data Tableau for an event model*

5. Click Process and then click OK to accept the dates.

6. Click the Graph icon on the toolbar.

7. Open the Graph menu on the menu bar, click Variables, highlight CP_PROMO, then click OK.

   Event variables are created by the user to indicate to the program the periods where events occur. In Figure 12-10, the event variable CP_PROMO takes the value of zero when CP_SALES is not promoted and the value of one when it is. Notice that the series includes the promotional schedule for the forecast period. When you use CP_PROMO to build an event model, an adjustment is included for the promoted months.

   CP_PROMO reflects the simplest type of event variable. Each month is coded as either promoted (1) or not promoted (0). At times, you may have more than one type of event. For example, suppose you had both price promotions and rebate promotions. In this case, you would create an event file coding months as not promoted (0), price promoted (1), or rebate promoted (2). When you build the event model, it will include two different adjustments, one for price promoted months (type 1 months) and one for rebate promoted months (type 2 months).

8. Click the Model icon on the toolbar.

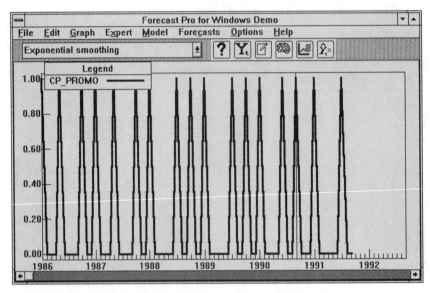

FIGURE 12-10. *The CP_PROMO event variable*

9. Select the Automatic option and click OK.

Notice that the model now includes an event index and that the adjusted R-square is 0.79 (indicating that the model explains 79 percent of the variation in the data). The values of the event indexes at the end of the historical data are printed in the Audit Trail. These figures can be interpreted directly. They represent the multiplicative or additive lift associated with each event type.

10. Click the Graph icon on the toolbar.

The graph incorporating the event adjustments (Figure 12-11) reveals a much better fit to the data, and forecast peaks that correspond to the months indicated as promoted rather than the "seasonal" pattern. It has also adapted to the decreased response to promotions towards the end of the data set. (This was due to the product switching to everyday low pricing for several large accounts.) If, in addition to being driven by promotion, CP_SALES had also been seasonal, the model would include both seasonal and event indexes.

To exit Forecast Pro:

1. Open the File menu on the menu bar and select Exit.

2. When the Audit Trail dialog box appears, click Discard.

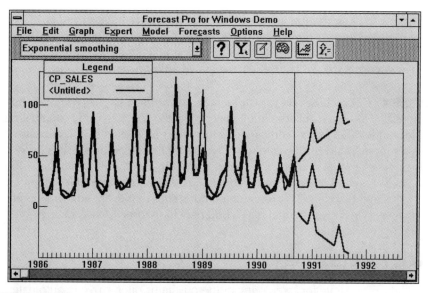

FIGURE 12-11. *The CP_SALES forecast with event adjustment*

Event adjustment models provide a very flexible framework to handle problematic data sets and to model promotional effects of many kinds. The following examples briefly note some possible directions you may want to take with your own business data. The examples require coding additional event types into your event variable. Each new event type provides the ability to explain your historic data by making the event variable more complex. Keep in mind that if your event description is overly complex, the out-of-sample performance of your model may deteriorate. You must strike the right trade-off between goodness-of-fit to your historic data and model complexity. This requires experimentation and monitoring of actual model performance.

Example 1   A one-time occurrence causes an outlier (extreme value), which "throws off" the forecasts. By assigning the outlier a unique nonrecurring event code, you can eliminate its impact.

Example 2   Moving holidays, such as Easter, fall in different periods from year to year. This problem is particularly severe when modeling weekly data sets, which include occasional 53-week years. The solution is to create an event variable that indicates where the holiday falls.

Example 3   A promotion in, say, September may have effects in August and October as well. Buyers may delay purchases in August and may be overstocked in October. You can code the pre- and post-promotional effects as event types of their own. These events will, of course, be associated with *decreases* in sales.

Example 4   Sometimes one SKU of a brand or product line is promoted, but closely related SKUs are not. The result may be that the promoted SKU cannibalizes the sales of the other SKUs. You can treat this effect by coding cannibalization events for these SKUs. But be cautious. Overuse of this technique results in an overly complex model and possible deterioration of forecast performance.

Business Forecast Systems has conducted extensive out-of-sample testing on event adjustment models. This research demonstrates that event adjustment models nearly always yield a substantial real-world benefit in forecast accuracy.

Batch Forecasting

Individuals responsible for forecasting numerous items often strive to automate the process. Forecast Pro includes a batch routine to allow you to prepare up to 50 forecasts automatically. Forecast Pro XE expands this facility to accommodate up to 100 forecasts. Forecast Pro Batch Edition is designed to forecast hundreds or thousands of items automatically. Its operation and capabilities differ from the limited edition of Forecast Pro XE that accompanies this book. If you are interested in learning more about Forecast Pro Batch Edition, contact Business Forecast Systems.

This lesson uses Forecast Pro's batch facility to prepare forecasts for five time series. In batch mode, each variable listed on the Data Tableau is forecast. Thus our first step is to make a list of the variables to forecast.

If you have already installed Forecast Pro onto your computer following the instructions inside the back cover of the book, all you need to do to start Forecast Pro is double-click on the Forecast Pro icon in the appropriate group in the Program Manager.

1. Click the Data icon (𝐘) on the toolbar.

2. Scroll the variable list box until SKU_001 through SKU_005 are visible.

3. Double-click items SKU_001 through SKU_005 one at a time. Your Data Tableau should look like the one in Figure 12-12.

   Often, you may wish to forecast all available variables or recall a tableau you defined earlier. Forecast Pro provides convenient and quick ways to perform these operations.

4. Click Process. The Fitting Set dialog box appears, allowing you to set the starting and ending years.

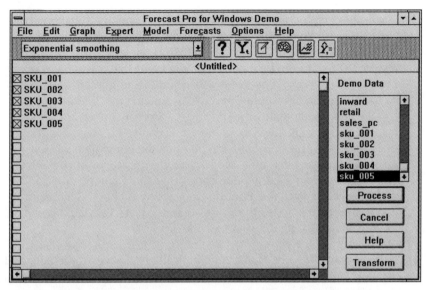

FIGURE 12-12. *The Data Tableau set up for batch forecasting*

The batch routine allows you to choose between using the data span defined in this dialog box or using all of the available data for each individual series. This latter option is useful when some series are longer than others, as in the present case.

5. Click OK to accept the dates.

6. Click the drop-down arrow (⬍) to open the Model Selection box and select Batch.

7. Click the Model icon ($\hat{Y}_=$) on the toolbar.

The Batch Forecast Options dialog box, shown here, allows you to select the forecast method. Notice that dynamic regression is not available in Batch mode.

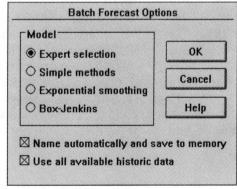

Expert Selection instructs the expert system to select the forecast model. Simple Methods, Exponential Smoothing, and Box-Jenkins all use the same automatic model selection algorithms as in interactive mode.

It is tempting to rely on the Expert Selection option throughout, but this choice may not be optimal when your data are highly irregular. Forecast Pro makes its choice of method at the item level, where irregularity may obscure the features to be modeled. If you know that, *overall*, exponential smoothing outperforms Box-Jenkins, then you should select it. The forecasts are likely to be more accurate and will be created much more quickly.

If the Name Automatically And Save to Memory option is checked, then each forecast is saved to memory and named by preceding the original name with an exclamation point (in the nonlimited version, the user can define an alternative prefix character). Otherwise, you will be prompted for a name as each forecast is saved to memory.

If the Use All Available Historic Data option is checked, Forecast Pro ignores the starting and ending times from the Data Tableau. Instead, it uses all available data for each individual series.

8. Make sure that both the Name Automatically And Save To Memory and Use All Available Historic Data options are checked and set the model to Expert selection.

9. Click OK to create the forecasts. The program performs the analysis and writes the results to the Audit Trail file.

10. Click the Graph icon (▨) on the toolbar.

11. Open the Graph menu on the menu bar and toggle on All by clicking it. Forecast Pro displays a graph of the first series.

If you wish to view other forecast graphs or create forecast reports, you must select the current forecast to work with.

12. Open the Forecasts menu on the menu bar, select Fetch from Memory, highlight !SKU_003, and click OK. The program displays the forecast graph for !SKU_003.

Selecting Report from the Forecasts menu generates a report for the current forecast (!SKU_003).

13. Open the Forecasts menu on the menu bar, select Fetch from Memory, highlight !SKU_001, and click OK. This changes the current forecast to !SKU_001, allowing you to graph and report on this new forecast.

As you have seen, batch forecasting is a handy option when you have many variables to forecast and you wish to automate the process. This concludes the exercise; you should exit Forecast Pro before starting the next.

Multiple-Level Forecasting

Corporations frequently need to generate forecasts across different levels of aggregation. Products data, for instance, often involves SKUs, which sum to products, which in turn sum to product lines, etc. Service corporations may organize their data geographically into cities, states, regions, and countries. In this section, we will examine techniques to reconcile such forecast hierarchies and illustrate how information available at higher levels of aggregation can sometimes be used to improve the forecasts at lower levels.

Figure 12-13 illustrates a very simple product hierarchy that might be faced by a brewery. Generating consistent forecasts across the levels usually involves some combination of bottom-up and top-down reconciliation. Let's consider each approach using our current example.

A bottom-up approach generates group-level forecasts (levels one and two) by aggregating their component forecasts. For example, the forecast for CANS would be made by summing the statistical forecasts generated for CANS_6 and CANS_12. A top-down approach would begin by forecasting CANS, CANS_6 and CANS_12. These forecasts would not be consistent across levels, so the next step would be to

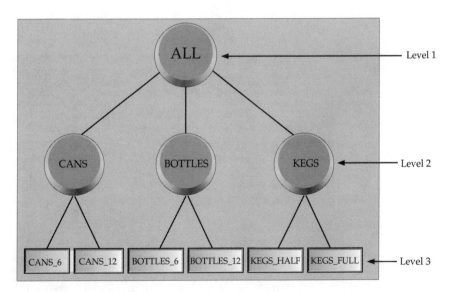

FIGURE 12-13. *An example of a product hierarchy*

adjust the CANS_6 and CANS_12 forecasts proportionally so that they sum up to the CANS forecasts.

Which approach yields more accurate forecasts will depend upon the data. If the components of a group have distinctly different behaviors (e.g., different seasonal patterns, trends, etc.) a bottom-up approach is preferable. If the components of a group are very similar, the top-down approach is generally preferable. In our current example, we would probably use a top-down approach between levels two and three and a bottom-up approach between levels one and two.

Figure 12-14 shows how the Data Tableau could be set up in Forecast Pro. The tableau contains four Group variables (ALL, CANS, BOTTLES, and KEGS). Group variables do not exist on the database. They are created internally by aggregating all data files found between the beginning of the group and its corresponding _END flag. Thus, CANS is defined as CANS_6 + CANS_12, BOTTLES as BOTTLES_6 + BOTTLES_12, KEGS as KEGS_FULL + KEGS_HALF, and ALL as CANS + BOTTLES + KEGS. The \TOPDOWN group modifier instructs the program to adjust lower-level forecasts to sum up to the indicated level.

There are two other group modifiers. \INDEXES instructs the program to estimate the seasonal indexes at the group level and use them for all members in the group. This is particularly useful when some members of the group have short histories or small demand, making seasonal factors difficult to calculate.

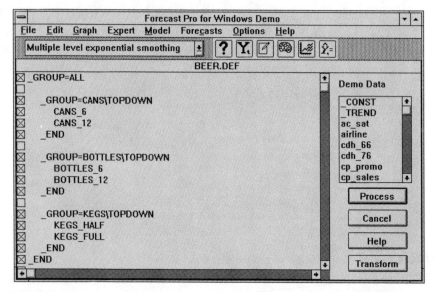

FIGURE 12-14. *The Data Tableau set up for multiple-level forecasting*

\MODEL instructs the program to select a model (Winters, Holt, etc.) for the group level and use it for all members in the group. The model parameters are optimized individually for each series.

After the tableau is defined, the procedure for creating the forecasts and examining the results is virtually identical to operating in batch mode. Thus a hands-on example has been omitted.

Applications for Multiple-Level Models

In many cases, the ability to work with a product hierarchy allows you to model behaviors that could not be addressed working with an individual time series. Several examples are given next.

Example 1   A manufacturer often maintains a product line for a long period of time but frequently changes the SKUs that make up the line. A laser printer manufacturer, for instance, introduces new models and retires old ones. The result may be that the overall product line can be accurately forecast, but the individual item histories are too short to support seasonal models.

We assume that SKU1 is phased out and replaced by SKU2, which is in turn replaced by SKU3. We also assume that at the end of the historic data, only SKU3 is alive. The manufacturer is interested in forecasting LINE and SKU3. The following tableau layout will take care of the problem.

```
_GROUP=LINE \INDEXES
    SKU1
    SKU2
    SKU3
_END
```

As a result, Forecast Pro follows this procedure:

1. Forecast LINE, obtaining seasonal indexes.

2. Use the LINE seasonal indexes to reject seasonal factors for the SKUs.

3. Forecast the resulting nonseasonal SKU level data. These nonseasonal models require very little data.

4. Use the LINE seasonal indexes to accept seasonal factors to the SKU level forecasts.

By default, the LINE forecasts are replaced by the summed SKU level forecasts. If you do not want this to happen, you can add the keyword \TOPDOWN to the first line of the tableau.

The tableau presented in this example can also be used when the SKU level histories are long-lived. The result is that seasonal factors are accounted for at the LINE level. This is desirable when the SKUs are likely to have similar seasonal patterns but the data are too irregular for accurate estimation of seasonal indexes at the SKU level.

Example 2   A product line consisting of aggregated SKUs is promoted as a unit. You believe that all the SKUs in the line will be affected similarly. You can deal with this by using the following layout on your tableau.

```
_GROUP=LINE \EVENT=PROMO \TOPDOWN
    SKU1
    SKU2
    SKU3
_END
```

As a result, Forecast Pro follows this procedure:

1. Forecast the group LINE, taking promotions into account.

2. Forecast the SKUs without taking promotions into account.

3. Adjust the SKU forecasts so that they sum to the LINE forecasts. This propagates the group level promotional effects to the SKUs.

Example 3   Now suppose that only one SKU of the group is promoted. A tableau of the following form can account for this promotion.

```
_GROUP=LINE
    SKU1 \EVENT=PROMO
    SKU2
    SKU3
_END
```

This causes Forecast Pro to forecast the SKUs individually. The forecasts are summed to obtain forecasts for the group LINE.

What if you were to add the keyword \TOPDOWN to the first line in this example? The effect would be that the promotion of SKU1 affects it but does not affect overall sales at the group level. This might be the case if the promotion affected sales only by cannibalizing other SKUs in the group.

Forecasting with Dynamic Regression

In this exercise, you will use dynamic regression to forecast SALES_PC, monthly residential electricity consumption per customer in a mid-Atlantic city. You will learn how to refine and improve your model in a sequence of steps, guided by the dynamic regression diagnostic batteries. Unlike the other modeling techniques in Forecast Pro, which can be built fully automatically, regression models must be built interactively in a sequence of steps. Although Forecast Pro provides a great deal of guidance as you build the model, experience and an understanding of the model and a few key statistics are very useful.

Exploring the Data

The following time series will be used in this exercise.

SALES_PC	Residential electricity sales (KWH) per customer
CDH_66	Cooling degree hours at base temperature 66 degrees
CDH_76	Cooling degree hours at base temperature 76 degrees
HDH_55	Heating degree hours at base temperature 55 degrees
DISP_INC	Disposable income per household
AC_SAT	Air conditioning saturation rate
_CONST	Constant term

1. Start Forecast Pro following the instructions found at the back of this book. Our first step will be to define a tableau identical to the one in Figure 12-15.

2. Click the Data icon (𝐘.) on the toolbar.

3. Double-click SALES_PC in the variable list box. (This will place the variable on the first line of the Data Tableau.)

4. Double-click CDH_66 and then each of the remaining five independent variables to add them to the Data Tableau.
    You have defined the dependent variable, SALES_PC, and six independent variables. The dependent variable is always listed first. CDH_66 and CDH_76 are measures of summer heat and HDH_55 is a measure of winter cold. The variable _CONST instructs the program to use a constant term in the regression. In general, you should include any explanatory variables that might possibly be significant. As always, our first step is to examine the dependent variable graphically.

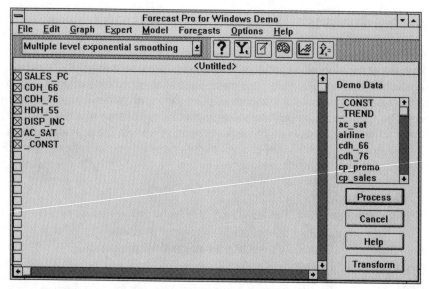

FIGURE 12-15. *A regression tableau*

5. Click Process, and then OK to accept the dates.

6. Click the Graph icon ( ) on the toolbar.

7. Open the Graph menu on the menu bar and toggle on ALL by clicking it.

In Figure 12-16, notice the strong seasonal patterns in the data and the varying heights of the summer and winter peaks. Much of the variation is due to air-conditioning and heating, which is primarily driven by the temperature. We will try to capture this relationship by using the weather variables.

8. Open the Graph menu on the menu bar and click Variables.

9. Highlight SALES_PC and CDH_66 and click OK.

The peaks in CDH_66 correspond to the summer peaks in SALES_PC. This suggests that CDH_66 is a powerful explanatory variable. Notice also that forecasts are supplied for CDH_66. You can fit a dynamic regression model without including forecasts of the explanatory variables, but you will not be able to use it to forecast. To do that, *you must supply forecasts for each independent variable.*

10. Try graphing some of the other variables to see how they relate to the sales data.

11. After you have explored the data graphically, click the Expert icon (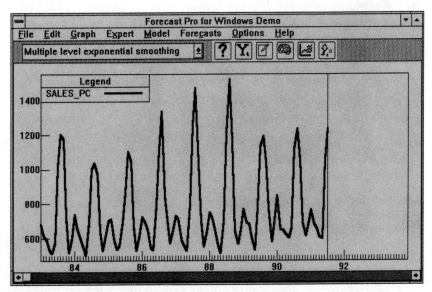) on the toolbar to determine which technique the expert system recommends to forecast SALES_PC.

You learn that the series is seasonal and trended, and that there are potential explanatory variables, which appear to be strong. Dynamic regression is the recommended technique.

There is actually very little need to consult the expert system when you already know that you have important explanatory variables. Dynamic regression is the only method that can take them into account.

Starting Out

You build your regression model in a sequence of rounds. You posit an initial model, diagnose it, and improve it. Then you diagnose that model and improve it. Finally, after several iterations of this procedure, you are satisfied with the diagnostics and accept the model.

There are many ways to build a regression model. Some people begin with a model that includes many terms, and weed out the terms that are not statistically significant. Others begin with a simple model and add variables one by one. We will take the latter approach. Start by including only the weather variables and a constant term.

FIGURE 12-16. *A graph of residential electricity sales*

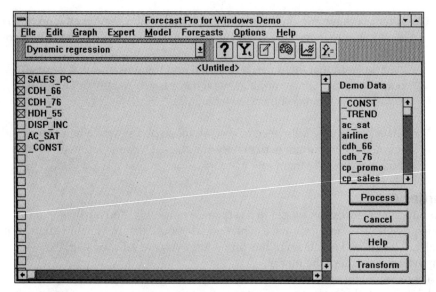

FIGURE 12-17. *A Regression tableau with inactive variables*

1. Click the Data icon (Y$_t$) on the toolbar.

2. Deactivate the variables AC_SAT and DISP_INC by clicking their check boxes. Your Data Tableau should now look like the one in Figure 12-17.
   Only the checked variables are included in the model. Later on, you will learn how to test unchecked variables for inclusion in the model.

3. Click Process, and then OK to accept the dates.

4. Click the Model icon (ŷ$_=$) on the toolbar.

5. The Ljung-Box statistic is marked with two asterisks, a warning that the model is poor. This indicates that the fitted errors are highly autocorrelated. Let's examine the error autocorrelation function directly.

6. Open the Model menu on the menu bar.

7. Select Diagnose and then Error ACF.
   You can see in Figure 12-18 that all the error autocorrelations are large, especially at the twelfth lag. This is because the model includes no time series features. It tries to explain all variation of SALES_PC in terms of the weather. However, the weather cannot explain the increasing use of electricity. The dynamics of this model must be improved.

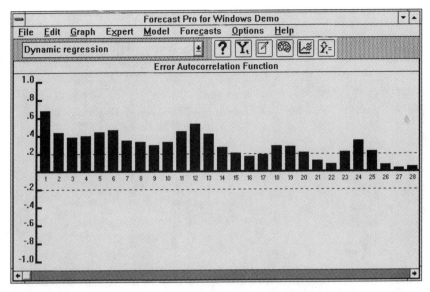

FIGURE 12-18. *The Error Autocorrelation Function window*

8. Open the Model menu on the menu bar.

9. Select Diagnose and then Dynamics.

The dynamics test battery (Figure 12-19) provides information on how to improve the model. You will see a large suite of statistics, each of which tests for some specific deficiency in model dynamics. You must respond to these statistics by deciding which deficiency to correct. If you are a beginner, it is best to make only one change at a time. Later, as you gain confidence, you will probably take some shortcuts.

Forecast Pro helps you decide what to do by examining the test statistics and finding the most highly significant. In this case, it recommends that you improve the model by adding the term _AUTO[-1], just as though it were one of your explanatory variables.

This is called an autoregressive error term, and the resulting model is a Cochrane-Orcutt model. When you add _AUTO[-1] to the model, it uses the fitting error from time t-1 to help predict the fitting error for time t. The predicted fitting error is then used to adjust and improve the forecast.

You can learn more about these models in the Forecast Pro user's manual or in an economics textbook.

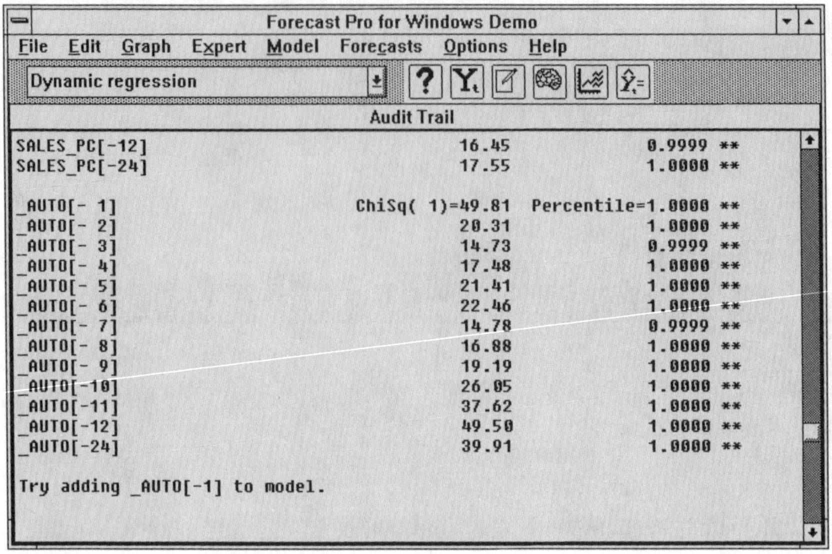

```
┌─────────────────────────────────────────────────────────────┐
│ —            Forecast Pro for Windows Demo           ▼ ▲     │
│ File  Edit  Graph  Expert  Model  Forecasts  Options  Help   │
│ ┌──────────────────────┐                                     │
│ │ Dynamic regression    │ ± │?│Yₜ│▱│▩│▨│ŷ₌│                  │
│ └──────────────────────┘                                     │
│                        Audit Trail                           │
│ SALES_PC[-12]                  16.45          0.9999 **    ▲ │
│ SALES_PC[-24]                  17.55          1.0000 **      │
│                                                              │
│ _AUTO[- 1]          ChiSq( 1)=49.81  Percentile=1.0000 **    │
│ _AUTO[- 2]                     20.31          1.0000 **      │
│ _AUTO[- 3]                     14.73          0.9999 **      │
│ _AUTO[- 4]                     17.48          1.0000 **      │
│ _AUTO[- 5]                     21.41          1.0000 **      │
│ _AUTO[- 6]                     22.46          1.0000 **      │
│ _AUTO[- 7]                     14.78          0.9999 **      │
│ _AUTO[- 8]                     16.88          1.0000 **      │
│ _AUTO[- 9]                     19.19          1.0000 **      │
│ _AUTO[-10]                     26.05          1.0000 **      │
│ _AUTO[-11]                     37.62          1.0000 **      │
│ _AUTO[-12]                     49.50          1.0000 **      │
│ _AUTO[-24]                     39.91          1.0000 **      │
│                                                              │
│ Try adding _AUTO[-1] to model.                            ▼ │
└─────────────────────────────────────────────────────────────┘
```

FIGURE 12-19.   *The dynamics test battery*

Improving Model Dynamics

After reviewing the dynamics test battery and the Forecast Pro recommendations on how to improve the model, you can begin to modify the model.

1. Click the Data icon on the toolbar.

2. Position the cursor on the line underneath _CONST.

3. Type **_AUTO[-1]**.

4. Click Process, and then OK.

5. Click the Model icon on the toolbar.

    You have completed one round of the model refinement process and are ready for another. This is the essence of fitting a regression model: you repeatedly estimate models, examine the diagnostics, and change them until you are satisfied. Thus dynamic regression is much more tedious than the univariate methods. If your explanatory variables are not very powerful, dynamic regression may not be worth the additional trouble.

6. Open the Model menu on the menu bar, select Diagnose, then select Error ACF.

Although the Ljung-Box test has improved somewhat, there are still some large error autocorrelations, especially at the seasonal lags. The model does not yet appear to accommodate seasonal factors adequately.

7. Open the Model menu and click Diagnose, then Dynamics again.

8. The expert system suggests that you add the term **_AUTO[-12]**. This will expand the Cochrane-Orcutt part of the model and will help explain the seasonal correlations left in the errors.

By now, you know just what to do. Return to the Data Tableau, add the new term, read in the data, and refit the model. Once again, there is noticeable improvement in the diagnostics. If you keep repeating the process, you will add **_AUTO[-24]**. Then the program recommends adding the autoregressive term **SALES_PC[-24]**, which is the Forecast Pro notation for SALES_PC, lagged by 24 periods. SALES_PC[-24] is the only significant (two asterisks) test, so you are closing in on a model with well-specified dynamics. Go ahead and add the new term.

Adding a new term sometimes causes terms that were already in the model to become insignificant. In this case, the _AUTO terms became insignificant when you added SALES_PC[-24], so the program marked the insignificant terms, and instructed you to eliminate them.

SALES_PC[-24] is not significant and its sign is negative. Its inclusion in the model now seems like a bad idea. Remove SALES_PC[-24] from the model by unchecking it on the Data Tableau. Then estimate the model.

Notice that two statistical tests looking at the same term have just contradicted each other. This is perfectly possible. Each test can incur either a Type 1 error (reject the null hypothesis when it is true) or a Type 2 error (fail to reject the null hypothesis when it is false). You must always use your common sense in interpreting statistical hypothesis tests.

Improving Variable Specification

The diagnostics for the current model are fairly good. The Ljung-Box test is not significant and with the exception of SALES_PC[-24], which we will ignore, the dynamics tests are clean.

The next step is to check the variable specification.

1. Open the Model menu on the menu bar and select Diagnose, then Variables.

The program performs excluded variable tests for each unchecked variable on the Data Tableau as well as the first lag of each explanatory variable. Significant (.01) tests are marked with two asterisks. The only significant test is SALES_PC[-24], which we already decided to ignore. Sometimes two variables that are individually insignificant are jointly significant.

2. Open the Model menu and click Diagnose, then Custom. You see a list box that displays the unchecked variables.

3. Highlight both DISP_INC and AC_SAT and click Test. Forecast Pro tests the joint significance of the two variables. As long as you remain in the dialog box, you can continue testing.

4. Select Cancel from the dialog box to write the results to the Audit Trail.

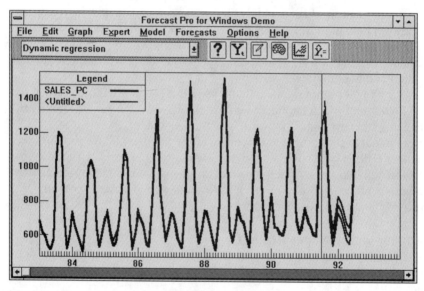

FIGURE 12-20. *Final regression model results*

Examining the Forecasts
Since the tests are not significant, we will declare this our final model.

1. Click the Graph icon on the toolbar.

2. Open the Graph menu on the menu bar and toggle on Fitted Values by clicking it.
   Notice how well the model fits the data and how tight the confidence limits are (Figure 12-20). You could also have examined effects on the forecasts as you fitted the model.

As a final exercise, try Winters exponential smoothing and Box-Jenkins on the same data. You will discover that, as the expert system predicted, dynamic regression yields the superior model.
   To exit Forecast Pro:

1. Open the File menu on the menu bar and select Exit.

2. When the Audit Trail dialog box appears, click Discard.

Fitting a regression model can be real work. In this case, however, most of the decision making was done by Forecast Pro. As you learn more about the program, you will be able to use your judgment to speed up the process.

Conclusion

The ability to create accurate forecasts translates directly into better decision making and increased profits for the corporation. Many companies have shied away from statistical forecasting techniques because of the high level of statistical expertise required to implement the techniques using traditional statistics software.
   With the advent of intelligent business-oriented forecasting packages, this barrier has been removed. Packages like Forecast Pro provide ready access to statistical forecasting methods regardless of the user's background in statistics or econometrics.

CHAPTER 13

Smart Solutions to Business Forecasting Problems

by Charles N. Smart
Smart Software, Inc.

As early as 1601, Shakespeare's *Hamlet* captured people's basic longing to know the future:

> We know what we are, but know not what we may be.

Just as individuals may wonder what is to come, so every organization anticipates its own future. And in today's world, a business often finds that its ability to function efficiently and to compete effectively depends on its ability to make better, faster forecasts of future events.

The New Wave of PC Forecasting

Decision-makers in almost every business and industry need reliable forecasts of critical variables, such as sales, revenues, expenditures, product demand, and inventory levels. For the many kinds of people who make these forecasts, new PC-based software solutions have something valuable to offer. To professional forecasters, they are a flexible, low-cost alternative to expensive mainframe forecasting models. To business managers and functional specialists, they offer independence from data processing backlogs, and the chance to incorporate know-how. Most important, these easy-to-use programs offer sound, helpful forecasting techniques packaged so that even someone who is not a statistical whiz can get useful results in a hurry.

Two Kinds of Forecasters

Larger manufacturing companies and service-based firms may have professional forecasters on staff with explicit responsibility for certain forecasting tasks. Professional forecasters typically have advanced training in statistics and economics. They use large mainframe computers comfortably and often rely on complex macroeconomic models to relate their company's future and fortunes to the entire U.S. economy.

But even in a large company, many others who would not consider themselves trained forecasters are called upon to make reliable forecasts. This is also true of small- and medium-size firms where, normally, no professional forecasters are on staff. Like the character in Molière's *Le Bourgeois Gentilhomme* who "spoke prose without knowing it," many business managers and specialists routinely make forecasts:

➤ Industry analysts forecast earnings per share and cash flow projections for brokerage account executives.

➤ Comptrollers forecast revenues and expenses for budget projections.

➤ Manufacturing managers forecast product demand, frequently for hundreds or thousands of items at a time, to drive production planning and inventory control processes.

➤ Strategic planners forecast industry trends to help determine total market size and their company's share of that market.

➤ Marketing managers forecast company sales, as well as the impact of planned promotions on those sales.

These "nontechnical" forecasters generally work without specialized statistical training. While the professionals may successfully use complex mainframe software (some of which has migrated to the personal computer), these solutions can be enormously expensive, normally require a great deal of time and effort, and separate the eventual user of forecast results—the manager or decision-maker—from control of the forecasting process. Until recently, most nontechnical forecasters have tried to make do with their familiar spreadsheet programs.

Beyond Spreadsheets

Before the advent of PC-based spreadsheets, and even before mainframe computers, companies still needed to forecast. Few, however, were able to do it in an efficient, systematic fashion. Before computerized forecasting, the two most popular approaches could be described as "seat-of-the-pants" and "numerical brute force." Under the seat-of-the-pants approach, managers relied exclusively on "best-guess" estimates of future key business variables, such as sales, revenues, and product demand. Little or no effort was made to analyze existing company data on these issues. Under the brute force approach, company data was certainly scrutinized, but the data had to be processed manually, and the forecasting methodology was normally limited to a simple average of the last few months' or few quarters' results. Both approaches suffered from a notable lack of precision, and the brute force approach, in particular, was quite time-consuming. It wasn't unusual under this approach to require numerous "bean counters" to labor for days crunching numbers with their calculators.

What computers have brought to the forecasting process is a much easier, faster way to organize and analyze data. On the PC, spreadsheet programs represent one of the earliest examples of this phenomenon. Over the last 10 to 15 years, spreadsheet use has increased exponentially in businesses of all sizes. During this period, spreadsheet technology has also become more powerful. In the area of forecasting, however, spreadsheets are still best known for supporting "What-if" forecasting. For example, you can note the growth of your company's sales by 5 percent last quarter and then simply extend this percentage growth over the next four quarters for a projection.

The problem is that a "What-if" projection does not use all the available data in an objective way. Consequently, important underlying trends and seasonal patterns, which may be crucial to developing an accurate forecast, can be overlooked. And the unwieldy graphics features of some spreadsheet programs do not readily permit nontechnical forecasters to make visual checks of forecasting credibility, nor to adjust results to reflect new market information or their own business judgment. While spreadsheet programs do organize data effectively and also permit certain rudimentary projections, they are poorly suited to squeezing the most out of available business data or eliciting a manager's best judgment.

Fortunately, a new class of PC software makes sophisticated forecasting capabilities available to nontechnical business forecasters. These programs make expert techniques easily available to the novice user and apply them automatically to create accurate forecasts of company sales, revenues, inventory levels, budget-line costs, and other key business variables, while significantly reducing the time and costs involved. They also employ graphics to display forecast results clearly, along with indications of their reliability. And, if a user decides that these results must be adjusted to reflect new market developments or managerial insight, the programs provide an easy, interactive means of accomplishing this. Examples of widely available business forecasting software include Autocast™ from Delphus, Inc. of Morristown, New Jersey, Forecast Pro™ from Business Forecast Systems in Belmont, Massachusetts (see Chapter 12), and SmartForecasts™ (profiled in this chapter) from Smart Software, Inc. in Belmont.

This new PC forecasting software is starting to have a major impact on who forecasts, how they forecast, and how well they forecast. To learn more about how this type of software works, let's step back and begin with the ultimate source of good forecasts: good data.

Forecasting with Company Data

To peer into the corporate future, forecasters have three sources of guidance: internal company data, information about the world outside their company, and their own business judgment. Advances in computer technology make it easier than ever to combine all three to arrive at reliable projections that contribute to company planning and decision-making tasks.

Internal company data on sales, revenues, expenses, and product demand is the backbone of the systematic forecasting process. Nowadays, it is commonplace to find this data inside electronic spreadsheets or database programs. It is a simple matter to transfer the information from the spreadsheet or database to a forecasting program. Later, the forecasts can be transferred back to the originating program or to another computer-based system for further analysis and use.

Time-Series Analysis

There are a number of well-known statistical techniques for converting a sequence of historical data values into projections. Such a sequence of data values is called a time series (e.g., company sales organized by month), and forecasting such sequences is part of a discipline known as time-series analysis. Time-series analysis rests on two premises: that there are patterns in the data that will repeat in the future, and that these underlying patterns are obscured to some degree by random fluctuations.

For example, the level of sales in a given month can be thought of as the combined effect of several factors:

> ➤ A starting point determined by the sales level in the previous fiscal year

> ➤ A trend reflecting the growth of the company and perhaps the growth in the economy at large

> ➤ A repetitive seasonal pattern corresponding to established rhythms in consumer demand, company advertising schedules, trade shows, and so forth

> ➤ Unpatterned influences caused by such phenomena as poor weather, equipment breakdowns, trucker strikes, and other random events

It is these random events that mask the underlying levels, trends, and seasonality in the data. By averaging over all Januarys, all Februarys, and so on, the time-series analyst hopes that the random influences will cancel themselves out and reveal the underlying pattern. Once this pattern is revealed, it can be extended into the future as a forecast.

The Exponential Smoothing and Moving Average Methods

The most popular time-series analysis methods are exponential smoothing and moving average. These "smoothing-based" methods turn out to be the easiest to use and understand. Because of their resilience and versatility, they are also remarkably accurate in a wide variety of circumstances. They work in similar ways, canceling out random effects to reveal the underlying trends and seasonality in the data and then extrapolating these forward to create a future forecast.

Among the exponential smoothing methods, some of the more common techniques include single exponential smoothing, double (or Brown's) exponential smoothing, and Winters exponential smoothing. In the case of the monthly sales series discussed earlier, single exponential smoothing would be most appropriate if the data fluctuated around a level that does not change much with time, neither rising nor falling. In that case, the series has little or no trend, and the forecasting problem amounts to smoothing out, i.e., averaging the positive and negative fluctuations to uncover the basic level of the data.

The single exponential smoothing technique uses all the data in the sales series to create a forecast, but it gives successively lesser weight or emphasis to older data. By giving more weight to more recent data, single exponential smoothing adjusts to abrupt shifts in the underlying level of a data series, such as a sudden jump up to a new, higher level. Using PC forecasting software, a forecaster can actually choose the percentage weight to give to the most recent data but faces a tradeoff when choosing that weight. If the most recent data are weighted heavily, single exponential smoothing is better able to follow abrupt jumps in the level of the series and to reflect those jumps in the future forecast. On the other hand, it is less able to average out random fluctuations if the level happens not to jump.

The complement to single exponential smoothing among the moving average methods is simple moving average. Like single exponential smoothing, simple moving average is an appropriate technique to use for forecasting a trendless series, such as consumer demand for a basic food product like milk, bread, or eggs. However, unlike single exponential smoothing, the simple moving average method uses only a selected number of recent data values, weighting them all equally. In choosing how many data values to average, a forecaster faces a trade-off analogous to that with single exponential smoothing. If the forecaster averages only the few most recent values, simple moving average reacts better to abrupt changes in the underlying level of the data. However, it is less able to home in on a fairly steady level of change.

If the sales series has a steady upward or downward trend, such as may be found in industrial sales of high technology products like PC workstations, then single exponential smoothing and simple moving average consistently lag behind the trend. As a result, these methods would consistently underpredict or overpredict, depending on whether the trend is up (as for PC workstations) or down. In this case, two forecasting techniques that provide a more accurate solution are double exponential smoothing and linear moving average. Unlike single exponential smoothing, double exponential smoothing tracks not only the level of the data but also any sustained changes in the level, so it is well suited to predicting data with trend. Just as double exponential smoothing works better than single exponential smoothing with trending series, so linear moving average works better with trending series than simple moving average. Indeed, linear moving average is sometimes called double moving average.

Frequently a data series, such as a sales series, will have not only a trend component but also a *seasonal* component with predictable highs and lows recurring over time. For instance, retail toy sales tend to have a yearly peak in the weeks just before Christmas. Unfortunately, the exponential smoothing and moving average methods tend to average out these seasonal cycles and remove them from the forecast. However, a manager or planner might want to predict the seasonal variation along with the underlying level and trend of the data series. As an example, you might want to know not only next year's total demand for a product, but also how that demand is distributed from month to month. You can get this type of information by using Winters exponential smoothing; this method tracks seasonality and builds it into forecasting results.

While the exponential smoothing and moving average methods are relatively easy to use and understand, there are choices that have to be made regarding the optimal method to use, and the weights or number of averaging periods to select. As we have seen, that choice depends on the nature of the data: Does the data series have an underlying trend? Does it have a seasonal component? A professional forecaster would have little difficulty in making these determinations, but nonetheless would have to invest some time in making the necessary evaluation of alternatives and implementing the optimal solution.

For the nontechnical forecaster, unfamiliar with the details of time-series analysis, this choice and evaluation process is usually not feasible. Fortunately, it is also not necessary. Most of the new PC forecasting software packages fully automate time-series calculations. Each also contains a built-in "expert system," which *automatically* selects and applies, from among alternative methods, the one method that best predicts any particular time series. In short, they can handle all the statistics for you.

Advanced Methods

Before leaving this topic, we should acknowledge that there are more advanced time-series forecasting techniques beyond the popular exponential smoothing and moving average methods. One of the better known is Box-Jenkins forecasting. This is a mathematically advanced technique that performs ARIMA (autoregressive integrated moving average) analysis. Since ARIMA methods by themselves often comprise most of a graduate course in time-series forecasting, we cannot hope to explain them here. Suffice it to say that the Box-Jenkins/ARIMA forecasting techniques may offer interesting alternatives, under certain conditions, to trained professional forecasters. Because of their complexity and their requirement for *long*, stable data series (usually 75 data values or more), they have less relevance for the typical nontechnical forecaster who must solve business problems where no more than three or four years of monthly/quarterly data may be available.

Adding External Data

Internal company data are often supplemented by external data on industry trends, competitor's activities, financial markets, and national or international economic trends. Often, the goal is to find some external variable whose movements foreshadow changes in an internal variable, i.e., to identify a "leading indicator." For instance, government statistics on new housing starts may imply a coming surge in demand for household appliances. Knowing that X new homes will be built, an appliance manufacturer could expect that Y dishwashers would be ordered after a suitable construction delay.

The statistical basis for this kind of forecasting is known as regression analysis. Regression analysis codifies the relationship between new home construction and dishwasher orders in terms of a causal model expressed by a mathematical equation. Just as with other forms of time-series analysis, regression analysis begins with the twin premises that there is a stable, underlying reality that will persist into the future and that this structure is obscured by random influences that must be removed by some sort of statistical averaging.

Regression Analysis

Unlike the exponential smoothing and moving average methods, regression analysis is, by definition, a multivariate (not a univariate) forecasting technique. This means that regression analysis not only examines the historical data of the variable you want to predict but also the data of other variables that may help in making that prediction (i.e., predictor variables). In essence, regression analysis exploits patterns that relate changes in the variable you need to forecast to changes in other variables. In the case of the dishwasher orders/new housing starts example, you might find that a regression model successfully relates past levels of dishwasher orders to levels of new housing starts occurring four months before. If so, you could then use this historical relationship to predict the future demand for dishwashers from the known values for new housing starts during the last few months.

The goal of any regression analysis is a regression equation that quantifies the historical patterns relating the variables. A regression equation for the relationship between dishwasher demand and new housing starts might take this form:

DISHWASHER.ORDERS = 12 + 1.12 x NEW.HOUSING.STARTS (4 months before)

All the numbers in the regression equation are products of the regression's mathematical analysis. In this example, 12 is an equation constant and 1.12 is the regression coefficient for the leading indicator, NEW.HOUSING.STARTS. In general, regression analysis selects the regression coefficient(s) that produces the best "fits" to the actual historical values of the forecast variable. In the technical jargon, this is called *least squares fitting*, because it minimizes the sum of the squared errors obtained in fitting the historical data (where each squared error is the square of the difference between each fitted value and the corresponding actual value).

Provided that there are no major changes in the way the world works, the historical relationship codified in the regression equation should be a good guide to the future. Given values of NEW.HOUSING.STARTS during the *last* four months, you can convert them into forecasts of DISHWASHER.ORDERS during the *next* four months via the regression equation.

Besides the regression equation, regression analysis also provides statistical measures of how accurately the equation will predict the forecast variable. They include, among others: the R-square statistic (a summary of how well the predictor variables work using the historical data), the standard error of estimate (the typical error made when estimating the forecast variable using the regression equation), and the Durbin-Watson statistic (the measure of the degree to which there is additional information in your data that the regression equation has not captured). In order to determine whether you have an appropriate regression equation for predictive purposes, you should review and evaluate these accompanying statistical measures. For this reason, the process of regression analysis cannot be entirely automated.

Although it is impossible to fully automate regression analysis, several PC forecasting packages do provide regression capabilities at various levels of sophistication, appealing to the needs of both professional forecasters and nontechnical managers. For business managers, the relative ease-of-use of these packages together with their ability to convert regression results quickly into usable forecasts makes them valuable analytical tools. And, their regression analysis capabilities not only accommodate the case of external leading indicators but also that of internal predictor variables, such as pricing, advertising, and staffing levels, which may relate strongly to the future values of other key business variables.

The Need for Business Judgment

Relying exclusively on objective statistical models to forecast—even when they are guided by an automatic expert system—requires that reality be simplified to permit mathematical analysis. However, the world of business today is both complex and dynamic. Especially in the context of forecasting, it is not always prudent to indulge the urge for simplicity.

Your competition is hard at work, and they may have announced new products that will influence your market share. Your own company may be planning sales promotions that will influence your future sales figures. Outside forces may change your cost of goods, forcing consideration of future price changes and inventory control modifications.

Under the circumstances, there is a clear need for expert insight and knowledge of future events and their possible effects to add a measure of realism. And in fact, business forecasts based on statistical analyses are still usually tempered by management judgment before they are officially adopted. Indeed, businesspeople agree that any system that stifles a manager's ability to interact easily with the forecasting process normally diminishes both the effectiveness and reliability of the forecasts.

Here is where the personal computer makes a unique contribution to business forecasting. By virtue of its flexible, interactive graphics, a PC can engage the mental model that the businessperson has of the firm and its market. Showing both historical data and forecasts graphically, the PC makes it easy to decide whether the results pass what one of our customers calls the "straight-face test" of forecast credibility: could you present these forecasts to your boss with a straight face?

If you cannot, PC forecasting software is available that lets the forecaster redraw and adjust the forecasts directly on the computer screen. This "eyeball" adjustment of statistical forecasts is an easy, intuitive way to blend objective statistical analysis with mature judgment and special knowledge. In a very real sense, this type of software provides a double expert system: the software provides the technical expertise during phase one of the forecasting process and, in phase two, the user becomes the expert, incorporating his or her business judgment.

The Need for Speed and Connectivity

In business, time is money. Managers who must wait for their forecasts to be developed are often managers who miss the chance to capitalize on those same forecasts. Even with an automatic system to select and apply the right forecasting method, an effective forecasting package must be fast to efficiently perform the myriad of calculations involved. This becomes especially important when the forecasting job moves beyond a few items to hundreds or even thousands of items.

Besides speed, most forecasters also need *connectivity*—the ability to share software programs, raw data, and results with colleagues in the same organization via a local area network (LAN). If your company has more than one manager or business analyst doing forecasting (and most companies do), the benefits of using a networked application on a LAN can be significant. They include improving access to essential data for multiple users, enhancing the efficiency of workgroup computing by easily sharing forecast results among several individuals, and reducing overhead, since the cost of a network software license can be considerably less than the retail price for multiple individual copies.

Solving Business Forecasting Problems

For most organizations, obtaining accurate sales and product demand forecasts is a very important objective. This is easy to understand since forecasts of these variables often drive a variety of financial, marketing, production planning, and inventory control systems within a company. For that reason, we have focused our attention in this section on presenting different types of sales and product demand forecasting problems, along with the types of business data representative of each. Bear in mind that these three examples are generic; the solutions discussed here are applicable to similar forecasting problems involving other types of business variables.

Forecasting a Single Business Variable Based on Historical Data

Let's consider the case of a medium-size sporting goods manufacturer that makes and sells a specialty brand of snow skis. The company has gathered accurate sales information on the number of pairs of skis sold on a quarterly basis by sales region. It now wishes to forecast future ski sales for one of the sales regions. The database on ski sales for this particular region is presented in Table 13-1.

Table 13-1 indicates that data on ski sales exist from the second quarter of 1991 (91:Q2) to the second quarter of 1995 (95:Q2), a total of 17 quarters' worth of historical information. The company's objective is to obtain a statistically based sales forecast, again by quarter, extending six periods into the future until the fourth quarter of 1996 (96:Q4). The question is, how can the product manager in charge of ski equipment best obtain an accurate sales forecast over this six-quarter horizon?

If the product manager were to look just at the numbers in the table, the answer to this question would not be obvious. There might be an initial tendency simply to average the last six quarters' sales results (from 94:Q1 to 95:Q2) or even all of the sales data (from 91:Q2 to 95:Q2), obtaining an average result per quarter that could then be applied to each of the six quarters in the future. Unfortunately, this would not take into account any underlying growth trend that might exist in the sales data or any seasonal aspect of that data. Each of these components is important in making an accurate sales forecast.

A better approach would be to graph the historical sales data first to see if a trend and/or seasonal pattern exists. This can be done easily using several of the existing PC forecasting software packages. A *timeplot* of the historical ski sales data (i.e., a graph of the sales values over time) would take the form shown in Figure 13-1. In this figure, time runs along the horizontal axis from 91:Q2 to 95:Q2. Sales for each quarter are measured in pairs of skis on the vertical axis.

	1ST QUARTER	2ND QUARTER	3RD QUARTER	4TH QUARTER
1991	not available	48	52	57
1992	63	42	57	60
1993	71	50	56	64
1994	86	53	59	68
1995	76	53	???	???
1996	???	???	???	???

TABLE 13-1. *Ski Sales (in Pairs) by Quarter*

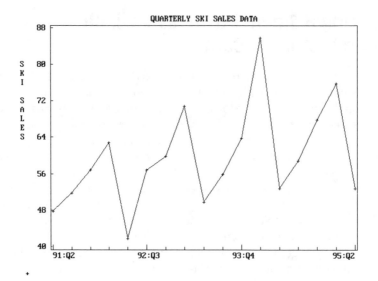

FIGURE 13-1. *Timeplot of ski sales*

Even to the eyes of a nontechnical forecaster, a number of things are readily apparent from the timeplot that were not apparent from the table of data values. First, there is a pronounced seasonal pattern in the data. Predictable highs and lows recur each year, with ski sales climbing in the third and fourth quarters of one year, peaking in the first quarter of the following year and then dropping off significantly in the second quarter. This corresponds to the seasonal buying patterns one might expect for this type of product. Second, while not overwhelming, an underlying growth trend in sales does exist. The manager can see this easily on the timeplot by comparing the first set of high and low sales figures (those for 92:Q1 and 92:Q2, respectively) to the corresponding sets of sales figures in later years.

For a professional forecaster, the results of this type of graphical analysis supplemented by the numerical values in the table would indicate that Winters exponential smoothing is an appropriate statistical forecasting solution. As you may recall, the Winters method not only tracks the underlying level and trend of a data series but also tracks seasonality, building it into the forecasting results. Of the five exponential smoothing and moving average methods described earlier in the chapter, only Winters is capable of predicting seasonal variation. Its application in this case will provide the sporting goods manufacturer with not only an estimate of total demand for skis over the next six quarters but also an indication of how the demand is seasonally distributed from quarter to quarter.

While a professional forecaster would have little difficulty in selecting Winters exponential smoothing as the optimal solution to this problem, the company's product manager might not have this level of statistical insight. Like other nontechnical forecasters, the product manager probably would (and should) rely on the automatic forecasting capabilities built into many of the available PC forecasting software packages. Later in the chapter, we will demonstrate exactly how the ski sales forecasting problem can be solved using an expert system that automatically selects and applies, from among alternative methods, the one method that best predicts a particular data series.

Forecasting Multiple Product Items Simultaneously

Let's assume that the sporting goods manufacturer also produces a group of racquet sports equipment. Included in this product group are tennis, squash, and racquetball items. Sales of these product items are considered by the manufacturer to be related to each other and, thus, to form a meaningful group total. Again, sales history on each item exists on a quarterly basis by sales region. A snapshot of the sales database for a particular sales region might look like Table 13-2.

The data table indicates that historical sales information exists for each of the three product items from 91:Q2 to 95:Q2, a total of 17 quarters of data. In this case, the company's goal is to obtain not only an accurate statistical forecast for each of the items during the next four quarters (95:Q3 to 96:Q2) but also an accurate forecast of total sales for the entire product group over the same period. Furthermore, there may be an additional factor to consider regarding price promotions that have affected sales of the product group in the past and may be planned in the future. Finally, the product manager in charge of racquet sports equipment will undoubtedly want to review the forecast results in real time and possibly will want to make judgmental adjustments based on knowledge of

	91:Q2	91:Q3	91:Q4	...	95:Q1	95:Q2	95:Q3	...	96:Q2
Tennis	78	66	69	...	102	95	???	...	???
Squash	48	42	31	...	70	66	???	...	???
Racquetball	32	23	19	...	40	44	???	...	???
Total	158	131	119	...	212	205	???	...	???

TABLE 13-2. *Racquet Sports Sales (in Units) by Quarter*

changing market conditions. How should the company proceed in order to satisfy all of these forecasting requirements?

Perhaps the most critical difference between this example and the single business variable example described earlier is the switch from a single-level to a multilevel perspective. The company is no longer concentrating simply on the best forecast results for individual variables at the item level, but also is concerned about the best group-level forecast for the total of those variables/product items. This begs the question of whether the multilevel forecasting problem should be approached on a bottom-up or top-down basis.

In a bottom-up approach, each product item is forecasted independently and the total group forecast is obtained by summing the item forecasts. This approach is considered most appropriate when item sales histories are relatively stable and emphasis is placed on reflecting the trends/seasonal patterns of the individual items. In a top-down approach, the product group history is created first by summing across item histories (as shown in the data table). The group forecast then is generated statistically based on the group history and the results distributed proportionally among the individual items to create item forecasts. This approach is considered more appropriate when the items are very strongly related, and/or the emphasis is on reflecting the trends/seasonal patterns apparent in the total group's sales history. Regardless of the approach, the final results show the item forecasts consistent with the total group forecast during each period in the future.

Even for a relatively small number of product items, such as the three in this example, multilevel forecasting brings an added layer of complexity to the forecaster's job. When the number of product items in a group increases from a few to a few dozen or a few hundred, the complexity becomes even greater. Furthermore, the multilevel sales forecast must be able to take into account the effects of planned price promotions, and the manager must be able to adjust judgmentally any forecast result (at either the item or group level) in real time. The solution to this type of problem cries out for a high level of automation. This would be true regardless of whether a nontechnical forecaster, such as a product manager, or a professional forecaster were performing the analysis. Later in the chapter, we will demonstrate how the multilevel, racquet sports forecasting problem can be solved by a business manager using automated multiseries forecasting.

Batch Processing Numerous Items in One Session

Many manufacturing companies face the constant problem of developing timely and accurate forecasts of their product demand. This requirement can extend to hundreds, thousands, and sometimes tens of thousands of product items in their inventories. Without an accurate assessment of the demand for these items, a company's manufacturing planning and control systems are severely limited in recommending how much product to produce and to stock at any point in time.

The old adage "Gold in, gold out, and garbage in, garbage out" has great significance for production planners and inventory control managers who are searching for quick, accurate solutions to their demand forecasting problems.

A representative forecasting problem for a manufacturing company that produces and inventories 5,000 stockkeeping units (SKUs) tracked on a monthly basis is displayed in Table 13-3.

The goal for this company's management is to take the recent record of product demand measured at the SKU level and deduce what they can expect individual SKU demand to be over the next three months, since three months is the production lead time for this general class of SKUs. While we do not have space here to present the specific results for each SKU, this problem speaks to the important role PC forecasting software can play in performing large batch-processing forecasting jobs. For example, in less than eight minutes, a 32-bit forecasting package running on a standard 80486 or Pentium PC can take a forecasting job of this size, read the electronic file containing the product demand data, automatically create future statistical forecasts for each SKU, and store the forecast results plus a summary audit report on the PC's hard disk. The results are then ready for immediate transfer, perhaps via a LAN, to a company database or other software system for use in various production planning activities. This type of speed and performance rivals that of mainframe software solutions but without the added expense and hassles normally associated with mainframe use.

Now that you know a bit more about how to generate a useful forecast—how to approach different kinds of forecasting problems, what data to use, which analysis methods are appropriate, the role of personal insights and judgment—we will turn our attention to how SmartForecasts can be used to solve a range of business forecasting problems. The next section of this chapter outlines

	JUL93	AUG93	SEP93	...	MAY95	JUN95	JUL95	AUG95	SEP95
SKU 1	23	21	33	...	45	41	???	???	???
SKU 2	3	5	18	...	34	45	???	???	???
SKU 3	76	84	106	...	54	69	???	???	???
.	.	.	.	.	.	.	.	.	.
.	.	.	.	.	.	.	.	.	.
.	.	.	.	.	.	.	.	.	.
SKU 5,000	34	89	124	...	189	202	???	???	???

TABLE 13-3. *Monthly Product Demand by SKU (in Units)*

SmartForecasts' features, followed by an instructional test-drive of the demonstration software found on the CD-ROM included with this book.

Features of SmartForecasts

We recognize that you, rather than the computer, play the central role in creating accurate, credible forecasts. With that in mind, we designed SmartForecasts to make the most productive use of your time. Our design grows out of two major observations about the forecasting process. First, forecasting is an art requiring a mix of sound professional judgment and objective, statistical analysis. And, second, forecasting is often a part of a larger process of planning and control. In other words, the forecasting process receives data from other business activities and normally feeds its results back into those same activities. Because we developed SmartForecasts with these observations in mind, it has a style and content well-suited for turning a personal computer into an effective forecasting and planning tool.

SmartForecasts was the first PC forecasting software to combine automatic statistical forecasting with interactive, graphical adjustments of forecast results (i.e., eyeball, or judgmental, forecasting). This means you can first obtain accurate statistical forecasts based on your historical data using the software's built-in expert system. Then you can adjust the statistical results to take account of your own special knowledge and insight. This synthesis of professional judgment and automatic statistical analysis is important for managers and analysts who must make reliable business forecasts.

Some of the special forecasting features that characterize SmartForecasts' integrated design include:

> **Popular Time-Series Forecasting Techniques, Including Single, Double, and Winters Exponential Smoothing and Simple and Linear Moving Average** These techniques are easy to understand, easy to use, and remarkably accurate in a wide variety of situations.

> **Automatic Forecasting Expert System That Provides Accurate Forecasts** SmartForecasts' Automatic forecasting feature automatically selects and applies the most appropriate statistical method to create a forecast of sales, product demand, budget-line costs, or other key business variables. Selection is made from the five exponential smoothing and moving average methods mentioned above, each tested with four different sets of weights (or averaging periods) for a total of 20 possible forecasting solutions. For example, the technique that most accurately predicts most recent sales from earlier sales history would be the one selected to forecast future sales.

> **Promotion-Driven Event Models to Reflect the Effect of Special Business Events** With SmartForecasts' Promo feature, a product manager can

automatically select the most appropriate forecasting method to predict sales of a particular product item and simultaneously adjust its results to reflect the effects of past and future promotions.

➤ **Eyeball Forecasting Capability That Permits Users to Make and Adjust Forecasts Directly on the Computer Screen**   This allows the business user to make real-time, onscreen adjustments to any statistical forecasts created by SmartForecasts.The Eyeball feature permits the user to see both a graph and the numerical values of the forecast at the same time. Modifications can be made instantaneously based on percentage changes, incremental unit changes, or simple management overrides. A manager is able to refine a forecast by applying insight or knowledge of a special sale, upcoming competitor actions, or other new market developments.

➤ **Multiseries Feature for Making Rapid, Multiple-Level Forecasts**   The Multiseries feature in SmartForecasts blends the capabilities of the Automatic, Promo, and Eyeball features to tackle the challenging task of forecasting not only a large number of related product items but also their group total. Depending on the edition of SmartForecasts, the user can create forecasts for groups with up to 1,200 product items, each of which may contain up to 520 weeks, months, or quarters of data.

➤ **Regression Analysis Solutions Specially Tailored for Forecasting Applications**   The SmartForecasts Regress command can quickly process regression models with up to 20 independent/predictor variables. For managers concerned with the causal relationship between the item they need to forecast (e.g., sales) and other independent variables strongly affecting future values of this item (e.g., leading indicators of sales, price, staffing levels, etc.), this forecasting feature becomes a valuable analytical tool.

➤ **Automatic Batch Forecasting of Hundreds, Thousands, or Even Tens of Thousands of Items**   Using SmartForecasts 32-bit Batch Edition, any business user can combine the Automatic forecasting feature with rapid batch processing of line items to forecast hundreds or thousands of items in one forecasting session. This capability is useful for companies with massive forecasting problems, such as manufacturers that must predict the demand for many thousands of items in their inventories.

➤ **Advanced Statistical Forecasting Methods to Whet the Appetites of Power Users**   SmartForecasts offers professional forecasters advanced Box-Jenkins (ARIMA) forecasting techniques to help them in their work.

➤ **Fully Integrated Graphics Displays and Tabular Forecast Reports**   SmartForecasts provides high-resolution graphs of all forecast results. Any graphics screen can be annotated (edited) to note special characteristics, and all forecast graphs are supplemented by forecast reports in tabular form.

➤ **Graphical and Numerical Reports of Forecast Uncertainty** Even the best statistical forecast must be accompanied by some measure of its uncertainty and degree of reliability. SmartForecasts provides measures of average forecast error and ranges (as well as best point estimates) of future forecast values. In inventory control applications, there is also the opportunity to convert estimates of forecast error automatically into more efficient estimates of safety stock requirements for any desired customer service level (e.g., 95 or 99 percent). This can lead to a significant reduction in inventory costs.

To support the forecasting capabilities discussed earlier, SmartForecasts provides excellent ease-of-use and compatibility with existing computer systems. SmartForecasts for DOS makes use of the standard point-and-shoot user interface familiar to most managers and business analysts who have ever worked with a spreadsheet or database. This interface, plus the program's streamlined menus and online help system, ensure a short learning curve for new users. It is also fully compatible with standard 80386, 80486, and Pentium PCs now used in most businesses. SmartForecasts for Windows, scheduled for release in the fourth quarter of 1995, is a 32-bit system compatible with the Windows NT and Windows 95 operating systems. An example of an onscreen display from this software package is shown in Figure 13-2.

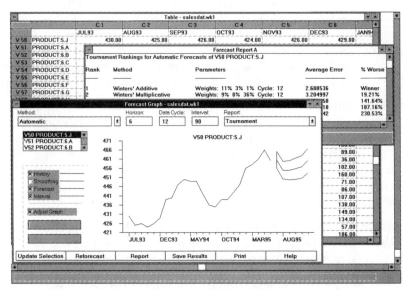

FIGURE 13-2. *A SmartForecasts for Windows display of product data, forecast graphs, and reports*

A Test Drive of SmartForecasts

A copy of SmartForecasts' demonstration program has been included on the CD-ROM accompanying this book. This *working* demo program is a full-featured version of SmartForecasts Standard Edition product, with only two exceptions. It can neither read (import) nor save (export) data in electronic files. In all other ways it is a complete, functioning copy of the Standard Edition program. The demo program comes with a built-in tutorial database that you can use to do the Automatic Forecasting Tutorial and Multiseries Forecasting Tutorial exercises presented in the following sections. Together, these two exercises will give you an excellent introduction to the Automatic, Multiseries, and Eyeball forecasting capabilities discussed earlier. They also demonstrate the program's user interface and general ease-of-use. Total time required for doing these tutorials is about one hour.

Once you have finished the tutorial, you can even enter some of your own data. This will show you how SmartForecasts can forecast your sales, product demand, or budget data. Instructions for doing this can be found right after the tutorials.

Before you start the tutorials, however, we must first transfer the SmartForecasts program from the CD-ROM to your personal computer's hard disk. To do this, follow the instructions found at the end of this book.

Starting the SmartForecasts Demo

To start the SmartForecasts Demo program, just follow the steps listed in this section. This procedure assumes that you have installed the SmartForecasts Demo in the C:\SMART directory. If you installed the program in another directory, simply substitute that directory's name and path in the place of C:\SMART.

Please note that if you have already changed some of the system defaults, your output screens may not match our tutorial samples. Therefore, if you have made changes, we recommend that you reset certain options back to their default settings: the Rounding option (in the Configure command on the Main Menu) should be set to no rounding, and the Nonnegative option (in the Configure command) should be set to allow negative forecasts.

To start the tutorials, follow these steps:

1. At the DOS C:\ > prompt, type **CD SMART** and then press ENTER.

2. At the C:\SMART > prompt, type **SF** and then press ENTER. Wait while SmartForecasts loads into the computer. After a brief period, SmartForecasts displays the screen shown in Figure 13-3.

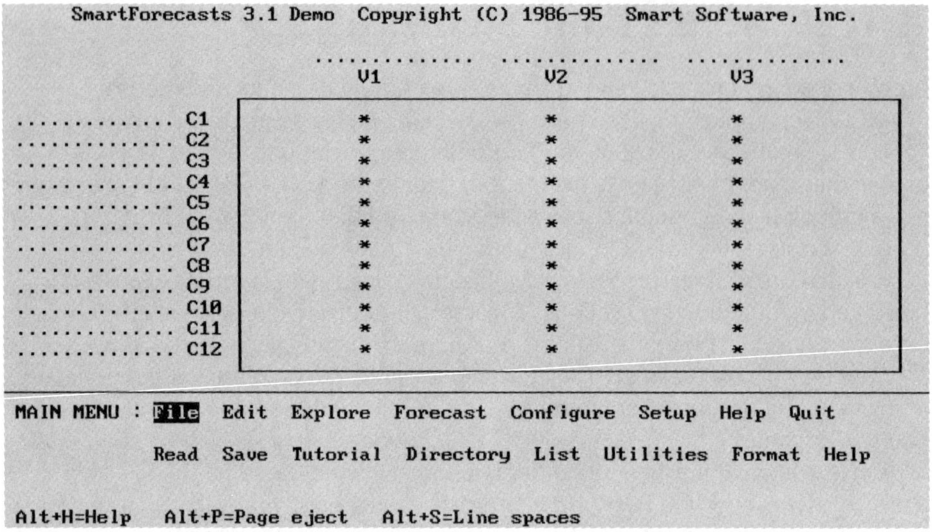

```
SmartForecasts 3.1 Demo  Copyright (C) 1986-95  Smart Software, Inc.

                     ..............  ..............  ..............
                          V1              V2              V3
............... C1         *               *               *
............... C2         *               *               *
............... C3         *               *               *
............... C4         *               *               *
............... C5         *               *               *
............... C6         *               *               *
............... C7         *               *               *
............... C8         *               *               *
............... C9         *               *               *
............... C10        *               *               *
............... C11        *               *               *
............... C12        *               *               *


MAIN MENU : File  Edit  Explore  Forecast  Configure  Setup  Help  Quit

            Read  Save  Tutorial  Directory  List  Utilities  Format  Help

Alt+H=Help   Alt+P=Page eject   Alt+S=Line spaces
```

FIGURE 13-3. *The main menu and an empty data table*

The lower part of the screen holds the main menu, which serves as the entry point to SmartForecasts. The top portion of the screen is the upper-left corner of an empty data table. What you see are the first twelve cases (C1 to C12) of the first three variables (V1 to V3) in the data table. When you look at a portion of the data table on your display screen, we say that you are *looking through the data window.*

The tutorial data table is stored on your hard disk. You will now read the tutorial data into the data table. To do so, follow these steps:

3. From the main menu, highlight **F**ile and press ENTER.

4. From the File Mode menu, press the RIGHT ARROW key until you highlight **T**utorial and then press ENTER. To protect against mistaken loss of data, SmartForecasts issues a warning at the bottom of your screen that the tutorial data table will replace the data table now on the screen. It then asks if you still want to read the Tutorial data table.

5. At the prompt asking if you still want to read the Tutorial data table, press the RIGHT ARROW key to highlight **Y**es and then press ENTER. After a short wait, SmartForecasts returns to the main menu and the Tutorial data table appears on the screen.

Now you are ready to begin the tutorials. We've created the tutorial data table to be small, simple, and illustrative. We ask you to assume the role of a sales forecaster for a sporting goods manufacturer. Our aim is to make you comfortable with SmartForecasts and to show you how quickly you can get to the point of doing useful work with SmartForecasts.

The Automatic Forecasting Tutorial

This tutorial shows you how quickly and easily SmartForecasts can forecast a data series. It also introduces you to the point-and-shoot method of choosing commands. With the point-and-shoot method, you use the arrow direction keys to highlight a command and then press ENTER to choose it. You will soon have both tabular and graphical forecasts of variable V2 SKI.SALES on both your screen and printer.

Viewing the Data Table
Let's start by looking at a list of the variables stored in the data table:

1. From the main menu, press the RIGHT ARROW key to highlight **E**dit and then press ENTER.

2. From the Edit Mode menu, press the RIGHT ARROW key until you highlight Variables and then press ENTER. SmartForecasts displays the screen shown in Figure 13-4.

```
Tutorial Data Table
List of variables:
─────────────────────
V1 :RETAIL.INDEX    V16:           V31:           V46:
V2 :SKI.SALES       V17:           V32:           V47:
V3 :TENNIS.SALES    V18:           V33:           V48:
V4 :SQUASH.SALES    V19:           V34:           V49:
V5 :RAQTBALL.SALES  V20:           V35:           V50:
V6 :                V21:           V36:           V51:
V7 :                V22:           V37:           V52:
V8 :                V23:           V38:           V53:
V9 :                V24:           V39:           V54:
V10:                V25:           V40:           V55:
V11:                V26:           V41:           V56:
V12:                V27:           V42:           V57:
V13:                V28:           V43:           V58:
V14:                V29:           V44:           V59:
V15:                V30:           V45:           V60:
─────────────────────────────────────────────────────────────────
EDIT MODE : Replace    See      Sequence   Label   Title   Variables   Help
            Define     Insert   Delete     Oops    Print   Clear

            Enter, change or review any numbers in the data table.

Alt+H=Help    Alt+P=Page eject    Alt+S=Line spaces    Esc=Main Menu
```

FIGURE 13-4. *The list of variables*

This screen shows a list of all variables and their labels. RETAIL.INDEX is a measure of local retail sales activity. The other variables are unit sales figures for two product groups: ski equipment and racquet sports equipment. The racquet sports product group has three individual components: tennis, squash, and racquetball.

Now let's get the data table back on the screen:

3. From the Edit Mode menu, press the RIGHT ARROW key to highlight **S**ee and then press ENTER.

The message area of the screen instructs you to press ENTER to see the upper-left corner of the data table. These messages help you to respond correctly to a prompt.

4. At the prompt asking for the variables you want to see, press ENTER. SmartForecasts erases the list of variables and redisplays the upper-left corner of the data table.

The cases in the data window range from the second quarter of 1991 to the first quarter of 1994. The message area also provides instructions on moving the data window. Let's move the window to see the more recent cases:

5. Press the DOWN ARROW key until you reach the last case holding data. Note that the data ends with case C17, the second quarter of 1995.

6. Press CTRL-PG UP to return to the top of the data table.

When you press the DOWN ARROW key, the data window moves down one row at a time. When you press CTRL-PG UP, it jumps back to show the first twelve rows in the data table. You can practice using UP ARROW, DOWN ARROW, PG UP, PG DOWN, CTRL-PG UP, and CTRL-PG DN to move the data window up and down. When you finish, press CTRL-PG UP to return to the top of the data table.

Now return to the main menu:

7. From the data window, press ESC to return to Edit mode, then press ESC again to return to the main menu.

NOTE
When you press ESC, SmartForecasts ends the current command and returns you to the previous screen.

Forecast Mode

The following steps will help you become familiar with the Forecast Mode commands:

1. To switch from the main menu to Forecast mode, press the RIGHT ARROW key until you highlight Forecast and then press ENTER. Notice that **A**utomatic is highlighted on the Forecast Mode menu.

2. Press the RIGHT ARROW key to highlight **E**yeball.

3. Continue to press the RIGHT ARROW key to highlight each command, then read the message describing that command. When you return to Automatic, leave it highlighted. You will now use the Automatic command to forecast ski sales (V2):

4. With **A**utomatic highlighted on the Forecast Mode menu, press ENTER.

5. At the prompt asking for the variable(s) you want to forecast, type **V2** (the variable number for SKI.SALES) and then press ENTER.

   You always type the variable you want a command to operate upon—in this case, V2. As a convenience, you can also specify more than one variable to forecast. For example, instead of typing just one variable (V2), you could type **V2 V5-V25 V34** and then press ENTER. In this case, the Automatic command would execute anew for each variable in turn. This ability to forecast multiple variables is called the Repeat feature.

   The Automatic command conducts a tournament among five different forecasting techniques, trying each technique four different ways before selecting the winner. The winner is the method that best predicts more recent values of the data series from earlier values. Note the advisory message at the bottom of the screen that warns against forecasting more than eight periods ahead in this instance. As a rule of thumb, you should avoid forecasting ahead more than half the length of your data series, because the degree of accuracy for forecasts far in the future can be noticeably less than that for earlier forecasts. Where necessary, prompts have advisory messages to help you respond sensibly.

   Next, let's specify how far ahead to forecast and the type of data:

6. At the prompt asking for the number of time periods ahead you wish to forecast, type **6** and then press ENTER.

7. At the prompt asking which type of data is V2 SKI.SALES, press the RIGHT ARROW key to highlight **Q**uarterly and then press ENTER.

The tournament begins as soon as you choose Quarterly. Because the data is quarterly, the forecasting tournament includes a technique that tries to exploit any pattern of repetitive quarterly variation in the data (the technique is called multiplicative Winters exponential smoothing). When the tournament is over, the program has selected a forecasting technique appropriate for the data. It uses that technique to forecast V2 and presents its results in a graph. Figure 13-5 shows the graph of the automatic forecasts of V2 SKI.SALES.

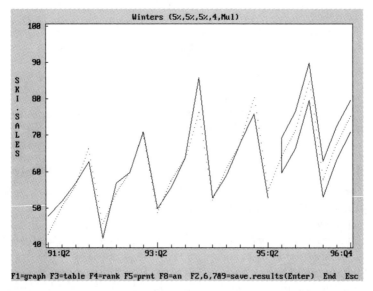

FIGURE 13-5. *Automatic forecasts of SKI.SALES*

An abbreviated version of a function key menu appears at the bottom of the screen. Whenever this menu (the short function key menu) appears, it serves as a reminder (or prompt) that you can perform one of the following steps:

➤ Press one of the function keys to invoke the function.

➤ Press ENTER to see the menu of function key options in expanded form (the full function key menu).

➤ Press ESC to end the command and exit the current screen.

You will use the function keys throughout the tutorials to produce graphs, tables, and so on.

Viewing Tables and Graphs

If you have a color graphics monitor, the graph in Figure 13-5 shows the historical data in red. On a monochrome graphics monitor, the historical data appears as a solid white line starting on the left of the graph and extending with repetitive quarterly variations for 17 quarters.

The dotted green line (dotted white line on a monochrome monitor) is the *smoothed* version of the historical data, which has random effects averaged out. The dotted green line extends into the future as the forecast. The solid yellow lines (bright white lines on a monochrome monitor) that bracket the forecasts indicate their high and low margins of error, respectively. The legend above the graph signifies the method that won the forecasting tournament. In this case, the winning method is multiplicative Winters exponential smoothing with weights of 5 percent.

You can send the graph to your printer (this step is optional):

1. With the short function key menu on the screen, press CTRL-PRINT SCREEN. SmartForecasts sends the graph displayed on the screen to the printer.

   You can print any graphics screen produced by SmartForecasts by pressing CTRL-PRINT SCREEN. Note that if your printer does not eject the graph, simply press ALT-P and then press ENTER to send a page eject (or form feed) to your printer. These keys are active in the main menu and in the File, Edit, Explore, and Forecast Mode menus, as well as in any function key menu.

   To produce a tabular display, let's use a function key:

2. With the function key menu on the screen, press F3. The table of forecasts shown in Figure 13-6 displays.

   The table header shows the forecast variable, the winning forecasting technique, the data cases used in making the forecast, the average forecast error expressed in units, and the average forecast error expressed as a percentage. The error results provide valuable forecast evaluation

```
Forecasts of V2 SKI.SALES using multiplicative WINTERS' METHOD
with weights = 5%, 5%, and 5%  and seasonal cycle length = 4 periods.
Based on 17 cases: C1 91:Q2 to C17 95:Q2.
Avg forecast error = 2.576       Avg percent error = 3.6%

                          Approximate 90% Forecast Interval
      Time Period        Lower Limit       FORECAST     Upper Limit
      _____        _____       _____     _____
      95:Q3                59.780          64.620         69.460
      95:Q4                66.612          71.621         76.631
      96:Q1                79.813          84.973         90.132
      96:Q2                53.089          58.128         63.167
      96:Q3                63.587          68.147         72.707
      96:Q4                71.112          75.478         79.844




F1=graph   F3=table  F4=ranks  F5=print  F2,6,7&9=save.results(Enter)  End  Esc
```

FIGURE 13-6. *Automatic forecasts in tabular form*

measures that show how accurately SmartForecasts would have predicted the forecast variable in the recent past. As we noted, the winner of the forecasting tournament in this example is the multiplicative Winters method.

The screen shows the forecasts, flanked by their upper and lower limits representing margins of error, in the three columns labeled Approximate 90% Forecast Interval. Based on historical experience, there is about a 90 percent chance that the actual value of the forecast variable will fall between the high and low estimates. (If you wish, you can change the 90 percent forecast interval to some other figure, such as 95 percent or 99 percent, by pressing ALT-F1 whenever the function key menu appears on the screen.) The middle column holds the best bet forecasts that appear in Figure 13-5 as a dotted line.

Let's go back briefly to the function key menu to switch to the expanded form of the menu:

3. With the short function key menu on the screen, press ENTER.

Figure 13-7 shows the full function key menu. Remember, whenever you see the short function key menu displayed along the bottom of the screen, you can get the full menu simply by pressing ENTER.

Now, let's send the forecast table to your printer (this step is optional):

4. With the full function key menu on the screen, press F5. Make sure your printer is on and set properly; then press ENTER to send the table to the printer.

SmartForecasts sends the forecast table to your printer. Wait until the screen clears and displays the full function key menu before you take the next step. If your printer does not eject the table, simply press ALT-P and then press ENTER to send your printer a page eject (or form feed) command.

```
Special Function key options for the AUTOMATIC command:

F1 = see graph of forecasts          F2 = save forecasts + smoothed data
F3 = see table of forecasts          F4 = see tournament rankings
F5 = print table of forecasts        F6 = save upper + lower forecast limits
F7 = save forecasts only             F8 = annotate (if graph is displayed)
F9 = save forecasts + history        F10:

Alt+F1 = change % level of           End = repeat forecast command
         forecast interval                 for next variable
Alt+F3 = save forecast table         Esc = return to FORECAST mode
         to a TBL file
Alt+F5 = print forecast table
         with page eject
```

FIGURE 13-7. *The full function key menu for the Automatic command*

5. With the full function key menu on the screen, press F4. The screen shows the final rankings of the techniques competing in the tournament.

The technique in second place was double exponential smoothing with a weight of 5 percent given to the most recent data. It had an average error 232 percent worse than the winner's.

Now let's end the Automatic command and return to the Forecast Mode menu:

6. With the short function key menu on the screen, press ESC. SmartForecasts escapes from the Automatic command and returns to Forecast mode.

If you don't want to quit SmartForecasts now, simply continue directly to the next tutorial, and skip these next steps:

7. From the Forecast Mode menu, press ESC to return to the main menu.

8. From the main menu, press the arrow direction keys to highlight **Q**uit and then press ENTER.

When you quit SmartForecasts, the program reminds you that you can quickly get back into the demo by pressing any key (except ESC).

9. Press ESC to return to DOS.

The Multiseries Forecasting Tutorial

This tutorial teaches you how to use the Multiseries command to simultaneously forecast several well-related data series. Our example focuses on variables V3 (TENNIS.SALES), V4 (SQUASH.SALES), and V5 (RAQTBALL.SALES), which represent the sales of related items in a racquet sports product group. Although we use only three variables in this tutorial, the Multiseries command lets you simultaneously forecast up to 60 variables at a time. (In SmartForecasts' 32-bit Batch Edition, this number increases to 1,200 variables at a time.)

This tutorial also gives you the option of using the method you prefer to choose a command—the point-and-shoot method introduced in the previous tutorial exercise, or the typing method, where you simply type the command's key letter (which is highlighted in red on a color monitor). Instead of indicating to you which method to use, we will simply tell you to choose a command.

First, let's rejoin the tutorials. (Skip the first two steps in this section if you are continuing directly from the previous tutorial).

1. Follow the instructions in the "Starting the SmartForecasts Demo" section earlier in this chapter to restart the demo and read the tutorial data into the data table.

2. From the main menu, choose Forecast.
  To make simultaneous forecasts of V3 through V5 and their total:

3. From the Forecast Mode menu, choose **M**ultiseries.

4. At the prompt asking for variables you want to forecast, type **V3-V5** and then press ENTER. SmartForecasts first asks you whether you want to adjust forecast results for promotional effects and then if you want to forecast using a bottom-up or top-down approach.

  In this case, there are no promotional effects, and you will choose a bottom-up approach where the total group-level forecast is created by summing forecasts of the individual variables.

  SmartForecasts also asks you how far ahead to forecast and what type of data you are forecasting (monthly, quarterly, annual, or other). Then it forecasts V3, V4, and V5 individually using Automatic forecasting (as in the previous tutorial).

  SmartForecasts then computes the total of the independently forecasted variables. At this point, you have the option of manually adjusting the forecast of the total group (using the program's Eyeball forecasting capability).

  Finally, the program automatically distributes any adjustments made to total group sales among the individual variables and lets you manually adjust their forecasts too.

5. At the prompt asking about adjustments for promotional effects, choose **N**o.

6. At the prompt asking about a bottom-up or top-down forecast, choose **B**ottom-up. SmartForecasts will not adjust forecast results for promotional effects, and will create the forecast of total group sales using a bottom-up approach.

7. At the prompt asking for the number of time periods ahead you wish to forecast, type **4** and then press ENTER. SmartForecasts will forecast the three related variables and their total four quarters ahead.

  You must now specify what type of data you are forecasting:

8. At the prompt asking for the type of data, choose **Q**uarterly. SmartForecasts runs the Automatic forecasting tournament on each of the three racquet sports variables, generates their forecasts individually, and then adds them to form forecasts of the total group.

  When the tournament is complete, the results for the total appear graphically. The screen shows the historical values of the total in red and the forecasts in green (on a monochrome monitor, both the historical data and the forecasts are shown as solid white lines separated by a break, with the forecasts to the right of the break).

  The cursor for manual adjustments appears as a small box whose horizontal and vertical positions (95:Q3 and 209.074, respectively) appear at the bottom of the screen. Suppose that the only revision you want to make is to lower the first forecast of the total.

9. At the prompt asking for the new number, press the DOWN ARROW key twice, and then press INSERT. These changes lower the forecast for the third quarter of 1995 to about 205 units.

   Figure 13-8 shows the result of the manual adjustment of the forecasts of total sales.

REMEMBER
After you move the cursor, you must press INSERT to insert the adjustments into the forecast.

   Now you can let SmartForecasts distribute this adjustment to total sales among the individual sales series.

10. At the prompt asking for the new number, press ESC.

As soon as you are finished adjusting the forecasts of the total, SmartForecasts automatically and simultaneously distributes any changes made to the total among

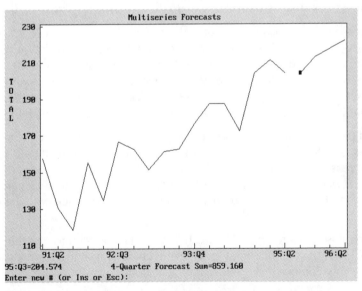

FIGURE 13-8.   *Multiseries forecasts of total after manual adjustment*

V3, V4, and V5. It makes the forecasts of the individual sales series consistent with any manual adjustment of the forecasts of the total.

SmartForecasts then displays a list of the individual variables. It prompts for any variable whose forecasts you might want to review and adjust. These individual adjustments are optional.

Reviewing and Adjusting Forecasts of Individual Variables

To review and adjust the forecasts of V3 TENNIS.SALES:

1. At the prompt asking for the V# or Vlabel of a variable to review, type **V3** and then press ENTER. SmartForecasts graphs the historical values of V3 and its forecasts.

   The cursor appears at the first forecast value. You are free to revise the forecasts manually if you wish. The bottom of the screen shows that the first forecast calls for sales of about 94 units in the third quarter of 1995.

   To revise the forecast of V3 upward for the second quarter of 1996, use the following sequence of keystrokes at the prompt asking for the new number:

2. Press PG UP. This gives more room at the top of the graph.

3. Press END to jump the cursor to the last forecast.

4. Type **110** and press ENTER. This moves the cursor up to 110.

5. Press INSERT to insert the change into the forecast.

6. Press TAB. This ends the manual adjustment of the forecasts of V3 and moves on to V4. SmartForecasts moves on and graphs the historical data and forecasts of V4 SQUASH.SALES, the next variable on the list.

   To review the forecasts of V4 SQUASH.SALES, you do not need to enter anything; simply examine the forecast of V4 on the screen. Let's assume that the forecast looks OK to you, so you want to leave it unchanged.

7. At the prompt asking for the new number, press TAB to leave the forecast of V4 as is. SmartForecasts moves on and graphs the historical data and forecasts of V5 RAQTBALL.SALES, the last variable on the list.

   Suppose you expect the next quarter's sales to be about 10 percent higher than predicted, but then expect sales to drop back onto the trend line.

8. To revise the forecast of V5 RAQTBALL.SALES upward for the third quarter of 1995, use the following sequence of keystrokes at the prompt asking for the new number:

9. Type **10%** and press UP ARROW. This increases the third quarter of 1995 forecast by 10 percent to 49.911.

10. Press INSERT to insert the change into the forecast. Figure 13-9 shows the result of the manual adjustment of the forecasts of V5 RAQTBALL.SALES.

11. Press ESC to end the manual adjustment.

Your revisions are now complete. To stop reviewing the forecasts of individual series:

12. At the prompt asking for the V# or Vlabel of a variable to review, press ESC.

At this point, you have forecasts of all the individual product items and of the product group total. SmartForecasts displays the full function key menu for the Multiseries command.

Viewing Tables and Graphs
Let's display the forecasts on the screen in tabular form.

1. With the full function key menu displayed, press F3. SmartForecasts displays the four forecasts of the total and all its component series, as shown in Figure 13-10.

Instructions for moving about the display window appear in the message area. To display the remaining forecast results:

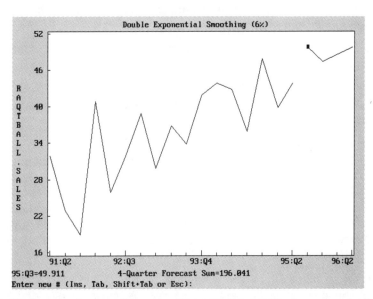

FIGURE 13-9. *Multiseries forecasts of RAQTBALL.SALES after manual adjustment*

```
BOTTOM-UP forecasts based on 17 cases: C1 91:Q2 to C17 95:Q2
Method for TOTAL: Sum of subseries    Method for SUBSERIES: Automatic

VARIABLE               95:Q3           95:Q4           96:Q1           96:Q2

TOTAL                209.111         213.635         218.196         231.794
TENNIS.SALES          94.027          97.718          99.340         110.000
SQUASH.SALES          65.173          68.376          70.146          71.915
RAQTBALL.SALES        49.911          47.541          48.710          49.879




Use the arrow keys to move the display window one step in any direction.
To jump right, press Ctrl+Right or End.  To jump left, press Ctrl+Left or Home.
To jump vertically, press  PgUp  or  PgDn  or  Ctrl+PgUp  or  Ctrl+PgDn .
Press  Esc  to return to the MULTISERIES menu.
```

FIGURE 13-10.   *A tabular display of Multiseries forecasts*

2. Following the instructions in the message area of the screen, press the
RIGHT ARROW key to see the remaining results, in particular the cumulative
four-quarter sum of the forecasts.

3. Following the instructions in the message area, press ESC to return to the
Multiseries menu. Now you will save the forecasts back in the data table.

4. With the short function key menu on the screen, press F9. SmartForecasts
displays a prompt asking whether you want to save the forecasts of the
individual data series.

5. Choose **Yes**. SmartForecasts immediately saves the forecasts of V3, V4, and
V5 at the end of their historical data. Then it prompts for your intentions
about saving the total and its forecasts.

   Because of space limitations, the Multiseries command must save
the forecasts of the individual data series back in the same variables as
their historical data. This is an exception to the general rule that you can
save forecasts anywhere in the data table, either with or without their
historical data.

6. At the prompt asking if you want to save the total and its forecasts, choose
Yes. SmartForecasts displays a list of variables so you can decide where to

    save the total and its forecasts.
       You will save the total and its forecasts in V6.

7. At the prompt asking for the V# or Vlabel for the total and its forecasts, type **V6** and then press ENTER.
       Because V6 has no label, SmartForecasts prompts you for one. The fifteen dots after the prompt show how long the label can be.

8. At the prompt asking you to enter a Vlabel for V6, type **TOTAL.SALES** and then press ENTER. SmartForecasts briefly displays the updated list of variables, showing the new label for V6. Then the full function key menu appears on the screen.
       Now let's examine a graph of the forecasts of TENNIS.SALES (V3).

9. With the full function key menu on the screen, press F1. SmartForecasts displays a list of the variables that have been multiseries-forecasted and their total.
       You can select any one of these variables for graphing. You will select V3 TENNIS.SALES.

10. At the prompt asking for the V# or Vlabel of a variable to graph, type **V3** and then press ENTER. Figure 13-11 shows the graph of tennis sales.
       A break in the curve separates the historical data on the left from the forecasts on the right. The short function key menu appears below the graph.
       Now end the Multiseries command and switch to the main menu.

11. With the short function key menu on the screen, press ESC. SmartForecasts checks that you really want to leave Multiseries, as a precaution against leaving without saving results.

12. At the prompt asking if you really want to escape to Forecast mode, choose Yes.

13. From the Forecast Mode menu, press ESC to switch to the main menu.

We will now quit SmartForecasts. (Skip these steps if you intend to enter data into SmartForecasts to create your own forecasts at this time.)

1. From the main menu, choose **Q**uit.

2. Press ESC to return to DOS.

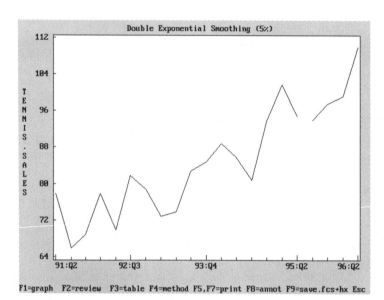

FIGURE 13-11. *A graph of Multiseries forecasts*

NOTE
When you quit SmartForecasts, the program reminds you that you can quickly get back into the demo by pressing any key (except ESC).

What the SmartForecasts Demo Can Do for You

Now that you have completed the tutorial exercises, we encourage you to take some of your own sales, product demand, or budget data and enter it into SmartForecasts. You can do so easily by following these instructions:

1. From the main menu, choose **E**dit to switch to Edit Mode.

2. From the Edit Mode menu, choose **C**lear and then choose **Y**es. This will clear any preexisting data, such as the tutorial data, from the SmartForecasts data table. You are now ready to enter your own data into the program.

3. From the Edit Mode menu, choose Replace.

4. At the prompt asking for the variable and/or case you want to edit, press ENTER.
   The Replace command is SmartForecasts' data entry and editing system. It works just like the data editors in popular spreadsheet programs.

5. Use the arrow direction and number keys to enter (and edit) your data in the same manner as you would in a spreadsheet. Just remember to enter each variable's data *column-wise*, not row-wise, into the data table.

When you are finished with the data entry you can begin your forecasting by doing the following:

6. At the prompt asking for a new value, press ESC to return to Edit Mode.

7. From the Edit Mode menu, press ESC to return to the main menu.

8. From the main menu, choose Forecast to switch to Forecast mode.

You are now ready to forecast your data by choosing a forecasting command, such as Automatic, and following the command's onscreen prompts. (You might want to refer to the "Automatic Forecasting Tutorial" presented earlier for a quick review of how to do this.)

If you feel at any time that you need more help in operating SmartForecasts, simply choose the Help command and then select an appropriate topic from the program's online help index. We recommend that new users of the program look at the Overview Help topic to see a brief summary of SmartForecasts' menu structure and operating conventions. The Help command itself is available from the main menu, as well as the File, Edit, Explore, and Forecast Mode menus.

Remember that while the tutorial exercises used data organized on a quarterly basis, SmartForecasts can also analyze and forecast weekly, monthly, accounting month, and annual data, as well. Also, because the Read and Save commands in SmartForecasts have been deactivated in the demo program, you will not be able to save your results in an electronic data file. However, you can use the program's print capabilities to send forecast graphs and tabular reports to a computer printer.

Conclusion

In today's competitive world, the ability to make better, faster forecasts of future events can be critical to your business' ultimate ability to function efficiently and succeed financially. Applications like SmartForecasts bring the power of accurate forecasting to the desktop, where it can be tapped by any business manager or decision-maker charged with planning your company's future. This provides your key personnel not only with more cost-effective planning strategies, but also with more control over the forecasting and planning processes. Benefits like these can lead to major improvements in your company's bottom-line results.

APPENDIX A

Selected Bibliography

Chapter 1

Benson, William, and Edward Kappus. *Managing People: Your Competitive Edge in the 90's.* Emeryville, CA: Avantos Performance Systems, Inc., 1992.

Blanchard, Kenneth, Donald Carew, and Eunice Parasi-Carew. *The One Minute Manager: Building High Performance Teams.* New York: William Morrow and Company, Inc., 1990.

Boone, Mary E. *Leadership and the Computer.* Rocklin, CA: Prima Publishing, 1991.

Certo, Samuel C. *Supervision: Quality and Diversity Through Leadership.* Homewood, IL: Austen Press, 1994.

Maddux, Robert B. *Effective Performance Appraisals.* Menlo Park, CA: Crisp Publications, Inc., 1993.

Mohrman, Allan M., Susan M. Resnick-West, and Edward E. Lawler. *Designing Performance Appraisal Systems.* San Francisco: Jossey-Bass Publishers, 1989.

Sachs, Randi Toler. *Productive Performance Appraisals.* New York: Amacom, 1992.

Swan, William S. *How To Do a Superior Performance Appraisal.* New York: John Wiley and Sons, Inc., 1991.

Vroom, Victor H. *Manage People, Not Personnel: Motivation and Performance Appraisal.* Boston: Harvard Business Review, 1990.

Chapter 2

Bird, Frank E., and Robert G. Loftus. *Loss Control Management.* New York: Institute Press, 1976.

Church, Frederic C. *Avoiding Surprises.* Boston: Boston Risk Management Corporation, 1982.

Tarrants, William E. *The Measurement of Safety Performance.* New York: Garland STPM Press, 1980.

Chapter 3

Cohen, Herb. *You Can Negotiate Anything.* Secaucus, NJ: Stuart, 1980.

Dawson, Roger. *You Can Get Anything You Want: But You Have To Do More Than Ask.* New York: Fireside, 1985.

Fisher, Ury. *Getting To Yes: Negotiating Agreement Without Giving In.* Boston: Houghton Mifflin, 1981.

Hall, Lavinia, ed. *Negotiation: Strategies for Mutual Gain.* San Francisco: Sage, 1993.

Lax, David, and James Sebenius. *The Manager as Negotiator.* New York: Free Press, 1986.

Lewicki, Roy, and Joseph A. Litterer. *Negotiation.* Homewood, IL: Irwin, 1985.

Raiffa, Howard. *The Art and Science of Negotiation.* Cambridge, MA: Harvard University Press, 1982.

Singer, Linda. *Settling Disputes: Conflict Resolution in Business, Families, and the Legal System.* Boulder, CO: Westview Press, 1994.

Susskind, Lawrence, Lawrence Bacow, and Michael Wheeler, eds. *Resolving Environmental Regulatory Disputes.* New York: Basic Books, 1983.

Susskind, Lawrence, and J. Cruikshank. *Breaking the Impasse: Consensual Approaches to Resolving Public Disputes.* New York: Basic Books, 1987.

Tannen, Deborah. *You Just Don't Understand: Women and Men in Conversation.* New York: Ballantine, 1990.

Ury, William. *Getting Past No: Negotiating with Difficult People.* New York: Bantam Books, 1991.

Williams, Gerald. *Legal Negotiation and Settlement.* St. Paul, MN: West, 1983.

Chapter 4

Adams, James. *Conceptual Blockbusting.* Stanford, CA: Stanford University Press, 1974.

Cynwyd, Bala, and James Halcomb. *Planning Big.* Los Altos, CA: Los Altos Publishing, 1990.

Graham, Robert J. *Project Management as if People Mattered.* New York: Primavera Press, 1989.

Mattimore, Brian. *99% Inspiration.* New York: Amacom, 1994.

Miller, William C. *The Creative Edge.* Reading, MA: Addison Wesley, 1987.

Nierenberg, Gerard I. *Fundamentals of Negotiating.* New York: Harper & Row Perennial, 1973.

_____. *The Art of Creative Thinking.* New York: Simon & Schuster, 1982.

_____. *The Complete Negotiator.* New York: Berkeley Books, 1986.

_____. *Negotiating the Big Sale.* New York: Berkeley Books, 1992.

Nierenberg, Juliet, and Irene S. Ross. *Women and the Art of Negotiating.* New York: Simon & Schuster, 1985.

Thompson, Charles. *What a Great Idea!* New York: Harper Perennial, 1992.

von Oech, Roger. *A Whack on the Side of the Head.* New York: Warner, 1983.

Chapter 5

Kotler, Philip. *Marketing Management: Analysis, Planning, Implementation, and Control.* Englewood Cliffs, NJ: Prentice Hall, 1994.

Porter, Michael. *Competitive Strategy: Techniques for Analyzing Industries and Competitors.* New York: Free Press, 1980.

_____. *Competitive Advantage: Creating and Sustaining Superior Performance.* New York: Free Press, 1985.

Chapter 6

Rouse, William B. *Design for Success: A Human-Centered Approach to Designing Successful Products and Systems.* New York: Wiley, 1991.

_____. *Strategies for Innovation.* New York: Wiley, 1992.

_____. *Catalysts for Change.* New York: Wiley, 1993.

_____. *Best Laid Plans.* Englewood Cliffs, NJ: Prentice Hall, 1994.

_____. *Enterprises in Transition.* Englewood Cliffs, NJ: Prentice Hall, 1995.

Chapter 7

Berstein, Leopold A. *Analysis of Financial Statements* (revised ed.). Homewood, IL: Dow Jones-Irwin, 1984.

Drucker, Peter. *Innovation and Entrepreneurship.* New York: Harper & Row, 1985.

Haller, Leon. *Making Sense of Accounting Information.* New York: Van Nostrand Reinhold, 1985.

Hawken, Paul. "Mastering the Numbers." *Inc. Magazine* (October, 1987): 19-20.

Mancuso, Joseph R. *How to Start, Finance, and Manage Your Own Small Business.* Englewood Cliffs, NJ: Prentice Hall, 1978.

Chapter 8

Baird, Bruce F. *Managerial Decisions Under Uncertainty: An Introduction to the Analysis of Decision Making.* New York: Wiley & Sons, 1989.

Behn, Robert D., and James W. Vaupel. *Quick Analysis for Busy Decision Makers.* New York: Basic Books, 1982.

Bunn, Derek W. *Applied Decision Analysis.* New York: McGraw-Hill, 1984.

Clemen, R. T. *Making Hard Decisions: An Introduction to Decision Analysis.* Boston: PWS-Kent Publishing, 1991.

Holloway, Charles A. *Decision Making Under Uncertainty: Models and Choices.* Englewood Cliffs, NJ: Prentice Hall, 1979.

Howard, R. A., and J. E. Matheson, eds. *The Principles and Applications of Decision Analysis.* Menlo Park, CA: Strategic Decisions Group, 1989.

Oliver, R. M., and J. Q. Smith, eds. *Influence Diagrams, Belief Nets, and Decision Analysis.* New York: Wiley & Sons, 1990.

Raiffa, Howard. *Decision Analysis: Introductory Lectures on Choices Under Uncertainty.* New York: Random House, 1968.

Samson, D. *Managerial Decision Analysis.* Homewood, IL: Irwin, 1988.

Von Winterfield, Detlof, and Ward Edwards. *Decision Analysis and Behavioral Research.* Cambridge, England: Cambridge University Press, 1986.

Watson, Stephen R., and Dennis M. Buede. *The Principles and Practice of Decision Analysis.* New York: Cambridge University Press, 1987.

Chapter 9

Peterson, S. "Software for Model Building and Simulation: An Illustration of Design Philosophy." In Morecroft, J. D. W., and J. Sterman. *Modeling for Learning Organizations.* Portland, OR: Productivity Press, 1994.

Richmond, B., Peterson, S., et al. *Business Applications.* Hanover, NH: High Performance Systems, Inc., 1994.

_____. *Introduction to Systems Thinking and ithink.* Hanover, NH: High Performance Systems, Inc., 1994.

_____. *Process Improvement Module.* Hanover, NH: High Performance Systems, Inc., 1994.

_____. *Re-engineering Using ithink: Helping to Make Effective Change Happen. Hanover, NH: High Performance Systems, Inc., 1994.*

_____. *Technical Reference.* Hanover, NH: High Performance Systems, Inc., 1994.

Chapter 10

Gogg, Thomas J., and Jack R. A. Mott. *Improve Quality and Productivity with Simulation.* Palos Verdes Peninsula, CA: JMI Consulting Group, 1992.

Hammer, Michael, and James Champy. *Reengineering the Corporation.* New York: Harper Collins, 1993.

Hansen, Gregory A. *Automating Business Process Reengineering.* Englewood Cliffs, NJ: PTR Prentice-Hall, 1994.

Senge, Peter. *The Fifth Discipline.* New York: Doubleday, 1990.

Siprelle, Andy. "Space Transportation System Near-Term Manifest Simulation Model." Society for Computer Simulation Western Multiconference proceedings. Tempe, AZ, 1994.

Whitman, Alan R. "Virtual Reengineering." *Industrial Engineering* (March, 1994): 17-18.

Chapter 11

Clemen, Robert T. *Making Hard Decisions.* Boston: PWS-Kent, 1991.

Law, A. M., and W. D. Kelton. *Simulation Modeling and Analysis,* second ed. New York: McGraw-Hill, 1991.

Megill, R. E. *An Introduction to Risk Analysis.* Tulsa, OK: PennWell Books, 1985.

Murtha, James A. *Decisions Involving Uncertainty: An @RISK Tutorial for the Petroleum Industry.* Houston, TX: James A. Murtha, 1993.

Startzman, R. A., and R. A. Wattenbarger. "An Improved Computation Procedure for Risk Analysis Problems with Unusual Probability Functions." SPE Hydrocarbon Economics and Evaluation Symposium proceedings. Dallas, TX, 1985.

Winston, Wayne L. *Operations Research: Applications and Algorithms,* third ed. Belmont, CA: Duxbury Press, 1994.

_____. *Introduction to Mathematical Programming,* second ed. Belmont, CA: Duxbury Press, 1995.

Chapter 12

Box, G. E. P., and G. M. Jenkins. *Time Series Analysis: Forecasting and Control,* revised ed. San Francisco: Holden-Day, 1976.

Gardner, E. S., Jr. "Exponential Smoothing: The State of the Art." *Journal of Forecasting,* vol. 4, no. 1 (Jan.-Mar., 1985): 1-38.

Goodrich, R. L. *Applied Statistical Forecasting.* Belmont, MA: Business Forecast Systems, Inc., 1989.

Makridakis S., and S. C. Wheelwright. *Interactive Forecasting,* second ed. San Francisco: Holden-Day, 1979.

Newbold, P., and T. Bos. *Introductory Business Forecasting.* Cincinnati, OH: South-Western, 1990.

Stellwagen, E. A., and R. L. Goodrich. *Forecast Pro for Windows User Manual.* Belmont, MA: Business Forecast Systems, Inc., 1992.

Wheelwright, S. C., and S. Makridakis. *Forecasting Methods for Management.* New York: Wiley, 1985.

Chapter 13

Armstrong, J. Scott. *Long Range Forecasting: From Crystal Ball to Computer,* second ed. New York: Wiley, 1985.

Bails, Dale G., and Larry C. Peppers. *Business Fluctuations: Forecasting Techniques and Applications.* Englewood Cliffs, NJ: Prentice Hall, 1982.

Hurwood, David L., Eliot S. Grossman, and Earl L. Bailey. *Sales Forecasting.* New York: The Conference Board, 1978.

Levenbach, Hans, and James P. Cleary. *The Beginning Forecaster.* Belmont, CA: Lifetime Learning Publications, 1981.

_____. *The Professional Forecaster.* Belmont, CA: Lifetime Learning Publications, 1981.

Smart, Charles N. "Foreward-Looking Software for Business Forecasting." *Journal of Financial Software and Hardware* (May/June, 1985): 28-30.

Willemain, Thomas R. *Statistical Methods for Planners.* Cambridge, MA: MIT Press, 1980.

Index

E

F

G

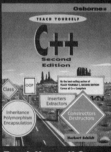

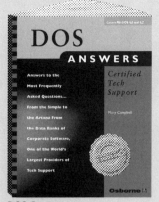
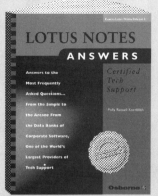
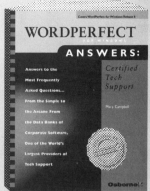

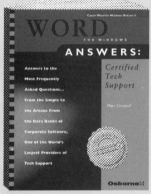
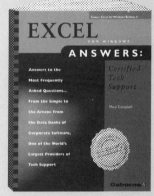

Yo Unix!

Think Fast
PASSING LANE AHEAD

ORDER BOOKS DIRECTLY FROM OSBORNE/McGRAW-HILL

For a complete catalog of Osborne's books, call 510-549-6600 or write to us at 2600 Tenth Street, Berkeley, CA 94710

Call Toll-Free: 1-800-822-8158
24 hours a day, 7 days a week in U.S. and Canada

Mail this order form to:
McGraw-Hill, Inc.
Customer Service Dept.
P.O. Box 547
Blacklick, OH 43004

Fax this order form to:
1-614-759-3644

EMAIL
7007.1531@COMPUSERVE.COM
COMPUSERVE GO MH

Ship to:

Name _____

Company _____

Address _____

City / State / Zip _____

Daytime Telephone: _____
(We'll contact you if there's a question about your order.)

ISBN #	BOOK TITLE	Quantity	Price	Total
0-07-88				
0-07-88				
0-07-88				
0-07-88				
0-07-88				
0-07088				
0-07-88				
0-07-88				
0-07-88				
0-07-88				
0-07-88				
0-07-88				
0-07-88				
0-07-88				
	Shipping & Handling Charge from Chart Below			
	Subtotal			
	Please Add Applicable State & Local Sales Tax			
	TOTAL			

Shipping & Handling Charges

Order Amount	U.S.	Outside U.S.
Less than $15	$3.50	$5.50
$15.00 - $24.99	$4.00	$6.00
$25.00 - $49.99	$5.00	$7.00
$50.00 - $74.99	$6.00	$8.00
$75.00 - and up	$7.00	$9.00

Occasionally we allow other selected companies to use our mailing list. If you would prefer that we not include you in these extra mailings, please check here: ☐

METHOD OF PAYMENT

☐ Check or money order enclosed (payable to Osborne/McGraw-Hill)

☐ AMERICAN EXPRESS   ☐ DISCOVER   ☐ MasterCard   ☐ VISA

Account No. ☐☐☐☐ ☐☐☐☐ ☐☐☐☐ ☐☐☐☐

Expiration Date _____

Signature _____

In a hurry? Call 1-800-822-8158 anytime, day or night, or visit your local bookstore.

Thank you for your order   Code BC640SL

Ordering the Software Products

Try-Before-You-Buy

If you would like to purchase *Try-Before-You-Buy* software featured on this disc, call 1-800-576-1559 between 6:00 A.M. and 10:00 P.M. (Pacific Standard Time, 7 days per week) and have your VISA, MasterCard, American Express, or Discover card ready. (Outside the United States, call 707-522-2385.) The operator will ask for a code that appears on the opening screen of the software you wish to purchase. Provide this code, your credit card number, and your name and address. That's all there is to it!

Demo Products

If you would like to purchase any of the demo products featured on this disc, call the phone number that appears on that product's page of the disc.

WARNING: BEFORE OPENING THE DISC PACKAGE, CAREFULLY READ THE TERMS AND CONDITIONS OF THE FOLLOWING CD-ROM WARRANTY.

DISCLAIMER OF WARRANTY AND LIMITED WARRANTY

OSBORNE, A DIVISION OF MCGRAW-HILL, INC. ("OSBORNE"), AND CD DIRECT, INC./MEPI SPECIFICALLY, DISCLAIM ALL WARRANTIES, EITHER EXPRESS OR IMPLIED, INCLUDING BUT NOT LIMITED TO, ANY IMPLIED WARRANTY OF MERCHANTABILITY OR FITNESS FOR A PARTICULAR PURPOSE. OSBORNE AND CD DIRECT, INC./MEPI DO NOT WARRANT THAT THE OPERATION OF THE SOFTWARE WILL BE UNINTERRUPTED OR ERROR FREE; THIS SOFTWARE IS LICENSED ON AN "AS-IS" BASIS.

Osborne warrants the physical compact disc enclosed herein to be free of defects in materials and workmanship for a period of sixty days from the purchase date. If Osborne receives written notification within the warranty period of defects in materials or workmanship, and such notification is determined by Osborne to be correct, Osborne will replace the defective disc. The entire and exclusive liability and remedy for breach of this Limited Warranty shall be limited to replacement of the defective disc.

Limitation of Liability

IN NO EVENT SHALL OSBORNE OR CD DIRECT, INC./MEPI BE LIABLE FOR LOST PROFITS, OR INCIDENTAL, SPECIAL, CONSEQUENTIAL, OR PUNITIVE DAMAGES ARISING OUT OF OR RELATED IN ANY WAY TO THE USE OF OR INABILITY TO USE THE SOFTWARE, EVEN IF OSBORNE AND CD DIRECT, INC./MEPI HAVE BEEN ADVISED OF THE POSSIBILITY OF SUCH DAMAGES. IN NO EVENT WILL CD DIRECT, INC./MEPI'S OR OSBORNE'S LIABILITY FOR ANY DAMAGES TO YOU OR ANY OTHER PERSON EVER EXCEED THE LOWER OF THE SUGGESTED LIST PRICE OR THE ACTUAL PRICE PAID FOR THE LICENSE TO USE THE SOFTWARE, REGARDLESS OF ANY FORM OF THE CLAIM. THIS LIMITATION OF LIABILITY SHALL APPLY TO ANY CLAIM OR CAUSE WHATSOEVER, WHETHER SUCH CLAIM OR CAUSE IS IN CONTRACT, TORT, OR OTHERWISE. SOME STATES DO NOT ALLOW THE LIMITATION OR EXCLUSION OF LIABILITY FOR INCIDENTAL OR CONSEQUENTIAL DAMAGES, SO THE ABOVE LIMITATION MAY NOT APPLY TO YOU.

This agreement constitutes the entire agreement between the parties relating to the use of the Product. The terms of any purchase order shall have no effect on the terms of this Agreement. Failure of CD Direct, Inc./MEPI or Osborne to insist at any time on strict compliance with this Agreement shall not constitute a waiver of any rights under this Agreement. This Agreement shall be construed and governed in accordance with the laws of New York. If any provision of this Agreement is held to be contrary to law, that provision will be enforced to the maximum extent permissible, and the remaining provisions will remain in full force and effect.

ABOUT THE CD-ROM

This CD-ROM includes six encrypted programs, which enable you to experience the full features of MBA-ware in the privacy of your own home: **ManagePro**, **Review Writer**, **OSHALOG.200 Plus**, **OSHALOG.200 Manager Plus**, **Negotiator Pro**, and **Product Planning Advisor**. Order these conveniently on CD Direct, Inc./MEPI's toll-free number: 1-800-576-1559.

In addition, the CD includes DEMO versions of the following software products (in this order):

1. Review Writer	Avantos Performance Systems, Inc.
2. OSHALOG.200 Plus	Safety Software
3. The Idea Generator Plus	Experience in Software, Inc.
4. Business Insight and Plan Write	Business Resource Software
5. Destiny Business Information and Planning System	Planet Corporation
6. DPL	Applied Decision Analysis, Inc.
7. ithink	High Performance Systems, Inc.
8. Extend+BPR	Imagine That, Inc.
9. @RISK 3.1	Palisade Corporation
10. Forecast Pro for Windows	Business Forecast Systems, Inc.
11. Smart Forecasts	Smart Software, Inc.

While we do everything we can to ensure the quality of this CD package, occasional problems may arise. If you experience problems with this CD, please call CD Direct, Inc./Micro Electronic Products, Inc. at 707-522-2385 between 6:00 A.M. and 10:00 P.M. (Pacific Standard Time, 7 days per week).

Instructions for Using the CD-ROM

The CD-ROM that comes with this book can be accessed by Windows users only. Please follow the instructions below to install and run the software.

System Requirements
386-33 MHz or higher, Windows 3.1, 4 MB RAM (8 recommended), 640 x 480 256 Colors (SVGA).

To Install the CD
1. Insert the CD into the CD-ROM drive.
2. From the Program Manager, choose Run from the File menu.
3. In the Command Line box, type **d:\install** (where *d* is the letter assigned to your CD-ROM drive). Click OK.
4. From the Program Manager double-click the icon in the *Digital MBA* group.
5. The first time you execute the program, a screen test will run (approximately 2 minutes).

To Run Windows Demos
Find the product you would like to install and simply click the demo button.